# THE ENNEAGRAM
# INTELLIGENCES

# THE ENNEAGRAM INTELLIGENCES

## Understanding Personality for Effective Teaching and Learning

JANET LEVINE

**BERGIN & GARVEY**
Westport, Connecticut • London

**Library of Congress Cataloging-in-Publication Data**

Levine, Janet, 1945–
    The enneagram intelligences : understanding personality for
effective teaching and learning / Janet Levine.
        p.   cm.
    Includes bibliographical references (p.   ) and index.
    ISBN 0–89789–561–4 (hardcover : alk. paper).—ISBN 0–89789–562–2
(pbk. : alk. paper)
    1. Enneagram.   2. Typology (Psychology)   I. Title.
BF698.35.E54L48      1999
    155.2'6—dc21            98–20129

British Library Cataloguing in Publication Data is available.

Library of Congress Catalog Card Number: 98–20129
ISBN: 0–89789–561–4
        0–89789–562–2 (pbk.)

First published in 1999

Bergin & Garvey, 88 Post Road West, Westport, CT 06881
An imprint of Greenwood Publishing Group, Inc.

Printed in the United States of America

The paper used in this book complies with the
Permanent Paper Standard issued by the National
Information Standards Organization (Z39.48–1984).

10  9  8  7  6  5  4  3

*To June Wilson Jones,*
*my first teacher*

# CONTENTS

viii  Contents

# PREFACE

This book is the result of many years of my own work in the classroom using the Enneagram model. Since 1994, I have had my experiences, insights, and reflections verified and expanded by many other educators (and students) who have attended the workshops I have led around the country and internationally, on what I call "the Enneagram edge in education." What are some conclusions?

First, teaching is an inexact profession that is often measured by an intuitive feel on the part of the educator for what we sometimes call the "chemistry" between ourselves and a group of students, at whatever level education is taking place. By good "chemistry" we understand that the learning dynamic is a positive and rewarding experience. Bad "chemistry" implies the opposite. Many teachers develop a range of skills and interventions to help that good "chemistry" manifest itself. On an instinctive level they deploy their understanding of how their personality impacts others. Most often it is a shot in the dark. *Inherently every educator knows how invaluable precise understanding of the patterns of personality behaviors is to them.* The descriptive accuracy of the Enneagram model provides us with exact information on personality—our own, and the other possibilities contained in the range of human behavior. The power of the model is enhanced by its predictive ability. The Enneagram system explains where we each shift under conditions of stress and security. In pinpointing these qualities, among much else, the book provides the know-how for educators to become true facilitators. It is filled with examples by educators (for educators) on how to understand, respect, connect with, motivate, and work most productively with each student (and colleague).

Second, using the Enneagram model provides a new lens for the 21st century through which to view diversity and difference. The Enneagram model lies at so essential a level of human individuality that the Enneagram types transcend race, ethnicity, gender, age, and socioeconomic status. This book goes beyond current theories of personality, multiple intelligences, learning styles, teaching styles. It takes their conceptual underpinnings to an entirely new level, deeper and more applicable to the whole person than the MBTI, or any of the other learning-style schemas and inventories. It is pioneering work of the order of A. S. Neill, Maria Montessori, Rudolf Steiner, John Dewey, Isabel Myers and Katherine Briggs, and Ernest Boyer.

Third, we should be placing greater emphasis on educators and teaching styles. Again and again, as I go around the country conducting workshops, I hear from teachers at all levels that accurately understanding their own teaching style is a vital, important missing piece. There is receptivity among educators to find out how they teach. The Enneagram offers a different perspective on the teaching/learning continuum—a new perceptual lens.

The Enneagram edge pioneers a study of the impact of personality on education. This book is a practical guide to understanding and applying that knowledge in all educational dynamics.

I know from my own experience that this work is sometimes received with puzzlement. On the most basic level the Enneagram is a personality typology describing nine strategies, or worldviews. The idea of "typologies" raises many red flags, for many reasons, for most people (myself included). Yet, this is not a reductivist system, rather the opposite. As soon as people are exposed to an explanation of the model, and they begin to see the intricacies and accuracy of the system, many are turned on to the possibilities it holds. In the introduction to the book I write that when I first came across the Enneagram system I saw that education and the Enneagram belonged together. I still do, and more so than ever as I see so many other educators becoming aware of, and beneficially using the power of, understanding personality. It is my belief that no educator after having encountered the system can approach teaching the same way again.

If you need assistance to pioneer this educational path, and for support, and information on materials and workshops, contact Learning & The Enneagram, P.O. Box 505, Milton, MA 02186 and/or the Educators Institute for Enneagram Studies at Milton Academy, 170 Centre Street Milton, Massachusetts, MA 02186. Our e-mail address is JLevinegrp@aol.com, and the phone number is 617-965-2926. Visit our web-site at www.enneagram-edge.com

# ACKNOWLEDGMENTS

My heartfelt gratitude to the following people for their help in completing the book: Ed Fredie, for his unwavering support, and encouragement. Judy George, for her friendship, belief in me, and inspiring creativity. Ilyce Glink, for her friendship, and getting me jump-started when I was stuck. Kay Herzog, for her love, support, and devotion to the profession we espouse, and the children we co-teach at Milton Academy. Antony J. Levine, for his love and support. Your editing skills were invaluable. Roger S. Levine, for his love, support, and sane words of comfort and wisdom. Wendy Palmer, for her friendship, and encouragement. Regina S. Pyle, for her love, support, friendship, attention to details, and endurance.

My thanks to the following people for reading sections of the manuscript, and for their thoughtful feedback: Terry Cetrulo, Kay Herzog, Jane Moss, Annette Wyandotte, Jody Fahrenkrug, Jennifer Starr, Kim Hourihan, Ruthanne Wrobel and Regina S. Pyle.

To Dave Franzen, fellow Enneagram teacher, certified Myers Briggs (MBTI) practitioner, organizational consultant, and visiting faculty at the National Educators Institute for Enneagram Studies at Milton Academy, my thanks for conversation, ideas, and making available your lecture notes on the Enneagram and the MBTI.

To Jane Garry, and Katie Chase, my editors at the Greenwood Publishing Group, my thanks for your positive attitude and cooperation.

To Helen Palmer, my appreciation for your pioneering work in paving the way for others to follow. Your original insights, theoretical understanding, energetic teaching, and comprehensive writing have set the standards in our burgeoning field.

To the many workshop participants around the country whose words grace these pages; truly, this book could not have been written without the honest sharing and generous giving of yourselves on panels.

# THE ENNEAGRAM
# INTELLIGENCES

# INTRODUCTION

People often ask me how the Enneagram has influenced me as an educator. This is a provocative question because I did not set out to be an Enneagram educator, or a pioneer. I was not trained to integrate what in essence is a model of personality used for personal awareness and growth into an application to education. Yet when I first came across the Enneagram system I saw that education and the Enneagram belonged together.

Why do I hold so dear this conviction and vision about spreading knowledge of the Enneagram model and the impact of personality in education? In essence, it simply makes unquestionably good sense to me to provide these practical tools for enhancing educational dynamics. In my native South Africa, since adolescence I was an antiapartheid activist. If I distill my motivations for political activism, it is to an idealistic belief in human rights and the notion of equal opportunities for all people. In many ways this belief system spills over to my current embrace and advocacy of the Enneagram model: an idealistic drive to bring the gifts of this knowledge to as many people as possible. I want especially to reach young people through educators (teachers, educational psychologists, parents, caregivers), so they may mature with a positive sense of self, a deeper understanding of why they do what they do, and how to be effective in the world.

Since 1986, I've taught English at Milton Academy in Massachusetts. Some 1,000 students attend Milton Academy, and 160 teachers work there. There are 65 million students enrolled in all educational institutions in the United States and 3.8 million teachers at all levels. Around the world there are billions more students and millions more educators. With all the possible combinations of teaching situations that exist, how can it be acceptable that essentially one way of teaching and one way of learning have become the worldwide standards by which all educational opportunities are measured?

The Enneagram system presents a meaningful shift from the standard hierarchical model in which it is the educator's job to impart content and material in the same way for all students, as if one shoe fits all. The Enneagram system provides an alternative model from traditional and limited perceptions about education that ignore personality idiosyncrasies and learning styles, to a laser- clear understanding of *why* we teach the way we do, *how* we learn, and the nine intelligences that make us *who* we are.

Over the past decades, the ongoing crisis in American education—falling standards, overcrowded schools, demotivated and disaffected students and teachers—has spawned a growth industry in innovative educational ideas, all aimed at reforming education. Some work and others do not. The Enneagram edge in education is one that has proved to work well. In this climate of reform the time is ripe to incisively and insightfully explore the impact of personality on education.

The Enneagram edge proposes a new educational paradigm that recognizes there are multiple intelligences and multiple personalities that need attention and validation. If all educators understand a model of personality that can pinpoint with detailed accuracy why students behave the way they do, whole generations may grow into adulthood with their self-esteem intact and a welcome sense of responsibility for their own learning and their own lives. In a world where educators use the Enneagram conscientiously, a new sense of self will emerge, a full sense of self-identity and self-esteem donned as one's birthright.

When I did my graduate work in education the Enneagram was unknown. At that time—the late 1960s—the Enneagram had yet to surface anywhere as a workable model that related to any existing psychological framework, let alone to educational psychology. My training in pioneering educational ideas included the work of A.S. Neill and the Summerhill school in England, the Montessori schools in Italy, the work of Jean Piaget in Switzerland, Rudolf Steiner and the Waldorf schools in Germany, and John Dewey in this country. Later, as a professional educator, I came across the work of Seymour Papert on children, computers, and the development of the computer language, LOGO; Howard Gardner on multiple intelligences; and Isabel Myers and Katherine Briggs on Jungian typology that produced the Myers Briggs Type Indicator (MBTI), and Ernest Boyer on recasting the historical precedent of faculty roles and rewards in higher education.

Despite the attraction that innovation in education holds for me, I never envisaged that I would be pioneering innovation myself. Central to this book, therefore, is an attempt to answer the question: How has the Enneagram influenced me as an educator?

At first the Enneagram influenced me privately. When I read my first book on the Enneagram in 1990, I was shocked to recognize how well the system described me and the others in my life. When I began to understand my subconscious inner drives and motivations and how these influence my emotional and mental habits, I turned a somewhat startled gaze to see how my personality impacted my classroom. For me as an Enneagram-type (E-type) Performer Three, the key characteristics of my personality are achieving goals to gain approval, being successful, and mastering an image of how I want the world to be. My attention goes to tasks to get things done. Energy follows attention. I therefore organized my teaching around tasks to help move me toward achieving goals.

My English classroom, like the classrooms of other Performer Three teachers, was dominated by task, task, task: "We must finish thirty pages of this text today," "You must write a paper every 10 days to two weeks." And image: "You've got to learn to package your ideas, to present them as effectively as possible." It never occurred to me to question if mine was the one right way for everybody. I assumed because my way worked for me, it could work for everyone else. And I was regarded as a good teacher. However, for almost twenty years in college and high school classrooms while I always connected with some students I kept missing others. Accepting pedagogical conventional wisdom which tells us "you always do," I regretted it had to be that way, shrugged my shoulders, and taught on.

I underwent a customary five-year peer evaluation process in 1992. The assessment was favorable. My teaching style was described as strong, focused, high-powered, intellectually rigorous, results-oriented. Year by year, student evaluations echoed this view: "she makes me think," "she's a strong presence who teaches by personal example," "she drives us to do our best," "she taught me to believe in myself and my abilities." The comments of both my peers and students reinforced my Performer Three self-image. I was unaware of how much my personality bias alienated many others.

A year after my peer evaluation, one of the evaluators returned for a follow-up visit. She was taken aback, "You've turned your teaching 180 degrees. What's happened? There's a whole different feel in your classroom, so hands off, so relaxed."

I struggled to find the words to encompass the transformation that was taking place in my thinking and behavior.

"I've been working with the Enneagram. It's a personality system. In Greek, *ennea* means nine and *gram* graph or model. It describes nine strategies or ways to view the world, but it allows fully for individual differences within those strategies. I've tried to become aware of how my personality biases affect my teaching and interaction with all my students. I'm conscious now that I share the classroom with individuals who fall into the behaviors of these eight other strategies. I'm really excited. You're right, the shift is quite remarkable actually, both for me and the students. You should read an Enneagram book."

My Performer Three students had flourished in my Performer Three classroom. We were in sync because we liked each other's efficiency and shared the satisfaction of completing tasks in a timely manner—milestones that marked the passage of the school year. But what about the others? Perfectionist One students who get caught in a right/wrong mind-set and hung up on the details? Helper Twos who want to please authority and have to be encouraged to think independently, rather than meet a teacher's needs? Royal Family Fours who want to be distinctive and different, who need encouragement in order to participate in ordinary classroom routines? What about the privacy-minded Observer Fives who want a quiet place in which to assimilate information in depth? Questioner

Six students whose logical minds rove back and forth until a cast-iron argument emerges? Optimist Sevens who like to brainstorm multiple options rather than work toward a predefined goal, their minds racing with many possibilities and resisting limits? Boss Eights who challenge preset goals and agendas, wanting to set the rules for themselves? Peacekeeper Nines who have little ability to motivate themselves and who absorb information indiscriminately?

Enneagram awareness directed me to exercise vigilance over my task-oriented Performer Three focus and to rein in its effect on others. I had always known the word *education* is from the root *edu*, to lead out. Henceforth I would be an educator. I tried to be less dominant in my classroom and found ways to facilitate my students being themselves. I ceased to be the Performer at the center of my stage and became a facilitator, a true educator. My students' comments at the end of that year reflected the seismic shift: "I've never been in a classroom where I can be so much me," "she makes me feel safe to be myself," "I feel appreciated for who I am," "I feel I can learn in a way that is me," "she's empowering," "she supports everyone's different ways of learning."

This set of comments reinforced my sense that I was on the right track. The adjustment from performer to educator was not an easy one. Often my behavior in the classroom felt counterintuitive. Many moments of panic almost overcame me when I felt the momentum of interactions about to swing forever beyond my control. But I allowed an energetic flow to take its course and the results were affirming for myself and my students. The realization that I was onto a powerful discovery with enormous potential for real change in education thrilled me.

At the time of my initial forays with the Enneagram in education, the fledgling field of Enneagram Studies itself was about to take a giant step forward. The First International Enneagram Conference in 1994 was cosponsored by and held at Stanford University in California. The call for papers presented a perfect opportunity for me to take my private experience with the Enneagram in education into a more public arena.

Claudio Naranjo, a psychiatrist based in Berkeley, California, and the father of the Enneagram movement in this country, told 1,400 conference delegates in a video interview (1994):

> Beyond the world of psychotherapy, I think a most important domain is that of education. I think the province of education is of crucial relevance to the transformation of society. It is very easy to imagine what a living and rich tool an experiential program in protoanalysis would be to future schools of education; what it could be for an educator to be aware and sharpen his perception of character and of the invisible pathology that we are not usually aware of because we have idealized the different characters so much. This would be a long subject to dream about, "the future of the Enneagram in education."

Naranjo's words washed over me with powerful force. I, too, was dreaming about the future of the Enneagram in education. My briefcase held a video I had made for the conference with nine of my sixteen-year-old students called *Nine Perspectives on What Motivates Learning in Adolescents*. Later that day I showed the video as part of a presentation in the Education Track at the conference. The forty people in the audience from all walks of educational life received the presentation with acclaim and immediately wanted to obtain the material. Excited by my vision, I recognized the great hunger the Enneagram's application to education could feed.

My burgeoning interest and involvement in the Enneagram coincided with the appointment of a new head, Dr. Edwin Fredie, at Milton Academy, an independent school outside of Boston, where I teach. Fredie was open to my ideas and dreams of the Enneagram and education and became a champion of the model. He encouraged my explorations in the classroom, in my own professional development, and for the institution. I worked with the administrative board of the school, with the faculty, and with the students. I learned a great deal and began to formalize the material. With Fredie's support I ran a summer program at Milton Academy in 1996 for educators to explore the Enneagram. Out of that remarkable week the permanent National Educators Institute for Enneagram Studies at Milton Academy emerged. The work of the Institute includes teaching week-long intensive programs to study the system, leading inservice training programs at all levels for professional development of educators around the country, initiating research projects for peer review, and creating on-going development of materials geared to help educators and those in related fields apply the Enneagram to education.

Imagine an educational setting—teacher-student, parent-child, intercollegial, professional training, psychologist-client—in which educators are completely aware of how their personality styles affect the way they teach, and understand how the personalities of their students affect the way they learn and interact with authority. In such a situation all educators and learners "fit," and feel part of, rather than alienated from, the educational process. Understanding the Enneagram's nine intelligences creates such a dynamic.

Young people coming of age in the early years of the next century, if educated in Enneagram-conscious environments, may affect a seachange in how they regard themselves and others, individually and globally. The Enneagram cuts through race, sex, socioeconomic, ethnic, and national differences. In the classroom and in the world, it gives space to allow all worldviews, all intelligences, all personality strategies, to be present and validated fully. The Enneagram provides a new lens for the 21st century through which to view individual diversity and differences.

In offering personality descriptions that account for these differences and useful tips about interacting with E-types, this book provides powerful, yet easily accessible, information for teachers and learners to understand themselves and to approach what they do from different perspectives. Many educators struggle in situations where teaching is not about content and curriculum, but about connecting across the divide of human differences. Those educators who know their own E-type can project themselves with wisdom and integrity into the personality patterns of the other eight E-types. Being aware of personality intelligences and strategies provides insights that mobilize everyone's resources. The system allows people to reconcile, humanely, the differences between themselves and those with whom they interact.

Education is about people—touching the essence of other people, facilitating a full awakening of their abilities. As I've mentioned before, the word *education* is from the root *edu*, to lead forth, or to lead out. It is analogous to the Enneagram system of personality types which leads people out of the boxes created by their narrowed attentional focus and into the realization of the 360 degrees of human possibility.

People teach by being themselves. Their choices, decisions, behavior —their lives—are the daily lessons they impart to others. Basically life is about teaching, because we are always teaching one another, positively or negatively. Learning from one another is one way that enables us to function in the world and, in many instances, to grow. Since time immemorial life's wisdom has been passed from generation to generation through unwritten lore—orally transmitted teachings of family, religion, community. In an essential sense we are all teachers and learners.

With the Enneagram edge educational leaders and administrators who recognize their own personality strategy are likewise freed from habitual patterns of behavior and a narrowed worldview. This knowledge can help them deal with problematic aspects of the overall institutional culture and improve interactions with other administrators, faculty, and students.

With all of this in mind, I have organized this book into a logical sequence that facilitates reader's discovery of their E-type. Readers can then begin to page through the other strategies, so that the personalities of colleagues and students become clearer. This new knowledge leads to compassion for ourselves and others, and makes possible a new paradigm for understanding differences. Practical advice and exercises allow readers to best accommodate to their E-type and, it is hoped, offer possibilities for awareness and growth.

Chapter 1 gives a brief historical background, psychological context, and explanation of the inner dynamics of the Enneagram model. Chapter 2 is the Enneagram Triads Personality Indicator for Educators and is followed by profiles of the nine strategies. Chapter 3 explores each of the nine E-types in-depth. Testimony from workshops and seminars with educators across the country offers examples of people bearing witness to their own forty-degree slice of reality. The poignancy and power of the human condition unfolds for readers, as people reveal their inner world. Helpful to educators and students, at the end of each description are practical suggestions on how to work with that particular E-type strategy. Chapter 4 gives practical exercises using the Enneagram triads to access the three energy centers and how to use their energy for oneself and one's students. Chapter 5 contrasts the Enneagram to the MBTI and other personality models and distinguishes the Enneagram as a tool for understanding the impact of personality in the classroom. The philosophical discussion in Chapter 6 ranges over the educational possibilities for the Enneagram model as a perceptual lens for the 21st century through which to view diversity and differences.

Sharing visions close to one's heart is affirming; to watch a dream unfolding is both humbling and exciting. In South Africa, I learned how holding the vision around an idea—the basic belief in human and individual rights—can change a country. I feel privileged to make available this application of the Enneagram system to education, to actualize my vision, so close to Claudio Naranjo's in his words at Stanford University in 1994:

> Future educators with a good grasp of character formation may one day help children to put on this mask of the ego, to develop a personality (for nobody can live in this terrible world without developing one) more consciously; to help our children know what they are doing so they may not forget who they are as they adapt consciously to the psycho-pathology of the environment.

# 1

# BACKGROUND TO
# THE ENNEAGRAM SYSTEM

The Enneagram system is a model of personality that describes nine worldviews or strategies—nine intelligences. In Greek *ennea* means nine and *gram* graph or model. Fully accounting for individual differences—race, sex, age, ethnicity, socioeconomic status—the Enneagram describes nine strategies to the *nth* degree. The model is based on nine patterns of thoughts, feelings, motivations, and perceptions tied to a central feature of narrowed attention (Palmer 1988). The Enneatypes broadly align with current personality theory, such as the categories of the current *Diagnostic Survey Manuel* (DSM-IV), but describe normal and high-functioning people rather than pathologies.

Empirical evidence for E-types is found in many hundreds of actual interviews with people. The psychological profiles of the E-types constellate around a central feature, or fixation. Other Enneagram authors describe in detail how these fixations approximate the psychological states described in many major religious traditions like the seven deadly sins of Christianity, the mind-states of Buddhism, the sacred psychology of Sufism, and the kabbalah.

No E-type strategy is better than any other—they are all equally valid—but each encompasses a distinctive way of perceiving the world. All people embody one basic strategy, yet they may see part of themselves in each of the strategies, because each represents an aspect of personality they all can relate to. The Enneagram system provides a framework and conceptual vocabulary for understanding people and behavior. Knowing the system enhances all interactions including educating/teaching/training (see Figure 1.1). Listed below are the nine E-types and a brief description of each strategy.

## Nine Unique Ways of Being in the World

*One—The Perfectionist*—is conscientious and moral, honest and idealistic. Perfectionists focus on doing the right thing and avoiding error. This can lead to procrastination and a lack of spontaneity. Communications can be preachy and zealous.

*Two—The Helper*—is empathetic, nurturing, relational, and can give of him- or herself with true altruism. Helpers focus on giving to others in order to meet their emotional needs—for love, approval, admiration—and to avoid rejection. Helpers can come across as manipulative.

*Three—The Performer*—is self-assured, competent, efficient, an accomplished team-builder, and driven to achieve "success." Performers avoid failure. They focus on results and are task-oriented. Image-conscious, they often deceive themselves and others and can suspend experiencing emotions.

*Four—The Royal Family*—is individualistic, creative, sensitive, and able to experience the highs and lows of deep emotions. The Royal Family avoid ordinariness. They focus on what is unavailable; the glass is always half-empty. Melancholia gives an attractive edge to life but can lead to depression. Fours envy others who seem to have what they are missing.

*Five—The Observer*—is private, measured, logical, and an intellectual seeker. Observers avoid (emotional) attachment. They focus on gaining knowledge. Fives can be retractive, overly self-controlled, detached from their emotions. Predictability is safety; Observers do not like surprises.

*Six—The Questioner*—is thoughtful, rational, loyal, dutiful, and responsible. Questioners avoid deviance, being seen as different. Sixes focus on scanning for hidden dangers. They are fearful, scared of success and vigilantly doubtful, which can lead to indecision, procrastination, and unfinished projects.

*Seven—The Optimist*—is upbeat, enthusiastic, charming, spontaneous, and entertaining. Optimists focus on being active, engaged with life, and having many pleasant options to choose from. They enjoy spending time planning and fantasizing. Optimists avoid pain. They have trouble making and keeping commitments. Optimists can be self-involved and do not deal well with others' needs, the routine and the mundane.

*Eight—The Boss*—is confident, powerful, a take-charge leader, honest, direct, and protective of "turf" and those who fall within their ambit. Bosses focus on power and control, who has it, and if they'll be fair. Bosses hate being dependent and avoid vulnerability. They can live "go-for-broke," excessive lifestyles.

*Nine—The Peacekeeper*—is compassionate, energetic on behalf of others, noncompetitive, patient, and sees all sides of an issue. Nines avoid conflict. Peacekeepers are reluctant self-starters, and procrastinators. They find difficulty in establishing priorities and making decisions. Resignation, inertia, zoning out with TV: Peacekeepers fall asleep to their own needs and agendas.

# Figure 1.1
## Diagram of Basic Enneagram Model

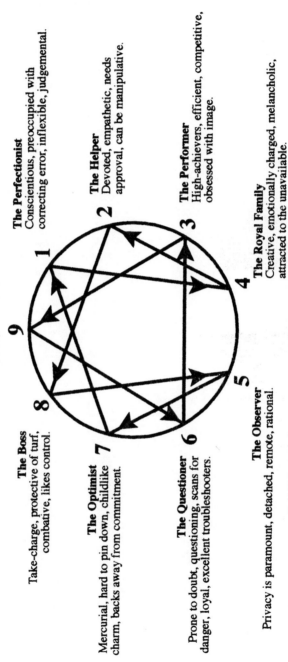

**The Perfectionist**
Conscientious, preoccupied with correcting error, inflexible, judgemental.

**The Helper**
Devoted, empathetic, needs approval, can be manipulative.

**The Performer**
High-achievers, efficient, competitive, obsessed with image.

**The Royal Family**
Creative, emotionally charged, melancholic, attracted to the unavailable.

**The Observer**
Privacy is paramount, detached, remote, rational.

**The Questioner**
Prone to doubt, questioning, scans for danger, loyal, excellent troubleshooters.

**The Optimist**
Mercurial, hard to pin down, childlike charm, backs away from commitment.

**The Boss**
Take-charge, protective of turf, combative, likes control.

**The Peacekeeper**
Calm, seeks consensus, takes on others' agenda at expense of own position, obstinate and stubborn.

© 1997 Janet Levine: *Learning and the Enneagram Workshops*

## A BRIEF HISTORY

The field of Enneagram Studies as a credible psychology is a somewhat recent development in the social sciences. Although the system has been taught to private and public, large and small classes since 1972, there was agreement among the early teachers that it remain an oral teaching. Breaking this agreement in 1984, Maria Beesing, a nun, and two priests, Patrick O'Leary and Robert Nagosek, wrote *The Enneagram* (1984). A simple primer, the book was meant to help Catholic clergy living in communities, but quickly found its way to a larger audience. Several years later more books on the Enneagram system were published for the general market. There is no doubt that the Enneagram is steadily making its way into the mainstream. Despite the many books on the model, there is little consensus among the authors as to its history. Sifting through the various texts produces several broad theoretical strands.

What are the antecedents of the system? In 1972, a group of psychologists, psychiatrists, and students gathered in the living room of a house in Berkeley, California, to learn from Claudio Naranjo, a prominent University of Berkeley psychiatrist, about a psychological system called the Enneagram. Naranjo had recently returned from Arica, Chile, where he had spent time studying with a spiritual teacher, Oscar Ichazo. Ichazo gave Naranjo fragments of insights into this tantalizing psychological model.

What Naranjo brought back from Chile were some sketchy theoretical underpinnings of an ancient system of psychology based on nine personality types, each organized around a central feature or fixation and placed on a nine-pointed star diagram called the Enneagram. On a psychological level these central features are the core emotional energies bound up in personality. On a spiritual level these energies are the engines for personal awareness and can, if properly trained, power the way to spiritual growth. In a synthesis of ideas, Ichazo named the fixations after Christianity's seven capital sins—anger, pride, envy, avarice, gluttony, lust, sloth—and added two more, deceit and fear. This metaphorical nomenclature of the Enneagram energies has become widespread, but it does not imply that it is a system of Christian psychology, although the Enneagram fixations were known in the Christian morality plays in the form of the seven deadly sins during the late Middle Ages in Europe.

Week after week the group met in Berkeley and painstakingly tried to align the central features of Enneagram type with the then DSM-1 (1952), a canon in the psychological community used by all American and Canadian clinicians for diagnostic purposes. They made hypotheses and drew conclusions through a "hit and miss" process of induction, discussion, and by careful interviewing of individuals on panels by Naranjo to elicit their inner psychological worlds. Putting together the two templates—the Enneagram central fixations and the DSM-1 categories—he provided the Rosetta Stone for understanding and presenting the Enneagram system of personality in its modern form.

While the DSM describes pathologies, the Enneagram describes the broadly correlating fixations of normal and high-functioning people: Point One's *anger* at the world not being perfect lines up with the *compulsive* pathology; Point Two's *pride* in acting out with other people and repressing their needs lines up with the *histrionic*; Point Three's identification with what they do and self-*deceit* lines up with the secondary *narcissist*; Point Four's *envy* for what is unavailable leading to self-attack and capitulation lines up with the *depressive*; Point Five's *avarice* in withholding and retractive behavior lines up with the *avoidant*; Point Six's constant *fear* and vigilance lines up with the *paranoid*; Point Seven's *gluttony*, the escape into enjoyment and pleasure away from darkness and pain, lines up with the true *narcissist*; Point Eight's *lust* in excessive behavior and action without thought lines up with the *sociopath*; Point Nine's *sloth* in being asleep to themselves and caught up in others' agendas lines up with the (passive aggressive) *obsessive-compulsive*.

The pervasive influence in psychological work since its inception a little over a century ago has been identifying personality traits through pathology. Although this influence remains at the root of psychological training and practice, since 1972 the Enneagram has offered the first alternative — a credible model for identifying personality in normal and high-functioning people without first seeking to identify low-end pathologies. It is a dramatic shift which holds great promise for developing extraordinary self-understanding of ordinary people.

Unfortunately the historical picture is not as simple and clear as the Berkeley living-room explorations imply. There is another strand of Enneagram influence in this century. In fact the first person to bring the diagram to the West was a Russian mystic and charismatic teacher, George Ivanovich Gurdjieff, who settled in Paris after the Russian revolution in the late 1920s and established a spiritual school there. Gurdjieff painted a huge Enneagram on the floor of the Institute for the Harmonious Development of Man, the name of his school where students practiced dance and movement on the diagram. Much of Gurdjieff's teachings centered on what he called Chief Feature, personality characteristics akin to the central features Naranjo describes (1990). Gurdjieff purportedly attributed the Enneagram diagram to Sufi sources. It is interesting to note that Oscar Ichazo, Naranjo's teacher, studied in Gurdjieffian Fourth Way schools in South America before starting a spiritual school of his own.

Following Gurdjieff's lead, many of the first wave of Enneagram authors declared that the Enneagram has its source in Sufism. They are correct up to a point. Central to Islamic esotericism is a system of psychoethics based on a version of the Enneagram diagram. A well-known Sufi scholar and writer, Laleh Bakhtiar, notably in her book *Traditional Psychoethics and Personality Paradigm* (1993), exhaustively explores the dynamics of this paradigm. But it appears the Enneagram may be even older than its Sufi version. Sufi adepts kept the diagram and the psychoethical system alive through the dawn of Islam, in much the same way as Medieval monks kept Latin and Greek alive in the early Middle (Dark) Ages in Europe.

Rabbi Howard Addison (1998) in ground-breaking research on the overlay of the Kabbalah, the Tree of Life of Jewish mysticism (geometric diagrams of the *Sefirot*, Kabbalah's manifestations of the divine personality which are also understood as a symbolic representation of traits that make up the human psyche) and the Enneagram, states that the two personality systems share numerous common sources which derive from antiquity. These include Pythagorianism, Neo-Platonism, Gnosticism, and Sufism. He makes the point that while Gurdjieff credits the Enneagram to the secret Samoun brotherhood that lived near Mesopotamia around the end of the Third Millennium B.C. E., clearly predating Sufism, kabbalah views the Old Testament figure Abraham as its founder and claims that his sons, born of his concubines, brought this secret knowledge East to the same region at approximately the same time.

Addison builds a convincing argument for recognizing connections between the Enneagram and the Kabbalah. Without going into the details of his argument here, he correlates the nine Sefirot with the Enneagram in the following way: Point One aligns with *Hochma* (All knowing, Correct, Internalized father, Abba), Point Two with *Bina* (Understanding, Controlling, Supernal Mother, Ima), Point Three with *Gedula* (Impetus To Be Great), Point Four with *Tiferet* (Beauty, Romantic Longing), Point Five with *Din* (Bound, Enclosed, Limited), Point Six with *Nezeh* (Enduring, Seeking Authority), Point Seven with *Hod* (Splendor), Point Eight with *Yesod* (Seminal Force), and Point Nine with *Shechina* (Accepting Presence).

The fact that ancient personality systems are contained in variants of the Enneagram model in esoteric Christianity, Sufism, and Judaism implies an even older, common source (see Figure 1.2). It is apparent that there is a "missing link" in the history of the Enneagram. There are other strands that lead into the modern-day Enneagram. For instance, the Platonic tradition describes a philosophy which resonates with the Enneagram—Plato's ideal forms: nine perfect essential states and a tenth state called unity.

The Hermetic schools of Egypt with their links to ancient cosmology are surfacing as another possible source for the diagram. Whatever that source may be, what is certain is that deep in the human psyche is an impulse to understand the personality of others, and the leaders, initiates, and adepts of many sacred traditions over many centuries used a form of secret knowledge to gratify this impulse, including the 2,500-year tradition of Buddhism. "Even Buddhism," as Mark Epstein (1995), points out in his book *Thoughts Without a Thinker*, "is, in its psychological form, a depth psychology. It is able to describe, in terms that would make any psychoanalyst proud, the full range of the human emotional experience." Depth psychology, too, the full range of human emotional experience, is the territory of the Enneagram model.

How can it be that a contemporary psychological system has its roots in these sacred traditions? Is it possible that there is a link between personality type and spirituality? Not only does the Enneagram system posit that understanding Type can be accomplished without first accessing pathologies, but also it takes another revolutionary leap in viewing psychology and spirituality as two sides of the same coin. Finding one's E-type is only the initial step; learning how to work with one's strategy, to grow in understanding, compassion, and acceptance of oneself and others, is the journey. To this end, the technology of the sacred traditions—such as training awareness, using the practices of breathing and meditation, developing a sense of ground and presence by employing principles of, for instance, the martial arts—becomes viable and within reach of ordinary people, many of whom do not necessarily consider themselves spiritual seekers. Chapter 4 describes the theory for these practices and details exercises on how to develop an awareness and how to practice ground and presence.

## Figure 1.2

### Table of Correlations Between Enneagram Type, the Kabbalah's Sefirot, Christianity's Capital Sins, and DSM-IV Categories

| ENNEAGRAM | KABBALAH | CAPITAL SINS | DSM-IV |
|---|---|---|---|
| Point One Perfectionist | Hochma-All knowing, Correct | Anger | Compulsive |
| Point Two Helper | Bina-Understanding, Supernal Mother | Pride | Histrionic |
| Point Three Performer | Gedula-Impetus to be Great | Deceit (Self) | Narcissist (Secondary) |
| Point Four Royal Family | Tiferet-Romantic Longing | Envy | Depressive |
| Point Five Observer | Din-Bound, Enclosed | Avarice | Avoidant |
| Point Six Questioner | Nezeh-Seeking Authority | Fear | Paranoid |
| Point Seven Optimist | Hod-Splendor | Gluttony | Narcissist (Primary) |
| Point Eight Boss | Yesod-Seminal Force | Lust | Sociopath |
| Point Nine Peacekeeper | Shechina-Accepting Presence | Sloth | Obsessive-compulsive |

## PSYCHOLOGICAL CONTEXT OF THE ENNEAGRAM SYSTEM

What is Type? There is a large body of literature in psychology on personality type. Essentially people have to survive in the world and need to organize traits and characteristics that will enable them to make their way and form relationships, both with themselves and others. Personality is about defense mechanisms, characteristic habits of thought, emotions that underpin thoughts, interpersonal aptitudes and abilities, and a way of handling the body to manage energy. While all people have access to all these areas, in many instances one area predominates and the literature describes people falling  broadly into body, mental, and emotional types. The Enneagram recognizes these distinctions, too, and the diagram is organized in triads that are made up of these distinct energies. Points Two, Three, and Four are the emotional triad; Points Five, Six, and Seven are the mental triad; and Points Eight, Nine, and One are the body-based triad.

The nexus of energies of E-types are powerful habits kept in place to help normal and high-functioning people manage their existential fears that can range from mild anxiety to outright nihilism. Ordinary people spend great energy in keeping these habits intact. Going on automatic, reproducing the psychological conditions that keep panic at bay, these feel like sensible activities, life-preserving instead of life-dulling. In an Enneagram frame these energetic habits can be described as the narrowed attentional focus which underpins the survival strategy of each individual and becomes their view of the world. They are the inner behaviors of normal and high-functioning people, people who do not relate their personality habits to descriptions of pathologies. Yet these same people in Enneagram classes—listening to others like themselves who have developed some degree of self-awareness and can describe their inner world—resonate with what they are hearing as the familiar patterning of their own lives. Panels of self-observers talking about themselves is a potent methodology for Enneagram public education.

Traditionally Type has been identified through pathology. The psychological world has found pathology helpful because if someone can be brought to see how their personality disintegrated, they can be helped to reintegrate themselves. Psychotherapists are trained to find how the personality defense mechanisms have broken down, rather than to concentrate on what's working. The Enneagram system provides a format for normal and high-functioning people to examine through close self-observation what component of anxiety their compulsive behavior papers over. Enneagram psychology pinpoints nine patterns of avoidance—error, emotional needs, failure, ordinariness, connection, deviance (being different), pain, vulnerability, and conflict. Our sense of self is manufactured largely out of one of these avoidances in our emotional experience. When we face up to, process, and integrate those aspects of ourselves we have been denying, the self can emerge as a whole, and the grace of compassion for self and others becomes possible.

The system offers the choice for proactive, rather than reactive, behavior and the opportunity to cease going on automatic without realizing what one is doing. Knowledge of their E-type frees people to expand the way they think about themselves, to find compassion for themselves and others, to manage emotional energy with more skill, and to begin to end habitual behavior.

In many ways Enneagram psychology is akin to Buddhist psychology. The Enneagram diagram and the Buddhist mandala of the Wheel of Life are both images that can be easily understood. They both make the point that as long as one is driven by the Enneagram central fixations, or driven by greed (attachment), hatred (aversion), and delusion (the forces at the center of the Buddhist Wheel of Life), we will remain oblivious to the means for release or relief from these forces. The paradox is that what people take to be so real, their *selves*, is constructed out of a reaction against what they wish to avoid. People become anxious around what they are avoiding, and experience themselves through their anxiety. According to Enneagram theory, peoples' fear of experiencing themselves wholly creates emotional suffering. This is also a central tenet of Buddhist psychology. It is widely accepted in the psychological field that the formation of character, the personality, is built on aspects of self-alienation. Inherent in both the Enneagram and the Wheel of Life is the idea that, as Epstein (1995) says, "the causes of suffering are also the means of release." It is peoples' subjective perspective that determines whether these forces are energetic drivers for bondage or freedom. Both systems offer a shot at transformation.

John Oldham, M.D. the Director of the New York State Psychiatric Institute, with Morris published *Personality Self-Portrait* (1995), in which they aligned the normal functioning person with DSM-111-R and DSM-IV categories. They show that it is acceptable in psychotherapy to see traits and tendencies of pathologies in normal people and no longer necessary to view people in their full pathologies. "The personality styles that we identify are common, utterly human, nonpathological ... we describe here equivalent categories of orderly human functioning."

Oldham and Morris' observations mark a significant moment in psychotherapy, the increasing acceptance that if normal and high-functioning people can create changes within themselves, they can change their relationships with self and others. In 1972 this was the promise the Enneagram held for the Naranjo group in Berkeley—a practical transformational psychology for normal and high-functioning people. It is possible that in the first decade of the new century this promise will begin to flower in earnest.

## INNER WORKINGS OF THE MODEL

The in-depth descriptions of the E-types that follow in Chapter 3 are each preceded by a banner of descriptive terms. This section offers an explanation of each of these terms.

### Triads

In psychological literature many authors have different ways of observing what they call body, mental, and emotional types. These are three distinct modalities of being; three broad patterns of behavior; three primal, intuitive motivations driving how people operate in the world. The Enneagram model accounts for these three basic ways of behavior in the Enneagram triads, which I call Attachers (emotional triad), Detachers (mental triad), and Defenders (instinctual triad). (See Figure 1.3.) My nomenclature is based on the work of the pioneering psychologist Karen Horney, who in *Our Inner Conflicts* (1945) describes three broad personality patterns as those of moving toward people, moving away from people, and moving against people.

One modality—of the Attachers—can be described as outer-directed attention, *moving toward people*, a way of making sense of, and operating in, the world through connection to people and relationships. The emotional context is the Attachers' environment. Points Two, Three, and Four are Attachers.

Another modality—of the Detachers—can be described as inner-directed attention, *moving away from people*, detaching, a way of making sense of and operating in the world from inside one's head. The mental context is the Detachers' environment. Points Five, Six, and Seven are Detachers.

The third modality—of the Defenders—can be described as self-protective attention, *moving (brushing up) against people*, a way of making sense of and operating in the world with an awareness of intrapersonal space and boundaries. The body-based context is the Defenders' environment. Points Eight, Nine, and One are Defenders.

These three modalities are primal patterns of behavior; people make their way in the world primarily as Attachers, Detachers, or Defenders. This does not mean that Detachers and Defenders are not emotional, or that Attachers and Defenders are not intellectual, or that Detachers and Attachers do not also struggle with boundaries of *self* and *other*-ness. People are a complex fusion of these three ways of being, but one is always dominant. Within each of the broad patterns presented by these modalities are three versions of how emotional, mental, and instinctual attention manifests in personality. These are the Enneagram triads.

### Attacher Triad

The Attachers' predominant mode of being is emotional. Being outer-directed, moving toward people, and knowing where they stand emotionally in relation to others are central preoccupations—*do they like me?* The dominant issue is approval. Attachers are activated by their feelings: how they feel about themselves each day, what moods and emotions they are dealing with affect all they do. These inner triggers direct their behavior. They are aware of the feelings of others and how they are coming across to them. Issues of image are important. Their defenses are marshaled around feelings; to make their way in the world, they have to learn to deal with feelings.

Some Attachers take pride in denying to themselves that they have feelings. Other Attachers suspend their feelings so they don't interfere with getting the job done. Yet others are constantly aware of their feelings and can lose their agenda if they allow feelings to overwhelm them. All Attachers use feelings to open their hearts to others and to the deepest parts of themselves.

### Detacher Triad

The Detachers' predominant mode of being is mental. Being inner-directed, moving away from people, and seeking to make sense of the world through mental processes and activities are central preoccupations. The realm of the mind is where Detachers feel most comfortable. Living in the imagination, conceptualizing, fantasizing, analyzing, forming contexts and synthesizing, all are based on mental activity. Even when they are with people they tend to escape into their minds—planning other options, running other scenarios, looking for new concepts to make ideas lock together. Their energy is mental. Some Detachers escape into the imagination where ideas swing freely, a state of mind called monkey-mind. Other Detachers question everything in their minds and voice their doubts. They like to think through the hard questions to build a fail-safe argument. Yet others live in an investigative mental mode: seeking knowledge to build interconnections among ideas and come to new understandings.

### Defender Triad

The Defenders' predominant mode of being is instinctual. Being aware of boundaries around themselves, their tendency is to feel brushed up against people. They need to establish their space—*here I am, deal with me*. Intuition, "gut" feelings, and nonverbal information are important. The body is where Defenders sense their relationships to others and to the world. They have an intuitive information gathering system. They say, "I feel it in my body ... I have a gut feel for that." They have a belly laugh. It is easy for them to lose themselves behind their boundaries, a state of mind called self-forgetting (acedia), sometimes they can feel like a mouse rattling around in a great suit of armor. Some Defenders make their presence felt by being confrontational and combative. Other Defenders are stubborn and signal that they won't be pushed around when they take a passive-aggressive stance. Yet others establish their self-identity and protect interpersonal boundaries through being critical and judgmental.

**Figure 1.3**

**Diagram of Enneagram Model With the Triads**

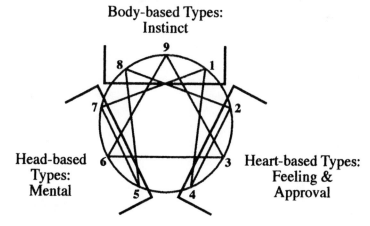

**Attentional Focus**

- Point One—Error
- Point Two—Needs of Others
- Point Three—Tasks
- Point Four—What's Missing

- Point Five—Acquiring Knowledge
- Point Six—Scanning for Hidden Dangers
- Point Seven—Pleasant Plans and Future Options
- Point Eight—Power and Control
- Point Nine—Others' Agenda

Much of what makes the Enneagram such a powerful model of personality is its ability to pinpoint an unconscious, characteristic narrowing of attention in each strategy. Helen Palmer is a leading author and teacher of the Enneagram. Palmer's (1988) original contribution to the field is the classification of the foci of attention of the E-types. This attentional focus directly impacts behavior in all its forms, including motivation, learning, communication, leadership, relationships with others, and so on. The narrowing of attention ordinarily operates as an involuntary response until we become aware of its grip on our lives. The narrowing lens of attention through which we perceive the world most often looms so large in our unconscious awareness that it becomes our entire worldview: "My attention is on gaining approval for what I accomplish, therefore so is everyone else"—the Performer. "My attention is on seeking safety and certainty in every situation therefore so is everyone else"—the Questioner. "My attention is on taking on the agenda of others therefore so is everyone else"—the Peacekeeper.

Recognizing when attention narrows and the lens takes over allows people to see themselves anew and to work constructively with their perceptual bias. Once we understand its power we can consciously use it in positive ways, and modify its tendency to induce worldview myopia. A Performer Three will always remain a Performer, but the attentional narrowing to tasks and getting the job done regardless of human cost (their own and others) can be modified to take cognizance of personal feelings and the input and concerns of others.

We can understand and appreciate the intentions of those whose attentional focus makes them see the world differently from ourselves. Knowing their own strategy and understanding the eight others with whom they share the world incrementally increases understanding and compassion and vastly reduces misunderstandings and misapplied motive.

A situational example follows in which a student, or your own child, or someone else confronts you: "This grade is unfair, I don't deserve this," (or some similar confrontational accusation).

All E-types will react to this provocation—attentional narrowing takes over. Perfectionist One teachers will want to gain the moral upper hand and prove that they are right. Helper Twos will change the grade to meet the student's needs. Performer Threes will want to get on with the agenda and try to sell the student on the grade. Royal Family Fours will be challenged to look behind the grade—"what's missing here"—to find a way to connect with the student on an emotional level, the grade is irrelevant. Observer Fives will want to gain more information about the grade, downplay the emotions of the moment, and set up a schema for the grand design of all the grades for the academic year. Questioner

Sixes will feel attacked, on shaky ground, suspicious of the student's motives, and try to build a logical hypothesis for exactly *why* that grade. Optimist Sevens will reframe the confrontation and give the student several options of how to look at the grade, alternatives mostly laced with optimistic silver linings. Boss Eights will raise the ante and be disappointed if the student backs off. Peace-keeper Nines will buy the student's agenda, broaden the discussion to an over-view of what is really important in the student's life, and leave the grade issue unresolved.

In the same situation, an educator (or parent) with some Enneagram knowl-edge will be aware that they are about to act from their myopic attentional focus, and know that what they have to do is pay attention, observe their attentional shift, find a neutral place where they can go to quickly in their mind and say, "OK, what's going on here? Why is this grade so important to this student that they're willing to do this, come up to me, argue with me?" Inner awareness may seem like esoteric behavior, but it's good common sense and there are practical ways to develop its presence. They're called attention practices, paying attention to oneself. In an essential way discovery of our E-type begins a process of learn-ing to live with ourselves, to pay attention. In Chapter 4 on attention practices, these techniques are introduced, along with much else about self-awareness and self-control.

No E-type strategy together is better than any other. Not only Performer Three students feel achievement when they do well, or only Peacekeeper Nine baseball coaches take on the team's agenda. The important fact is that energy follows attention and our attention habitually returns to the nine foci listed above.

A frequent question in Enneagram workshops involves the nature/nurture di-chotomy of developmental psychology. Both propositions are evident in E-type development. Most Enneagram authors and theorists currently agree that people are born with a disposition toward one of the nine strategies (nature). If their childhood is tense and stressful, the E-type characteristics go deep. If their child-hood is secure, the E-type characteristics appear more lightly (nurture).

### Gift

- Point One—Moral Compass
- Point Two—True Altruism
- Point Three—Leadership on Behalf of Others
- Point Four—Creativity and Uniqueness
- Point Five—Rationality
- Point Six—Logic
- Point Seven—Optimism
- Point Eight—Harnessing Their Energy to Empower Others
- Point Nine—Universal Love

It is a truism that people have low and high sides to their personalities:

"This brings out the best (or worst) in me." The classification of the gifts of the E-types is another of my original contributions to the system. The gifts of the E-types come to the fore when people are feeling secure within themselves and managing their anxiety threshhold. When they are not in the downside of their fixation, not avoiding their central preoccupation, they are in a sense more whole, more able to utilize the positive flow of their personality traits. Each description of the E-types later in the book discusses these implications indepth, two illustrations follow here.

In this stance, a Perfectionist One educator will drop the constant criticality and judgment of herself and her students as not measuring up to the inner right/wrong standard she upholds. Now she teaches with an almost objective certainty, knowing she is correct in trying to lead her students' thinking in a certain direction. She has an intuitive sense of the morality of issues.

Likewise, a Questioner Six educator drops his constant scanning and suspicion. He teaches material with conviction gained through hard-won back-and-forth argument. He can move students with the power of the clarity of his thinking. He has an intuitive sense of the pure logic behind what he is teaching.

### Avoidances

- Point One—Error
- Point Two—Own Emotional Needs
- Point Three—Failure
- Point Four—Ordinariness
- Point Five—Connection
- Point Six—Deviance (Being Seen as Different)
- Point Seven—Pain
- Point Eight—Vulnerability
- Point Nine—Conflict

Enneagram psychology pinpoints nine pivotal avoidances. These avoidances play a major role in our habitual, or unawakened, personality. Our sense of self, our very defense mechanisms, are largely put in place around the avoidances. Much of what drives people to behave the way they do, and how they experience their emotional world, is a consequence of avoiding, or denying these preoccupations. People become anxious around what they are avoiding and experience themselves through their anxiety.

A first step in self-awareness can be to begin to examine what component of anxiety a person's compulsive behavior covers over. When those aspects of ourselves that have been avoided and denied are owned up to, processed, and integrated, the self can begin to emerge as a whole.

For example, an Observer Five educator avoids connection—with emotions and people. Fives are aware of a need to manage (hoard) their time, energy, and private space. Connections are unpredictable, they can lead to unexpected and unwanted drains on the Observer's reserves. Each day in the classroom, the Observer educator expends just so much energy and time. Surprises and unexpected demands can derail the Five who is managing/avoiding connection with a mental control switch.

A Boss Eight educator avoids vulnerability. Being vulnerable means not knowing who is in control, whether they'll be fair, and opening oneself to the risk of being jumped. This sounds like suicidal behavior to the Eight. So Bosses make sure they are safe by taking control, seeking confrontation and often moving into action without thinking. At the beginning of the academic year the Boss's classroom can be rife with tension around issues of confrontation. Perhaps by the end of the semester, if the Boss is comfortable with her students, she'll let down her guard and share the softer, more open side of her personality that not many people know.

**Growth Path**

- Point One—From criticality and judging to serenity
- Point Two—From pride to humility
- Point Three—From self-deceit to honesty
- Point Four—From envy to equanimity
- Point Five—From hoarding (guarding) to allowing
- Point Six—From fear to courage
- Point Seven—From no limits to restraint
- Point Eight—From excess to trusting sufficiency
- Point Nine—From being asleep to oneself to right action

The Enneagram model describes nine ways of inner growth, each based on the central feature or fixation and moving toward its essential opposite. This has obvious implications for everyone who discovers their E-type strategy and who, through self-awarness and attention practice, transforms their core energy from the bondage of habitual behavior to the relief of freedom from its charge.

Educators daily encounter these fixations in their students. Good educators have probably already intervened in charged situations. In a sense inadvertantly they've enabled their student to think about working with their core energy (fixation) in a more constructive way. The Enneagram provides sophisticated interventions for what educators grope toward almost instinctively. Most students are fearful in a gymnastics class the first time they work on parallel bars. Gymnastics teachers often work long hours with the most fearful students—catching them again and again until they have certainty that they can manage the moves and do them without the teacher. These teachers will never know that they have broken through the personality defense mechanisms of the Point Sixes in their classes. At that moment when Point Six students leap into the air their fear is transformed to courage.

A college professor meets weekly with a student who is bright but struggles to keep deadlines. In their discussions the professor allows the student to fly any ideas, including those which certainly will be questionable in a paper. In allowing a free-form discussion, she gives the student a safe place to fail. By introducing ideas from the outside, she demonstrates she is aware the student has trouble with self-motivation and needs a frame to work up against. The professor will never know she has broken through the personality defense mechanisms of the Point Nines in her class. When the paper is delivered on time that Point Nine student has awakened to himself and transformed sloth (*acedie*) to right action on his own behalf.

### Essence

- Point One—Perfection
- Point Two—Freedom/Will
- Point Three—Hope
- Point Four—Universal Belonging
- Point Five—Omniscient Awareness
- Point Six—Faith
- Point Seven—Commitment to Work
- Point Eight—Truth (Fairness and Justice)
- Point Nine—Universal Love

Essence is that quality of being that arises when people are totally present in the moment. No thoughts, memories, associations, emotions, or sensory perceptions interfere in the experience of being fully present. These moments are commonly know in our culture as *being in the flow* or *being in the zone*. In sports, athletes talk of being in the zone, a phenomenon that occurs when time and space take on a dimension akin to slow motion. The *real* split second timing to gather instinct, training, and reactivity to accomplish the athlete's goal seems to take place in a *virtual* pocket of enough time to do what has to be done. Essence qualities occur when people speak or act before they know they have spoken or acted. In essence it is almost as if there is no sense of a dualistic self that can be observed. These are peak moments of our life experience. The above list attempts to name the essence qualities, but these are only approximations. Our perceptual language does not have words for these qualities. Ephemeral, fleeting, they disappear the moment awareness of them arises.

### The Arrows

While much of the psychological value of the Enneagram lies in its descriptions of the E-types, much of its predictive power lies in the patterns of interconnecting lines. These lines point away from and toward any one point on the diagram. In other words, every point is connected to two others with the arrows (see Figure 1.4). The arrows' direction mirrors predictable shifts in our E-type strategies, as when people feel personally secure, or when they find themselves in stressful situations. For example, educators teaching a course where everything "clicks" relax their inner defenses. In that situation they may move against the arrows into behavior patterns of the E-type behind their own. Teaching a class where the chemistry is "wrong" is stressful. Following the flow pattern of the arrows, they are likely in this situation to move with the arrow and adopt the characteristics of the type ahead.

In these situations a task-driven Performer Three can come across as almost a different teacher. In a secure mode the Performer Three goes to the Questioner Six and teaches more slowly, thoughtfully, and allows more time for process. In the shift to Peacekeeper Nine under conditions of stress the Point Three teacher may come across as if acting in a daze—spinning his wheels, unable to prioritize, struggling to move into action. Once we know our basic strategy, we can connect the arrows to our stress and secure points. When people find their E-type strategy they also discover these two other places they go to on the Enneagram and they gravitate naturally into them.

**Figure 1.4**

**Basic Enneagram Model with Arrows**

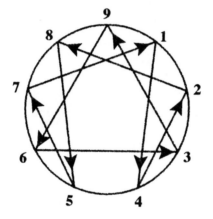

## Wings

People also have wings, the points on either side of their E-type. One wing may predominate, or both may be equally available, and they color or flavor the E-types. The Points Three-Six-Nine triangle have wings that can be seen as variants of the core preoccupations of that E-type triad, or even as a more inner-directed and outer-directed version of the core point. For example, Point Six with a Point Five wing (inner-directed) may be more private, withdrawn, and overtly fearful. Point Six with a Point Seven wing (outer-directed), may be more outgoing, friendly, less overtly suspicious, and doubtful.

Similarly, a person with an E-type that falls on the hexagon (the figure formed by the interconnecting lines), still acts out his or her preoccupations, but with a specific coloring. Point Eight with a Point Nine wing handles confrontation in a more stubborn, passive way, while Point Eight with a Point Seven wing is less overtly confrontational, more jocular, disarming the anger with a little charm.

## TYPING OTHERS

Knowing that there are nine intelligences, nine strategies, nine basic ways of being in the world, and providing that spectrum of possibilities for students or whomever we are educating and interacting with, we can provide a large canvas for people to create themselves fully. I strongly believe that we need to keep the spotlight of inquiry on ourselves and work with that. If we know ourselves we can keep coming back to self-awareness, to our fixations, to an informed understanding of how we are impacting others. Then we can minimize our negative impact by finding a place of choice from which to act, to allow ourselves options as to how we respond. With that level of self-awareness we provide an empathic, supportive space for our students, for all the people in our lives. To me that is the way the Enneagram edge can be used to the greatest advantage in education—indeed, in all walks of life.

A journey of self-discovery, recognizing one's E-type is part of the process of awakening and best left to each person. We should not go around typing others. There are obvious dangers and consequences of mistyping and stereotyping. Young people especially, as they grow in knowledge of the inner behaviors of their personality, need to find the strategy they embody for themselves so as to see clearly this *self* we all wear. Let us make the means of discovery available, but leave the gift of that discovery to each individual.

## NOTE

The names Perfectionist, Performer, Observer, and Boss are attributed to Helen Palmer. The name Helper is attributed to Don Riso and Russ Hudson. The names Royal Family, Questioner, Optimist, and Peacekeeper are attributed to Janet Levine.

# 2

# ENNEAGRAM TRIADS PERSONALITY INDICATOR FOR EDUCATORS

This inventory is designed to help you understand your basic patterns of behavior—how you think and how you feel.

This vital information underlies what motivates you, why you make the decisions you do, what sort of educator you are, why you interact with others the way you do. I authored the inventory (Levine, 1997), by compiling data from interviews, and tested it initially on over 1,200 educators at all levels. Refined from their feedback, the instrument directs you accurately to your Enneagram strategy. It pinpoints the many behavioral traits that make you who you are, explains *why* you do what you do, and demonstrates how you do it. Understanding yourself and what drives you is among the most valuable assets you can have as an educator.

## Instructions

Choose one of the three categories following each question. At the end of this section you can ascertain your score. Your personality modality is indicated by the majority of your choices. Detailed descriptions and explanations of the personality strategies within each modality follow. Do not think for long about your response. Read the question and accompanying statements, and circle one without further thought. If you cannot decide on an option, chose the one that fits you the closest.

Then read the accompanying explanation and descriptions. Read the three profiles in your triad first. Find yourself, then go on to read the others.

### *How I Think? How I Feel?*

1. *You are part of a team evaluating colleagues in the classroom. Observing another teacher gets you thinking about your own teaching. You assess your*

*teaching style as:*

a. My teaching style has to do with interaction and energy, with con necting to people. I ask myself, am I getting through on an emotional level? Do students understand where I'm coming from? How am I coming across, how do others see me? It's important that we connect in a meaningful way.

b. My teaching style is intuitive, I have a "gut" feel about what is right and wrong, fair and unfair. I don't like the sense that I'm being crowded—whether by institutional rules, expectations of others, demands that are extraneous to the job I'm doing. I don't always like conflict, but I have a great need to say what I have to say, to be heeded.

c. My teaching style is intellectual, no question. I'm interested in how people think, process information, work with ideas. I live in my head—conceptualizing, fantasizing, thinking things through are important to me. *Rationality* is a big word with me.

2. *In thinking through the details of your teaching style, how do you assess the way you communicate and present materials:*

a. What you see is what you get. I don't use guile or fancy gimmicks. I present the way I understand it; I give it my best shot. Students get my honest sense of how it is.

b. Presentation, connection, and performance are important to me—the medium is the message, that kind of thing. So I try to put on a show, highlight the work, find the nuances of expression that will enhance the basics. I use emotion and show-time, anything that will help students become engaged learners.

c. I try to keep things as conceptual, uncluttered, and intellectually pure as I can. I teach them to ask questions, to practice skepticism, to be discerning thinkers. I try to probe below the surface: If we can stick with what's rational and logical, we're on solid ground.

3. *If you were being evaluated, how would you answer the question: Why do you teach?*

a. I teach because of the mental activity, of finding answers, of the excitement that comes from seeing young minds open to the possibilities, to big-picture connections, to new conclusions. The mental energy in the classroom stimulates my own thinking.

b. I teach because I value people, and I love the possibilities of all sorts of human contact and connection: the emotional highs and lows, the feeling of achievement when we all "click" and experience some profound interconnection in the moment. The classroom is like the theater when the audience and the actors become one—unity built on empathy, human understanding, little else.

c. I teach because in a profound way I want to develop young people and help steer them in a direction where they can make capable, competent life-choices for themselves. People need a sense of themselves, of where they stand in the world. The world is difficult to understand, you can lose your way all too easily. I want to give people some skills, some tools, some road maps to take on their journeys.

4. *Although you get along with most students you teach, every so often one comes along who clashes with your style and doesn't like you. What would they say to you?*

a. I come on too emotionally when I present things; they often feel like I'm trying to manipulate them into interacting with me. Why can't I just say things out straight? I try to shine it on; it's almost like I need their approval.

b. I'm too abstract, too theoretical, too detached. They need more emotional, personal interaction from me. We're talking, I'm listening, but they have this sense that I'm not really there, that I've moved to somewhere in my head. The harder they try to know where they are with me, the more I distance myself. They ask if anything gets through to me emotionally.

c. I have a sense of boundaries around myself. I can come across as an immovable force, solid, implacable, although I'm not usually aware of this. I know I can dig in and nothing people say or do will shift me. I've been accused of being overly defensive, stubborn, critical. I'm not usually aware of my impact on people.

5. *One of your students is in serious trouble because of a grave misdemeanor. You are the one who gets to break the news. How do you approach this difficult meeting?*

a. I'll send her a memo detailing all the reasons why this outcome is inevitable.That way she'll have time to think things over and we can have a rational discussion and not get caught up in emotions. She knows what I feel for her personally, this has nothing to do with that—it's a disciplinary decision, based on school rules.

b. I'll call her in and tell it to her straight. We've known one another long enough, we know where we stand. This does not affect my relationship with her, it's school rules. It will be hard, but face-to-face, saying it straight without any extraneous talk, that's always the best way to do these difficult encounters.

c. I don't like doing this, it strikes at the core of me. We know one another well, have a good understanding, a good connection. I know what she'll be feeling, as if it were myself. How best to put this across? I'm more anxious about this than I want to admit—emotional upsets really get to me. She'll accept it any way I tell her.

6. *The Principal/Dean informs your department that due to budget cuts one teacher is to be let go. You think it might be you. How do you react?*

a. Disbelief, I can't accept this at all. I knew cuts were coming, but not in this department. I've been with the school since I started teaching. I feel like my heart has been wrenched out of me, I'm so connected here. I can't get beyond my feelings. I'll never get over this one.

b. I guess I should have seen this coming. All the signs were there, I just didn't think they were pointing in my direction. If you think about it rationally and logically, it's a perfectly legitimate business decision. I allowed myself to be blind-sided. I've learned a lot here, I'll get good references, I know a lot of people in education. Maybe it's time to move on anyway: it's a shove I need. I won't take this personally.

c. I'm uncomfortable; I have so much anger in me. There's no place to feel you belong in this world. I did everything anyone could ask of me here. You get slammed one way or the other. The anger is overwhelming, I feel it in my whole body. This just reinforces my sense that life is unfair, life is hard. My mistake was to leave myself open to be kicked around.

7. *You want to be a great educator—your dream reflects the deepest parts of yourself. Your passion for your vision stems from:*

a. A feeling that I've got something people can relate to. I believe I've got what it takes to put across my vision in a way that's honest, good, and effective. It's all about people. I can get through to people, I'm in tune, I understand people. In my heart I know this is true.

b. A hunch, an instinct that I'm in the right place at the right time doing what I'm supposed to be doing—when my head, heart, and belly are aligned behind something, I can trust that sense. I can put my full force behind it. I would never commit myself if I didn't feel 100 percent about it.

c. The knowledge that I have thought through first-rate ideas that will be of benefit and break new ground in terms of concepts. I wouldn't be teaching if I wasn't convinced of the validity of my ideas. If I wasn't one hundred percent sure of my thinking I wouldn't be putting myself on the line.

8. *You are sitting opposite the recruitment head of a school trying to convince her to give you a position. You feel confident you can land the job because:*

a. Of my proven record as an ideas person. No one can question that what I do is conceptually thought through and mentally sound. My references attest to my theoretical ability and know-how. I'm as intellectually solid a teacher as any on the market.

b. Of my track record of getting through to people. Whether it's in the classroom, the soccer team, the library committee, running the PTA auction, I've always been able to put across what I believe in a way that people feel they want to be part of it. I know people, people are my life. I can get the world on board.

c. Of the fact I just know this is the right job for me, I can fit right in here. I have reliable instincts. I've proven it to myself and others time and again. Lots of people have made good from my instincts. Only something that I believe in 100 percent would get me into this chair to ask for a job. Students know where they stand with me, that makes them feel safe.

9. *Your peers nominate you for a Teaching Excellence award. What is your response?*

a. The award is objective validation that the way I think about what I teach, my intellectual energy, and the highly mental approach I bring to teaching are verifiable, something others can measure. I'm pleased.

b. Public recognition for my efforts is gratifying, but it's not about me, I'm not what I do. This award won't change things one way or the other, make me a better person, or bring meaning to my life. I'll just go on teaching the way I always have.

c. I know I'm a good teacher, so I deserve this, but many of my colleagues are good teachers, too. What is important about this, is that I was nominated by my peers. That means the world to me. Enough people know me, value me, are connected to me and want to acknowledge me this way. That really gets to me.

## SCORE

The following majority of choices indicates your modality. You may find you have several choices in different areas. There are sound Enneagram reasons for this that have to do with the stress/secure shifts from your core point. For example, many educators are secure in their teaching style and the inventory can reflect this. Nonetheless your primary triad is the one that shows the most choices.

*Attacher:* 1a, 2b, 3b, 4a, 5c, 6a, 7a, 8b, 9c
*Detacher:* 1c, 2c, 3a, 4b, 5a, 6b, 7c, 8a, 9a
*Defender:* 1b, 2a, 3c, 4c, 5b, 6c, 7b, 8c, 9b

## THE ENNEAGRAM TRIADS PERSONALITY INDICATOR

### Explanation

People are different. We all know this to be true. Not just the obvious differences of age, sex, race, life circumstances, ethnicity. But different personalities, different behaviors, motivations, actions and reactions, different ways of understanding, of deciding what's important, of communicating. We all know people feel differently about the same situation. Let's talk about feelings—there are different responses to, for instance, personal feedback. *Some people respond on an emotional level:* Dawn tries to empathize with the person giving the feedback. Jack adjusts his persona to accommodate the feedback to his image. Paul wants to connect meaningfully with the person giving the feedback. *Some people experience feelings mentally:* Betty tries to make sense of the interconnections in the ideas around the feedback. David doubts what he's hearing. Suzy hears several options in the feedback. *Some people experience feelings in the context of intrapersonal boundaries:* Chris confronts the feedback. Bob concentrates on avoiding conflict generated by the feedback. Laura feels criticized by feedback and becomes moralistic and judgmental.

Different people think differently. What about the news that there is an earthquake in San Francisco? Dawn thinks about the victims and seeks ways to help through relief agencies. Jack thinks he's lucky not to be there, groveling in the ruins of all he's built. Paul thinks of the high drama, and connects with the suffering, pain, and heroism of those involved. Betty thinks about earthquakes: where do they come from, how do they occur? David thinks of all the times he's told people he knows in the Bay Area that this would happen. Suzy thinks of the different ways she'd go about rebuilding. Chris reacts with rage in the face of his vulnerability when it comes to natural disasters. Bob takes the long view that events like the earthquake are part of life and life goes on. Laura thinks of how much death and destruction could be avoided if people adhered to stricter building codes.

How we think and how we feel—habits of heart and mind—show different personalities.

There are three distinct modalities of being, three broad patterns of behavior, three basic motivations driving how people operate in the world. One modality can be described as outer-directed attention, a way of making sense of and operating in the world through attachment to people and relationships. The emotional context is the Attachers' environment. Another modality can be described as inner-directed attention, a way of making Detachers' environment. The third modality can be described as self-protective attention, a way of making sense of and operating in the world with an awareness of boundaries. The instinctual context is the Defenders' environment.

**Personality Profiles**

*Attacher Triad*

### *Key Issues for Attachers*

- Image: central concerns are tied up in image—how am I coming across to others, what image am I conveying, how are people responding to me?
- Connection: reaching out, getting through, making contact is affirming to Attachers.

- Approval: gaining approval is a major motivation for Attachers.

*Attachers—The Helper (Point Two).* Helpers struggle to know their own needs, but instinctively know the needs of others. They are sensitive to other people's feelings. What motivates them at work and at play is knowing what others need. Helpers convey feelings of warmth, understanding, and genuine concern in their interactions. Sometimes they feel frustrated because they're not able to do as much for others as they would like. To feel comfortable with others, Helpers rely on interpersonal alignment; they can be sweetly effusive, sincere and quietly empathetic, firm and plain-talking—all at the same time depending on the person with whom they are interacting. Helpers can juggle several personas concurrently. They pitch their conversations to elicit approval from others. The subtext of their conversation is based on personal appeal: "Look what I can do for you. You need my help. I am here to serve you." They feel misunderstood if others think they're trying to manipulate them: they want to be perceived as warm-hearted and sensitive.

Helpers develop a gracious environment whether at home or at work built on mutual approval. They pick protégés, or champion persons of consequence. The selected person is wrapped in a cloak of largess and service. Helpers work long hours to open doors, and keep them open, with anticipatory expectations of gratitude and heightened emotional responsiveness in return. Yet helpers can feel harried by their constant need for approval and acceptance. Often Helpers recognize that they have a need to give, but far more subtle insight is required if they are to see that their subtext in giving is a need to be loved, to be popular, to be admired. If they feel underappreciated Helpers can become emotional and demanding.

Helpers project a positive persona and turn on stellar performances day after day. They are usually popular. Their excellent communication skills, the special care and attention they turn on for bosses, or peers they deem significant, elicit admiration, popularity, and love. Helpers breathe approval like oxygen. This is the bottom line—the need to be approved, even loved, is the reason for giving.

Helpers appear to be independent but internally know how much time they spend attending to others. They attend to the needs of a group as a whole, but they assiduously monitor the progress of several "favorites." They can keep a mental tab running of different peoples' schedules and agendas—and manifest unexpected, but appreciated, behind-the-scenes support. They value the private confidentiality and emotional resonance such support engenders.

Helpers do not like their efforts to appear self-serving, but will give unstintingly of themselves on behalf of the organization for which they work. It is tempting to devote too much time to a job that has interpersonal appeal. They will volunteer to do the additional assignment, or spend extra unforeseen hours on a project. They devote time to developing peers' potential, and welfare, and take pride in others' accomplishments, while often thinking: "They couldn't have done that without me." They work hard at making relationships happen. The allure of someone else's needs always seems more important than the Helper's own emotional needs. However Twos do take care of their physical needs.

*Attachers—The Performer (Point Three).* Performers literally *perform,* both in the sense of getting the job done, and constantly seeking to be the center of attention. Performers like to think of themselves as the role models of their professions—the image is of confidence, brisk efficiency, solid skills, and leadership. They believe who they are as people is tied up with what they accomplish. Coming first, being a winner, is strong motivation for Performers, who get a lot of recognition and reward for what they do. Performers play a central role in their undertakings, they are unmistakably present; they create the environment, set tasks, direct interactions, achieve goals. They communicate by persuasion: "This model works for me, it'll work for you." They get a lot done, most of it successfully.

Performers play to their peers and colleagues, basking in the applause and approval. They play their "audience" with skill and a finely tuned ability to pick up on pockets of resistance to their message. They adjust their voice, vocabulary, emotional range, and body language until they feel they have their "audience" (even if it's one other person) "in their hand." Performers are goal-directed: they drive themselves and expect the same commitment from others.

The results are what count—get the job done, efficiently, without fuss or fretting. Performers will not be bothered with their own or others' feelings or emotional responses; not if these stand in the way of completing the task at hand. They are impatient with people who waste their time through bad planning and inefficiency. They hate being held up—by illness, incompetence, whatever—and will rather complete the task themselves. Natural leaders, they are also team players when they respect the leader.

Performers sweep up others in their forward-driving energy. They move directly from idea to action with little time lag to accommodate the hesitancy of more skeptical or cautious peers. They know from experience how hard it is for others to resist their goal-directed momentum. Performers thrive on the energy and excitement generated by their interactions with others. It is a high when the energy drives a meeting along.

Performers see the overall goal as getting from Point A to Point Z. This goal is sorted into various tasks, prioritized, and assigned a time frame—two hours, within a week, this quarter. The larger goal is made manageable in sequential blocks of time. Performers can juggle several tasks at the same time. Time not used to do something is time wasted. Performers think in terms of deadlines—an objective measure of progress at any given time.

Performers feel an illusion of control when there is constant activity around them. In the downtime after attaining a goal, often Performers can be at a loss what to do with themselves. There is time and space to regard peers and colleagues, not as units to fulfill the Performers' agenda, but as people with their own priorities, problems, and responses. This is when Performers experience feelings and become aware of their exhaustion, accompanied by an unwelcome insecurity. Doubts can arise that affect the Performer's overarching self-confidence. But the time can be used by Performers to think things through, replacing their tendency to what is often glib superficiality and quick-fix answers.

*Attachers—The Royal Family (Point Four).* The Royal Family live in a rich emotional world. They have a sense of their own uniqueness, yet, paradoxically, Royals focus not on what they have, but on what's missing. The Royal Family think of themselves as different from others, and can often feel lonely and misunderstood. They feel they bring the gift of themselves—unique, creative talent and depth—to both what they do and to the people with whom they interact. They care deeply about people and seek emotionally meaningful connections. They take pride in their own and their peers' achievements and experience a fulfilling emotional connection at being part of meaningful and valuable creativity: "Something special." Royals devalue themselves in comparison to others who seem to have more, or better. This self-denigration can manifest as competitive envy.

The Royal Family embodies emotionality, and a dramatic tone imbues their relationships. Relationships are all-important. They regard themselves as sensitive, with the ability to experience feelings deeply. Royals are aware of a push-pull in relationships: they can come across as aloof and self-absorbed or, conversely, as vitally interested—this inconsistency is often bewildering to others.

Royals often violate boundaries in other people because they yearn for connection both to deep feelings and relationships. They can overdramatize their feelings to the discomfort of others. They like to be liked and to have their efforts appreciated. Yet often when praise comes their way, Royals deflect it—the glass is always half empty. They experience a cycle of expectation and then regret. The Royal Family need to learn to value the flat, ordinary moments in all undertakings, and take their attention off the dramatic high-low extremes. The unavailability of emotional sustenance can lead to melancholy, even depression.

The daily passage of time with its routine tasks is of little consequence to the Royal Family. They live for the grand-scale occurrences that color what they often feel is the dull oblivion of the rest of their lives. The time when deep feelings emerge in interactions, or on projects, is memorable; yet Royals cannot recall the ordinary matters of everyday life. It is hard for the Royal Family to stay in the present moment. Now is filled with nostalgia and associative memories of options not exercised, and "if only" thinking. This year's highlights are seen in the rosy-hued mythic light of significant moments of the past. The Royal Family measures their lives by dramatic interpersonal events beyond the passage of time.

### Detacher Triad

### Key Issues for Detachers

- Interconnections: seeking the key among ideas to unlock life's big picture puzzles.

- Mental argument: seeking certainty through logic and rational think-ing.
- Imagination: fantasizing, creating pleasant options, with a major emphasis on planning.

*Detachers—The Observer (Point Five).* Observers move away from people. By detaching from the outer world and realizing their thoughts and emotions in a rich inner life, Observers feel secure. They minimize participation as a way of keeping their inner selves intact. They need more privacy and private time than most people do. When alone they relive experiences and can find it easier to get in touch with feelings than when living them the first time.

Observers are interested in finding answers and making connections. They seek radical approaches to problem solving that goes beyond traditional ways of thinking. Gaining knowledge is finding pieces of the puzzle—each piece might be incomplete in itself, but locks together, creating the whole, or larger picture. Observers look for a new, or particular, way to get across a complex idea. They appreciate working with others who also struggle to create, to synthesize ideas, and admire those who step outside the bounds of packaged, conventional think-ing. They like to watch events rather than be involved in the thick of things. Observers interpersonal style is to play it "close to the vest," they are not emo-tionally expansive and forthcoming in their interactions. They value privacy and respect the privacy of others. Observers prefer to communicate in closely worded notes, conveying their feedback and appreciation in comments on papers, or pri-vate correspondence. They prefer to work in an almost silent environment, silence signals evidence of real thought.

Observers connect with others through an exchange of ideas. They try to be impassive and objective, stone-faced in meetings, to convey that everyones' ideas are equally valid. Often accused of being unresponsive, the rejoinder is that all ideas are listened to without value judgments. Observers maintain that by not talking unnecessarily; they empower others who need to be listened to. From the Observers' point of view their detachment shows respect for their peers' boundaries. Yet colleagues may interpret their noninvolvement as negative lack of interest.

Observers are careful about how they spend their time and energy. They ap-portion time to anticipated demands—being in the office, attending a meeting, traveling to a client. Unexpected demands and spontaneous invitations are jar-ring; they assess the demand with a reactive response: "What will I get for my time?" Time spent in mental pursuits is time well-spent: Observers hold dear the notion that knowledge is power. Knowledge is never given away wholesale; people have to earn access to the Observers' hard-won treasure-house through diligent effort and evidence of real thinking.

*Detachers—The Questioner (Point Six).* Questioners regard the world as in-herently unsafe, and they seek certainty and safety, their attention focused on po-tential threats. Highly imaginative, they are as good at locking onto what is potentially, as well as what actually is, dangerous. Questioners either run away from danger or meet it full force. If something is thought through in a logical way, the conclusion is reliable. Thinking things through, and skepticism are high on the Questioner's list. To feel safe with people, Questioners want evidence that they can interact with their own thinking. Doubting peoples' intentions, they generate an interrogative climate around themselves, where argument and counterargument are welcomed so that everyone ends up with clear conclusions, albeit drawn from different perspectives.

Questioners believe that everyone can think deductively. They want peers to come up with probing questions that reveal thought and skepticism. Their own questioning attitude to life can make them come across as sharp and critical. People often misinterpret anxious prodding at their thinking as personal attacks, or as being treated with unwarranted suspicion. Questioners can be perceived as setting up a case against a peer.

Questioners are ambivalent about themselves in positions of leadership. They alternate between being rigidly authoritarian and nonauthoritarian. Their own inner doubts cause the swing. When they are afraid of being challenged, they exert control; when they are filled with inner conviction, they relax and become permissive. Seeking predictability and safety, they view the authority of their bosses with skepticism. Periods of blind allegiance oscillate with rebellious insurrection.

Questioners are constantly vigilant; an inner radar system seeks out the hidden intentions of others. This wariness is often perceived as reactive negativism. Unanswered questions, or unexpressed anger, undermines the basis of trust they have built with colleagues. Procrastination sets in until doubts are resolved, until the Questioner can separate negative feedback from a personal attack.

Questioners can put aside personal doubts in service of a cause—they are loyal to the institution, or an idea. Once established, their inner conviction lets them feel certain in promoting their cause. They trust objective data far more than personal assurances. Questioners see danger in acting openly, but inaction, procrastination, is equally dangerous through missed deadlines and failed enterprises. Yet Questioners can act on behalf of others, and rally the troops behind a person or ideal in which they believe. Once committed, they are generally loyal.

Questioners experience time as an authority looming over them and which they must obey. In fact most of the people and circumstances in their lives become the authority with which they must wrestle. They perceive themselves as constantly on the rack of responsibility to satisfy *the authority,* whatever form it takes.

*Detachers—The Optimist (Point Seven).* Optimists are focused on future plans and new and exciting options. When reality bites, Optimists escape into an inner world where there are no limits; being occupied with upbeat ideas obviates painful circumstances. High-energy Optimists have many balls in the air. They focus on keeping them up there. Optimists are fascinated by ideas and interesting options, such as the way to change a process, or design a new plant.

They dislike doing the same thing the same way twice—new input, new ideas from articles, new problems present exciting directions to try.

Optimists are process people, planners. The plan's the thing, the doing of it is left to lesser beings. They can spend hours at their desks thinking through how to present material or a promotion plan. Optimists never feel they have exhausted the possibilities of their subject—the layers, the variety, the complexity are fascinating. Optimists imbue positive mental energy and alertness, their minds race with myriad ideas and responses. Often their associative mental leaps to creative conclusions are too fast for others to follow. Peers need to tell them to slow down their thinking. Colleagues can feel swept away by the Optimists' mental intensity.

Optimists are fluid, multioptional thinkers; they assume that others are also comfortable with shifts in direction, choosing between options, and moving among ideas. Optimists exercise mental ellipses and reframe concepts in ways that baffle other thinkers. There is always another way to present the material; and to the Optimist, on-the-spot ideas—as they arise—seem brilliant and important to throw into the mix, now. It is hard to pinpoint the Optimists' position; they are mercurial; ideas and concepts do intersect and connect, and options change as new information is acquired and processed.

Optimists try to grasp at the pattern of another person's thinking: how that person sees themselves, what are the components of their thinking, what issues fascinate them; are they detail or big-picture thinkers, open to new possibilities, or conservative? They subconsciously classify people by how they think. Discovering how others think allows Optimists to get on with them by mirroring a perspective, or framing an approach. The ability to form patterns and make mental connections is of basic concern to Optimists. Optimists can come across as having a sense of personal entitlement: they believe people are entitled to a pleasant life. Your time, effort, and attention are at their disposal. They'll charm and disarm you.

Optimists experience time like an elastic band with an almost infinite capacity to expand. Time expands to enable them to fit in all their plans and options. Time does not impose limits around their commitments.

### Defender Triad

#### Key Issues for Defenders

- Instinct: trusting their intuitive sense of how they feel about something is the only way for Defenders to feel comfortable.
- Being heard: it is important to Defenders' sense of self that people listen when they have something to say.
- Feeling respected: this helps Defenders establish their space, and enables them to be present.

*Defenders—The Boss (Point Eight).* Bosses live with an innate sense of power and control. Confrontation for the Boss is a way of reading the world, of establishing where the power is, and of knowing who has control. Exerting control is a way of moving through what to the Boss is an inherently unjust world. Bosses use confrontation as a way of connecting with others. They assume that confrontation is part of interactions; those who stand up for themselves are most able and most open. If Bosses sense that someone is not being honest, they will push and push, to provoke a response. When Bosses feel a connection with someone who stands up for what they believe, they will become a protector and do everything to support that person. Bosses empower those under their protection with a mixture of challenge and support. They do not tolerate weakness in people, unless they see where it's coming from. Their anger can be devastating and abusive. Bosses commit themselves with passionate conviction to what they do. Often their anger arises in defense of a belief system, but they come across as personally confrontational—Bosses spend a lot of time mending fences.

Bosses make their own rules. They believe rules are to be broken. This often causes a dilemma: how to hold the structure of the organization, while believing those rules and regulations are not always productive or beneficial. Bosses take charge. They do not realize their own force. Control is a survival strategy: peers and colleagues either fall in line or resist. Bosses want to establish how people operate under pressure. Bosses are invested in finding out where people stand. Cower, defy, resist, comply—this information is vital to those who are constantly judging if it is safe to lower their guard and be vulnerable. Vulnerability means exposure, feeling fragile, being open to people coming after them. Bosses come across as powerful. It is difficult for peers to know that the other side of the bombastic Boss is soft sentimentality.

As with rules, Bosses control time: if the Boss's meeting runs late, that's okay, but don't be late for their meeting. Dominant Bosses like to be on center stage, such as when they are in charge, then people know their impact. Times of less-high-intensity are of little consequence and can be forgotten, fudged, or ignored. Bosses think they own time; and that delusion of control often blindsides them when they are caught in the consequences of their power rushes—deadlines and appointments missed, angry or anguished colleagues, bosses and peers knocking at the door, demanding an explanation.

*Defenders—The Peacekeeper (Point Nine).* Peacekeepers are reluctant self-starters, their attention is focused on the agendas of others. They have forgotten themselves, energy and motivation arise from without, not from within. They try to create a climate of harmonious interaction wherever they are—don't rock the boat—there are many sides to every question. They are natural mediators, although conflict and dealing with conflict is distracting and exhausting. A satisfactory day at work has more to do with watching others work productively together than a feeling of self-achievement. Peacekeepers easily establish rapport and laid-back comfort with colleagues. They take pride in getting along with others; bosses, peers, and subordinates alike respond to the warmth, concern and noncompetitive nature of Peacekeeper relations. They find it difficult to motivate themselves, but are easily motivated by the agendas of others. It is the expectations of colleagues, of the job, that gets them moving. They plan, process, initiate, execute, and perform, to meet the expectations of others, and avoid the consequences of nonaction. Peacekeepers are easily distracted and lose their agenda.

Peacekeepers believe in the concept of a level playing field—it is hard to establish objectives and priorities when every person, every idea, every project gets equal time. Others' demands can be too pressing, but Peacekeepers become obstinate and obdurate rather than display overt anger. They believe expressing anger is damaging, so they rarely allow themselves to be overtly angry, hence others do not always take their anger seriously. Anger usually takes the form of passive-aggressive behavior—a go-slow attitude to work deadlines, procrastination in getting things done.

Peacekeepers see the world as a flat, even place—setting priorities, for example, is difficult because all demands are equally important, as are making choices or reaching decisions. Peacekeepers delay by constantly weighing up the pros and cons and seeking advice. This gives them breadth of information, but makes action even more difficult. Peacekeepers feel comfortable sitting on the fence, but colleagues can feel mired in the Peacekeeper's indecision.

Peacekeepers believe everything happens in its own time; given enough time, priorities, choices, and decisions, will sort themselves out. Time sets its own course and carries Peacekeepers to where they are going to end up anyway. Whatever is not completed that day, or week, or quarter, will be done thereafter. There is always more time to attend to everything.

*Defenders—The Perfectionist (Point One).* Perfectionists live in world where a sense of inner direction drives them to achieve. They seek perfection in an imperfect world. They live with an innate sense of what's right—they think they know what's wrong and how to fix it. Things must be done the right way, they do things right and are judgmental of those who don't. Perfectionists believe in what they say and do. They feel they owe it to themselves and others to be competent to handle any details, whether it's a presentation or a process. They focus on the details and facts. Ideas and materials are conveyed in ways that model precision, ethics, and responsibility. They have a convincing, albeit preachy, way of communicating, underscored with "right thinking" messages. Others can feel judged if they disagree with Perfectionists. Yet their moralistic energy, which may sometimes be overzealous, is largely appreciated as authentic and inspiring.

When they are committed, Perfectionists are inspiring leaders and colleagues, imbuing others with the force of their own inner conviction. Perfectionists are obsessively self-critical. They spend hours  preparing material, deliberately building a model from intricate details. They struggle to make complex notions orderly, and are uncomfortable with open-ended options. They also do not like changing gears halfway through a process. Nonetheless plans B, C, and D, while not written out, are at their fingertips to cope with the unexpected.

Perfectionists have to deal with a severe inner critic that produces an unrelenting commentary on their lives. They realize the critic is a feature of their own consciousness, but find it extremely difficult to ignore such a familiar manifestation of their thinking. Paying attention to the inner critic is a major drain of time and energy. Any activity and its progress is monitored against the critic's measure of perfection: "Do it right, or don't do it at all." Deadlines are a struggle, because the inner pressure to produce a perfect piece of work also has to be perfectly timed. They can resent others who don't do things properly, although they try not to show open anger.

Perfectionists live under the whip of time. The inner critic drives them to account for themselves. Their work schedules mirror their preoccupation with correctness—good people work hard and play later, maybe. Procrastination arises with fear of making mistakes. Time is siphoned away from a project by a Perfectionist paying too much attention to time-consuming details. Work schedules reflect time well-spent—meetings, appointments, preparation—the "must dos." There is no free time to schedule "time off" for pleasure and fun.

# 3

# THE ENNEAGRAM
# INTELLIGENCES IN-DEPTH

The Enneagram is a complex model and there are several ways to introduce the E-types. A way that works well for me in workshops is to describe the basic E-types in their triads. This way we get the full force of the key issues for that triad and how they vary and play off one another.

Each description begins with two vignettes of that E-type in action. These are followed by a general description of the E-type. The words of people on panels at workshops around the country describing their inner world, anchors the key characteristics of each E-type, including both teaching and learning styles. As far as comprehension and rules of grammar allow, I have kept their comments in the vernacular, so as to illustrate the different speech patterns of the E-types. In a brief interview near the end of the section, educators each answer the same set of questions, so we have nine E-type strategy responses to compare, a type of gold standard. A list of helpful tips for that E-type to work with themselves, and for others to work with them, concludes the description.

## *ENNEATYPE TWO: THE HELPER*

- TRIAD: *ATTACHER*
- ATTENTIONAL FOCUS: Needs of others
- GIFT: True giving
- AVOIDANCE: Own needs
- GROWTH PATH: From pride to humility
- ESSENCE: Freedom
- SHIFT TO SECURE POINT: *THE ROYAL FAMILY FOUR* (Attacher —against arrow)
- SHIFT TO STRESS POINT: *THE BOSS EIGHT* (Defender—with arrow)
- WINGS: *THE PERFECTIONIST—ONE* (Defender)
  *THE PERFORMER —THREE* (Attacher)

## EXAMPLES OF HELPER TWO EDUCATORS: MEETING THE NEEDS OF OTHERS

### Giving to Get

Caroline A. teaches six year olds in the first grade. This is all she ever wanted to do. From her childhood she can remember lining up her dolls and those neighborhood children (usually younger and willing to go along with the game) in neat rows in front of her while she stood and taught them from a toy blackboard, a birthday gift from her parents. Even then she took care of snotty noses and scraped knees. Her reward: voluble approval from neighborhood parents who sang her praises to herself, to her parents, and to her teachers at Sunday school meetings. As a young girl, Caroline deliberately lingered behind her peers after school so she could "just happen" to be in a particular teacher's path and help carry books and materials to the car. But she did not make herself available to all teachers, only those into whose good graces she wanted to fall, like the music teacher, whose approval she valued. She barely paid attention to others like the gym teacher.

A model student during her teacher training, Caroline carefully chose the arenas of college life where she believed "her gift of giving" (as she has so often heard her prevailing personality trait described) would be most appreciated and appropriate. Community service and volunteer work, a stint in the dean's office where she became all but indispensable to the dean's secretary, secretary of the women's à capella singing group, these activities garnered praise for her helpfulness, devotion, care, and unselfish generosity in giving of herself. It was flattering, and she took secret pride in her ability to please others.

Caroline always knew the learning environment she wanted to create in her classroom. A fifteen-year veteran of the classroom now, the physical aspects of the space are attended to as if they belong in a beloved room in her own home. Entering her classroom every child feels safe—this is a safe place to be oneself, to take risks and stretch, to explore the world. Art, fabrics, rugs, maps, small animals, books, musical instruments, computers—all come together in an inviting, gently stimulating, self-contained world. She loves being the one who opens the door of formal learning to her students, teaching reading and writing skills as great gifts she is giving to each one.

Caroline does not let on that she is aware her praises are sung by grateful parents far beyond the walls of her school as "the best first grade teacher you'll find anywhere." Administrators, too, in addition to acknowledging her teaching prowess, count on her to undertake many extra duties. Despite knowing deep down it isn't true, she still enjoys the feeling of being regarded as an indispensable asset to the school. But she does acknowledge her delight when old students drop by, many in high school and some even in college, especially those whom she singled out in first grade as being worthy of "special" attention—attention paid in a subtle way, so those chosen know of her extra attentiveness, but also know it was not given at the expense of the others.

## Tender Loving Care (TLC)

George P.—middle-aged, affable, and a psychologist for the past twenty years—has been the stalwart force in student counseling services at a well-known college. The phrase "the helping services" was what drew his interest to pursue a career in counseling when he was a student. Early in life he knew that he was the one who gave, the one who took exceptional care of others. For all these years to earn his way by doing what came so naturally to him, George regarded this as a minor miracle. Directors of the counseling service have come and gone, as have other psychologists, social workers, and administrators, but George seemingly rolls on forever. He is the repository of the lore of the services, knows what's in the files, and where to find everything. Several times the dean has asked him to take on the directorship himself, but George smiles and demurs. He dislikes being in the frontline, but loves being the 2IC (second-in-command), the power behind the throne. "I couldn't have done that without you," says his boss or a grateful co-worker or student, words that are music to George's ears. He knows this to be true, acknowledges it to himself, but will never make such a statement publicly. Hearing the words is motivating and keeps him going, for George breathes approval the way other people breathe oxygen.

The counseling office offers a range of services and George counsels students on a continuum: from the severe cases of deep trauma suffered from sexual abuse incidents such as rape, or severe drug problems, or alcohol abuse, or full-blown or minor depression, or pathologies, to the less-severe cases usually stress-related from too heavy course loads and time management problems. George feels more present and alive in these one-on-one sessions than in any other area of his work; he cares, deeply. The students know this and under his guidance many have experienced remarkable readjustments in their lives. His favorite coffee mug, a gift from a grateful student, reads "Thanks Dr. P for the TLC Extra."

George also volunteers his services on college policy-making committees and boards and seems to have a natural ability, which over the years he has honed to an art, of knowing what each member (and especially the chairperson) needs by way of support to help the committee move forward. "Now that George is on the committee, we'll make real progress," is often heard on campus. George knows this to be true, but would never lay claim to such a statement himself.

### THE HELPER STRATEGY

| *Strengths* | *Weaknesses* |
|---|---|
| On-the-job support | Emotionally needy |
| Effective gray eminence/2IC | Flatterer |
| Potentiator | Constant need for approval |
| True altruist | Constant need for acceptance |

| Care giver | Plays it safe/not a risk-taker |
| Capable of real connection | Curries favor |
| Emotional support | Manipulative |
| Empathic | Selective about whom to help |
| Nurturer | Can become resentful and angry |

## THE E-TYPE TWO PROPOSITION

### General Description

*Giving of Yourself and Looking Good; False Pride and True Altruism*

Point Two Helpers seek connection so they can gain approval from others under the guise (often hidden, especially from themselves) of helping them. Helpers will single out selectively those individuals with whom they want to forge a connection. Twos pick a few people with whom to connect, a marked difference from their E-type look-alike the Point Nine Peacekeeper who takes on the whole agenda of, for instance, an individual, class, or institution.

Helpers are the most outer-directed of the Attacher triad: life is not real unless there is a connection "out there" with someone. Even in an impersonal arena such as delivering a speech to an audience of strangers, the Helper presenter will find someone, one person in the audience, who will become of such significant importance to the Two that he has to feel connected, bound up in that person. The presentation devolves into a test of the Helper presenter's ability to sway that stranger and make sure she's on the Two's side. (It's quite unlike the Performer Three who's trying to carry the whole room.)

In the classroom this ability to shift energetically plays out by allowing the Helper teacher to naturally change personas so as to meet and match the personas of the various students in his class. The Helper teacher has the ability to adjust his energy level in an instant in order to connect with the silent boy on his left, while not losing connection with the overeager girl on his right, while at the same time keeping connected with the energy of the class as a whole. Twos have an almost uncanny ability to shape-shift.

A Helper Two university department secretary describes how on arrival for work, in the elevator from the garage, she meets a janitor and feels herself changing: her subjective cues and judgments, her vocabulary, her whole approach while trying to match his energy in order to talk to and connect with him. On the first floor several lecturers enter the elevator and she is aware of herself changing and adjusting her energy and her way of being in order to be able to connect to them. On the fourth floor, the administrative dean, her boss, enters and she realigns herself once again in whatever it is she perceives he needs in order for her to make their connection. By the time she reaches her office she is quite ragged because she's gone through all these different shifts so quickly.

Part of the Helper's gift is an ability to bring to fruition the potential in others. But this is a trap for Helpers, too, a door through which a false sense of pride can enter. The conundrum works like this. Twos feel deeply that they have enabled their "selected" people to succeed. They take pride in acknowledging this to themselves. *You're* autographing the book at the book signing, but you wouldn't have had it published without *me*, thinks the department secretary, a Two, of her boss, the dean. "You couldn't have done that without me," pride sings, "you couldn't have done this without me." *I* don't need to be up front to get the prizes, *you're* getting the prize, and you couldn't have done that without me," thinks the Helper teacher of a student.

Pride also takes another form for Twos in a forgetfulness around their own emotional needs, or often a denial to themselves that they have any emotional needs. Pride is a two-sided coin. Helpers feel pride in meeting the needs of others and pride in avoiding their own needs. An inner dialogue can sound often like this: "I don't have needs—me? You have needs, I want to take care of you—that's my need. My need is to take care of you. But I don't have any needs." The sting in the tail for those connected to Twos is that resentment can build if the Two feels they've been taken for granted. The inner dialogue continues: "Why haven't you attended to my needs?" A dance evolves: "I don't have needs, but you're not paying any attention to my needs, and therefore, I don't like you very much and I'm going to get angry about this soon and move off."

In the classroom Helper Two students are those who give back to the teacher exactly what was given to them. The teacher is pleased with herself and the student: he's gotten the entire point of my lesson, he's a model student. Helper students achieve "A" grades a good deal. They have used their intelligence—the innate Enneagram intelligence inherent in their Helper strategy—to root out what the teacher needs in order for that teacher to give them back approval. An Enneagram-savvy teacher intervenes with Two students by gently throwing them onto their own resources. On returning their history paper, or physics quiz, she says, "This is beautifully done, but this is what I think and this is what I have said. Now I want you to go back and redo this, and for you to tell me what you think, or how you would solve this."

It's difficult for Twos to take risks—that's why they haven't handed in their own thoughts and responses in the first place. They feel that if they hand in a paper that's not going to be what the teacher likes, they're not going to get approval and they're not going to be liked. Disapproval, and dislike are devastating to Twos. So part of the Helpers' self-defense mechanism is an ability to give and to keep giving and giving and giving—a feedback loop to ensure that they are loved, have approval, are liked, and validated. The relief of gaining approval and therefore feeling good about oneself reassures the Two that there is a self at home. It's a long process of inner growth before the Helper can say: "I'm doing this for myself."

Early steps on the growth path for Twos are to move from the false pride about not having their own needs, into acknowledging with humility that they are human like everyone else and have needs. Twos have grown when they can state their need: "I need your attention." "I need you to tell me that you love me." "I need from you a sense that you value me without me having done any-thing for you."

From the outside each of these growth paths seems so obvious, but for the people involved in the process these seem like major, survival-threatening changes. Yet they are essential if we are to become awake to ourselves. For the Two these steps are a way to grow into a sense of freedom and will to be them-selves and not to live with the obligation that they exist for others. Twos gain freedom in understanding this essential lesson.

Helper Twos who can work with their fixation and begin their personal growth process are outstanding educators. For the gift of the Two is true giving, true altruism, true allowing.

### Shift to Point Four (Security)

When Twos feel secure they experience their emotions more deeply, direct-ing their attention and energy away from others onto themselves. In the Point Four stance Helpers allow their own emotional needs to surface and they find ways to satisfy them. They are more in touch with themselves, and from this position can claim their own power, rather than being the gray eminence, the power behind the throne.

> At times when I feel more secure in my life, I notice that I change in my dealings with people. It's hard to change, because people don't like you. Colleagues and students are used to me spending hours and hours on the phone counseling them, but I'm learning to cut it short. They say, "Wait a minute I don't feel good yet." Then I have to deal with that. It's a problem because I want people to like me and it's hard to say, "Well, I'm taking care of myself." It's been a real growth pro-cess to set boundaries and not let everyone take a piece of me, and I can only do it when I feel secure.

Even though Point Twos shift to Point Four when they feel secure, they can also access the defense mechanisms of this E-type, experiencing a sense of longing, feelings of shame and of being a victim.

### Shift to Point Eight (Stress)

When Twos shift to Point Eight under situations of stress they access the Eight energy, aggression, and anger. In a positive use of this energy, Helper Twos will move to confrontation on behalf of others. On their own behalf, what they perceive as ingratitude or lack of appreciation and approval from those they've tried to help are stress factors that move them to Point Eight. Helper Twos in stress experience a desire to exact revenge by increased manipulation and even deceit—for instance, by withholding information, not sharing import-ant reports and data. Aggression, anger, and confrontation are difficult for Twos. They deny the need for these dangerous weapons, and often fall back on hypocrisy to mask their real needs and feelings. However, stress situations can help the Twos establish their own position and priorities, when they move to honest confrontation.

My co-teacher in the other fifth grade is difficult to work with, and we've worked together for thirteen years. Lately our situation was stressful to me. I'd come home and say, "I can't stand this and it's so terrible because if I tell her then she won't like me and we won't get along anymore." Finally this spring the level of discomfort I felt was so stressful, I had to confront her. I said, "I'm not pleased with the way this process is going and we should speak about it a little more." And that took so much courage, but I felt as if I got my two legs back. Now I know I can speak as long as I have my intentions clear and that's a hard thing for me if I'm afraid I'm going to lose a friend. As long as I can say that clearly, early on, I'm not afraid to press a point.

Even though Point Twos shift to Point Eight when they feel stressed, they can access the gifts of this E-type, harnessing energy for others, and truth-telling.

### Key Characteristics

#### Giving: "I'm Just a Girl Who Can't Say No"

I think there's a serious danger of getting overcommitted. "I'm just a girl who can't say no, can't say it at all." That's me.

Of the three E-types in the Attacher triad, Helpers are the most outer-directed, their attention and energy moves out toward others. They are relational, Twos' lives revolve around their relationships to others. Helpers give of themselves to others from a deeply held subconscious belief that giving is the way to ensure their progress in the world, to gain approval and love from others, and protection against life's exigencies from those to whom they give.

I'm not sure what motivates the need to give. It's something that I actually recognized quite overtly in myself from a very, very early age: my role was to be the one who gave. Although I know now what I didn't know then, this is a bargain. If you're the generous one and give your brother the last chocolate biscuit, you will get the reward, which is more important to you, of your mother's approval.

Many Helper educators regard their profession as being "the business of giving," creating the means whereby exciting self-discoveries enable students to grow.

What I feel about teaching is that it is the business of giving, that you are actually giving people a present: to a great extent, it is giving a gift, enabling people. The great reward, or a teacher's greatest reward, is

that moment when somebody's eyes light up and they say, "Oh, I get
it." Or, someone else says, "Oh yeah, I've always known that," but
they haven't in fact and you've hit on something which is true for
them.

Point Two educators like to create an environment of personal comfort in
their classrooms where they can extend to students an invitation to be at ease
surrounded by the special touches the Helper teacher has created for their time
together.

> I like my room to be the most beautiful place for students to learn
> in. My classroom to me is my home. Sometimes I think it's more my
> home than my real home. Everything I care about goes on in that room
> and I want those children to care in their own way as much as I care
> about everything that goes on there.

Helpers need to be made aware that in their desire to move toward others
they can smother the recipients of their giving with too much energy and attention.

> A colleague once said to me, "You're like a hypodermic needle, jab
> 'you need this, it's good for you' jab." There is a level of not over-
> whelming people with all that you want to give them, or teach, or let
> them take in—you have to pace it. It's hard personally to keep the
> boundary.

Often Twos are aware of and, many times, baffled when they glimpse their
mixed motives in this "business of giving," at how their giving comes with
strings attached.

> It's interesting how something I give becomes mine rather than
> the other person's. For instance, I gave a friend some flowers and ferns
> in a vase and she took them to her car and emptied the water out. I
> thought, so the roses will die. Suddenly, they were my flowers and my
> arrangement, it wasn't a real gift—it was about me.

### Giving to Get

Two Helper educators strike a subconscious bargain that ensures they get
their emotional needs met in the classroom. For the educator the dynamic works
in the following way: if I give my students energy, attention, caring, love, and
help them to succeed academically, then I will be identified with their success,
buoyed by their appreciation, gratitude, and love.

> I've certainly felt, most of my career, I think, that I'm doing
> something of critical importance. In fact, I never have the feeling that
> we are underpaid or overworked, or don't have privileges, or that it is a
> miserable little job, or that it is a job. It's difficult to give a rational
> reason why I teach, or why I want to give, because it's so much woven

into the fabric of my being that it's not even a question. I know that in my teaching my subtext is to be loved, to be popular, to be successful. I'm not sure that it's altogether a bad motive. I feel that I'm giving them something that will last a lifetime and be important to them.

It never is a question when someone asks, "Will you take this difficult person, this difficult child?" and I say, "Sure," or "Will you chaperone the event on Central Avenue?," "Oh, certainly." I also do more than I want to do in the way of library duty, chaperoning, or driving to community service, or bits and pieces, because I'm defenseless when it comes to someone asking me to give them a service. Often I find that it's perfectly okay, that when I actually drive people to the picnic I have a wonderful time, so it is all right, but I do secretly find myself doing more than the basics.

While many Twos experience feelings of pure joy in being able to give to others, to help them grow, the sense of self-fulfilment can be undermined quickly if Helpers feel their efforts are not appreciated.

When I'm driving to school each morning I think of each child as a mystery I'm going to try to solve that day. When I see their faces as each child comes into the room it gives me a great deal of pleasure to know I am helping them to be enthusiastic and happy. At the kindergarten level I'm not motivating them for SATs or anything, but I just want them to be enthusiastic and in love with learning. I think I can see where I need to touch them, that makes me happy. I don't feel *that* unhappy if I distress them because they're so young and sanguine that you can pretty much rid them of that bad feeling in one second. But I do feel very, very distressed when I put a great effort into a child and it's not appreciated by their parents—that's a tough one for me. I feel abused, misunderstood.

### Meeting Others Needs: "You Made Me Love You"

Inherent to the Two E-type intelligence is an innate seductiveness, an instinctive ability to put the moves in play so as to make others like the Helper. It does take a certain degree of self-awareness on the part of the Two to acknowledge this pattern of behavior.

If I was intent on figuring out what you needed, I would work every single angle from every single part of the circle to get you to be aware that you needed what I was giving you. It's like somebody once said to me, "You made me love you" and I said, well, that song was written for people like me.

For the Helper educator this intelligence is used in any number of ways to ensure the Two is coming across as caring, as someone with whom a student can feel safe because the Helper knows what the student wants often before the student himself.

As a teacher I elicit approval from my students by meeting their needs. I have to pace things for whomever is sitting across the table from me I ask, "Do you need a break now?" "What is going on?" because I can feel something. I used to think I knew what they felt, but now I have to check it out. I'm usually accurate; they need something.

Another way Twos meet others' needs in the classroom is by sustaining a juggling act.

I've became increasingly aware of the different ways people are learning, are proceeding, seated around the table. Increasingly I've became sensitive to the needs and myriad styles that I am confronted with. I'm communing with the person who doesn't want to talk, the person who is momentarily distracted, the person who is answering the questions all the time. I become more able to juggle these things. In the last years it's become increasingly easy to juggle all — the text, the eager kid, the difficult kid, their yearning to be outside, the fact that it's lunchtime. I seem better able to weave all the distractions and all the different paths into a single purpose as time goes on.

Two educators report that they see themselves playing different roles to meet others' needs — the welcoming figure whose classroom is her home, the hostess at a dinner party, the students' servant in one-on-one conferences — part of the Two intelligence is to seamlessly fit these roles, to become what the other needs, so that the self is subsumed into the role.

One of my roles, as it were, is as a hostess. I consider every lesson as if it is a dinner party; the children are the guests to be treated with the utmost generosity and courtesy. I learned from my mother (who was also a teacher) an enabling style, in another sense the skilled hostess. She would receive a suggestion from a student, and however absurd the suggestion was, she always had the skill (and I've tried to learn this from her) to turn it into something wonderful. "I think what you're thinking then is ..." And then she would bring in some quite sophisticated thought and the student would say, "Yeah, that's what I was getting at, that's exactly right." And the reward of this is that wonderful moment when the child is lifted, or the other human being (I mean it happens just the same with a friend), it's something shared. You've shared an emotion, shared an insight.

Where I've had the most difficulty is in being challenged when I have a student who doesn't want to be at this dinner party, and of course, naturally, there are some. I don't do a particularly good act with that role. I mean it is hard for me, if someone makes a snide remark, or tries to destroy, say, the school's character. I can cope with this on an intellectual level, but not well on an emotional level. This sort of conflict makes me extremely uncomfortable.

It is frightening to Helpers when they find themselves without a role to play as a ploy for securing the good graces of others, a feeling akin to being caught naked: there *is* no self at home.

My friends ask me, "What do you want?" I answer, "I want what you want." "But if we weren't here what would you want?" I can't often answer that question and it's scary. I just want to please them and I don't have anything that I want that I'm in touch with. Sometimes it's not a projection, I'm on target with what other people are thinking and feeling, but I'm out of touch with myself.

Helper Two educators use their E-type intelligence to put themselves into the "skin" of others, to take on the persona, or play the role of another as if it were their own being. There is a subconscious feeling of pride in this ability. Not many Twos are aware of being prideful in this meeting the needs of others, they deny the pride element, their awareness to this is blinded by their sense of giving. Albeit to those on the outside it can be seen as a false altruism.

I will prepare a lesson carefully, not in terms of the material, but thinking about those people to whom I want to give the gift of the material. My exercise in preparing classes has been trying to put myself into the skin of three, or four, or five of the children who I know I'll be teaching the next day, so that I can feel how long that piece should be, or how the material will be received. Sometimes I'm wrong, but it's quite uncanny how I can put myself in the skin of the children and give them what they want. I think what they want is what they need.

Helper Two teachers take pride in reading subconscious signals.

Quickly I've got feelers out, like a lobster or something, and I'm sensing their energies, what they're bringing into the classroom. It's probably arrogant of me to believe that I know what they're bringing in, but at the same time, after doing twenty-thirty years of teaching there are almost subliminal signals that students bring in with them that the teacher can read more or less subconsciously: how they get their books out, where they're sitting, how they interact with their next-door neighbor, what kind of looks they are giving to you, what snide or other remarks are being made, and I think the teacher has to be full of tentacles of awareness. Experience leads you to know where the soft spots are around that table and where the hard places are.

### Own Needs

As we have seen, Twos are experts at maneuvering others (by giving to them) into getting their own needs met. Yet Helpers experience intense discomfort if they have to ask directly for something, so they don't put themselves in that position.

Neediness is the feeling that somebody is not with you, or can't sustain it with you, so that you will lose the very thing you need the most—that connection with them. If I've called someone whom I know well and feel comfortable with and asked them to help me, it almost brings tears or choking, it's just hard. I can't tell you why it is, but I'd rather do anything myself than ask for help. If you ask me to do something for you it will be a pleasure, it won't be an imposition, I'll feel good having done something for you.

In the classroom even if the Helper is aware that her need is to be needed (and this is a major step in self-awareness for the Two) this very awareness is seen as deficient, acknowledging one has needs is shameful.

My needs in the classroom are approval and enthusiasm and, I hate to use the word, "love." I am there because I know I can elicit enthusiasm, I know that I can give a large number of the students an exhilarating forty-five minutes—"time out" in a way, a time when we are sharing something that is exciting and new and moving and beautiful, and my reward is that they say, "Oh, isn't she cool, what a cool lady." I find it rather difficult to admit but that's the bottom line, the fact that you're popular, the fact that they tell their parents what a wonderful person you are, the fact that you get bouquets at the end of the year. These are peripheral in a way, but I'm afraid that they are the signs and symbols of a need to be needed.

It is easier for Twos to state their needs definitively if they do not include asking for help. This teacher's need is to make a difference through providing an emotional context for her students' learning.

I wouldn't want to sit in a classroom and hear dry, straightforward material, so I think about how I can involve them emotionally in a way that they care about the material. In everything I teach I try to bring in something that's going to capture them emotionally. That's my need. I want to make a difference to them so that when they walk out of the room and remember my lesson, they've been emotionally touched.

While this teacher's need is for structure.

I'm in trouble as a teacher if I don't have structure, so I've learned to lean on it, count on it, and I hope that in the structure there will be room to breathe and talk and relate.

And, likewise, for this Helper whose need is to be seen as creative in designing her lessons.

In kindergarten life is of the imagination, feeling, and will. So I organize my lessons very carefully to appeal to those aspects. Through an artistic way of reaching them I give them skill upon skill, it's not an intellectual approach at all. We do movement to develop motor skills, we act out stories we create from listening to music, and so on.

## *Potentiating Others*

Part of the highest intention of a Two is the desire, almost an obligation, to assist others to reach their potential. Helpers direct their energy, will, and creativity to this end. Even in situations beyond the teacher-student dynamic (as in intimate relationships), Twos become the facilitator, helping their partner to structure an agenda and attain goals. In an educational setting when embodying this high intention the Twos become gifted teachers—for in this instance what they give, how they meet needs, is a natural fit and they become what they are, true teachers.

I think the best thing about being a teacher is giving the love of whatever we teach; people come to me because they want to learn how to play tennis. One of the things I like about it is finding out how to say the same thing ten different ways for different individuals. I get a lot of pleasure out of figuring out what the student needs in order to learn this wonderful game.

This Helper puts forth great effort to help others reach their potential.

If I see potential in someone and I decide to bring it out, heaven and earth will move. Making a difference is very important to me, so those ways I make a difference, positively, I role model that a difference can be made.

This Two educator believes that by helping her students to reach their full potential, she will model for them that they can do the same for their students.

I teach both psychology and social work interns, and sometimes psychiatry residents, and I think that one of the talents that I have is to see potential. I see the positive side and I'm able to help people see what *they* have to offer, as opposed to them looking to me as the authority. It is an approach that allows students to learn that they can be on a more even level with the people with whom they work. As I empower them it allows them to learn how to empower others. I think there's a way in which I can almost sniff out potential, whereas other people look out there and unless it's right in front of them, they go riding right over it.

I had a student this year, a psychology intern, who was so self-critical that at the beginning of the year she was literally almost afraid to go into a room with somebody for fear that she wouldn't do it right. What I saw was her potential for warmth and acceptance of others, and I wanted to encourage her to accept herself, too, without being so critical. So I helped her see her warmth, while also helping her to realize that her ability to seek perfection was a gift and a talent, but that her propensity to be super-critical of herself could interfere with that gift.

While this Two teacher acknowledges the Catch-22 she creates: helping others reach their potential is self-validating, and validation is what she wants.

I've always known there is a part of me that wants to help some-body else reach their potential. There are several things involved in this. Firstly, I always felt I was overdependent at a younger age so if I could help someone not have to go through those same feelings and inspire them to greater independency, that is something that turns me on. Sometimes I succeed to such an extent, as with some of my own child-ren, that they became so independent they don't need me anymore, that is something I've had to adapt to. Secondly, helping people reach their own potential is getting the validation that I desperately want, because I feel I've succeeded in doing something great which is probably a form of self-validation.

### Selectivity

From the reports of Helper Twos we know that they lack a central belief in a sense of self, and in its place are aware of a marked sense that they can *become* what other people want and need in order to get back the approval and love they need. Twos know they lack self-esteem and self-image, which is not surprising since their self-esteem and self-image are tied up in the responses they receive from people with whom they are in relationship. Their E-type intelligence di-rects them to whom they should align with in order to gain this sense of self. For instance, the Two teacher who buys the school principal's agenda and finds a sense of self in being his right-hand person in implementing that agenda, or the assistant professor who aligns with the brilliant authority in the field and finds himself in putting out his best effort through research, writing, and teach-ing to further the "authority's" reputation.

Part of the selectivity is that you know you want to help some-body who's also going to help your image. At work it might be someone who is a leader or who's well respected. In a social situation, it might be someone who is either well known, liked, dresses well, or entertains well. In a teaching situation I want to align myself with the people who are good at what they do, who get respect, who get appro-val because that will ensure me that I will probably get approval. But I also have a soft spot for the underdog. It's seeing the potential again, like the struggling student who can't get out of his own way. The stud-ent who maybe gets overlooked. In a teaching situation I'm often drawn to the student who's struggling more because there's a way in which I can contribute more. So it's both altruistic and for my own good, be-cause I feel good if I can help someone and the more they're struggling, the more I can make a contribution and feel good about what I do.

This selectivity process does not always involve a person who can enhance the Two's image in the eyes of others, but it can be used as self-defense strate-gy.

If I'm particularly needy, then I'm going to perhaps focus on somebody who will let me express that by letting me give to them. I remember that I was withdrawn at a younger age and had trouble coming out of that space I had gotten myself into. One of the ways that I did so was to look outside myself when I was in a social circumstance and find a person who seemed to be distressed or nobody was talking to. I would seek that person out and try to make them feel more comfortable. That helped me to start talking a little more publicly.

### Pride

Twos move out toward others, their E-type intelligence directs them to a belief that they intuitively know what others need, often before they do themselves. Helpers have a sense of self-pride and importance around this, as if their empathy and ability to give is a gift. Those they choose to share it with are fortunate to receive, while those from whom it is withheld are somehow diminished. This perception notwithstanding, in reality Helpers do give away a part of themselves, for a sense of being worthy is created by how they are reacted to by others, so if approval or love is not forthcoming, or is present and then withdrawn, Helpers experience the loss as personally devastating. They are worthless, they have no meaning or significance.

There's a pride in having an intuitive predisposition to know another's state empathically and when that's used well it's a beautiful thing. However if you've got someone on the other side of this who doesn't want what you're trying to give them, you have a real problem and no communication. I would say as a kid I didn't even exist. My identity was anyone I was with at the time. I got their energy, I'd experience a puff of pride: *I got them.* The work is to build an identity alone. Only by being alone do I know who I am without this other thing I keep circling through. Then when I get you alone, I might be able to hold onto that a little more each time.

As this Two educator reports, pride can take the form of denying one has needs.

I take pride in making sure that you don't know what I need. In other words I prove to myself that I can do anything. That's sort of a sad thing in a sense, because it's not acknowledging that I do have needs, and anyway what's so terribly wrong about being needy? Other people can indulge in their neediness without feeling the same distress that I do.

Pride can also be a sense of self-importance.

A story of false pride involves the reunion of a group of graduates whom I taught ten-fifteen years before and who came to see me in my classroom. I thought, how lovely it is to see them and how kind they are to come. One said, "There are some things about your classroom i will never forget." I was all open for some wonderful compliment. "You told us that Wordsworth had long-distance vision and that Tennyson was near-sighted."

*Approval*

We have spoken about how important approval is to Helpers; they report that approval is like oxygen, a necessity of life they have to have in order to survive and make their way in the world. Each E-type has blind spots; gaining approval is a blind spot for Helpers. Twos believe that approval is something that's gained from or withheld by others. This is one of the mechanisms through which Helpers become dependent on other people, and a reason why they experience such panic when thrown onto a dependence on their own sense of self.

I don't think my attention goes to approval, my attention goes to where the approval is not. Lecturing in front of a group of a hundred people, if there is one person in terms of my projection (because a lot of times this could be wrong) who looks to me as if they aren't interested, or they don't like the lecture, I can play to them. I feel I can win their approval through the will of my incredible intention that they like me. Unfortunately this can backfire if you get someone who doesn't buy into it, they can withdraw even further which is devastating. It's an intense feeling. I feel manipulated by that energy sometimes.

and
Giving flattery leads to approval.

This Two educator describes clearly both the maneuvering to be liked and gain approval, but also how problematic it is when approval is lacking.

I think I get approval from them by making them feel special. Because I work one-on-one with my students for eight hours a day it's easy to know what special is: spending time with them to try to bring out the best in them and make them feel they can do their very best. Years ago in graduate school I went to Europe with a friend and after about three weeks she said, "I've finally figured out your trick of how you get people to like you." I said, "I have a trick? Please tell me." She answered, "You make the person you're talking to feel like they're the most important person in the world and your life wasn't complete until you met them." I think that's probably what I do with my students: they're wonderful students who complete my life. In many ways that's reflected back to me. I think what I want back is to be psychologically seen, I want to be seen that I have the ability to do that which is special. I get that from a lot of students. Not all students want what I have to give, so that's a conflict for me. It was painful when I first started teaching because I didn't want not to be liked and it took me about five years of getting evaluations to figure out that no matter how I did it, there were a certain number who were not going to like me. Finally I decided I'm just going to please myself. Teaching became a lot more fun when I didn't have such a focus on everyone having to like me. It got in my way initially; I'd look at evaluations and I'd change. I'd do it one way and those people would complain. They're still complaining twenty years later. But I've become a lot more relaxed about it.

This Two educator describes the inner dance around articulating her needs.

The paradox is that I need everyone's approval. I'm hard-wired about neediness, the good stuff is providing for others. I don't tell you what I want or need; first because I don't know, but second because it's automatic. I assume that since I know what you want, you'll know what I want and you'll provide it without my having to ask.

### *Image*

Self-image is tied in with the Helper's preoccupations with pride, selectivity, and approval. While image—looking good to others—is in part fueled by the Helper's highest intentions to perform to the best of what others need in order to help them reach their potential under the Two's guidance. So for this Two educator the activity of teaching takes on the outer trappings of a performance.

I'm always there before them, so there is a degree of stage management. I always ask people to sit around the table, or if there is free seating, in a tight pattern so that there is a dynamic interchange. I sit at the round table and I'm careful to move every day so that there is no seat left out. I feel that you're on stage, that you owe your audience—the ten-fifteen kids, all that you've got—just as much as an actress does on stage. I feel stage fright at the beginning of every morning, I feel that elation after a class, even sometimes after a not very good class. I don't at all like people sitting against the back wall, because that's too far from the party.

This Helper teacher is convinced of the image of herself giving a gift to each student in the classroom.

I feel on a good day, when things are going well, at the end of the period everyone has a present, everyone is getting a gift. There is extreme frustration on the days when it doesn't work. This can happen, there can even be a class where it seldom works. I don't think I've had a class where it never works, but it's a balancing act for me. Everything in the balancing act is on the plus side. I'm almost incapable of disappointing people, so that I can't be very nasty.

This Two educator carries an image of herself as a sympathetic facilitator.

I had one boy in a recent class who was resistant. I couldn't make an end run around him, and he either wouldn't talk or was very, very challenging. That's hard for me. I did my maneuver of last resort, which is to keep him at the end of the class, not in a challenging way, but to engage him with something that he had said earlier. I said, "I don't think I'm understanding what your objections are to this class" or something like that, and we got in quite a debate, an interesting conversation about his viewpoint, which indeed had a good deal of validity. Perhaps because he realized I was taking him seriously, he did in fact begin to become a participant in the class, I felt wonderful about that.

While this Helper sees herself as being the image of a teacher's teacher.

Teaching takes all the energy I have. I mean it must be what a dancer feels in dancing or a singer feels in singing—it's what I'm supposed to be doing. So the reward is just that: it's doing what you were made to do. It does have peripheral rewards as well. When students are responsive and enthusiastic, and this still goes on after thirty-five years that you get a paper or a remark which is absolutely enigmatic, something that you never dreamed of yourself—you feel there's a spark that went all the way to produce this insight. It's flattering, and that's not a very good word to use, it makes you feel good.

### Changing Personas/Shape-shifting

Many Twos report that they are aware that they alter themselves to match energetically with, and so connect to, the people with whom they interact. This can be achieved by shifting to approximate the outer physical characteristics of speech and other mannerisms of the other person, as well as to the more subtle inner intimations of energy, needs, and desires. The Two E-type intelligence tells them this is how to make their way in the world, and Twos find it difficult to believe that relationships can be forged in any other way.

I'm very conscious of altering. I have a lot of friends and they're from different walks of life and places in life and so forth. A number of years ago a dear friend threw a surprise birthday party for me, and while she only knew friends from the group where I'd met her and the activities that we were involved in together, she invited people that I was working with at the School of Government and she invited people from my neighborhood. Oh my lord, what a stressful evening. It wasn't fun because I'm aware that with some friends I'm more lively, or louder, or talkative, and with others I'm a little more intellectual, or serious, and there they all were in the same room and it was stressful.

Twos can be helped to grow when they recognize an overt elliptical tilt toward others, experiencing what others are feeling, while lacking a sense of their own feelings.

> It's hard when your identity is tied up with everyone else. I know the definition of identity is that you are separate, but it's hard to know where I leave off and other people begin, where you are and what's yours.

Many Twos are aware of this shape-shift inside themselves.

> I can date the moment when I knew this about myself. I was on my bicycle coming home from school, and suddenly I realized as I turned the corner about halfway in my journey that I was putting on my home persona which was the "good" girl, who wouldn't make waves, who wasn't bossy, like my oldest sister, or retracted and whiny like my younger sister, I was going to be good. It was a conscious decision, I can remember the moment. Then bicycling back to school I was going to be outgoing and fun and a leader. It's rather disturbing to think how early and how aware I was aware of this degree of manipulation—it goes on still.

and

> At about age twenty I was troubled because I wasn't constant, because I changed all the time with other people. It was a distracting feeling for me, I felt inside my heart it was not right. It's easier when you're older to find what you want and who you are. Not easy, but easier, not so difficult to keep to who you are. It's good to be alone. I have found it a blessing to be alone and to feel what I need and just to be as I am.

For this Two educator shape-shifting is seen as a plus, as an ability to meet the needs of all her students at the same time. There is a certain pride in being "all things to all men."

> In a classroom I think I do encounter each child with a somewhat different persona. It's obviously more marked when you have them alone in a conference or something similar, because then you become their servant. What they want to convey about their writing or about their problems in comprehension, you're enabling them in that process. In the classroom I've often had the experience that I was juggling, that there are a large number of balls in the air and that you had to be careful about balance because the great enthusiasm that you might express for that eager person—who is usually a girl on one side; might be too gushy, too sweet, too silly for the resister—a boy perhaps or a girl over on the other side. So you're sort of all things to all men. I'm probably not as successful all the time as I experience myself to be.

The following Helper's report demonstrates a high degree of self-awareness around this shape-shifting characteristic of the Two E-type intelligence. She is aware that an element of manipulation is present.

I am my husband's wife, my mother's daughter, my children's mother, my grandchildren's grandmother, I am a patient advocate. I can assess the needs of people whom I selectively select—terrible as that sounds. I have a habit of saying that givers need takers and what we look for sometimes we don't get back, because takers take and givers give, so you don't always get back what you give. It is hard to verbalize what I need myself—you are supposed to know that by what I do. Compliance is a two-edged sword for me because I feel underneath compliance is real aggression and the capability to manipulate and so forth—so what you see is not always what you get.

### Confrontation — Setting Limits

Confrontation is usually not an option for the Two educator. If you confront the student you run the risk not only of them not liking you any longer, but of losing their approval. Even though you may not like yourself for doing so, because it's hypocritical, you feel complying with their need seems a far safer tack.

I find it near impossible to be confrontational, to be tough, and one of the downsides of my teaching is that even when I know a student is stringing me along, and he needs some limits set, I find it practically impossible to set those limits and I think it's a weakness and I think it's a shortcoming in a teacher.

and

I play with it in a joking way and that's the closest I can come to confrontation.

This Two educator knows she is too lenient with grades, but rationalizes her unwillingness to hold the line as being bad for that student's development.

I'm too lenient in grades and sometimes too lenient in deadlines. I always give people extensions and the benefit of the doubt, which is not always wise, because some people are manipulative. I think I'm overgenerous in being objective: contests, competitions, that's the part of the work I don't like. Partly because I don't think there are always objective standards and I think that you can do tremendous damage by saying that a child's work is lazy or stupid or sloppy or inefficient. I think what you ought to do is pick out what's good and use that as a growth point.

### Growth Path: From Pride to Will/Freedom

Growth for Helpers occurs when awareness dawns that the pride they take in being able to meet others' needs is a trap that keeps them from developing a sense of self and robs them of their own identity, the freedom to act spontaneously on behalf of themselves.

What freedom means is an ability to know what is the appropriate relationship between us and the appropriate measuring out of giving and taking. For instance, to take my talent and ability to sense what you need and want, but in the context of recognizing who I am in relationship to you, as opposed to something that gets inflated. To me that's been one of the greatest gifts of studying the Enneagram, that I've begun to acquire a real ability to sense with someone what is my true relationship to them, what is my true contribution to them.

### Quality of Essence: Humility

Humility comes with being able to give to others without expecting anything back. Helpers are aware of how pure this feeling is. They also know the difference between true giving (from a sense of self-identity and intact boundaries) and giving from a sense of false pride (self-sacrifice.)

What I've learned over the years is I can tell when I'm giving out of just a genuine giving, or when I'm giving to get. I can identify this in my body. If I'm genuinely giving to you, it won't matter what you do. I don't need anything back from you and there's no angst, there's nothing, it's just pure pleasure. But certainly when I'm in the other situation where I'm giving and I'm unconscious that I'm doing it because I want something back from you, I can go ballistic in about a millisecond if I don't get back what I want.

### What Helper Students Say

### Getting My Needs Met: Making Me Feel Special

The classes that I enjoy the most are with the people who feel love for their subject and *are eager to bring it to me* and who can explain it well and have joy in the subject.

and

There are teachers in high school who take a special interest in me, or give me what I think are special tasks to do and have a specific way that I feel I can contribute to them. Even though it is in the context of school work it might be that I stay late and help them organize something, or copy things, materials for the next day. If I have an opportunity to help and assist them in some way I feel special. If I have a teacher and I'm not making an "A," but I want approval, there's a way in which I can be either helpful or committed so that I get that approval even though I don't get it necessarily from grades. There are some courses I will get "As" in—but a lot of others I don't, yet I'm always recognized for effort and for being pleasant. People like having me in the class because I can get things going. I can get conversations going, I will do whatever is necessary to contribute to that class. I think the teachers I remember the most are ones who pay attention to me. It seems as if I'm always connected to a teacher who is in high standing, I seem to usually be around those teachers who are known as the best teachers.

### Approval and Appreciation

The most difficult situation is if someone doesn't see me as a person. If I'm not understanding and there's no room for me to be acknowledged, I will get exhausted. If I have a teacher who only relates to me from an intellectual position, I get worn out and exhausted and then I get frustrated. Then what you see is not a compliant, cooperative student, but someone who is sullen. I've been known to get angry even. I keep it under wraps at school but, yes, the teacher who's just on an intellectual plane and there's no emotional connection, is difficult. It's not so much about the material, or the question of can I understand the material, but rather how it is presented and whether or not there is any connection or affirmation in that. I often understand the material but there has to be an emotional engagement, there can't just be an intellectual connection. And I'll sense that like that.

and

I always sit near the front of the room. I'm always prepared, I can always engage the teacher by asking pertinent questions, and making their work a little easier for them. One of the things that turns me off is the teacher who says, "Well, I know that you know the information, so I want somebody else to answer." This other person probably hasn't prepared half as hard as I have. The thing that I like the least is when a classroom is held in an auditorium and there are many, many people and virtually no interaction with the teacher. Some people actually like that but for me, I sort of need that connection.

### Meeting Teachers' Needs

I like being a student because I can please and I know how to do that and I know if I work hard I can get a good grade. I don't get much recognition at home, so school is the place it can happen. It is a comfortable place to be and I can succeed at it and I know how to do that.

and

I love being a student when I love my teacher. I remember loving my kindergarten teacher and then not till 6th grade when a teacher came into the school with whom I totally identify: he's the reason I want to be a teacher, he changed my life. He is just a wonderful man, full of energy, full of love, full of compassion for the students, he loves the subjects he teaches. I come from a tiny school, four rooms in the country with no exposure to anything. This man brings in so much life to our school that is never given to us by any other teacher, this is the last-resort school, nobody wants to work here and this man turned my life around. He was everything, still is.

and

I'm a flirt, I try to seduce all my teachers. I organize everyone in the class to do something nice for the teacher, so we are always giving gifts and having parties and that's how I make my way through.

### Empathy

I don't think that their (the teachers') expectations motivate me, I think I motivate myself, but it's important for me that I uphold standards that people uphold for me. I hate the feeling that both of us know I'm the one whose let them down.

and

I know what people want to hear and then I can tell them that. I think that happens with adults also. In a sense that almost makes it easier for me to OK things that other people do, when it's not OK with me. If they do something that gets me upset it's pretty easy for me to be understanding because I can say, "Oh well, the type of personality they are, that wouldn't be such a big deal for them"—it's easy for me to adjust.

and

In history recently we watched a movie on the Vietnam War and for me it was so hard to watch that I wanted to get up and leave a few times, it was just very, very difficult to watch and not so much because of the war, but just seeing the kids, they were kids before they went and how naive they were. I could relate to that in a sense. So I wrote about that because it was very significant for me.

### Changing Personas

In school I sometimes find I'm a completely different person in different teachers' classrooms. My history teacher is a man who fought in the Vietnam War, he's a war hero or something, and he runs his class like the military. So I behave like a soldier, neat and tidy and I always respect his orders and the way he likes to do things. My math teacher is old and I feel he needs help with the class, so I look after him a little, I guess. He knows he can always rely on me to tell him what homework is due. I don't care if the other kids don't like that, he reminds me of my grandfather. Our English teacher is young and hip, and she wears these snazzy clothes and we listen to rap music a lot, to understand the "now" culture. In her class I become so cool, so with it, my history and math teacher would never know it was me. It's only when I'm with my friends that I'm myself and then that can change too, depending on whom I'm with and what I'm feeling.

### Brief Interview with a Helper Educator

*Q: What is your teaching style?*
A: My teaching style is a performance style. It is not a one-man performance, because it relies greatly on arousing enthusiasm, appreciation, input, and improvement. What I think of as a good lesson is one that contains a performance ingredient often near the beginning of the lesson. This then gives rise to real interaction, not so much between me and the students, as between one student and another. I find that a successful class is one where I will set the ball rolling and the students run with it. That's the ideal and doesn't always happen.

*Q: What do you look for in your students?*
A: What I look for in my students can be called commitment. But what I want more than anything is their willingness to be engaged—to be there and to like what we are doing, dislike what we're doing, express an opinion, fight, agree, laugh, cry, whatever. What I find difficult is lack of interest, passivity, and particularly a kind of sarcasm which some teenagers find cool and I find annoying.

*Q: What is important about the way you present the material?*
A: What's important to me in the way I present material is two things, and they're equally balanced. One is the nature of the material: I'm careful about the material I choose. I never teach anything I don't think is good in its way, if possible the best in its way, so I have great respect for my material and often a great love for it. Equally, it's important to me that each person in the class should have breathing space, should be able to encounter that material and should himself be treated with absolute respect.

*Q: What will students say of you?*
A: Students will say of me I'm a sentimental old thing. That they've had a wonderful time in my classroom and may not remember a thing.

*Q:Why do you teach?*
A: I teach because it is the place and the activity where I feel most alive.

*Q: How do you communicate?*
A: My communication style is verbal, I elicit responses on a cerebral level.

*Q: What is your attitude to preparing teaching plans?*
A: Preparing teaching plans has changed over the years. In the beginning it was a performance. I prepared absolutely so that each class was designed for a fifty minute perfect parabola. So that it started at one point, moved through certain activities, moved along to an epiphany, and wrapped up five minutes before the bell. It was highly timed and planned. Now I plan less and less. I have a starting point in my head, but I'm much more interested in what the students bring. The lesson plan often goes by the board.

*Q: What do you like about the classroom?*
A: I like being stretched and revitalized by using all my powers of imagination, persuasion, and passion.

*Q: What don't you like about the classroom?*
A: What I don't like about the classroom is whenever the relationship with students becomes, or can be perceived as, adversarial—for instance, handing out grades, or returning papers at exam time.

### Practical Tips

*For Helpers to Work with Themselves*

- Find a way to refocus on your own needs and feelings.
- Be aware when you are helping students without their asking for help.
- Try not to be selective in your attention—either with the young superstar, or the lame duck.
- Try to forge your own path instead of helping "the authority" with theirs.
- Hold the line with students with regard to deadlines and grades.
- Uphold institutional rules although this may mean confrontation with colleagues or students.
- Learn that flattery is self-serving and be more demonstrative with spontaneous warmth.
- Be aware that many colleagues and students are put off by the emotionality of your manner.
- Pay more attention to a purely intellectual context, remember you are biased toward the relational.

*For Others Who Work with Helpers*

- Encourage them to take risks in presenting their own ideas and work.
- Allow time to make personal contact, nothing is more important in motivating Twos.
- Show them you've noticed them, comment on little things, Twos thrive with that sort of acknowledgment.

- Structure an interactive component into their class work and study.
- Don't let them help you if it is not appropriate.
- Help them build boundaries by directing them back to themselves.
- Encourage them to articulate their needs and desires, to make "I" statements.
- Make it clear that your approval is for themselves, not for how they've helped you.
- Encourage them to spend time alone to get in touch with themselves.

## *ENNEATYPE THREE: THE PERFORMER*

- TRIAD: *ATTACHER*
- ATTENTIONAL FOCUS: Tasks
- AVOIDANCE: Failure
- GIFT: Leadership on behalf of others
- GROWTH PATH: From self-deceit to honesty
- ESSENCE: Hope
- SHIFT TO SECURE POINT: *THE QUESTIONER SIX*
  (Detacher—against arrow)
- SHIFT TO STRESS POINT: *THE PEACEKEEPER NINE*
  (Defender—with arrow)
- WINGS: *THE HELPER TWO* (Attacher)
  *THE ROYAL FAMILY FOUR* (Attacher)

### EXAMPLES OF PERFORMER THREE EDUCATORS: GETTING THE JOB DONE

#### How Far Can You Go, How High Can You Climb?

Doug D. is known in the educational world as Alexander the Great. This is because at the age of twenty-six fresh out of Harvard's Graduate School of Education and with no formal classroom experience, he was appointed supervisor of a large suburban school district in an East Coast city. Doug spent summers during his undergraduate college career working with teenagers in Washington, D.C. On the strength of that experience and his work in the Civil Rights movement before graduate school, he was appointed to a Presidential Task Force on inner city youth at risk. A natural leader and organizer with an open, easygoing manner, an ability to listen, and an excellent speaking style, he always gathered a loyal following.

Rising to the challenges of leadership as a schools' supervisor, Doug soon earned the respect of his older colleagues in the district. By dint of hard work, organizational efficiency, team-building skills, and making the tough decisions, within several years he was running a model suburban school district. His next career move, in his early thirties, was to become president of a large urban college for education and teacher training. During his tenure the college gained national attention for innovative school/community programs with students teaching in city schools at least once a week.

After a ten-year stint as college president, Doug took on the job of top administrator in a statewide Department of Education, working closely with legislators and educators. Doug's networking skills are an integral part of his persona. He is an SRO feature on the national educational conference circuit as a keynote speaker. His speeches and articles combine his love for pedagogy (and safeguarding national educational standards) with a call for activism in education as America enters the 21st century with an increasingly diverse population.

Doug has been approached many times to run for national office, or to serve in the nation's top educational administrative jobs. With years ahead of him as an influential educator and with his innate skills as an administrator and spokesperson, many performances lie ahead for Alexander the Great.

## The Role Model

Martha C. is cited as a role model of her profession. An outstanding scholar-athlete and leader, in her academic career she embodied achievement, reliability, and determination in all she undertook. Her first professional appointment was as a history teacher in a small, but well-known rural independent high school. In addition to a full load of teaching, she helped coach both the speech and tennis teams, ran a dorm, and volunteered for community service. Married with two small children, after two years in the classroom, she took on increasingly larger chunks of school administration, until in her third year she was appointed assistant head. In addition to her traditional duties, during that year she initiated, developed, and ran a summer program for junior-high- school students based on the premise that if you teach skills such as concentration, commitment, risk-taking, and technical know-how, both in sport and academics, you will bolster self-esteem and individual performance.

At age thirty, she applied for the position of administrative dean at a large independent school with an international reputation, and not unexpectedly beat out the competition for the job. During the interview process she heard from student leaders of their perceived gap of communication with administrators. She settled on this as one of her priorities. In her first weeks at the school, she made herself visible, for instance, by taking delivery of the newspapers from the startled driver at 5.30 a.m. and doing the deliveries around campus with the students. Her office door was always open and she kept meetings going with students until all were satisfied that there was nothing left to say, even when it meant coming back at night to finish up.

Martha set new systems in place that made her peers and students alike responsible for administrative decision-making, she streamlined older procedures and in an institution hidebound by over two centuries of tradition, she was not scared to rock the boat and hold her colleagues accountable. Her major weakness was impatience: rather than delegate and wait for others to perform tasks for her, she took on more and more herself. Burnout engendered a health crisis. Chastened, Martha learned to pick people she could rely on as her support staff. In five years at the school she achieved an almost legendary and much-loved profile among the student body. Of her peers, some loved her, others positively disliked her, most admired her energy and leadership.

Three years later, she was appointed the youngest head ever of a prestigious independent girls' high school. This is her current position. She inherited the legacy of a recalcitrant faculty whose agenda drives the school. In giving her the appointment, the board made it clear that her primary job was to take back the moral authority and vision of the school from the faculty without alienating and demoralizing them. Martha loves the challenge.

## THE PERFORMER STRATEGY

| Strengths | Weaknesses |
|---|---|
| Efficiency | Can brush aside feelings |
| Reliability | Impatience |
| Self-confidence | End-product by any means |
| Focus on tasks | Manipulates facts |
| Natural, leader | Can be deceitful |
| Goal-orientated | Believes own propaganda |
| Competitive | "Watch my tracks on your back" style |
| Polyphasic thinker/doer | Switches tracks in midstride |
| Driven to succeed | Avoids failure |

## THE E-TYPE THREE PROPOSITION

### General Description

### Performance and Achievement; Self-Deceit and Hope

The name Performer arises from the fact that Threes act out a persona and also that Threes get the job done—they perform on the job. There are two types of Threes who may appear at first glance to be different; however, the underlying psychological patterning is the same. For the Beaver Three—"what I do speaks about who I am"—performance is subsumed into what they do. The Peacock Three is a more obvious form of the Performer—"image and how I look are of essential importance." For both these variants of the core Three energy, performance is the *modus operandi*. For Performers, identification with what they do is so strong that they run the risk of imagining they are the role model of whatever they undertake. Performance is tied into image and the right image is projected to ensure approval (including self-approval) by getting the job done.

More self-aware Threes are conscious of when they don personas and can separate out the pseudo from an essential self. There is an awareness of performance, some Threes do know the difference. One of the life tasks for Threes is to be on the lookout for the times when the illusion of who they are fuses with what they do.

Attention and energy can be highly selective, Performers naturally gravitate to situations where they fit their energy and task orientation to further their own agenda. Underneath this energy there is a great deal of passion, and while they may suspend their feelings for the sake of doing the job, feelings are powerfully energizing when they can gain access to them. Threes need to pay more attention to their feelings, to slow down long enough so they can recognize what they are feeling.

In the Enneagram lexicon Threes are often named the *deceit type*, but it's not so much a case of overt lying—Threes are actually quite truthful. The core issue revolves around self-deceit. Performers reframe reality to their advantage, because it's so hard for them to admit failure. There's never a failure, Performer's never fail: "Well, it didn't work out, but this is good, because now I can use this material. In fact it was great that opportunity closed for me, because now I can go and do with this what I wanted to do anyway." Performers reframe what they think others see as failure into success, even partial success. It is an intense experience for Threes when they realize most of the other E-types don't think of life in terms of failure and success—either something works, or it doesn't. Success or failure are a Three construct on life. Performers put enormous store on success and achievement and this is usually a major sticking point for other E-types in interactions with Threes: "Why do Performers always have to be the first to ask a question?" "to get up and perform?" "to dominate discussions?"

In the classroom Performers play to their audience. A subtle inner mechanism operates to draw in students—changes in voice, gesture, and manner—make sure the Three has everyone's attention. These adjustments are quite automatic: "Once I have you, my belief is that I can sell you anything, because I know how to package ideas." This as an essential Three illusion, a projection, a blind spot. But most Performers hold onto this belief and they can come across as phony. While the Three thinks they're on a roll and everyone is on board their bandwagon, others see them working so hard to sell!

Performers don't listen very well; they filter out negative criticism as well as what they regard as extraneous information. In a classroom setting, or a departmental meeting, if Performer's are not the ones talking then they're not particularly interested in what anyone else is saying. Performers report that their minds are spinning in several different grooves: "What I'm going to do, how I'm going to do it, and what are the alternative ways for doing it."

If as a teacher you're not directly addressing what is of interest to the Three student—"what is the goal, why are we here?"—Performers are not going to listen. If you're going to insist on the steps through a process, Three students are going to think you're a bore. Performers line up in their heads the most efficient way to do something and if, according to the Three student, a teacher is floundering they're going to dismiss the teacher and do it their way anyway. Three students are the ones who doodle, who look down their noses at teachers as if to say, "Well, how long is it going to take you to say this?" Cultivating listening skills is something educators can point out to Three students, they need to pay special attention to listening skills.

Performers are natural leaders, their energy is controlling, but control can be disguised as teamwork, *doing* in the interests of the team. Performers do not wield control for the sake of power, like Point Eights, or to feel safe, like Point Sixes, but in order to reach the goal: "If things spin out of my control then everybody's going to be so inefficient that we're not going to get this job done. So I'll hold all the pieces together."

Everything in life comes back to completing tasks. Performers expect others to work as hard as they do. Results count, not how one get's there. It's okay to cut corners, to machinate, never mind if others working alongside the Performer feel short-changed, pressured, or cheapened by the process. For Threes time wasted is time lost forever. This is another illusion of control, more evidence of self-deceit, a belief that one can actually prioritize and schedule life into blocks of sequential time.

In whatever arena, self-deceit abets the Three's drive to accomplish. When you believe you're the one who's going to get everything done for everybody else, there's a sense of self-importance. It is hard for Performers to accept and learn that in fact the world operates quite well without them.

The gift of the Three is leadership and on-the-job performance on behalf of others. When Threes can step back and put their energy and talents at the service of a cause, or other people, when Threes can feel they are genuinely part of a team and everyone else is as important as they are—both in their ability to contribute and execute—then their gift truly draws out the best of the Three. Tied into the Performer leadership style is the embodiment of the quality of hope. Threes bring hope in their drive forward style to manifest a vision and attain goals.

### Shift to Point Six (Security)

When Threes feel secure they slow down, stop driving themselves and everyone else. There is space for feelings to surface and time to think about themselves and others. But for a Three to be in Six can also be discomforting, because doubts emerge. Faced with fears, questions, and doubts, bubbling emotions can be overwhelming. When the discomfort level is too high Threes quickly kick into action mode again.

> I'm so focused on reaching my goal. Last semester I had to prepare a report on faculty advisors at very short notice. I went on automatic to get it done, ignoring all thoughts or feelings of being tired, or having downtime. When I handed in the product, I felt great. Then, I let go and relaxed. I was overwhelmed with feelings of how tired I was, of almost annihilation, because I didn't have anything pressing to do. I'd worked myself to a standstill, and there I was awash with feelings—fears and doubts about the project, my image as the author, the reaction of my colleagues, so on. It was frightening.

Even though Point Threes shift to Point Six when they feel secure, they can take on the defenses mechanisms of this point, such as doubting and worse-case-scenario thinking.

### Shift to Point Nine (Stress)

When Threes are stressed their attention is split onto an internal taskmaster counting off all the tasks that have to get done, while they find themselves losing their ability to prioritize. For the Three in Nine there's a sense of not being able to move into action, of spinning one's wheels, of becoming more and more frustrated and frightened.

When I have a difficult exam coming up in a class I hate, I get to this place where with one day to go before the exam, I'm taking the notebook and rearranging all the papers and putting in tabs. Rewriting the headlines, all the stupidest, irrelevant things because I'm swimming in this swirl of a lack of direction, when of course what I need to do is focus on the three or four key points that will be on the exam and I should master. It's almost like I become paralyzed in inactivity which is so uncharacteristic of me under normal circumstances, but happens under times of particular stress.

Even though Point Threes shift to Point Nine when they feel stressed, they can experience the gifts of this point: unconditional love and support of others.

## Key Characteristics

### *Taking on a Persona*

Threes take on a persona, the more impressive the better, to become what they do. It is a form of role-playing, except that the role becomes the self. Performers can take on many roles during the course of one day—the practical, concerned teacher, the conscientious soccer mom, the supportive wife. Often Threes will change clothes several times a day as they subconsciously flex themselves into these roles. This Three educator needs to wear a coat and tie and turn himself into Mr. X, teacher, because to get the job done his way he needs to wear an air of authority and formality in the classroom. Note that it is in the process of thinking through what he has to *do* each day that he becomes Mr. X.

So that over the years I've developed Mr. X. I'm never Y, I'm always Mr. X and in the morning I always get dressed up. I wear a shirt and a tie everyday, as a kind of teaching uniform that actually separates me from them and gives me an element of formality that allows me to have some authority in the classroom. I leave home in the morning and I walk up the street to school, and in that process, in that time of walking up to school, I become Mr. X, teacher. Sometimes people who know me pass in their cars and they say, "I tooted my horn at you this morning and you didn't even wave back." I never wave, because I'm oblivious to what goes on with the traffic that is passing me, because I'm going through my day and I'm thinking through what it is I have to do. In those few minutes I make the transition from myself as a private person to myself as a public person, and by the time I get to school, I'm ready to be Mr. X. I fear without this uniform, something about me is too informal, too friendly, too casual, too full of laughter, that I won't gain the students' respect.

### *Achieving Goals*

Threes want to be in control, they establish their authority through the image of being efficient achievers. With an almost limitless capacity for hard work, they organize their lives by breaking goals into tasks. Efficiency, seeing a way to do things more quickly, more competently, is a trap for Threes. Not too many colleagues, or students, take kindly to being shown, over and over, a *better* way to do a task. Threes need to realize that others will do the job, even though the way they go about it may look inefficient and time-wasting to the Performer.

I can have a very long-term vision, but I can't tell you how I'm going to reach the goal. When the pieces start to fall into place, I know exactly which are the right pieces to go with—so I can adhere to my vision as a goal, but I can't tell you how I'm going to get there step-by-step. I wait for the right people to show up, I wait for the time to feel right—is this a time to push, or hold back? Then I break everything into manageable tasks. I have an intuitive understanding of how to get to my goal, but I can't plan it out for you.

This goal orientation and focus on tasks has many implications for Threes. Performers gain approval by achieving their goals, but they run the danger of becoming human *doings*, not human *beings*. Performers get many rewards in our American society with its emphasis on energy, achievement, image, being a winner. Performers definitely want to be seen as winners.

I've got to see short-term wins in order to see long-term goals. I'll never get there unless I achieve short-term goals, I'm very task-oriented, and set things up so I win along the way. Every time we finish a course unit, that's a win. Reaching the end of the first semester, handing in my grades and comments, that's another win. My school year is laid out on my calender, each time I cross off another deadline, that's a win. The goal is summertime, end-of-school.

When you get right down to the bedrock inner mechanisms of the Three, living life itself is a goal, and gaining approval has its place in the life-goal matrix.

Of course I'm focused on goals, and I assume the whole world is, and I'm continually surprised that other people are not as goal-orientated. Looking for response and approval is achieving goals, isn't it?

Performers make sense of existential, objective reality by working toward a goal as a way of organizing life.

Both short- and long-term goals are important. If I do not see a purpose to something, it becomes senseless to me. Take Latin: I never saw any purpose to it, as a result it was one of the most difficult subjects for me, because I kept on thinking, what am I going to do with this when I get out of school? I couldn't study it just for the sake of learning something new and different. It has to have a practical purpose, a goal, for it to make sense to me.

For the Performer life is lived through order and structure which is symbolic of a steady step-by-step forward momentum to achieve goals. It is hard for Threes to stop moving forward, not unlike the ubiquitous Energizer Bunny.

I tend to get the little things out of way, so that I can feel a sense of accomplishment. I have a friend who makes a list and the first thing he does is to write down, #1. *Make a list*, so that after he makes the list he can then cross off number one, he already has done something. I don't go that far, but I do order my life. I said to someone yesterday—she had asked me to make a phone call, we had a discussion last week, and I had said, yes, indeed, I would make the phone call—yesterday, I said it's going to happen. It made the list, and that's a way of my saying to myself that I'm actually going to do it. I may not get it done instantly. I may not get it done tomorrow, but I get it done when it hits that piece of paper.

For outer-directed Performers the sense of an inner self is often nonexistent. When Threes are not at work, they assume the role of a person of leisure, but the underlying driver of achievement through a well-ordered life is still intact. This is how one Three educator *does* summer and fulfills his summer goal of being laid-back, being his *essential* self. Note how often forms of the verb *to do* appear.

As soon as the summer comes, I don't have any order or organization anymore and it's very hard to get any tasks done, because that's when the essential me happens. This other me that I've learned how to do and feel comfortable doing and is now habitual happens during the school year. I don't mean I become a slob in the summertime, but I relax much more and my schedules are much looser and freer and to people around me who have schedules, I say, "You are the one with the schedule, what do you want me to do? Do you want to go for a picnic this afternoon—sure?" "Do you want to have lunch tomorrow? It's summertime. I've a lot of time, sure, let's do it now."

### *Motivating Others*

Performers gravitate naturally to leadership positions. They enjoy being authority figures, with the commensurate recognition and sense of importance this brings. They feel they deserve success because they work so hard. Threes are competitive, good self-promoters, and natural net-workers. When it is important for them to do so, they back up the hype with solid results—from childhood they've gained approval for what they do. With a Three in charge there is a sense of unstoppable forward momentum. One way in which Threes motivate others is to embody what they do, even if consciously they're playing the part.

To motivate others, I have to walk the walk, promote a sense of honesty and integrity about what I'm doing. As educators we have to be what we say we want them to be. Young people are so much more intuitive, they haven't been damaged yet by society. They can quickly pick up fakes and phonies and I don't think the message ever gets to people, unless there's a real true thought process that says what I'm telling you is real, because I live it.

Another way Threes motivate others is to become the container of a vision, and to hold that vision and keep moving forward until it (even if the vision is revised several times along the way) manifests itself.

To motivate I hold a vision; I have inner certainty. I make it happen because I believe in it, or I believe in it so I make it happen—in my mind I can't separate the two. I think it's my energy around holding a vision and taking the small steps that will get me to that place. It's an energy and an ability to look at setbacks and not take them personally. In a way I can see how this can come across sometimes as cold, cold and calculating, but in reality I feel very deeply. I can't achieve a goal unless I absolutely believe in it. Now that may be my illusion, but it's what I believe and I will make it happen. So that's my vision, and I hope it's motivating for my students.

### Polyphasic Ability

Threes have an ability to do several tasks at the same time. They practice this behavior not only because to them it seems an efficient use of time, but because it is a rush to do so. Others may look at the Three student or teacher and see a hamster unable to get off a wheel, but the Three feels great.

It is my responsibility to teach them things, ideas, skills, whatever, so I'm very present in my classroom. I direct things, I keep the discussion going, I set up the lessons, the pieces that we'll do during the course of a class. It's my job to figure out the process that gets them from their lack of confidence and their lack of skills into being successful in a way that is powerful and propelling, interesting and imaginative, and I take the steps, and I do that. When the discussion in an English class is moving like crazy and I'm interjecting something, moving it along and pushing them and asking the right questions and drawing things together, and when that's all over I'm exhausted, and I have the sense of a tremendously satisfying experience.

From the following Three we get a definite sense of the intrinsic confluence of energy, effort, and polyphasic activity in order to achieve.

I can do two, three, four, even more things at once, always have, I'm always doing multiple projects at the same time. My entire life, achievement is a driving force. I always had to be at the head of the class, the one who won the award, with the biggest and the best of whatever it was. And I'm willing to put in time and effort and hard work necessary to make that happen. And it sure helps to be able to do more than one thing at the same time.

The polyphasic Performer predilection can turn the classroom into a peripatetic place filled with activity and interaction.

A multimedia style; I don't think I ever speak for more than five minutes at a stretch, just talking, I always have overheads, or video, or some kind of exercise that people are going to do. I studied psychodrama and I set up psychodramas in my teaching where people do role-playing in front of the group. It turns everybody on when people realize they're active participants in something going on in the classroom setting. It's nice for me to have the action going on. I hate to sit and teach, I want to move about among the class, I want to make contact with everybody. While teaching I want to keep on moving, so people don't get bored, and some of the ways are role-playing and other interactive exercises. Breaking things up is important to me, and then stopping for short breaks. I try to create for other people the learning environment that turns me on.

The ability to organize plays a major role in the achievement of tasks.

So that during the course of a double period, I have five, or six, or seven different activities and I am to that extent the director of that class. It's all these pieces that interweave and overlap and don't necessarily go from point X to point Y, but come back and around and go on again and then come back again, and hopefully, then it gets to endpoint, Z.

### Tasks and Organization

For Threes reaching the goal, achieving the vision, manifesting the end product are of major importance, the source of their approval. Performers throw everything at the given job: flexing into the appropriate image so they become identified with what they do, clamping down on feelings, bringing the full bore of their polyphasic abilities into play, but no attribute is as powerful for the Three as their ability to perform through organization and task-orientation. This Performer thinks of teaching in terms of lessons, not in terms of students, or course content, or other criteria. He is focused on tasks.

I do tasks well, because I keep things organized, and teaching is exactly the same way. There are papers to be graded and classes to attend to and lessons to be planned. My wife says, "What's on for tonight," and I say, "I have to plan my lessons." I think of teaching in terms of lessons, so order and structure and organization are all terribly important to me because it's a way I believe ultimately in education of getting skills out to kids in a reasonable fashion. I'm very much—I hope this doesn't sound too egotistical—but I'm very much the center of my own teaching, and I feel comfortable with that, and I enjoy it.

The ability to prioritize plays a major role in achievement of tasks. Other E-types also run lists, but for different purposes than the Performer.

At the beginning of every week I may have a little card with my schedule on it, and I write when my classes are, and my appointments with students, or when I have a meeting. I always have a list of things. I write down what my homework is and I write down whom I have to call and what has to be done, and I move along task, by task, by task, by task. I was told years ago that I was supposed to do my most important tasks first when I had energy, but I don't do that, I tend to do my most important tasks last. That way I have a sense of accomplishment by doing less important things first.

The ability to organize plays a major role in the achievement of tasks.

Organization: I live with it. I once said to a friend that I like schools and I feel comfortable with schools because schools are orderly places. I have to be there every morning at 8:00, the bells ring and things start and things end, and the semester is over, and the new semester begins, and the endlessness that can happen in life doesn't happen in schools, because it's all very orderly. When I talk about my teaching, which others sometimes describe as chaotic, but I know there's an order and a plan to it, and I think actually that's not a contradiction—it actually goes together because it's a kind of organized chaos. I allow the chaos to happen while also marching along. I always know what I'm going to do tomorrow, I always like to do things. When I'm at school I do things, when I'm at home I do things.

### Identification

Identification means aligning oneself with a person or group with a resultant feeling of close emotional association. For other E-types identification may go no further than a feeling that one would like to be like a mentor, or identifies with a place, or ideal, or religious idea. For Threes identification takes on another level of meaning, merging the persona they create to do the task, with becoming the task itself. This educator teaches us well, he is so identified with the role of being a teacher that he has become what he does.

If you all taught like me, what a place this would be! We'd get everything done, the kids would be upbeat, we'd have wonderful presentations, they'd learn how to get out in the world and sell themselves. Every other teacher should be like me, I should be the role model for the whole institution.

Identification can extend to Threes seeing themselves as the institutional moral authority and quintessential role model.

As an administrator a big part of my job is getting my 400 staff people to understand what is the mission and philosophy of this large institution, so that's where my teaching comes into play. Being the leader of this institution is in some ways being the first teacher, the lead teacher. When people first show up here, to teach or to learn, I start off and teach them what my institution is all about and what my philosophy is.

### Failure

Threes avoid failure. It is well-nigh impossible for Threes to take Rudyard Kipling's advice from the poem *If*, "If you can meet with Triumph and Disaster and treat those two impostors just the same." Triumph and Disaster are not impostors to the Threes, they form a solid reality in their world. This Three identified herself on the Enneagram model from simply seeing the word "failure" on a list of the avoidances of each E-type.

In an Enneagram book I read, the word "failure" aligned with the Three just jumped out at me, and I thought, oh my God, somebody has actually caught the secret of myself. I could not say the word "failure." It's something I kept at absolute arm's length. Later, I went through a two year process of integrating failure into my psyche—I asked questions of failure, such as, "What do I have to learn from you? And why do I have these feelings about you? How can I incorporate you into my life, so that you become less frightening to me?" It took me two years to say, "I can fail, and there's still me intact."

In my teaching, even with knowing the Enneagram, I'm still not going to get through to every kid but I don't regard that as a failure any more. They have their journeys and I have my journey, and I can only facilitate theirs with compassion and understanding, I can't sell them my journey.

Threes do not take easily to living in the flat, even plateau between the peaks of Triumph and the valleys of Disaster. In a world where failure is inadmissible, even the word must be reframed as a "downside" or "disadvantage."

A failure in my classroom is that I overdo it, this being so present. Because I love to talk I tend to go on at length, and I think that in a discussion classroom I don't allow for enough of them. I try very hard. I ask a lot of questions. When answers come, I applaud those answers. I am enthusiastic and positive as new perceptions come up, even if their perceptions I have perhaps thought of a long time ago myself, or heard others students give. It's not as if I'm giving the dramatic lecture ever, there is always this exchange, but I think the exchange—the failure—the downside of it, the disadvantage, is that some students can become a little lazy in my classroom because they know that if they don't come forward with the energy I will, because I can't stand silence in the classroom.

The depth and pathos of the Three dilemma around failure is eloquently captured by this Three. She is coming into a dawning realization of a sense of self that does not have to be navigated by her constant compass readings of Triumph and Disaster.

My biggest fear is not cancer or losing my kids, but boredom and failure. I have an internal mechanism that when everything goes wrong I judge myself a failure, instead of accepting that there are times when I have no control over events. I'm not in control of this whole universe. The "aha" came after I sat down, did some deep thinking, and began to realize that to get to the same point there are other ways than what I've been doing for so long. Now there's hope, real hope.

A successful image is intrinsic to the Three strategy. Here is an inside account of how Threes amalgamate energy and attention to achieve success. Donning blinders to blot out that which will not be conducive to success allows Performers to home in almost relentlessly on what will be successful.

I will drop whatever I'm not successful at. In school I was hopeless at math so I dropped out. I had to be in the classroom, but I paid no attention whatever. We had a matriculation exam, a public exam which I failed. I didn't bother, I wasn't any good at it, so I wasn't going to put any time into it. I look successful because I only do what I can succeed at. I was good at sports so I put a lot of effort into tennis and field hockey, and at performance—public speaking and the debate team. I was a star in the humanities, but I never ever studied physics, or chemistry, and math was a nightmare. I drop or go around what I'm not going to succeed at, and never tell anyone about it. So you only know what you see on my resume and assume that I was great at this, and great at that, and I trot out my prizes and publications. If you asked me to, I could even reframe that I was successful that I failed at math.

### Image and Approval

As children Performers gained approval by doing well, by achieving, by believing that they were loved for what they accomplished, rather than for who they were. This belief leads to a lifelong dance with issues around image—winners are loved, approved of—there are no prizes for those in second place. Performers project an image in which they can believe and sell to others, so they become caught in a self-fulfilling loop of projection, image, approval. An edgy layer of anxiety underlies the Three drive to success, which also translates as approval. Threes can be panicked and mill around in confusion if the image they choose does not earn them the status and respect they feel they've earned by dint of hard work, their own competency, and the thrust of all their power and energy in the professional field in which they compete.

Rather than face the feelings that arise around a potential failure, Performers shift gears, adjust the image, find an alternate route to the success and approval they crave by becoming the prototype of the new role they've adapted. Others can see this swift change of costume as deceitful, as Machiavellian in the sense that "the ends justify the means." And, in most instances, the end is for the greater glory of the Three.

I want the sun to always shine on me. It's important for me how the outside world sees me. I am so driven. When I was a kid, I didn't know what I wanted to do, I just wanted to be famous. I want the world to tell me I'm okay.

Performers have an unslakable thirst for approval, it is as if they look in a mirror and are not alive unless someone else is smiling back.

It is embarrassing for me to admit it, but I do love to perform, and I do love to speak in front of groups, and I do look for your approval. I pick out different people in an audience when I'm teaching: who's smiling, who's laughing—and I can focus on them, and feed off of them. In a way it's very important to me to feel you're listening to me, and I haven't lost your attention.

Because approval is so important, Threes set up a comparative yardstick of how well they are doing. Unlike Perfectionist Ones who also compare themselves with others, but do so judgmentally, Threes compare themselves to others in their field and measure how much it will take to outdo the competition. Threes are proud of their achievements, because they are competent and have worked hard to earn them. Performers tune out negative criticism with what in extreme cases can be an almost narcissistic belief in their superior abilities.

I certainly appreciate it when people stop and say, "Oh I heard a good thing about you." And one of my reactions is, "More, more..." because so often in life we don't hear good things. No matter what else anyone has said about me, about something that happened last week that they liked, or some award my students have won, or whatever, it's what happened today and what happened in the aggregate of classes, and whether I made it happen or not. If I can't make it happen because of the weather, or because my students are angry with each other for things outside of the class, I still take it upon myself as important to make it happen. So my sense of image to myself is important.

Ultimately, for Threes it all comes back to achieving goals by adhering to tasks.

It's my following a process for myself that is my approval: my setting up the environment, my planning the tasks, my putting the curriculum together, my developing those lessons. I get my approval when

I know I've done the job well, that I can take students through a process and feel that they've got it at the end, then that's what important to me. i'm the one who judges that. I don't need a department chairman or a principal to sit in my class, or parents on Parents' Day to say, "Oh, just great."

### Feelings

Performers seem to be forever optimistic and upbeat. They do not often pause for long enough between an idea and moving into action to be ambushed by emotional reactivity. In an intrinsic way Threes have put on hold an interior life in the name of performance and activity. Habitual conditioning around how to win approval is in part what creates the need for constant activity and for the Three to suspend feelings. Performers fear that feelings will hold them back, drag them down, and they will not be able to *do*. As long as attention is outer-directed on tasks and others, being caught up in the discomfort of a swirl of emotions can be put permanently on hold. Performers have little practice at con-necting with their feelings.

I push down my feelings, because I need all that energy to take care of everybody else's feelings. I push all those feelings down and use that energy to take care of everybody else, those who I don't think can stand up to the pressure that I can stand up to. So I never let my feelings out, because I'm busy taking care of everyone else's feelings. Letting go is probably the most difficult thing for me and letting people fix them-selves. I'm fifty five years old and I'm just beginning to feel and not be afraid of what's going to happen when I feel. I trust now that I'm not going to fall apart, or not get up again.

This Three deceives those around her by diversifying her power, so there's a split between the more laid back public persona she projects, and her private per-sona with its deeply held conviction of her power. She is oblivious to the *self-deceit.

I've always believed that I have so much power that if I put all my energy into one enterprise, I'll totally blow everyone away, so I have always diversified and have three or four things going on at the same time, simply to protect the people around me, and in a way to protect myself from what I feel is this tremendous power I have and that I can pull through. I feel that I can use that power— be in the flow, let that power come through me—and use it for something. And that's hap-pened a few times in my life. But the way I explain it to myself is that I cannot let all my light shine at the same time, because it will blow everyone away.

The subconscious mind is a powerful register and Threes have conditioned themselves to believe that their value and worth are tied up in what they do, rather than knowing who they are. Performers have not sacrificed an inner life, they simply do not know there is one available to them. Threes keep the schedule filled: if there is no free time, there is no time for feelings to interfere. As this Performer says:

I squash my feelings and then I'm back to doing and everything is okay. Mostly I believe that I can't handle my feelings. They're so intense that it's overwhelming. When I have a strong feeling it's just so profound, I almost believe I'm not going to live through it.

### Growth Path: From Self-deceit to Honesty

Although there are Threes who are the exception in whom self-awareness rises naturally, most Performers come face-to-face with their feelings during an enforced period of inactivity—illness, or work-related or family induced crisis situations. Questions about self-esteem and worthiness, doubts around self-value gnaw at the Three, who is forced to stop and take a good look at herself.

Over time Threes learn to become aware of what the differences are between when they are stating and feeling the truth, or building and protecting an image they know will bring them approval. At first truth-telling can feel risky: "No one's going to like me for doing this," but then it becomes liberating and self-verifying.

Before I would sit in a meeting and rehearse carefully what I was going to say: both for maximum dramatic effect, but also to be supportive of the point of view of the person I thought was a winner, and therefore, the one I most wanted to work. Now, I find I blurt out the truth without thought, it's liberating, but it's also scary. People say things like: you've got courage, I could never be that brave. It doesn't feel courageous, or brave, it feels suicidal actually, but I can't help myself.

### Quality of Essence: Hope

Hope means desire with the expectation of fulfillment. Performers are adept at delivering the goods in terms of the image they project. In a psychospiritual sense, a mature self-aware Three embodies hope: both the expectation (vision) and the expectation of fulfillment (getting it done).

Threes report that when they are running on hope, they accomplish seemingly without effort. It is as if all they have to do is put themselves into an universal flow of energy and instinctively, they'll know the right moves. Hope, then, truly is embodied in the Performer.

I do hold the vision, I can provide the spark, the hope to get things going, to move it along. So the high side of my personality for me as a leader is holding that hope. But now I have the realization: "No, I'm not the one doing it, we're all doing it together," and that has been such a relief, that has been just an enormous relief. I still do leadership, but i'm a different leader now to what I was even a couple of years ago—hands off, providing space for people to succeed (I make sure I choose competent people), it's empowering to bring that hope.

and

The positive thing for me is the capacity to achieve, but to achieve in a way that is good for the world. I need to feel that somehow the world is a better place because of what I'm doing. And I have a good sense of self-satisfaction out of doing exactly that.

## What Performer Students Say

### Polyphasic Activity

In school I find it unbelievably painful and boring to sit in a classroom where the teacher stands in front of the class and just talks at you. It's all I can do to keep from getting out of the chair and moving around and doing something. I can't go to a lecture and sit for an hour and listen to one person talk, or grind on all the time, or reads the same material that's been handed out, or is in the book. I almost can't stay in the room, and in those classes I don't do well. I pass because I have to pass, but it is hell for me. It's excruciating for me to do that—I have to be moving, I have to be doing.

On the other hand if I'm in an educational experience which is a hands-on type of experience like a lab, or the teacher is doing a demonstration in front of the class, and people are participating, or a discussion or anything that get us up and moving around and involved, that works for me.

### Avoiding Failure

If I'm not good at something, if I can't do it, I get somebody else to do it for me, I'm good at selling. I don't feel great about that, but that's who I am. Physics is something that terrifies me, so I get someone else to do it for me, and that's the truth, and if that makes me a dishonest kid—I hope I'll learn about integrity as I get older. I have a very difficult time at school when it isn't something I feel I can win at, or be good at. If I'm going to be less than, I don't want any part of it, because my world is defined by people saying how good I am, how successful I am. I measure myself by how much I achieve. And if I'm going to be criticized, I run from critics, it hurt too much, causes too much pain.

and

Failure is a word everyone wants to ignore. I will admit that at times I fail. But I focus more on the fact that I might have failed, but it's all part of building character, building this huge picture, this blueprint of the future. Failure builds character and it also helps you; it motivates you to do better.

### Goal Directedness

I need somebody to engage me, I learn quickly, but you have to engage me, tell me what the end result is if I do all your good stuff. If I can't see the purpose of why I'm doing something, I'll go through the motions of doing it, but you won't get all of me. A teacher got my attention recently, he knew that to get my attention to work with him and listen to him was to make me involved in the outcome of what we were doing.

### Competition

If I'm in an ungraded setting, it is great for my emotional well-being, because in a graded setting I have to score highly, or else I'm not worthy. If the competition is taken away, I have to find self-value in other ways, and that's beneficial for me. But being who I am, I will always find a way to compete with the other students even in a non-graded setting so that I can feel I'm excelling.

and

Competition is not a negative for me. I want to have approval, I like to be pushed, challenged to perform, to take the very best of what I am and make me come alive. I don't think I'm trying to beat out the other guy, it's more that I'm trying to outdo myself, to achieve the goal, and be the first to get there. Sometimes I'm aware of how much I do is in competition with everyone else. I don't want to take someone specific out, it's more general than that. I just want to win.

### Focus on Tasks

Achieving tasks on a daily basis is important. At the beginning of this week I haven't gone to bed until three or four o'clock in the morning, not even worrying about my health, or how much I sleep I'm getting. What I'm worrying about is: I've got to lay out the newspaper, I've got to finish my history paper, I've got to do my math homework. I just lay down my schedule and it has to get done, regardless of what time it is, how I'm feeling, or whether I'm dozing off to sleep at my computer. It's actually funny, I'm sitting here at 3:00 a.m. looking at myself: I'm tired, I'm probably going to get sick, but I have to finish this. And that takes precedence over sleep, *I have to finish this.*

## Performing

Many people think that those who are attention grabbers, they're just showboats, they're out to make themselves look good at the expense of others. But I don't think it's necessarily a negative. I think it's interesting that when I ran for head monitor and I was up there giving a speech, standing in front of 600 people, it made me feel good. All those 1,200 eyes on you, it sends that feeling through you. It makes me nervous, obviously, but it gives me a feeling that is almost indescribable, a rush of adrenalin. Any place where you are the center of attention, it's important to me, it gives me a great sense of pride, it motivates me I suppose.

### Brief Interview with a Performer Educator

*Q: What is your teaching style is?*
A: My teaching style is dramatic and public.

*Q: What do you look for in your students?*
A: What I look for in my students are energy and engagement with the material.

*Q: What is important about the way you present the material?*
A: What is important in the way I present the material is that my students come to understand that a novel, a play, or a poem is something significant, something to be rescued from meaninglessness, something connected to real human experience. It may not be their human experience, and it may be that the style of the work is difficult for them, but what I want them to see is that they can get beyond the limitations of their own lives, as I had to get beyond the limitations of my own life.

*Q: What will students say of you?*
A: Student will say of me that I talk too much and that I like to hear my own interpretations. Even though I say my opinion in class, forcefully, students know that if they marshal their evidence in a powerful way, I'll accept their conclusion.

*Q: Why do you teach?*
A: I teach because I get a tremendous amount of satisfaction and pleasure out of taking this content, or these skills, and bringing them to these minds, and these people. The interaction between the information, the ideas, the skills, and the people have become endlessly fascinating and wonderful fun. I believe that as students move forward in their lives, they will move forward with a stronger self because of the instrumentality of having worked in my classroom. I think that sense of self-confidence is terrifically important in life, because there are lots of forces battling to push us down.

*Q: How do you communicate?*
A: My communication style is loud.

*Q: What is your attitude to preparing teaching plans?*
A: Preparing plans is frustrating, and I get annoyed when I don't have enough time to prepare lessons well.

*Q: What do you like about the classroom?*
A: What I like about the classroom is the interaction that happens, the excitement that we as people can generate among each other. The best days are when that energy just goes right up to the roof and by the time the bell rings everybody is bubbling and the energy spills out of the room into the hallway.

*Q: What don't you like about the classroom?*
A: What I don't like about the classroom is almost nothing. I have found for myself a place there. In the early days my physical reaction said "this is hard", but once I learned better how to teach and to know that my style and energy were going to be reasonably successful, I've found almost nothing I don't like.

### Practical Tips

*For Performer to Work with Themselves*

- Emphasize theory and context as well as action.
- Align yourself with the purpose and goals of the mission of your institution.
- Stop and consider the consequences of your forward momentum.
- Forestall burnout by learning to recognize when you are overextended and exhausted.
- Guard against being the instant expert who exaggerates positives and neglects negatives.
- Be aware of when you are acting as a role model, instead of a person.
- Don't overcommit when several enticing projects come to hand at the same time.
- Allow time to hear questions, doubt, suggestions, negative as well as positive feedback.
- Acknowledge others—as the leader don't take all the credit for a team effort.

*For Others Who Work with Performers*

- Make sure they hear praise as being for themselves, not for what they achieve.
- Point out that they'll be liked even if they don't always run for leadership positions.

- Show them how their focus on task rather than feelings can lead to unpopularity with peers.
- Define what you do in terms of purpose and goals, so Threes can align themselves behind you.
- Frame your questions in terms of goals: "How can we improve your performance?"
- State criticism in ways that they will not lose face: "This will be more efficient" rather than "That's a mistake."
- Remain firm in showing that alternative ways to do something are as valid as their own. Threes need to know that everyone has a contribution to make and that goal orientation is not universally admired.
- Get them to slow down and communicate clearly. Threes' multitask minds can shift between professional and personal concerns in ways that can come across as deceptive.
- Make sure Threes have covered the bases when they say they have; often they substitute assumptions for facts.

## *ENNEATYPE FOUR: THE ROYAL FAMILY*

- TRIAD: *ATTACHER*
- ATTENTIONAL FOCUS: What's missing
- GIFT: Unique creativity. Deep connection and empathy
- AVOIDANCE: Ordinariness
- GROWTH PATH: From envy to equanimity
- ESSENCE: Universal belonging
- SHIFT TO SECURE POINT: *THE PERFECTIONIST ONE* (Defender —against arrow)
- SHIFT TO STRESS POINT: *THE HELPER TWO* (Attacher—with arrow)
- WINGS: *THE PERFORMER THREE* (Attacher)
  *THE OBSERVER FIVE* (Detacher)

## EXAMPLES OF ROYAL FAMILY FOUR EDUCATORS: USING MY UNIQUE GIFTS

### The Authentic Article is in the Closet

Reyes B. is an artist, a sculptor, but he teaches physics. He grew up in a family that frowned on displays of feeling: joy, sadness, fear, tears. Reyes learned early on to control his feelings, but they roiled inside him, finding an outlet in his passion for art. His artistic pursuits and triumphs were acceptable to his parents: it is good for a man of substance to have interests. There was never a possibility that his father would support full-time study of art, Reyes knew better than to ever raise the matter, so he studied physics, seeking in the laws governing form and matter complementary understandings to his knowledge of the use of space and boundaries in sculpture.

As a young man, as an adult, the meaningful moments of Reyes' life were those of connection, experienced in his heart, when his concern, love, and soul touched the heart of another: albeit an animal, a feeling of union with the sky, his fourth grade teacher, the girl on the debate team who was in love with his best friend, or his philosophy professor.

Where love for his father should be Reyes felt a hole in his heart, although they had always gotten along. As the old man was dying Reyes tried to tell him that he loved him, words he knew all his life he was not permitted to say, and waited for his father to respond. What he got was a meaningful tightening of his father's grip on his hand and tears squeezed past the shut eyes, rolling down the lined cheeks. At home Reyes would hold close his young son, Rudi, named for his grandfather, and murmur over and over into the soft curls on his head how much he loved him.

Reyes taught physics in an urban public high school with many classes of over thirty students. The labs were ill-equipped. He could have had a career in higher education, but felt that in a high school he would have more opportunities to make a difference in students' lives. He chose to work in one of the poorest school districts. Many of his students did not speak or understand English well, but he communicated in the language of physics which he loved. His love for his subject matter and his love for his students, his gentle way in the classroom in the face of rudeness and disinterest, his concern and genuine interest in their well-being and lives soon garnered a solid reputation for him as a teacher which grew year by year. Long after his students graduated, many would return to see Reyes in the lab. With others he kept in closer touch as the years passed, sharing a beer in the pub, attending marriages and christenings, visiting them in their new family homes.

Whenever he thought of his art Reyes felt the familiar bittersweet ache of melancholy and loss posed by the great "what if" question. Close to his fiftieth birthday, he took over a small room near his lab at the school and began to sculpt again. He experimented with bold forms in steel, learning from the students in the welding shop how to work the tools, creating abstract shapes that portrayed inner space and feeling. He promised himself that when he retired he would devote all his time to his art.

## Look Carefully, You Won't See Another Like Me

Trudi G. teaches drama in the performing arts program of a prestigious, rural, small liberal arts college. Growing up Trudi had a love affair with the theater and wanted to act full-time. She graduated from Barnard College and in her undergraduate years landed parts in off-Broadway productions. Shortly after college her big break came: Trudi was cast in a play at Lincoln Center, but she didn't feel that she and the director had a good connect, he didn't understand her character as she did. Trudi left the cast one week prior to opening night. Her friends thought she was crazy to throw away the opportunity she had been working toward all her life—it was selfsabotage one said—but Trudi shrugged her shoulders: this event was to be anticipated, didn't they know the glass of life was always half empty?

"You are talented enough to accomplish anything you want to in the theater." Those were the words her drama coach at high school told her often as he encouraged her toward the acting career that had eluded him. More and more Trudi realized how significant he was in her life (they kept in touch all these years), how their connection sustained her through many dark and sad moments: I want to be like him, mean something to people. Trudi enrolled in a graduate program in drama and several years later was awarded a Ph.D.

She became a remarkable, controversial, and much-sought-after teacher. Her special gifts—love of literature and the craft of the theater, combined with her intensity in working with performing arts students—helped to fill her classes year after year. You had not acted until you were in one of Trudi's plays. You had to experience for yourself her intellectual rigor, her demands on your creativity, her warmth, the quality of her connection with you when you became one of "her" students. Almost single-handedly, or so it seemed to her, she lifted the moribund drama department to a place of national prominence.

On the campus where Trudi has taught for almost twenty years she is a celebrity, pointed out to freshman as she walks calmly (having mastered the art of lyricism in walking) across the quad and along the corridors. Whatever the season, no one has seen her in anything other than basic black clothes complemented by dramatic and colorful scarves and hats. Her dark, luxuriant hair in many-layered curls hugs her face emphasizing the dark eyes, black-fringed pools, in whose depths constant feeling wells. Her celebrity status arises from the fact that she has appeared in minor character roles in Hollywood movies over the years, that she acts in all the plays she directs, but more important, from her mystique as an extraordinary teacher. Trudi's hallmark is her ability to forge strong connections with students—such extraordinary relationships as to provide grist for the rumor mills of those on the "outside," rumors of amorous affairs with both men and women students. No substance has ever been found to these rumors. When pressed about this, Trudi answers with a melancholic smile that it's what she expects living with her celebrity and notoriety on campus. Teaching is her truest role.

## THE ROYAL FAMILY STRATEGY

| Strengths | Weaknesses |
|---|---|
| Connectivity | Feeling special |
| Creativity | Melodramatic |
| Empathy | Aloofness |
| Passion | Egocentricity |
| Compassion | Needing to be different |
| Intensity | Inflating emotions |
| Understanding | Feeling unworthy |
| Authenticity | Finding balance |
| Intuition | Romanticizing emotions |

## THE E-TYPE FOUR PROPOSITION

### General Description

### Being Special and Deep Connection; Envy and Universal Belonging

The name for Fours, the Royal Family of the Enneagram, came to mind because there's a sense of uniqueness, of authenticity, of being special for Fours, the idea of a life lived intensely—a rich and passionate life colored in mythic purple. The focus of attention of each of the E-types is one clear way to distinguish between them, and for Fours the focus of attention is on what's missing. The Four focus underscores the special quality, the drama of the Four's life —the glass is half-empty.

How does this pattern play out for Fours? Let's take the realm of relationships. Relationships have intense meaning for the Royal Family, they feel most alive when they sense a deep connection to, for instance, a person, a cause, or their own creativity. The idea of "what's missing" in these connections plays out as a "push-pull" mechanism. The pull is toward a situation, or a person, or to conveying the aesthetics behind certain material in teaching, but when you get there, you find still there's something missing, and that's the impetus for the push back to where you started from. The mechanism can result in a constant flow back and forth. Until the push-pull pattern is recognized, there is no fulfillment, no ripening to fruition, but rather a sense of, "I've done this now. Is this all there is to it? There must be more." Or, "can I repeat this next year?" Or, "how do I satisfy the expectations of other people—now what?"

The psychological phenomenon is quite unlike the sense of achievement Performer Threes' feel, "OK, I've achieved this goal, what's next?" The Royal Family achieve the goal, but achieving goals generates apprehension, for Fours the moment is shot through with anticipation that inevitably the flow is going to go the other way, to the emptiness. This phenomenon in a broad sense characterizes the Four penchant toward experiencing life as having a bittersweet melancholic flavor. At a subconscious level the Royal Family are all too familiar with the paradox that the seed of growth and fulfillment is also the seed of decay and disappointment. In addition, the focus of attention on what's missing characterizes the avoidance of the Four which is ordinariness. Fours have a sense of the highs (rising to achieving goals) and lows (falling back to emptiness) and little of life lived in the the middle, in ordinariness. One of the growth areas for the Royal Family is to try to even out and balance a life that is either "high" or "low" or both, and to find in the mundane, the ordinary, that which will help them to stay there.

Another important area to highlight in the Royal Family profile is the energetic charge around envy. Often it's not envy for another's material possessions, but a comparison between one's life and the lives of others and most often a feeling of diminishment arises. Envy often takes the form of competition and can manifest itself as full-fledged competitiveness. Competition for the Four can be compelling; if a Four wants a position, and it goes to someone else, or someone flirts with the Four's significant other, they want that other person *dead.* This is unlike Performer Threes who often seem to epitomize competitiveness. Threes will assess what they need to put out: how much energy, effort, will to beat out the competition, to be the first to do the job. Even in matters of envy and competition, the Royal Family are ruled by emotions around connection.

Life is experienced with a melancholic flavor by Fours which they report to enjoy. From the outside a more overt form of melancholia can look like the darkness of depression. For many Fours depression does not carry the negative charge placed on the term by society at large. A Royal Family speaker explains it thus, "There's a sense of I can stay here, no one else can. I can go into the deeper, darker parts of the human psyche, I can bring back and describe that experience for others. None of you can feel as intensely as I do, because I'm someone who has been there, I've gone into those places and I can stay in those places, I'm not afraid of them. I can stay there for a long time and resonate with the emotional pain of others." There is a profound interiority to Fours, and in the educational sector, many Fours who are in the counseling professions do excellent work with the most troubled teens and adults because at a deep level they can emphasize with the other's anguish.

The Royal Family's life is painted in mythic purple, a canvas they frame of the great moments of intense connection. When Fours look back over a career of teaching, it's to those moments of connection with a student, or a colleague, or something coming together that makes it worthwhile. Fours yearn for connection and yet, often, when they make the connection, life becomes too ordinary, so they don't want it anymore, they pull back. The more intense and dramatic the connection is for the teacher, the more meaningful the class becomes, but it's not always that way for students. Students often experience difficulty dealing with a Four teacher because they're not quite sure where the boundaries are in relationship to the material, or to the teacher.

An adjunct to this drama and intensity is that for the Royal Family time is not sequential. If you ask Fours to tell a story they will never begin at A and end at Z; what you will get is in order of importance to them the dramatic highs or lows of the event. This can create difficulties in teaching when in certain subjects some deductive, sequential thinking is essential and the Four educator is working from an inner terrain that feels and looks like a roller coaster.

### Shift to Point One (Security)

The Point Four shift to Point One allows Fours to know what is right, to provide a moral compass, a direction to move toward in making decisions and taking action. This is a great stress reducer for Fours who are often at the mercy of intense emotions, each one feeling overwhelming. Fours also shift to Point One when they need to organize their lives in order to bring some structure and sequential logic to what they're thinking and experiencing.

I don't think in words, I don't think in numbers, I tend to think in metaphors and symbols. So letting go the metaphors and translating my thoughts is like someone who is speaking poor French coming back to English. Where I get emotionally high and low is when I haven't had a chance to get everything congruent and I get stuck in the middle again. When I feel more extreme emotions it is from not knowing how to process, not knowing other people don't process the same way. If I jump into a metaphor, or symbol, they think I'm flaky, but I don't know how to interpret my interior being. It's learning more about myself that's enabled me to do so.

Even though Point Fours shift to Point One when they are secure, they do experience the defense mechanisms of this E-type. They can become self-critical, and their anger takes an internal, indirect form, expressing itself as judgment and criticism.

### Shift to Point Two (Stress)

The shift to Point Two comes from stress and can be uncomfortable. It usually occurs when too many people make too many demands on the Four and he loses his personal boundaries, his sense of balance. In the Two stance, the Royal Family are concentrating so hard on making connections to give other people what they want, the connection is no longer *forming inside* the Four.

In the helping professions setting up boundaries in all kinds of ways is critical. I feel real phony when I lose my boundaries, I'm helping and it doesn't feel as if it's from a deep place—I'm just on a roll.

and

I can design a good three-hour class, but if I go in and get swayed by a student I will totally abandon my plan in order to address the student's need, or give the person want they want. So I lose myself, I lose my equanimity, I lose my plan. My practice is to watch when I leave the lesson plan, I ask myself: why have I left the plan?

Even though Point Fours shift to Point Two when they are stressed, they do experience the gifts of this E-type. They can be truly altruistic, and use their energy to potentiate others.

### Key Characteristics

#### Connection

For the Royal Family life is connection: do I have it, is it missing? These are the parameters of life's possibilities; everything else is secondary. Fours yearn for connection because they are acutely aware from childhood that they feel a sense of something missing. This perception is tied to feelings of loss, abandonment, an inability to feel they fit in (shame), not belonging. It is easy to see how this blind spot can be overcome by developing an acute intelligence around connection, to scan for it internally, to come to know what authentic connection feels like, what it means, an ability to name different kinds of connection. Unlike Point Twos who are outer-directed, ellipted onto others by anticipating their needs in order to form a sense of self from the responses they receive, connection for Fours emanates internally. The following speaker articulates this phenomenon with clarity and insight.

My classroom is always in the form of a circle. I try to connect by engaging energetically with each person in the room so that I can match them. If you don't feel comfortable in the circle, I'm going to do everything to keep you safe, I'm going to try to connect to you energetically.

The key connection is down and in—the key compulsion is up and out, so if I'm up and out I'll start going faster and faster, stop breathing I have to shift and come back down and then I can reconnect because I'm in a centered place again, I'm reconnected with myself. Now I can say, let me experience you out there and see what your energy is like separate from what it is that I want to bring.

Eskimos have many words to describe the different conditions of the natural occurrence we call simply *snow*. Like Eskimos to snow, Fours have a finely tuned conceptual vocabulary to describe the nuances of connection. What follows are statements by Royal Family speakers precisely describing the intricacies of various kinds of connection. They all point to some intuitive knowing when it comes to connection, they speak easily of intuition, and energy—its presence, absence, or shifts. Such intuition is an integral part of the Four E-type intelligence.

Connection is a knowing that when you're with someone you know how they feel. They don't have to tell you, if they do choose to tell you, you'll understand. It doesn't matter what the background is, I'm intuitively connected on a feeling level. It creates problems when I have strong feelings, for then I'll feel connected with someone else and I'll project those feelings onto that person and go ahead with gusto even though I may be totally off base. So a lot of work on myself has been in clarifying my feelings and literally separating myself from other people, so that I can see and value others and hold onto myself and know where I'm coming from.

This is how a Four teacher describes connection in the body.

When I have a strong feeling, and I'm sure everybody has some feelings, I either get warm, or kind of giddy in my head, or feel fluttering in my stomach, or any of those signals that I have when I know that's a strong feeling. I can have that because someone else is feeling some way or because I am, or both. I've learned that when I have a physical reaction to check, literally, ask myself what just happened in my life, is this me, or them?

*Personal Connection.* When I'm teaching a class I can be working with students and get a real strong feeling from one of them. I'm a good teacher and can be pretty flexible, I can shift a class's momentum and move in a different direction if I think a student feels a certain way and can benefit by that. But if I do that all of the time, I risk losing the rest of the students. So if I feel a student is having a big shift and needs something, rather than respond to it then, I'll check in with him later and find out. If I'm wrong, of course it's a good thing I didn't change everything. But if I'm right, I have made the personal connection that I want and I haven't lost everybody else.

*Special Connection.* I'm a school psychologist and I usually deal with kids in a one-to-one situation, either testing or counseling, usually around issues of behavioral management. Inherent in this one-to-one is a special connection, unlike those teachers with a full class of students, I automatically have a connection. I rarely move forward in this connection until I've found a point of energy between us. In our interview I'll find something, a point that gives us both a rush, then I can go on to the cut-and-dried work, but until that point I'm kind of stagnant, searching for this rush that creates a bond between us.

*Meaningful Connection.* I work with adolescents in a counseling setting and I think the words "meaningful connection" intuitively resonate with truth for me. It's important to be able to communicate with adolescents in a way that helps them to understand the truth about themselves. When I feel valued in helping them is when I have some hints that form into a coherent pattern, when I start seeing congruence and can help them support their feelings about themselves. Recently a seventh-grade boy in this process was telling me he's probably the best basketball player in the school. He was elected captain, a position usually filled by ninth graders, yet he chose to drop that because he didn't think he understood how the intricacies of leadership worked from his point of view. After listening to all his summing up I was able to say, "Many kids your age aren't thinking about those things, you seem to think about that a lot, you're probably different from your friends." He said he thought that might be so. It was a sort of "aha" connection for both of us.

*Heart Connection.* I teach math and jazz: the meaningful connection comes when the students see the depth and the beauty of either field. I see math as an art form, there's an incredible amount of beauty that I find in mathematics. In jazz when some of the weaker students play something and they'll catch on from their heart, it might not be very elegant, but if it's right from the heart—that's a moment of real connection.

*Spiritual Connection.* If you're trying to establish a spiritual connection among faculty and students in a school that has a little take on it, for me it's built on respect, mutual respect, and tolerance and there's a lot out there around teaching tolerance and a lot of curricula that you can use. In relationships between student and faculty, if a teacher respects a student and looks him in the eye and gives him time and care, I think that has a ripple effect. I think that's how I feel about God, Buddha, or the sense of eternal spirit, it's about respect.

and

I have spoken about my desire to make connection with people.

Spirituality to me means attempting to make the same kind of connection with God and that's something I'm working on.

*Universal Connection—Bliss.* Sometimes it all comes together, quite often actually, and it's blissful. You see the students actually get it, no longer are they doing what you told them to do, but they actually understand it for themselves, they're creating without you, they're expressing themselves and communicating. What an honor and a privilege it is to help facilitate them getting from point A to point D or G or H, in some cases. They get excited and want to pursue that on their own and it's a real treat to have been of service in that capacity. I take a great deal of pride and I feel emotional about it too.

### *Boundaries*

With such an imperative drive toward connection, it is not surprising that many Fours have issues around personal boundaries, their own and others.

Sometimes some of the students feel a little more familiar, they don't know where the line is, because I haven't drawn it that clearly, or where the line changes. So that's something that I'm just starting to learn about, how to set boundaries. The thing I learned about boundaries is that they are something that I can violate in other people. I've started to realize that I need to learn all about setting boundaries. I care enough about the students to go after them in ways that might be uncomfortable for them. If I think that they want to learn I'm not shy about going after them. This might mean telling them things that they might feel uncomfortable with or hurt by. So, that's my style: because I care about my students I try to come after them and try to help them.

Other E-type educators need to allow Four students to set the agenda, to define the parameters and boundaries within which they want to accomplish an assignment.

Four students are the ones who always want to do the assignment a little bit differently. They're the ones who come to you and say, "Can I do it like this" or "I've been thinking, I don't want to do it the way everybody else is doing it, I think I can do it this way." Now that's certainly permissible if it falls within the constraints of the assignment. I remember that before I knew the Enneagram, a student put the above request to me and I answered, "No, no you can't, you have to do it the way I've told you to do it, because this is the way that you have to learn to do it if you are in my class, you have to do it this way." I've even had a senior boy, in retrospect I think he was a Four, in tears because he'd done outstandingly well over four years writing essays the prescribed way, had even been to a summer writing program, and he pleaded with me, "I've done that, can I do it this way?" "No." So there's

room for allowing learning to take place in the natural instinctive way
of each of the types. Certainly in the later years that I've taught, I'm
aware of allowing the Fours to do that special something. This is part
of the Four gift, an unique creativity.

### Something Missing

As has been stated repeatedly, the focus of attention for Fours goes to what
is missing. The following speaker gives a clear report of how this perceptual
lens underscores many of the other "classic" Four preoccupations.

There's no defense against feeling worthless, unauthentic, vulnerable, and I get depressed, I don't defend myself—I get depressed if that
sense of connection isn't there. Virginia Woolf is always writing about
missing—how men and women just miss connections. One of the joys
of learning about the Enneagram is to learn where people's attention
goes, because you can realize that people are trying to connect with you
by the way attention comes to them, how it comes to them. When you
realize that your attention is always going to what's missing in you,
and what's wrong with you, and you've actually developed this faulty
belief system that you are worthless, that you are less, that deep relationships aren't possible—then you basically have to start learning and
teaching yourself that that's not true. You learn that in fact we are all
interconnected, just in different ways.

More specifically in the classroom the focus on what's missing plays out
for this Four educator as not being able to receive approval when it comes his
way. There is a dance around wanting to be heeded, respected, and appreciated,
and an inability to assimilate that approval.

It is also nice to have the students appreciate your efforts. I don't
seem to be good about that one. I'm not sure what it is, but I think the
students take advantage of me. I don't think it's a malicious taking advantage of me. There's some quality or aspect in the way I do business
that attracts that sort of thing. It's a feeling of being taken for granted;
certainly some students are appreciative, but they're also a large number
of student who just assume, "Yeah, you're supposed to bring my equipment and set it up for me." So, I'm just starting to learn about what
role I play in this. The truth is also, when I do get appreciated, which I
do often, I'm a little uncomfortable in that role, so it's a funny place to
be in that I have this yearning for recognition and acknowledgment because I give so much of myself, and oftentimes what I get back is neglect; if not, sometimes outright abuse.

### Feelings

The Royal Family belong to the Attacher triad where the E-type strategy and intelligence include a matrix of characteristics that have to do with feelings. Even when Fours find themselves in environments where feelings are not part of the general institutional climate, they will find an outlet. Many Four educators, particularly in higher education, may know how this feels—to be a feeling type in a predominantly mental environment.

I am a feeling person who's attempting to function in a thinking environment and that makes it very difficult, sometimes it puts a lot of stress in my life. I have this secret side that is known in fact to very few of my colleagues and that's my touching feeling side. It's been a part of me since day one but I managed somehow to suppress it for nearly thirty years. But when I got to the university where I teach now it suddenly burst forth and I began working at the crisis call center, the university counseling center, taking courses in counseling, attending every Gestalt and sensitivity group I could find across the country. I became trained in leading Gestalt sensitivity training and sexual attitudes reassessment workshops. Ultimately I got a degree in counseling and became a licensed psychological examiner for the state.

### Emotional Reactivity

Fours perceive that they experience life more deeply than many other people; it is one of the ways in which they feel special. Certainly there is an element of emotionality and feeling close to the surface. When Fours form part of an interactive dynamic it is difficult for the Royal Family to be distanced and objective about the behavior of others in the group; they "take it personally."

They're not bad kids. They're just not used to focusing, and it's difficult for them not to noodle on the drums or play the piano when I'm trying to give the instruction. If I get this kid under control, then that kid turns around. I take it very personally. I'm not happy about that, but it's because I give so much of myself, I don't have a reservoir of patience. In fact, I think, given more ordinary circumstances, people think I'm incredibly patient, but in a situation where I've given so much of myself and I'm absorbing such stress from the environment and the structure in which I'm teaching, that my patience doesn't last long—I take it personally. If, for instance, the bass player doesn't show up for a concert, the whole team suffers, and because I care so much about the activity of the students and want the experience to be so positive, it's difficult to let go. I tend to hang on to, "Oh geez, so the bass player didn't show up, now what are we going to do?" I've already lugged equipment around for about thirty minutes. I'm feeling put upon. So I take it personally.

### Unique, Creative Gifts

Fours have a sense that they are somehow special, different, and, indeed, many of the Royal Family are uniquely gifted in the realm of creativity. It is difficult to define creativity precisely because it has so much to do with the intuition and intuitive energies. Many Fours seem to know this as a truth about themselves.

The gift I feel I bring to the classroom is the gift of myself in that I'm a little bit different than many teachers. I'm extremely interested in spirituality and believe that we have access to intuitive powers —energies that we don't have any understanding about, or most of us don't have any understanding about—and so I try to bring those into teaching without trying to make converts of the students.

This Four teacher describes on-the-job, spontaneous creativity. She trusts her intuition to tell her if something will or won't work.

There's creativity and change and it's fun to have variety, oftentimes I go into class and improvise. In other words, I've got a lot of tricks in my bag, so I'll say, "I feel like doing this, starting off with this." I'm skilled with that, I know a lot of different ways to connect to kids to help them to do drills. Sometimes it feels like I missed something, "Maybe I should have done it this way," or "I missed that." You can't do everything all the time differently. I often get frustrated in that I didn't get around to that one, but it is creative. I have to trust my intuition a lot. I think on my feet and I let their responses often dictate how the class will go. We'll start with an activity and if it goes well then we'll do that activity daily, if it doesn't go well, we might be able to back up and address what the issues were that we didn't do well.

### Envy

Envy is an intense desire for what is missing, or what someone else is, or has, that which is special. It is part of the unbalanced "high-low" swing of the Four. The growth path for Fours is from envy to equanimity. Having equanimity is being able to operate in the ordinary with a sense of inner balance. Fours report eloquently on how the passion of envy is ever-present and the forms it can take.

In every second of every delicious artistically designed moment in my syllabus, in every millisecond, I can imagine myself doing this better, differently, I can see other teachers doing it, hear another teacher in another classroom and there's a dynamic going on, "Oh God, we should be doing that." My attention is constantly going to what I could be doing, or what I wish I was doing, or I wish I had on the outfit that one of my students is wearing. It's almost as if you want to be somebody else. What happens then is you lose yourself and that reinforces the fact that you're lost and you have to struggle to gain yourself back again, it gets into the central issue of loss. You keep recreating it by wishing you were someone else; it's constant.

This Four teacher, aware of her own experience with envy, can help others to work through it.

> When I was a lot younger I was interested in art and I went through a number of years when I could not go through the Art Institute because I was too envious. I understand this with students: when they want to do something, they won't try because they just can't bear experiencing the loss of not achieving, it would be too great. I think it's a form of envy and I try to help kids with this distortion.

This Four educator describes envy as almost a One-like sense of the unattainability of perfection.

> Envy comes up when I think perfection is attainable. There are so many fantastic trips that I can go on during the day, what they have in common is that they're all terribly perfect. Life doesn't map that perfectly, doesn't measure up to fantasy, or how it is in its perfect realm.

While this Four teacher describes the envy he feels at his perception that everyone else's life is better than his own.

> I feel I give of myself so much in the classroom and outside of the classroom, sometimes I get envious of what seems like the more peaceful existences of other colleagues of mine. It's a feeling of, "How come I can't have that?" or "I'm a good person; why can't I just teach a normal load?" as opposed to being so driven and stressed out by teaching so many classes and managing such a huge program.

This Royal Family educator envies his own students, for having the teacher (himself) he wishes he could have had.

> If I could have had one wish as a student, it would be teachers who said, "I can be a resource for you so you can create whatever it is that you have to create. It's your vision and you're the expert not me." That's what I try to bring to the classroom, that each of these students, however they're going to do it, whatever they're going to do, is going to be the expert and not me. I was wishing for that, I got a little of it and I remember those teachers with a great appreciation.

### Competition

Competition for the Royal Family is tied in with being special, with envy of others, with proving they're good enough.

> Competition is big in my life. When I was going through school, where there was a clear structure, I was going to be the most special no matter what. If that meant I had to do it your way, I would do it your way because I was going to be the most special. I got lost in that. It didn't look like I did, on paper I was everything a dream student would ever be and I got lost. I don't think the teachers particularly knew it, I

sure didn't know it, but looking back that seems to be so.

### *Vulnerability*

For all the E-types vulnerability comes from being open and frank, from allowing other people to view us in the sense of our "true selves." For Fours vulnerability can mean being open about the need to connect with others and letting down the guard around one's longing for that.

Connection is extremely important in my life and I think the importance shows through to the point that it puts me at a disadvantage sometimes, it makes me vulnerable. I have a need for connecting that many people at work don't have and so I show that vulnerability. In the classroom the way I try to achieve this with individuals is to drop little hints, "I feel happy when such and such a thing happens" or "I feel sad." I hope they will pick up with that on the emotional level. But if I say that and they go off and start talking about a fishing trip, I'll know that the connectivity isn't there.

### *Authenticity*

Authenticity is a fertile idea that for the Royal Family often brings together many of the elements of this E-type intelligence, problems of what's missing, or unworthiness, or of the whole play between real feelings and pseudo- or trumped up, dramatized feelings. Experiencing authenticity and being able to tell us about it is another of the gifts of the Four. Authenticity is present in a number of layers of experience. For this Four it is the bedrock of her being.

Authenticity is clarity, it's totally lined up, there's no question about it—it's a feeling about somebody else, a feeling about an issue, or how do I act in a situation, or something as simple as I don't know where I'm going, but I know I have a sense to turn left. I turn left and the place is there.

This Four educator describes how authenticity is present when she does not avoid discomforting conversations—therein lies the kernel of what makes connection real.

In the multidisciplinary staffing situations in which I participate, parents are there, staff, the classroom teacher. If the real problem the child is having isn't being discussed, and often it has to do with something emotional, I will bring it up. It's the missing piece, what makes it authentic. Sometimes it makes people uncomfortable, but I have to do it, it wouldn't be real if I didn't do it.

Here a Royal Family educator describes what authenticity feels like in his body.

In music I feel I have a real fine sense of whether or not what's

coming from my students is genuine just by the way it feels in my
body. I play a lot of recordings for them of great musicians so they can
sense what it feels like when people are speaking from the heart.
Through singing, too. It's difficult, it's a foreign language, and they're
at the beginning stages of speaking this foreign language, and they
don't have a lot of skills. I ask them to imagine if it were Spanish and
they knew about ten words well, they could sound authentic in those
words. So I try to work in a context that has narrow confines, but get
them to try and feel it in their bodies, and try to learn that language.

### Authenticity and Image

Many Fours are aware that they present themselves as an image of what
someone else expects them to be, mainly as a cover-up for their own sense of
deficiency, rather than the authentic inner self they would like to present. Fours
experience this pull between authenticity and the creation of a pseudoimage as an
inner struggle. This Four articulates the struggle.

I think there are two levels of image and authenticity: something
that feels like pseudoimage and pseudoauthenticity and a deeper level
that has to do with what I might call image and authenticity. Pseudoimage and pseudoauthenticity have to do with someone else having a
standard for me and I'm going to try to create an image to match what
they have. I'm going to create a pseudoauthenticity my way. The next
layer down is the authentic one where I believe that I'm defective. What
I want is for you not to believe this truth that I believe about myself.
What you see is not going to be what you get, because I'm going to try
to make you feel that I'm special in order to avoid my own sense of de-
fectiveness. The real, the deepest layer of all is that in my mind, heart,
body I experience myself as being defective, I accept my worst nightmare about myself. Now I'm being truly authentic and I can contain it
for myself.

There is pain for Fours in not being perceived as authentic.

Image is also related to the question of "How did I do?" feeling afterward I screwed up, or I did not do that well. I have a lot of pain when
I hear the image other people have of me if it's not what I think I am.
It's painful because I spend a lot time on my physical image and the
sense of how I'm perceived by others. It's very important to me.

At times Fours experience a sense of bliss, when everything comes together
in a moment of authentic truth.

A feeling in my body is authentic, the *me* that's experiencing it is
authentic. I don't have to do anything with it, I can just allow it. Now I
don't have to create anything, I can just say this is what's so for me. At
this point, image, the projection of the image, the authenticity come

together. They come together in a still point and that's the deepest layer, that's the true authenticity.

### Image—Not Being Good Enough

The feeling of low self-esteem for the Royal Family, as with so much else in this E-type strategy, is tied in with the attentional focus on what's missing. If it is the truth (and the Four believes it) that something is always missing, how can the Four ever be good enough?

That's the story of my life I guess, not being good enough. The way it plays out for me is anything I do or accomplish I totally minimize, I don't value the string of accomplishments behind me, I still have a low sense of self. For instance, a strength of mine is relating to others. Recently my principal wanted me to take another position in the school. I said I hadn't completed my goals in this job. I *had* made the office a better place to work in, but that wasn't part of my job description, everybody was doing better because I had communication going which wasn't there before I came. That was one of the first times I started to realize that I was of value, I could see that my being there made a difference. It was enlightening for me.

### Getting Into the Emotional Depths

Where many of the other E-types (particularly the upbeat Seven, task-driven Three, and larger-than-life Eight) tend to shy away from the darker, more painful aspects of life, Fours are comfortable with the range of experience of the human condition, the full palette of life's emotional offerings; these include melancholy, sadness, and depression.

*Melancholy.* Being melancholic is often the preferred state for Fours, melancholy has a fullness, a bittersweet sense that is in keeping with the Royal Family's understanding that the glass is always half-empty. It speaks of sadness and loss and an eternal yearning akin to the affect of the heroine of Alfred, Lord Tennyson's Romantic ballad *The Lady of Shalott*. Fours often don't want what they have, don't think they can have what they want, which leaves them in a perpetual state of yearning that reinforces the melancholy aspect of their E-type.

I feel a lot of sadness, I'm dealing with a lot of sadness, but it feels safe to be in it. It's safe to be sad. Melancholy is fullness, it's not bad. It's fullness, it's depth, it's beauty; it's not depression, or dark, or sad, at least to me.

For this Four educator melancholy is a feeling of being intensely alive.

Melancholy is a state of being that's intensely alive. So is joy. Anything that is alive I like—the whole range. When I'm vulnerable I might feel anything, the whole range of life. When it gets too much, I leave it, go into my head, I become analytical and withdraw. My intention is staying with whatever is true in every moment. Right now I'm not feeling particularly melancholic, but I'm feeling alive, it feels just as good as feeling melancholy. If I can find any way of connecting with myself and connecting with you and staying present, I'm in my ecstasy.

This member of the Royal Family describes how bittersweet memories are often richer than the experience itself. Caught up in their reveries of the past, Fours can amplify their feelings around long-gone events, and give to them especial significance.

When I look back on my life I think some of my happiest moments were when I was sad because I was dumped by a girl. Ah to replay that: Oh how wonderful it was, and why did she dump me, and why couldn't it be, and so forth. But I think there's also another side to that, a tendency for me to overplay the good times. When my children were young we had marvelous times as a family on vacation and I'll look back on that with, on the one hand, great joy, but on the other hand, this sadness and revel in the sadness: Oh, those days are over. And, pardon me, why didn't I spend more time with the children? I didn't do a good enough job of being a father. There's a tendency even to look back nostalgically on the very best of times with a sense of sadness and to be comfortable in that sadness. The remembrance and the reveling in it can sometimes be fuller than the experience itself. I think, however, it may be partially a function of age, I think I was too young and stupid then to know what I had. But maybe I will say the same thing in another ten years.

*Sadness.* Fours report that they have a radar for sadness. They can walk into a room and sense that someone is sad. Until the Royal Family become aware of this transference they think it is themselves who are sad. Fours need to learn to get a reality check when intense feelings such as sadness arise. They need to question themselves, Where is this feeling coming from? To ask, "Am I really sad?"

I took a day trip with a friend to a charming New England oceanside town. In the middle of the afternoon as we were walking passed restored, historic homes I'm aware I'm not "with" my friend anymore. I'm thinking about my Midwest hometown, the buildings that weren't restored there, the irrecoverable past, and that this day is also transient. I'm feeling sad. Meanwhile my friend who has been uncharacteristically quiet, tells me that today is the birthday of her mother who died several years before. She apologizes for being quiet and says she's been feeling a little sick all day. Did my sadness begin with her sadness?

*Depression.* Whereas any of the E-types can experience clinical depression, including Fours, the Royal Family reports that depression is a black hole that you can't get out of. Because Fours operate at the extremes of high-low polarity in moods and emotions, they are prone to hyperactivity on one end of the scale and depression on the other. Depression is experienced as a disconnect with the outside, ordinary world, exacerbating an acute sense of loss and sadness. In a way as the depression, takes a deeper and deeper hold on the Four it reinforces their sense that no one understands their inner world anyway, or can help them. Many Fours never move into the real darkness of depression for when they recognize the signs of the downward slide they have become adept at structuring steps to lead themselves out. The Royal Family knows from experience of the darkness how to empathize with others in their pain.

> I don't enjoy being depressed, but I do enjoy wallowing in the darkness of any emotion. The fullness, it's like the ecstatic, it's all part of what is and especially sometimes it's almost as if I need to do it because everybody else has this false impression that it's not good to go there. It is a fullness: a wide range, but depression is not part of this. Depression is a deep, dark, black hole that you can't get out of, or you feel that way. So I wouldn't say I enjoy depression, but I'm perfectly fine with sadness, with somebody else's sadness or pain, I can be there with them.

This Four acknowledges that great personal growth can occur through experiencing depression.

> I've seen some of my greatest growth through extraordinary periods of pain or depression, wrestling and staying in the quicksand for a while, I see pain as full of possibilities. What's changed as I've gotten a little older is that I can look with optimism at seeing someone in extraordinary pain, whether with child or sexual abuse, they don't want to talk about it, own it, I let them lead me through their pain by staying very grounded so they don't feel either guilt or negativity about themselves, or some sense of unworthiness.

This Royal Family educator uses her firsthand experience of depression to share with others that they can overcome their pain. For this reason, Fours can often make excellent teachers and counselors of emotionally disturbed children and adults.

> In my past I've been much more a victim of extreme emotions and I could certainly write a book about depression. When I'm immersed in this feeling I'm analyzing my way out of it. If you've been depressed and found a way out you know at least something about how you got out. It's because I've been there that I know it can be done. I know we can come out of those places.

### Avoiding The Ordinary

The avoidances of the E-types are defense mechanisms: for Fours feelings of unworthiness and inadequacy can be defended against, paradoxically but quite logically, by listening to their E-type intelligence, and adopting a stance of feeling "above," better than, or special.

When I was younger I felt like I was the fairy princess who gets to rescue the kids out of the ordinary, boring classroom. I work with small groups of children and it's important for me to make them feel special. I don't want them to be ordinary, so if I notice they're doodling I'll do something to foster their talent for drawing.

This educator describes the exhaustion that comes from giving your all to make each class you teach an extraordinary learning experience.

If I'm teaching a class and I think it's ordinary, I'll muster and drum up something to get the juices flowing. The result is that I can spend a lot of my energy doing that, constantly trying to make these deeper connections, make sure that everybody is having a community experience, that they're going to leave saying, "I not only learned what I wanted to learn, but this teacher discovered who I am and helped me see who I am." I'm ready to fall on the floor with exhaustion and another class comes in and I start it all over again.

This Four teacher describes her realization of her need to avoid ordinariness, and that may not be what is best for her students.

Avoiding being ordinary can be a real Achilles heel, or a ball and chain. The work it can create for you is just enormous because you want the class to be so deep and meaningful. What I'm trying to learn is that I need to set my agenda, or I need to understand what the students' need to learn, what I'm supposed to be teaching, what our timeframe is, and try to keep myself focused on that and not always get pulled away when things feel ordinary. For example, this student, the more I'm hovering over him and coming up close up, the more he's going to say, "Please get this teacher out of my personal space." What feels ordinary to me may in fact be just the right thing for quite a few students. So it's important for me not to try to whip myself out of the ordinary all of the time and try to bring people into something that I think they need because I need it.

This Royal Family educator describes the downside he experiences when he knows his lecture is ordinary.

If I'm in a small classroom and things start getting ordinary I'll usually revert to trying to be personal by connecting with students on a personal level. That usually works. If I'm in a large classroom that's difficult—by large I mean some 140 students—I may attempt that but it's a little hard because even if you connect with a couple, a number of things can happen. At the worst my energy can disappear, just goes down the tube and then everything goes from bad to worse. The next worst thing that can happen is I start getting heartburn and talking louder and running around and being more hyper. The technique that I use most often now is to stop and say, "Hey I prepared a lecture and I thought things would go well, but this ain't going well, let's talk about this and see what we can do" and bring the class into it and do some problem solving. I think the class then rallies around and it may not completely save the day, but it's the best of the options I can come up with.

### Mood and Energy

Fours live on an emotional roller coaster, now high, now low, so their moods shift between these extremes with little experience of staying in the middle, of flat ordinariness. Feelings and moods are experienced intensely. Part of the Royal Family E-type intelligence is the ability to engage in an inner inquiry that allows them to come up with precise descriptions of where their energy is and what they are feeling about it.

My students tend to be quite passive, that's the Japanese way, but if I can get through, if I see I can get through, then a dynamic is established. They feed me and I feed them and it's a mutual process, it's exciting and that's when I know a connection has taken place. It's less on the basis of individual students than with the class as a whole. It usually seems to take place with my own dramatics, or passion for whatever I'm teaching, also my mood.

Four teachers are aware of how their mood and energy can infect a whole class.

I've had to learn that my own ability to throw energy can be strong. Before I go into a classroom I do a check on my feelings and make sure they're in balance, because if I enter taking some baggage from my last experience with me I immediately see the class disintegrate, or they'll directly reflect my feelings. In a classroom any intense feelings that I'm experiencing will press the buttons of every adolescent child in the class. If I clear and settle the emotional feelings, the class will also settle.

Despite trying to be balanced and calm, this Four shares an anecdote that shows she can't hide her moods from her students, and to her surprise finds that this is not a negative experience.

I will give myself lead time, I will try to compose myself, I do everything in the book so when I walk into the classroom I'll be logical, cool and collected, even-keeled. One day I did a task with my students, they were just learning how to describe someone in English and I asked them to work with a partner. I collected their papers, put on the overhead projector, and the other students, not the author, would have to try to identify who their classmates were from the descriptions. We went through these and then I got to one, "I'm thinking of a person who is never late for class and has a rich palette of an emotional life, intensive brightness and is sometimes moodiness on us." I thought this is fascinating, who can this person be. So I said, " OK, guess." About three-quarters of the hands went up. I thought: Wow this is great participation for a Japanese class. "OK, who?" "Sensei, sensei." I asked the author, and he nodded, "You, teacher." I thought: I'd spent all this effort to try to hide who I was and they knew right away. But it wasn't negative for them and that was something I needed to discover.

### Sequential Order

This characteristic is tied into the one above. Fours live a life of emotional extremes—inner states like imagination and memory reflect those extremes. For instance, the most dramatic occurrences are those recounted first in describing an event.

I've just come back from a trip to Sri Lanka, the Maldives, and India and when my colleagues asked, "Well, how was your trip?" "Guess what, I met the Dalai Lama, and I saw three dolphins in the ocean." "So what else happened?" Then I begin to tell the story once they get me into some kind of sequential order. Where I do bring clarity is in writing and while I say I'm a recovering lawyer, the law did give me discipline and bring order to the wilderness of my imagination.

This Royal Family teacher describes her penchant, reported by many Fours, to think in metaphors.

I use metaphors a lot, I think of teaching as an Amish quilting bee where we have a project and we're working, we're connecting and its community. I'm sure that's not the typical speech pathologist's thought about their work.

### Growth Path: From Envy to Equanimity

Growth for Fours occurs when they can experience equanimity. Equanimity can be defined as balance or calmness or tranquility. For the Royal Family it is balance that comes about when the extraordinary and the mundane are present together, and there's a richness in that. A growth path for Fours is to undertake, is a search for completeness and wholeness, for instance, to try to include the extremes of sadness and ecstasy as part of the same daily experience.

I used to define the physical sense as ordinary. Now I think it's profound actually. I'm sure it switches from person to person, but it's anything mundane like chores and getting them done. Once they're done, they become a known entity, even if it was extraordinary, now it's mundane. It's that balance, putting the two together, the every dayness where I keep trying to put myself.

## *Quality of Essence: Universal Belonging*

Essence for the Four is the sense of belonging in a universal way. Universal belonging, a feeling of connection to the universe, is the recognition of ultimate interconnection.

Since childhood there is this sense of some sort of disconnect, of not belonging and a longing to get back to a belonging. Being present in the moment, being essential, is a feeling of having found that place where you belong, of being there.

## What Royal Family Students Say

### *Avoiding the Ordinary*

I hated school until I was an adult, the traditional classroom was deadly for me. I hate sitting and listening to some one drone on. I like to interact with people. I love working in groups and role-playing, and bantering back and forth with teachers.

### *Being Special*

I'm a straight "A" student so I pretty much do what I need to do to get the good grades and maybe this plays into being special because I'm always top of the class and all of that. But I don't think so, I think I learn because I'm pretty curious, so that's good. I'm #1 and that's an achievement. Once I'm here I feel, "Oh well I'm not good enough to be here" and then I get attracted to relationships and all that takes me away from studies. Keeping us on track is a good thing.

### *Connection*

As a student a most important thing is for a teacher to recognize me, to recognize something that I've done. You can't just praise me, it has to be something that I have done well. It's vital if a teacher tells me, or responds to me, recognition gives me complete confidence, so much more energy. Often I feel that I'm not quite good enough, if the teacher says, "Wow this is a great job" or "I liked how you did this"—that loosens it up for me so that the creative juices can flow. If I have a teacher who is all lecture and doesn't particularly connect with me, I might not be apt to do well.

### *Emotions*

My emotions do affect my work. When I'm in a good mood, when I'm feeling positive about myself and about the materials then I do a lot better and focus more. When I'm in a bad mood I can turn off to what we're doing and I need to put myself in a better state of mind before I can do my homework. When something is bothering me I need to sort it out even just by myself.

### Something Missing

I like classes that are focused around discussion, but sometimes that can also get annoying. I like to talk a lot in class, but if no one's disagreeing, or the discussion isn't going anywhere, it doesn't feel as if we're accomplishing much. I like it a lot when the teacher notices this and tries to steer the discussion in a way where we will accomplish what's supposed to get done.

### Authenticity and Image

It is important to me how people view me: I don't like people to see me wrong. I don't like to be viewed as something I'm not. So I try and make it clear to people who I am. I like to get to know people who are from all different areas in the school, socially and stuff, because I hate stereotypes and I hate being viewed as something that's wrong.

and

Success is feeling comfortable with who you are and being happy about your accomplishments regardless of what other people think, or how successful you are in terms of money or grades. I don't care about grades, they're not important to me, except I do care about getting into college because I want to go to a place where I'm going to be happy eventually.

### Competition

I guess I don't like having friends in class, it's an obstacle for me, and that's because I find myself getting competitive and I don't like that at all. Before you know it you start comparing grades and then that gets important and I don't like to think of myself as a letter to somebody.

### Brief Interview with a Royal Family Educator

*Q. What is your teaching style?*
A: My teaching style is informal, it's personalized, it's also intense at the same time as being informal. It's both at the same time.

*Q. What do you look for in your students?*
A: What I look for in my students is interest and dedication. I want them to

make an effort. I don't expect them to be talented. I do expect them to show up on time and be present.

*Q. What is important in the way you present material?*
A: The important thing to me in the way I present material is that I reach the student directly, that I make sure the student is able to receive and process information and take away from it.

*Q. What will students say of you?*
A: Students will say lots of things about me; they'll say I'm a good guy; they'll say I'm a grouch; they'll say I'm a gifted teacher; they'll say I'm a taskmaster. They'll say I'm a competent professional musician.

*Q. Why do you teach?*
A: I teach because I love to.

*Q. How do you communicate?*
A: My communication style is pretty direct; I don't like to beat around the bush, and I like to have a good time. I want my students to feel they have a good time, but I don't want them to feel like they can be casual or neglectful.

*Q. What is your attitude to preparing teaching plans?*
A: Preparing teaching plans is fun. It's not hard and it's pleasant.

*Q. What do you like about the classroom?*
A: What I like about the classroom is the feeling of community, being able to direct the group from direction A to direction B.

*Q. What don't you like about the classroom?*
A: What I don't like about the classroom is the difficulty in having the students focused and present.

### Practical Tips

*For the Royal Family to Work with Themselves*

- Check if you are centered before you enter a classroom, or a meeting.
- Find ways to notice when your emotions and feelings are inflated.
- Be aware when you are romanticizing another person, or your own feelings.
- Anticipate mood swings, structure ways to check and balance your energy.
- Avoid depression. When feelings of sadness and loss become overwhelming, get a reality check, or ask friends to help pull you back.
- Don't lose yourself in the need to be special, that's when you most

need to be centered.
- Encourage yourself to undertake mundane tasks.
- Focus on facts as well as feelings.
- Remember the rest of the world runs on an orderly schedule set by the clock and the daily calender.

*For Others Who Work with the Royal Family*

- Establish connection.
- Reinforce worthy achievement.
- Help even out mood swings by structuring situations in terms of facts and logic and not emotions.
- Encourage creativity.
- Avoid harsh criticism; remember Fours feel unworthy and deficient to begin with.
- Encourage Fours to hear feedback by praising something that's worthy, as well as pointing to what's lacking.
- When the Fours' attention goes to what's missing, count the positives for them.
- Fours can procrastinate when they view tasks as mundane; help structure a creative solution.
- Help Fours see the value in what they've already achieved as a way to intervene when competitive envy arises.

## ENNEATYPE FIVE: THE OBSERVER

- TRIAD: *DETACHER*
- ATTENTIONAL FOCUS: Gaining knowledge
- GIFT: Rationality. Big picture thinking
- AVOIDANCE: Connection
- GROWTH PATH: From hoarding (guarding) to allowing
- ESSENCE: Omniscient Awareness
- SHIFT TO SECURE POINT: *THE BOSS EIGHT* (Defender—against arrow)
- SHIFT TO STRESS POINT: *THE OPTIMIST SEVEN* (Detacher—with arrow)
- WINGS: *THE QUESTIONER SIX* (Detacher)
  *THE ROYAL FAMILY FOUR* (Attacher)

## EXAMPLES OF OBSERVER FIVE EDUCATORS: GUARDIANS OF THE SELF

### The Conservationist — Only Connect

E. M. Forster, the famous English novelist, in his work *Howard's End* uses as a frontispiece the epigraph "Only connect..," then toward the conclusion of the book he writes of Mr. Henry Wilcox, a protagonist, "He had refused to connect." This is a comment on connection on many levels. As Wilcox's world falls apart around him, he realizes that his emotions and passions are forever trapped in his mind. Those he loves perceive him so differently from how he knows himself to be.

John E. is an English teacher haunted by Wilcox's dilemma, for the problematic thread of connection runs through his own life. For instance, students' evaluations pointedly refer to his unresponsiveness and lack of interaction in the classroom. Yet he feels quite passionate about his purpose in the classroom — opening young minds to see the world in new ways. The problem is that for many years (until he saw how it was backfiring) *he tried* to be unresponsive; so as to maintain objectivity around judging ideas, he did not want to imply by his enthusiasm that one student's idea was better than another's, so he cultivated a stone-faced persona for the classroom.

John places great value on the practice of nonattachment; he tries not to let emotion sway his judgment. So when adolescent girls come to him in tears about a grade it is hard for him not to become impatient, and he bites back sarcastic comments. Why, he asks himself, can't they see this is one grade out of several score for the year, and hundreds in their lives as students? How can a grade be worth tears? John does not trust that spoken communication is as pure as the written form, therefore he shows his approval or disapproval of students' work, not by a pat on the shoulder and remarks such as "well done," but in unambiguous checks on a page and neat notes at the end of papers. Often his classes are dreary, for John speaks in a slow monotone and relishes long silences when students cannot come up with glib responses and have to think through an answer. John says he connects with other people in order to find answers together.

Sometimes when he is energized by ideas, or the discussion, he can become animated, and his comments are bitingly funny as he pushes students to think through what they are saying. Many students try to hide from his sarcasm, but John maintains that his comments pertain to the limitations of a person's idea, not to the person themself. Why can't others understand that distinction, he asks himself. Often John feels he is a fish out of water in a dynamic such as education, where interaction and personal connection are so necessary. Perhaps I should have stayed with pure research, he muses, or followed my first inclination to become a brain surgeon. When you are operating on a brain, all interactions are essentially impersonal. But I was waylaid by literature, the power, passion, and possibility of literary creativity.

John does have a passionate side, his passion is for his hobbies—hiking, fly-fishing, and helping to conserve the planet's natural resources. He belongs to several nonprofit nature conservation organizations and has held high-level office. He is an effective advocate and his papers and policy statements reach a wide audience.

In many ways John feels most alive when he is hiking alone in one of the huge nature reserves in the West. At night sitting by his frugal campfire under the golden-fretted firmament of the heavens, he rests easy in the knowledge that it is his mind that is making sense of the infinitude around him. Simultaneously he feels infinitely insignificant and completely connected to the universe.

### Keeping Cool Under Fire

Sister Rosemary C. is the principal of an established, 100-year-old, K-12 parochial girls' school in the suburbs of a large Mid-Western city. She heads a faculty of 120 teachers, all women, ranging in age from new teachers in their twenties to many in their mid-sixties nearing retirement. Almost half the faculty have graduate degrees in their field, only 5 percent are in orders. Sister Rosemary is, of course, a nun. Nearing retirement age herself, she spent only a few years in the classroom early in her career before she was singled out for administrative work both in schools in the diocese and in the diocese itself. Her ability to assimilate and present detailed reports, on the one hand, while being able to carry a big-picture vision made up of those details, on the other, have been hallmarks of a leadership style that make her a notable asset to her order.

She is small in physical stature, retiring by inclination, yet her presence looms large. A historian by training; research and the ability to conduct research is of paramount importance to her "I trust the facts," she says. She adds that all her life she has been trying to find the one great mystical truth that will unlock the metaphysical puzzle. She has been an avid seeker of that truth since she was an adolescent growing up in an inner-city ghetto. A devoted religious practitioner, she embodies spiritual humility, a quality that makes her a beloved leader. Her eyes shine with love and compassion.

Sister Rosemary knows the names of all the girls in the school. She always has. She takes pleasure at recess to walk through the halls, hear the laughter and sense the energy of the older girls, while in the grade school playground the younger students flock around her as she strokes a curly head or straightens a gym tunic, talking eagerly with the children. Every term she blocks out time to teach classes in the grade school; she says the innocence and spontaneity of the little ones recharges her energy and enthusiasm.

Sister Rosemary has had to work hard at developing the people skills that enable her to handle (to her mind) the concerns of an often overly anxious parent body, but she is well aware of the sacrifices many parents make to provide a private-school education for their daughters, as well as the pressures on everyone in the college admissions process. Her faculty are independent-minded women who jealously guard their classroom autonomy. Sister Rosemary is mindful of the drain on her energy required to practice tact and diplomacy to manage both these groups. Often in the course of an emotionally charged or tedious meeting, she is aware of how she detaches from the situation and observes herself going through the interactions. If she could she would love to communicate solely through written notes, e-mail, and voice mail. She protects her time and privacy by using these means whenever possible. Sister Rosemary believes that minimal personal contact translates into rational thinking unencumbered by emotional overlays. She thinks that among the greatest compliments her faculty pay her in the periodic reviews she undergoes is that she is a rational thinker who is cool under fire.

Sister Rosemary was among the first school leaders in the country to see the potential of computer usage for interschool communication and implemented, among other uses, an all-school computer bulletin board, and a closed e-mail system for the faculty. She sought to enable all her students to become computer literate as quickly as she could. She did away with weekly faculty meetings; instead, every Monday morning she posts on the computer network a newsletter for faculty and staff. Through a gift from a giant computer company in her area, this year all the students in the upper four grades own laptop computers and, in a controlled study, are doing as much school work as is feasible on computers. Sister Rosemary likes the feeling of being on the cutting edge of technology, "You have to keep an open mind to make sense of this chaotic world," she says.

## THE OBSERVER STRATEGY

| *Strengths* | *Weaknesses* |
|---|---|
| Rationality | Private |
| Calmness and balance | Detached from emotions |
| Objectivity | Secretive |
| Big picture thinkers | Guard time and energy |

| Creative synthesizers of ideas | Control emotions |
| Nonjudgmental | Compartmentalizing |
| Taciturn | Non-communicative |
| Predictable | Lack spontaneity |
| Independent | Overvalue the self |

## THE E-TYPE FIVE PROPOSITION

### General Description

### *Rationality and Distance; Hoarding and Allowing*

If, as we have seen, Point Four is the most inner-directed of the emotional triad, the Point Five Observer is similarly the most inner-directed of the mental, fear-based triad. It is interesting to note where these points are placed on the diagram (see Figure 1.1). They form the two legs at the bottom of the circle with the gulf between them (they fall into different triads) bridged only by the fact that they are wings of one another. So a Point Four with a Five wing has the characteristic patterns of a deeply emotional *interior* life highlighted by reclusivity and privacy, while the Point Five with a Four wing, characteristically detached, reclusive and private, finds emotions much closer to the surface, more easily resonant in relationships than a Five with a Point Six wing.

This is the most internalized, retracted point on the Enneagram; defense mechanisms are built around avoiding connection. Observers are like citadels surrounded by moats of rationality. For one to enter they have to raise the drawbridge to let you in. There is a fear of a loss of self, of a draining away of one's essential energies by the demands of the intrusive, outside world. The great fear is invasion that cannot be contained—like a blotting stain seeping over and obliterating the Five's life. The literature describes Fives as hoarders, not necessarily in a materialistic sense, although they can be great collectors of physical goods and materials, but hoarders of their time, energy, and privacy. I prefer to use the word *guardians*. Observers are guardians of the self. To Fives, the world seems to demand something essential from them. The fear is that if you give in to the demands you're going to give your*self* away. Fives overvalue the self, and because they are afraid of emotions, they control them. They also guard their privacy, time, and energy, in order to conserve them*selves*. One conservation strategy is gaining knowledge; it is also the way Fives pay attention. The focus of attention goes to gaining knowledge to avoid an inner sense of emptiness. The need to fill this internal space is achieved by creating a rich inner world. Fives report that they experience life three times—the preview (anticipation) of the upcoming event, the event itself (where often they are detached from what is happening around them), and the review (reliving the event, the richest experience).

Unlike Point Sixes who ask questions as a way of scanning—like circulating radar antennae—to find zones of safety, Point Fives ask questions to gain knowledge. Safety is achieved through formulating a sane, rational grid to lay over an insane world. That this grid exists is the Five illusion and primary blind spot. Observers compartmentalize the different parts of their lives. They don't easily cross boundaries between them. This is an element of the habitual pattern of hoarding and privacy.

Basic to the intrinsic mechanism is an ability to detach, to move back, especially if something is frightening or makes an emotional demand. Fives like the idea of themselves as an objective observer, detached from an emotional bias that may obfuscate judgment. Observer teachers would prefer that the students talk to one another rather than address them, so they can watch the interaction. Fives bring a gift of nonjudgment, each idea from each student is equally valid.

A stereotype of Fives is that they detach from feelings (akin to Point Threes suspending emotions), yet neither E-type is unemotional, both have the capacity for experiencing huge emotions. For the Five these are contained in their rich interior world filled with feelings, ideas, nonlinear thinking, and creative new solutions for solving problems.

From the point of view of this E-type intelligence, the safest place to be in is the head. The E-type avoidance is connection; whatever the connection is in terms of people, situations, emotions. As long as Observers feel they can detach safely into their heads, they *can* operate on two levels, and many Fives function well in relationships, both personal and professional. Minimalists by inclination, Observers are shaped by an intelligence that directs them to put out the least; for then that is all people will expect of them. Nonverbal language translates into expressions of affection, a positive means of communication for the Five.

If a line is drawn on the ground between the Observer and another person and physically they are each standing two feet from the line, the Observer in her mind is twenty paces further back. In order to connect, Fives need to be aware they must take twenty-two steps forward to other peoples' two. Fives also need to work on accessing the energetic power source available to them at Point Eight (security.)

However Fives do connect to ideas like proverbial ducks to water. The mind is clear, rational, powerful, uncluttered by emotions and emotional demands. Here, the drive for hoarding can be satisfied fully by gaining and storing knowledge. Knowledge is power, because the more knowledge you have, the more you can use that knowledge to piece together the puzzles of life, make sense of the world, and hence make it safer. Five teachers will list what they teach in an order that replicates the way ideas connect, how it all leads to a bigger picture. The big picture, finding the essential ideas that will unlock the big picture, or bring it together, is key. Observer educators expect their students to be able to create the big picture.

Fives love predictability and order. Observers don't do well in teaching situations where there are unexpected demands, such as having to cancel classes in order to accommodate a request from the principal. This would be seen as a huge curve ball, not only in terms of having to cancel classes, but in terms of: Why am I being asked to do this? I knew how much energy I'd need for this week, now I have to undertake this other responsibility. How am I going to manage my time?

The Five energy is cerebral. Fives will hardly ever articulate a full sentence —it first has to be formed in the head before it is spoken. Of course they get fast and skilled at this mental preparation. This is often the root of verbal communication problems for the Five: the long pause before an answer, the pause in which the formulation of meaning and syntax is taking place. Many other E-types feel it's like drawing teeth to be in a conversation with Fives. Their speech patterns are treatiselike (rambling), and their articulation is clipped; and, most Fives do not display facial or physical expression. Observer teachers are aware that they need not only to respond more quickly to students, but to bring some excitement and inflection to their voice. But speaking out is an action fraught with danger for Observers, because once the words are out, you can't take them back.

How to get the Observer to talk in class? Observer Five students are those who learn by listening, they are simply not going to speak up in class. Calling on them creates tension as, red-faced, they seek to disappear under the desk. Daily, huge efforts by many teachers around the world are expended to get Observers to talk in class. It's as if there's a societal rule that you cannot pass school if you don't talk in class. Five students are not particularly interested in talking in class; they participate and learn by listening. Their internalized interaction with the material is as intense as that expressed by the more outwardly verbal, enthusiastic student burbling on. Observers receive negative feedback around what is one of their strongest suits: the mental ability to sort quickly through material. Ask Fives to synthesize the lesson at the end (but tell them the day before you are going to do this). When they know it is coming, they'll respond with a gift—insightful information and a way of creating a big picture. Other gifts are rationality, a coolness, a calmness, a balance, a way of being able to be above the fray, to detach.

Procrastination forms part of the pattern, too, arising because one idea can lead to three others and those three others lead to another three. Soon there are nine ideas, and then twenty-seven, which lead to other whole sets. A typical Observer Five doctoral student will spend weeks amassing 1,500 reference cards, weeks more sorting them, and freeze over the task of translating that knowledge into a sixty page term paper, "I can't hand in this paper, it doesn't scratch the surface of what's available."

### Shift to Point Eight (Security)

The shift to Point Eight occurs when Observers feel secure. They experience the Eight energy viscerally as a physical manifestation, a rush through their bodies. Fives report that they learn to trust their gut instinct.

As I grow older, I can observe myself a little better, I'm aware of a definite rush of nervous energy. One of the few times I can feel something down in my belly. I used to kind of back away from it, but nowadays if I get that I try to act right away with what I have to do. Previously I interpreted that feeling as basically nerves and it caused me probably to retreat even more. But once I took that chance, "When you get this kind of feeling, say what you're thinking." I got such positive feedback, I started to realize that we're not talking about nerves here at all, what we're talking about is not excitement, it's gut instinct. I still find it strange, but it's what happens.

Even though Point Fives shift to Point Eight when they feel secure, they can access the Eight defense mechanisms: avoiding being vulnerable, and engaging in confrontation.

### Shift to Point Seven (Stress)

When Fives feel stressed, they access the Point Seven energy. They retreat even further into their minds with their thoughts in a chaotic whirl. More and more possibilities open up for them, making it even more difficult to deal with the matter at hand.

When I get stressed, I find I keep expanding my time-frame in which to get tasks done. If a project is due tomorrow, I will watch TV, or procrastinate in other ways, because, in my mind, I have options around the deadline. After the TV program, two hours will suffice to do six hours worth of work. I also find myself thinking a lot, up in my head so to speak, with useless thoughts running around in there. I catch myself thinking, or worrying, or fixating on trivial matters, seemingly for the sake of the worrying and not for the sake of taking care of the matter.

Even though Point Fives shift to Point Seven when they are stressed, they can access the gifts of the Seven: optimism and formulating options.

### Key Characteristics

### Making Connections — A New Way of Seeing

Observer Five educators set great store on people's ability to make connections between ideas that can lead to big-picture thinking. They seek ways to interconnect information, to come up with news ways of seeing, to create new possibilities. This teacher articulates clearly this process.

One of the ways I begin each year, it doesn't matter what level I happen to be teaching, I use the analogy of the apple falling from the tree. I mean, obviously, people noticed that things fell for a long time, but someone like Isaac Newton is the kind of person who tried to make correlations between the fact that all things fall, from him you get that sense of connectedness. If students have a sense that the same law that governs the falling of an apple is the law that allows us, for instance, to get to Mars, they begin to see the ways in which things are all connected. They need a sense that represents different ways of looking at the world.

Note how this teacher tries to break down his students' conditioned patterns of thinking. He tries to decondition their world by promoting creativity in finding solutions. He connects with students so they can find answers together.

When I started teaching I was trying to demystify the teaching of literature. I was constantly looking for ways to get students excited about this material. The ideas are important to me. I went into teaching because my concern is finding ways to make life more palatable, or comprehensible for people. You know, it may sound as if I have the answer, but that's not it. That's one good thing about working with students, because they are in the process of finding answers, also. While they may begin with packaged answers, with answers from their parents, or whatever social institutions they have been connected with in the past, in the process of being in the classroom, looking at books together, reading newspaper articles, something else begins to happen. They become aware of their prejudices, whatever they happen to be, and that perhaps there are other ways of solving problems rather than just the traditional way of thinking.

### Big Picture Thinking

The Five mind works as if it were piecing together a puzzle, seeking the one piece that will unlock the whole when everything falls into place and a big picture forms. Observer teachers will talk about what they teach in terms of the way things connect, how it all leads to a bigger picture.

Achieving a big picture is probably the most exciting thing to do intellectually. I think that's what I'm always thinking about.

Five educators need to be aware that not all E-types think this way. Just as many Fives as students struggle with teachers' demands that they articulate their thoughts in class on-the-spot, many students in the Observer's class struggle with reconditioning their thinking to form interconnections and big pictures.

For me, the thing about knowledge is finding other ways of looking at a problem. That's what I try to do in a classroom. Oftentimes, you can't solve a problem unless you take some radically different approach to doing so. Most of us still grow from our experiences. I think that's the kind of truth that I like students to get at. It makes the world a lot more complex.

Even on the most minimalist level of deconstructing a sentence, Fives can find evidence of a big picture in the complexity of the differing points of view it carries.

What I look for when I grade papers is evidence of thought. I will always invite them to create their own thesis. On the basis of that particular thesis I will judge their papers. Of course, I am always pushing them to create more exciting and more complex theses. I show them the complexity of sentences, the way the thought moves from one point of view at the beginning and by the end of the sentence, it's embracing another point of view. I say this writer sees two points of view and can talk convincingly about both points of view. I think that is the essence of what I want to accomplish.

### Big Picture and Safety

The following speaker is someone who returned to graduate school in her middle-age after having practiced law for many years—and she is still disinclined to talk in class. She reports on how having a big picture makes her feel safe.

Often even in graduate school, as comfortable as I felt with the teachers and as safe as it was to talk, you'd usually have to call on me to get it out of me. What makes me feel safe is to have the big picture. Then I feel that I can go off in any direction and respond to any situation. I know that's an illusion, but it helps to have the confidence because that can boost me to the response of action. If I don't feel I have the big picture I feel uncomfortable, because I only see fragments and don't know where that fits in and therefore where I fit in.

### The Sound of Silence

Silence has a charge for many E-types. Some are comfortable in the silence, it allows them time to think, for others silence is uncomfortable because in it they are thrown back on their inner resources, unable to concentrate on outer actions, or ellipt onto other people. In the section on Performer Threes, one of our Point Three educators reported on how he can't stand silence in the classroom, if the students don't talk, he will to cover the gap. To the contrary, this Observer educator values silence as a signal that his students have to think about an answer. He finds these moments among the most successful of his teaching.

Success for me is silence when I ask a question. I know then that I have led them down the path which makes it impossible for them to answer the question with a simple "yes" or "no" answer. The silence is a signal that they have to think about it. Sometimes what they're actually doing is trying to figure out what the trick answer is. Often times I'll tell them that there is no trick, I don't know, I am interested in their ideas. That's frustrating for students. I like to frustrate them in that respect. They want to know what my opinion is, often I tell them that my opinion is not important: It's what you know, or you feel, or what you believe, that is important.

### Being Perceived as Distant

This Five teacher shares a most poignant statement about how she has to observe others in order to learn how to put her emotional affect out in the world. She has learned that it's not enough to think your emotions, you have to embody them energetically. Interaction is not spontaneous behavior for her, she has to think it through first.

> I was in the Peace Corps before we got engaged. When I came back I moved in with my husband, we were going to be married shortly thereafter. I had to observe his family, and watch how they were in relationship with him in order to figure out what does this man need from me, how am I supposed to be with him? Then I would mimic their phraseology, their expressions, because the feedback that I've gotten in my life is that I often have a blank face and people find me distant, yet I'm not feeling that way on the inside. So I know enough about myself to say: It's not enough to think happy face, I have to be conscious that I'm smiling, that I'm saying "Hi, honey, I'm glad to see you"—the energy has to be there. I have to be careful. It's not just the thought process, but that I'm actually carrying through with it.

This educator also discusses the value he places on ideas. He is aware that in his concern to be objective he comes across as dispassionate and unresponsive. There is pain in being misperceived.

> In the process of listening to a student I'm always listening for an idea. One student can give me an idea and I will respond one way to that idea. Another student will give what I consider perhaps to be a less sophisticated idea, and while I don't mean to say that's unimportant because this idea over here is more intriguing, I've been told, "Why don't you respond? That person said something and it's as if you're not hearing them." There's no doubt about the fact that I can come across differently to students than I mean to. There was a point in time when I was so stone-faced because I tried not to discriminate between the ideas that students were trying to communicate. They would ask, "Why don't you respond?" My response was, "Well, if you say something and I don't like what you say and I tell you, and that person over there says something, and I tell that person that I like what he or she says, then that's going to make you feel as if your ideas are not counted." That's not the way I like to teach anyway, because I would rather have the students talking to each other rather than talking to me.

### Rational Assessment

Evidence of detachment can also be found in Observers in the area of assessment. Fives value mental judgments, pure thought, intellectual ability, they tend to regard other manifestations of intelligence as suspect.

When I put comments at the end of a paper I have to consciously tell myself to put some stroking in with all the negative criticism, my eye and ear go to the critical flaws, not the good parts. What I've learned to do, I can suspend judgment, I can be both skeptical and doubtful, and suspend that to see what's on the other side of it. I can hold both positions at the same time and that feels comfortable and safe.

Observers can be sarcastic and judgmental as a cover for not wanting to expend emotional energy.

In one of my previous trainings as a Jesuit, one of the things that appealed to me in Ignatian philosophy was the idea of "indifference." This doesn't mean you don't care, it means it doesn't matter if you are rich or poor, happy or sad, this appealed to me. What gets me into trouble is if somebody comes to me with a problem that seems to me a minor problem, no big deal, my response can be sarcastic. I feel for them, but I feel maybe this much, because it's not worth a great deal of emotional energy. Junior girls come to me with concerns about grades, it's one grade out of twenty-five over the course of a quarter, and they're going to bother me with this? I say to myself: This is not worth tears. Why are you doing this to me? Invariably, I get concerned phone calls from parents.

This Five educator is open about how minimalist he is in showing approval to his students. He curtails interpersonal contact through confining his interactions to written remarks on students' work.

Students know I approve when I give them grades on their paper. If I see a good idea on the paper, I usually put a check in the margin, or a check plus, or a check check, or something like that. I think the comments that I put at the end of the page, or the end of the paper suggest that these ideas were first-rate. I saw that you were struggling to create something. I try to teach them that if they can interpret the world rationally through acquiring knowledge, nothing unexpected can happen to them, they can be safe.

### Living in the Mind

For Fives, the process of review in their minds after an event has happened is by far the richer experience.

Especially when an emotional or exciting event happens, I'll spend three times as much time afterward thinking about it and almost feel like it's a richer experience when I'm thinking about what happened than when I actually experienced it. When the feelings come in it can sometimes be overwhelming, sometimes I can react, go over the situation as I suppose anyone else would. Though even while I'm still interacting with the situation, I find I can separate and start thinking about it as it goes on.

This Observer shares with us her inner world, how she separates (detaches) from experiences and has no spontaneous connection with her emotions.

When feelings come up, the initial response in me is a knee-jerk reaction to separate, go somewhere by myself and figure out what's going on with me. Then I can put it into a context and have a plan for what I'm going to do the next time that happens to me, so I'll be prepared. When conflict comes up, I will think about it, I don't have a ready response such as I'm feeling love, or sadness. If I find myself sad, rather than feeling sad, I will think about everything that is going on around me, and try to figure it out. Then I realize, oh, I must be feeling sad. I have to put feelings into some sort of context or theoretical framework, I do a lot of journaling—that's how I flesh out how I am feeling.

### Detachment

Fives are among the three fear-based E-types. This Observer articulates how she can deal with her fear by having foreknowledge of her situation. She does realize that she can never acquire all the knowledge necessary to deal with every situation, that at some point she has to trust her instincts.

My way of feeling secure is to get a sense of not only what's happening, but what's going to happen, and all the possible ramifications. Not from a fear position, more from a knowledge base. It's a security issue; I don't know if that's connected to fear at all. But more crucially this preparation is in ways of relating, also in teaching. Generally I try to catch myself doing it because I realize I spend way, way, too much energy obsessing about the stupidest details (especially in the classroom) that when the situation arises I'm going to do what is right. There's no sense in needing to figure out way ahead of time what's going to be the case in a particular situation.

### Detaching from Feelings

This Observer describes how she is able to detach from her emotions at will.

I have a full coterie of emotions and I use them on a regular basis with a lot of enjoyment, sometimes with some frustration and pain. But I do like them, I can weep with the best of them. I have been an Emergency Room nurse, when you're in the middle of battle, if you get winged in the shoulder, you just can't stop because of your emotions, you just can't. You must go on because if you stop you become needy of attention too, and you are not the focus of the emergency, it's the poor sucker who's just been electrocuted. So you put aside what you're dealing with until later; then you begin to understand how close to death you stood looking at this patient. It's multiple tragedies at multiple levels. I felt sad for him, but if I allowed my emotions at that point I would probably have fainted.

Her report is verified by another Five speaker. Both speakers demonstrate that Fives *do have* feelings, but they can detach from them.

The feelings are always there, but when you detach from them, you're detaching from an overwhelming sense but you don't know what they are. You need time to sit back, review the situation, figure out what you knew at the time you were feeling. I'm thinking about three or four crisis situations. When my best friend broke his back, I was right there. Other people were freaking out and panicking. I was cool and clear, I made the right decisions. I was focused fully on the needs of my friend, even though I was surprised by some of the effects happening around me. At that time I suspended my emotions, later I reviewed them. I can't tell you about my emotions until I sit back and think about them. At other times, especially when I'm relaxed, emotions will overwhelm me instantly.

### Emotions

Although they are often stereotyped as being unemotional, Observers have plenty to say about emotions. This speaker offers us a dramatic description of how emotions can overturn his inner world.

I can sit back most every day, cruising along in my own mind, gathering ideas and knowledge, synthesizing, and interacting with people. If emotions come up unexpectedly it's almost as if my ship gets overturned, I capsize in a way. Emotions take over and throw everything else out of my mind to such a degree that I can't deal with it. The only way I can respond to something that's been emotional, is to sit back for an hour or more and after several hours I know how I feel. If someone comes to me with something emotional and asks, "How do you feel about this?"—I can't respond. I can say, "I need to think about it." If you come to me with a problem and say, "How do you feel about this," I'm going to run basically.

The following speaker also has a high degree of self-awareness and offers this whimsical description of how emotions play out for him both in professional and personal arenas.

In the teaching situation emotion and feeling are fine. One of the students I supervise (we meet about her work and her learning every week) recently said: "I'm not going to cry," and I said, "OK," and she reached for the Kleenex. I know this student, she's almost finished her residency, she's a wonderful person, she needed to speak to me about a serious matter in her family, she needed to clear it with me, before we got to academic matters. That's fine with me, but there's still a little part of me that wanted to say: "Let's do what you're here for." I have to be careful with that.

However if I go home and there's an outburst I have had to learn to ask for time, "Can we talk about this later?" I need to give myself some space and time to get ready to handle something that might be very small, but big to me because of what it brings up in me. I don't have the same structure at home as I have at work and can't expect that. So I have learned little phrases to use to get me time and, said properly, I get it.

*Knowledge*

Gaining knowledge is the Observer's focus of attention. Essentially this E-type intelligence directs Fives to seek more and more knowledge as the means of acquiring safety. Much of the habitual patterning of Observer behavior is rooted in this drive. The following speaker acknowledges that she has a need to acquire knowledge.

I don't feel as if I'm some kind of encyclopedia because half of the time I'll forget what I've looked up. That's a stereotype of Fives, that we keep everything in our heads. When the need arises, I need to know the answer, but then it recedes again. I can't say that I have more in my head than other people do, because I don't know what other people have in their heads. So maybe I do have a huge amount of knowledge, but I don't think so.

This Five has another take on the role knowledge plays in her life. Note her feelings of insecurity because she does not consider herself an expert (and therefore safe) in any one particular field.

Knowledge is a collectible. Some people collect records; others collect dolls, and I don't actively read books to obtain knowledge. I like having knowledge and knowing where to find it. I have many books in my house for that reason. I won't have read them all, but there are particular subjects that I'm curious about. It's a comfort to have the book there and know one of these days I want to be an expert on that subject (it's my secret desire to be an expert on a particular subject.) I feel like I'm too much of a jack-of-all-trades, so it's a professional desire of mine not just to be a social studies teacher, but to be an expert on a particular subject. It's an insecurity in me as a professional. As a teacher I want to call myself an "expert" in medieval history, or something.

The following statement from an Observer elaborates on the previous one.

This Five does not want to be an expert in the accepted sense of the word, rather he wants to redefine his field to accommodate all knowledge into the ultimate big picture.

Most people think that Fives are these book owls who sit in the library and study a particular subject. But I feel that way about other people. For instance, one of my great passions is fly fishing, but I run across people all the time who have so much more knowledge. They go into the insects and this and that. I find myself being more diffuse, my professional field is history; my goal in teaching and studying history is to broaden the focus, to incorporate all of the different disciplines into history. This could be a particular feature of my own mind, to paint the ultimate big picture.

This Five says she has learned that knowledge has to be experienced, you cannot learn it from books.

In my formative schooling years knowledge was a form of defense. The teacher looked at me and said, "What's the answer to this question?" I would be terrified not to know and became adroit in picking out details to weave together in an instant reply, not necessarily an answer, but anything to get me off the hook. The hook wasn't being right or wrong, the hook was being in the public eye, although being wrong in the pubic eye was excruciating, unbearable. But now I realize that knowledge is not something that comes from books per se, but from life experiences. Knowledge is like that; you can't get it reading a book, you must experience it.

### Searching for Knowledge

This Observer touches on one of the key drivers of the Five E-type intelligence. Observers can never acquire that final piece of knowledge—this is a classic Five blind spot, the illusion that the possibility of knowledge, that is totally certain, exists at all.

For me, when I'm doing research for putting out an article I never quite get to the final product. I never think I have enough knowledge yet for it to go out in a permanent form into the world, for the reason that I don't want to seem stupid, there might be something I've forgotten, there may be something discovered yesterday I don't know about yet, I haven't run my Web search yet today—all that questioning of myself. But I find on the other hand that if I get good feedback from the reviewer I get into my action mode of: they liked it, this is on track, I'm ready to go with this, and that has a lot of energy until in the writing stages I get down on myself again. But at least I can play the doubting game at a different stage. I have a believing game I play first to get it on paper and then my doubting game helps me to work with the first draft.

### Compartmentalization

For Fives by compartmentalizing the different parts of their lives they protect their privacy, store information in a manageable system, and ensure their defenses are intact against separate parts of their lives flowing into one another and hence out of their control.

> Compartmentalization is a wonderful mental construct. It's like having a bureau in your mind with many little drawers and each drawer has its own designation. It's wonderful to be able to store things. It's important to be able to remember where you put it, retrieve it, use it, blend it, mix it, mash it. You know, cook with it, do a Cuisinart with it, just to be able to have this potpourri is wonderful. I'm thrilled with it, I'm sure that other people have this, I can't imagine they don't.

For this Five, compartmentalizing is a way of conserving energy. Attention and thoughts stay focused on one compartment and don't spill over to others.

> Compartmentalizing is part of my life that if I'm focused on a task, or having fun, or interacting with a certain group of people, I'm not going to think about anything else . Especially feelings, they're not going to intrude. When I say that I know obviously there are certain times we all go through different exceptionally intense emotional times, when that's all we're going to think about.

This Five describes the mental process around compartmentalizing. It is important to note that to her (and many other Fives agree) the compartments in her mind are separate, but connected in a big picture.

> Compartmentalizing is in my mind. I have an inner sense that when I take in data bits I tend to sort them right then and hang them on pegs. When I need them, they make sense, and I know where to find them, where I might retrieve them. I don't like them in isolation, but part of a bigger idea. All my compartments are connected, part of the big picture. While I sit here I can think of many different things I'm going to do, or situations I'm in at the time. I guess other people don't think that way. If I know I have these options for the future and I'm doing this right now, I can hold all that in my head, but none are present in this point in time. But I know I've got them all sorted out.

### Privacy

Fives are aware that they can retract, be present physically, but have no presence. This way they can retain their privacy even when among other people, and so keep the ramparts to their inner citadel firmly intact.

> In middle school I learned how to become completely invisible. So invisible in fact that Mademoiselle used to mark me absent in her French class even though I was sitting in the third chair. That's when I

retract, you can't even see me, but going that far away from yourself may not be good.

Retraction and privacy, guarding oneself, Fives can come across as overtly secretive.

A good way of thinking of privacy is there are different "me's" interacting with different situations, different groups, different people with whom I have no compunction to share. I could have an intense experience with a certain situation, or a person, but with someone else who is equally important to me, I won't even mention it, because it's mine. I don't so much think that's hoarding, it obviously involves being private, it is something I realize I need to work on, perhaps being less secretive.

### Conserving Energy and Time

Outside intrusions are interpreted by Observers as a drain on their essential energy. Fives are aware of the need to withdraw, to be private, to recharge after a period of interaction.

Even if I'm in an energy-intensive, or energy-draining experience, I can go through it, no problem. But I have to know that I'm going to have that hour afterward to recover. So I can give of my energy, but only with the intention of a having the time to recharge. There have been times when I don't get that time, when the situation keeps going and going and going, I find then that I can just go with the flow. But it's difficult to put myself spontaneously into that mind set of flow, as opposed to being forced into it by situations.

This Five describes the physical measures she takes to ensure her downtime.

Time and energy management isn't just psychologically needed, it's emotionally a must. Otherwise it feels like crispy critter time and I have to get away if I've done too much. If I'm scraping the bottom of the barrel to put my energy out, it can feel very, very fatiguing, at that point I'll go home, close the door, lock it, go to the telephone answering machine, turn it off, go to the telephone bell, turn it off, and I'll have some downtime.

### Synthesizing and Brainstorming; Interactions Such as Role-playing

Many educators use brainstorming as a tool to stimulate thinking and role-playing as a relational exercise. This Five tells us why both techniques are problematic for Observers.

To those Attacher teachers who say that they think role-playing is a great way to reach all students, I can tell you from personal experience that is the last thing I want to do. I have forced myself to do it occasionally, but it is an unpleasant experience for me, it's good for teachers to know that not all their students are into role-playing. The other area is brainstorming, more and more people use it, you get people together and brainstorm ideas. It's hard for me to throw out ideas, I need to be able to think about them. The Five student in the group might want to go off by himself, write ideas down and then come back, I can't sit there and throw out ideas to other people, I find that hard.

### Natural Way of Learning

The same speaker makes a plea for us to keep the more traditional ways of teaching in the classroom; they model the way Fives think. But, Five students need to be stretched, too. The Five who is resistant to cooperative learning, may, in the long run, see that cooperation is truly, a better, quicker way to *get* the big picture.

Please don't throw out the traditional method of imparting knowledge and materials, of expecting students to synthesize and give it back—that's my natural way of learning, I wouldn't want to learn in these nontraditional ways such as a team project. If you give four people an assignment and tell them they're going to be graded on the final product, I'll be cooperative and give all my ideas up to the group. But, if there's a situation where a teacher says as part of the exam you should brainstorm a response and help each other out, I'll be honest with you, I'm not going to respond in that situation, because I feel any ideas I come up with that are good in response to a particular essay question are going to remain mine, there's no reason for me to give up that idea. I don't think that's necessarily a bad thing. If we're talking about an essay on an exam why should I be sharing my ideas with other people? I know the argument is it helps you to come up with more ideas yourself.

### Communication and Noncommunication

In the interactive educational dynamic, Observers, both educators and students, are out of sync with the accepted societal norm of being spontaneous, speaking in the moment, sharing ideas, articulating emotions. As we have seen, everything about this E-type intelligence directs Fives to be guarded, private, silent, until all the pieces of an argument are in place in their minds.

Even in those classes where most of the time I'm the one person who talks the most, there are several times when I won't say a thing for the entire day. If I don't feel like I have anything to contribute to the discussion, I won't. Of course I have been in teaching roles, and there you're the one who is required to keep things going, I can do that as well.

This Observer instructs us well in the following typically Five conundrum; how best to help Fives learn to express themselves. What comes through clearly is his pain and indignation at what he perceives is a major injustice on his teacher's behalf. All he was doing in class was being himself.

In ninth grade the history teacher decided to give me a "C" because I wasn't talking in class. He said he could tell by my essays that I had good ideas, but if I didn't speak in class he's going to give me a "C." I thought that was outrageous; I'm sure that's how I reacted. I know I didn't bump that grade up to an "A," I probably didn't say another word in the class, because I took it personally. If he had sat me down one-on-one and said, "Look, I think you have valuable ideas. Why don't you try expressing them." This is what he should have done, because as an educator you need to draw people out, especially Fives who need to learn how to express themselves and how to interact in a group. I think definitely the way to go is to sit students down one-on-one and discuss the issue. What would have worked is if he'd given me the reason. "Look you're going to need to learn how to express yourself, you have good ideas, you can contribute to the class, I would love to see you doing it." I'm sure that I would have.

Now I've graduated from college, I've learned the tricks. For sure, I made a point in every class that I was ever in to say something just so that the teacher would know I was there. But it probably took until I was a junior or senior in college, which is a long time. The way that teacher did it was negative, as if he was saying: "I'm going to punish you for not talking."

### Connecting to Fives

These Observers share with us what it feels like to be a Five in the classroom of other E-types. For this speaker, to feel safe, she has to know that the teacher is praising her for specifics of her output; bland generalizations won't do.

I would observe the teacher, figure out what was required for a good grade, and basically follow the plan. I hated being called on, I never raised my hand unless I was sure I had the answer. It's absolutely true that the worst thing you can do to somebody whom you suspect to be a Five is to put them on the spot. When I took a more visible role in the classroom, it was because a teacher went out of his or her way to have a special connection with me, to recognize me, to reach out to me one-on-one, to praise me, notice that I was doing a good job, or to pick out something specifically, not making general praise statements, but to actually pick out something I had done and praise me. Then I would feel more confident to raise my hand, feel safer in that class. When I was older I actually studied a process called voice dialog; there's a part of me I do now that is a social front. When I have to be in a social situation I call on that part of myself to engage with people, the energy can come out, I operate from that place. My whole life speaking up is not a natural act for me.

This Five speaker pinpoints another Observer dilemma: wanting to be included in the group, but not having the social skills to approach others.

I have few friends, few relationships, but a rich interior life. I had one good friend in grade school. If you're a teacher and you see a group of kids playing with balls or something, the person who's standing and watching them that's probably the Five child. Fives are not antisocial, we want to belong in a quiet way. If you are the teacher, draw Fives out; it's almost a relief if you're standing there apart from the group and someone comes over and pulls you in. You want to be included, but many times you don't have the skills to approach the group. It's good to be drawn in. If the child responds positively to your prodding, it's an indication that they want to join, but it can definitely become an intrusion if they don't want to and someone's always pulling on them.

Asking Five students what they have observed in the lesson is an excellent way to forge a connection between the educator and the student, and also between the student with the material.

I sit in the classroom and don't say a word, but I take everything in. There are a couple of times when I may want to add something, but it doesn't seem appropriate at the time, or important enough for me to say anything. There are other classes where I speak all the time (in fact I ran into an old teacher of mine yesterday who said I cotaught the class with her), but even in those classes I'm only going to say something when it's ready to be said, if I feel that I can put it out there.

If, after a class, a teacher comes up and asks me if I have any observations, in fact that's a good way to get at me, because it makes me think about it. I'm not articulate or coherent in the moment, but after two more hours I can respond with exactly what happened in the classroom, how it was appropriate, who seemed to bring up interesting points, where it flowed, and where I think the lesson can be emphasized. So my point is that it may take me several hours before I can respond, and, at the time, it may look like I'm just sitting there and I'm not present.

### Being an Observer

Five educators are comfortable with silences that imply thinking and with nonverbal communication. They tend to want to sit back and observe others as a way of assessing, of making judgments, and placing a value on what they are seeing. This educator states the stance succinctly.

As a teacher I sit quietly, I only intervene as absolutely necessary. I like my students to be self-directed, to learn on their own. I can observe and help and intervene, accompany and challenge, but I like to see them learning on their own. I can sit back and observe, listen and enjoy.

This Five speaks to how she responds fully in her mind, she does not see the necessity to share her thoughts.

Oftentimes, it's enough for me to think of an idea, to think: that's a good idea. In a classroom setting it wouldn't occur to me to put it forward; because I thought of it, it's a good idea, it's part of my knowledge now. I took something that someone said, I responded to it in my mind, I think I responded to it well, but there's no reason to share it with anyone.

This Five educator has the final word on being an Observer and how for him everything comes back to having the big picture.

I don't know I have observed while I'm observing, I have to let it happen, I'm not there putting all these thoughts together, they're putting themselves together and then I'll realize that later. The fear is the fear of not knowing, and looking stupid, and saying something stupid. I overcome the fear by having the big picture. The big picture for me is to believe that my students know, and that together we will know and find out and ask the questions, then I'm not afraid.

### Growth Path: From Hoarding to Allowing

The growth path for Observers has to do with the idea of guarding or hoarding—in the sense of energy and time management, of knowing they have so much to give, of being private and detaching from emotions in order to conserve energy. Growth comes from the sense of not being so attached to these habits, of letting go, of allowing, of letting spontaneity rise. This Five knows she is overattached to control and that there is a need for more spontaneous interactions in her classroom (and her life).

In a classroom situation, I'm definitely the person in charge. If a student is getting out of control, I have a guideline in myself of what I've worked on to prepare for that situation, and I kick in the plan. I do tend to obsess about situations that happen to me, personal situations that involve emotion or conflict, so that when I see that person again, or I have that student and they start acting up again, I'm prepared. I don't act spontaneously with my feelings in the correct manner. I don't trust myself to do that, I guess.

### Quality of Essence: Omniscient Awareness

The essence quality for Observers is omniscience, knowledge of a universal connectedness. The concept is akin to the Point Four essence quality of universal belonging. Both speak to a fullness of being in the moment, of being present, of the still point where being and belonging come together.

I was working in a garden, it was May, my shoes were off, I was up to my ankles in dirt and I was thinking as I looked at the trees: they're carbon atoms, the grass is carbon atoms, the dirt is carbon atoms, Mars is carbon atoms, and gosh, I'm carbon atoms! Suddenly I realized that I was part of something that is sublimely bigger than I am, the universe, the cosmos, and I'm part of this. I, who had not felt part of anything for long, was part of that, or it was part of me. I realized that no matter where I go, or what I do, or what I don't do, I'm connected to this. When I die I'm still connected to it. It lasts longer than life.

and

At times in my life I have a profound sense of being here, in my body. I'm not in my brain, but I'm in my body. I'm in this family, I'm in this world: this is why I'm in this world, this is my purpose. From the time I was a child, I felt I had a sense of purpose. That feeling never came from my head, it's something I've always felt in my body; one of the few feelings I could tag.

## What Observer Students Say

### Hoarding

If you assign me to a group of people and we have to come up with the answers to a test you're going to be giving in two weeks, I'm not going to say a word because it's my ideas, why should I give them to anybody else? This is avarice and hoarding but it does help you get through the world.

### Emotions

I can get very emotional, but I hide it as much as possible. There are two completely different planes for me: there's me and there's kind of me whose been rehearsed to behave this way. I prefer to kind of hide. I can't explain it, but in front of people I get this awful dread and I want to melt.

### Big Picture

I don't consciously get motivated to learn, but something will grab me. If I'm taken in by something I won't stop, I like to do the whole thing and just keep going. I have to be interested, then I like to focus on one thing and learn everything about it.

and

I like ideas and insights and new ways of looking at things. I like categorizing them systematically and connecting everything else and getting this big picture and this interconnectedness, it's exciting.

### Minimalism

I don't like writing prose, I can't write prose, prose gets ... too ... I get too carried away when I write prose. I don't write structured poetry, it's more controlled because every word has to carry something and fit in, and if it works right, it's great; and if it doesn't ... What you can do with poetry you can write something three pages long and then condense it to a paragraph and make it all work out. You can make something that can flow together and its kind of got *it*.

### Observing

I like to know where things are and I like to look around people's houses, so I know where absolutely everything is. Even something I wasn't supposed to know where it is, I would know. People ask, "I wonder where this is?" I say, "I saw it in X, Y or Z" and people will say, "That's interesting."

### Energy Management

There are two planes; people on the lower plane, I deal with them and then I get away as fast as I can. I dislike dealing with people. But if you can get me going I will get going; if you can't, I'll say the minimum and move along.

### Brief Interview with an Observer Educator

*Q. What is your teaching style?*
A: My teaching style is investigative.

*Q. What do you look for in your students?*
A: What I look for in my students is creativity, and a desire to question.

*Q. What is important in the way you present material?*
A: What is important in the way I present the material is that kids see as big a picture as I can allow them to see.

*Q. What will students say of you?*
A: Students will say of me that I want too much, especially at the beginning of the school year.

*Q. Why do you teach?*
A: I teach because I think the world is a screwed up place. I have faith that if kids have a sense of what are some of the things that are wrong with the world, they can begin to formulate solutions, solve some of the wrongs.

*Q. How do you communicate?*
A: There are definitely some glib teachers who walk into a classroom and can talk from the beginning of the class to the end of class. They start a sentence and they know exactly where the sentence is going to go. I think sometimes my kids must think I am an idiot or something because I'll start a sentence, I'll get into the middle of it and then just stop, because I've gotten into the middle and I realize that I've said something that isn't quite right. Somehow I want to fix it. That can be confusing to kids.

*Q. What is your attitude to preparing teaching plans?*
A: Preparing teaching plans is difficult for me because I am always looking for that particular way of getting across a complex idea so that a student can say, "Oh yeah, I understand." That's not easy to do because we are so used to thinking in conventional ways that it's difficult for kids to think any other way.

*Q. What do you like about the classroom?*
A: What I like about the classroom is the fact that at the school where I teach the students are incredibly bright, they are much brighter than I am. I appreciate that intelligence. My classroom is a place where ideas can be exchanged freely. I can't think of any other forum where people are actually forced to answer difficult questions and they can't leave until they have begun formulate those answers.

*Q. What don't you like about the classroom?*
A: What I don't like about my classroom is I'm afraid I've narrowed my bag of tricks down to a few and I don't feel that youthful energy when I go into a classroom anymore. I have to get the energy from the kids. If I'm not delivering that energy, they are not going to give it back to me.

**Practical Tips**

*For Observers to Work with Themselves*

- Be aware that you can come across as noncommunicative and secretive.
- Make an effort to connect with people, to share and enjoy interactive experiences.
- Tell people of the rich ideas and insights you have in your head.
- Push yourself to do role-playing, or act in plays, learn how to express emotions.
- Be aware that you share little of yourself, successful relationships are a

two-way street and demand much more of you.

- Manage your energy by building in downtime to be private and re-charge.
- Learn to access your instinctual energy and trust what it is telling you.
- Share your gift of rational thinking, of keeping a cool head in charged situations.
- Practice spontaneity, take risks, experience what it is to be fully alive in the moment.

### For Others who Work with Observers

- When you see Fives hovering at the edge of a group, structure a way for them to join. Often they want to participate but lack the social skills to approach the group.
- Don't assume that stone-faced students who show little enthusiasm are disinterested, if they are Fives they learn by listening.
- Let Fives establish a comfort zone for themselves by observing, before you demand participation.
- Encourage Fives to share their observations, utilize their gifts of synthesis and creativity with big pictures.
- When a Five writes a good paper, ask them to read it to the class, that way you let them share in the interchange of ideas, let others hear their voice.
- Take Fives aside and share with them your perception of how they are coming across to their peers, often Fives are oblivious to how retracted they appear.
- Set deadlines for Fives, to circumvent procrastination from gathering too many ideas.
- Realize Fives need time alone to regroup and recharge—help them structure that for themselves.
- Encourage Fives to engage personally, to interact beyond their comfort level.

## *ENNEATYPE SIX: THE QUESTIONER*

- TRIAD: *DETACHER*
- ATTENTIONAL FOCUS: Scanning to seek certainty
- GIFT: Sound logic, clear thinking
- AVOIDANCE: Deviance. Being seen as different
- GROWTH PATH: From fear to courage
- ESSENCE: Faith
- SHIFT TO SECURE POINT: *THE PEACEKEEPER NINE* (Defender —against arrow)
- SHIFT TO STRESS POINT: *THE PERFORMER THREE* (Attacher —with arrow)
- WINGS: *THE OPTIMIST SEVEN* (Detacher)
  *THE OBSERVER FIVE* (Detacher)

### EXAMPLES OF QUESTIONER EDUCATORS: BETTER SAFE THAN SORRY

#### A Cast-iron Argument

Gary L. teaches in an Ivy League university medical school. He has a small consulting practice, but his career is teaching. He has not published much in his field, the minimum to receive tenure, his intellectual energy has gone into teaching. Gary loves standing in front of a large lecture hall presenting his course material. This was not always the case. When in his first lecture in his first year of teaching he was faced with a room full of a hundred graduates, he was so fearful of the experience, on the edge of nausea, that he put down the chalk, closed his lecture notes, and dismissed the class.

Later, sitting at a fountain in the medical school quadrangle, he spoke severely with himself: you've invested twelve years to get your degrees, this is what you what you want, a career in academic medicine, it's a little late now to change your mind. That night Gary once again put his lecture notes through a rigorous mental process of review and refinement, until he proved to himself that the argument was ironclad. Nothing could go wrong, he could trust himself absolutely. The next day he delivered the lecture, and the next, and the next. Slowly it became easier for him to stand in front of a lecture hall, but he never forgot the feeling of relief he found in being able to rely on a cast-iron argument. Over the years Gary's lectures became well-known for their theoretical rigor. He inspired students to think with equal rigor. This was his goal for teaching: to teach people to think clearly, to build logical arguments, to apply rationality to their judgments, to find evidence to support conclusions.

In his fifties now, he has been a department chair, served on various administrative bodies in the school, and headed up taskforces on such areas as ethical practices and changing student attitudes over the years. Gary is loyal to the school where he has spent his career and, despite his lack of enthusiasm for committees, he sees it as his duty and responsibility to be part of the adminis-tration. Responsibility is a big word for Gary. His cautious approach, his ability to troubleshoot, and the gentle way he engages others who want to rush ahead with ill-thought through plans or positions, have made him a valued member of the faculty. In his understated way he looms large, his influence is more power-ful than he'll ever believe.

Gary has relaxed into teaching smaller and smaller seminars where his warmth and personability shine through in ways they never could in the larger lecture format. He joshes with his students, creates a safe space for them to ex-press opinions, treats all opinions with serious intent while he tests them for logic and feasibility. His seminars are full of humor, both his own quirky hu-mor and the quick wit and repartee of his students.

Although to many Gary appears as the epitome of a successful professional, which he is, he knows that at any moment Life can pull the rug out from under him, crises occur that will engender the familiar feelings of panic, self-doubt, double-guessing, even self-loathing. Gary relies on the energy rush that fear pro-duces so that he can rise to the occasion, cope with the crisis. But nothing works as well as being able to refine a cast-iron argument, or the way to proceed.

### Scared of Her Own Shadow

Pat J. is a mesmerizing teacher. There are no theatrics or performance in her presentation. She ignores the conventional wisdom of successful teaching: little eye contact, no attempt at ice-breaking when she first faces students, no evidence of establishing rapport, or warming the student audience to her. She stands firm-ly at the podium and speaks. She doesn't move from where she first starts speaking. Soon the students are drawn into a body of knowledge that becomes as concrete as if it were a real body in front of them. Vocabulary and tone construct the facts one on top of the other into an elegant structure whose foundations are unshakable. Pointed and often cutting humor underscore key issues. Time pass-es, there is no sense of building the lesson in a parabolic arc to finish with a well-timed crescendo. Each fact is as important as the next well-thought-through, concrete block. "I'm a literal thinker," she says. Usually she runs late, but it doesn't matter where she stops, the argument can be resumed the next day. Students emerge from her class as if they've been submerged in facts, solid theo-ries, telling evidence, a world of conceptual thinking that demands commensu-rate mental energy from them.

Pat is at her best in front of a class. It's as if she has a license to share her mental world. Away from the protection of being the class leader, she is suspi-cious and cranky. Students who seek her counsel as an authority in her field (she is a prolific and successful author) are often disconcerted by the sharp questions and suspicion which greet them. Pat is not comfortable as a mentor and advisor. She wrestles daily with herself—if she can't advise herself, she cannot see how she can advise anyone else. A stubborn individualist, she refuses to serve on committees and be part of a group, she is easily irritated by what she perceives as the slowness, shallowness, and power-mongering of her colleagues. In fact she is no longer invited to join—her reputation for prickly attacks and negative double-guessing precedes her. This is fine with her; her faith is in ideas and theories, people always let themselves and others down. "We are all equally untrustworthy," she says.

Pat lives in a bunkered world. Her hideout is a large house near her school where she controls contact through a flow of e-mails, faxes and voice mail. This way contact is minimized to mind-to-mind interactions. She has a family, those intimates know another side of her: loving, caring, funny, generous; there are a few friends, but none she would call close. "People always want something from you," she says. Yet students who attend her classes know she is passionate and emotional about what she teaches.

What drives Pat? She uses galvanizing energy rushes to drive her toward whatever it is that either interests and engages her, or tackling and confronting what discomforts or disturbs her. And there is much in life to be wary of. "Don't any of you read the newspapers?" she asks. The energy surges allow her to mobilize her defenses; they are invigorating, life-giving, dramatic, and offer relief from pressure. Any movement into action is better than having to sit around with the discomfort, thinking about it and thinking about it.

## THE QUESTIONER STRATEGY

| Strengths | Weaknesses |
|---|---|
| Questions incisively | Defensive |
| Logical | Self-doubting |
| Rationality | Self-sabotaging |
| Skeptical | Struggles with authority issues |
| | |
| Clear thinking | Suspicious |
| Troubleshooter | Distrustful |
| Loyalty | Thinking replaces doing |
| Protects the underdog | Fearful |
| Responsible | Procrastinating |

## THE E-TYPE SIX PROPOSITION

### General Description

#### Skepticism and Logic; Fear and Faith

Point Six is one of the mentally based types—among those who detach, not into an emotional shutdown in terms of what, for instance, Point Threes experience, but a withdrawal into the mind, where in fact there is a great opening up, a relief, a sense that the world is safe because one is in one's head. The retreat into the head is directed at containing fear, the whole momentum in Sixes is to find safety. But safety is a projection, an illusion, because nobody is more or less safe in objective reality. The sense of seeking certainty and finding it seems real to Sixes. But others look at the Sixes' life and think: Oh no, how can you be thinking that? The concepts of questioning, seeing the worst-case scenarios, being doubtful, are positive means whereby Sixes respond to their E-type intelligence that tells them the world is not safe. It seems to make absolute sense that the only way you're going to find security is though questioning. If you don't question, how can you ever be sure, and maybe the only surety you can have in your life is that you are not sure, and that's OK, for a Six that's a good place to begin.

Point Six is among the most difficult points on the Enneagram to understand because there are two variants of the Questioner—phobic and counterphobic—although most Sixes have elements of both variants to some degree. The phobic Six is easier to understand, this is the E-type intelligence that *knows* (the blind spot) that the world is a fearful place and the way to cope with fear is to figure out what's the worst that can happen: there's a degree of safety in knowing. Inherent to this strategy is a means of confronting your phobia by going toward people in a warm way, being friendly to mitigate dislike and potential harm from others. None of this fear is pathological; Sixes are as normal and high-functioning as anyone else, but their E-type intelligence tells them to keep up their guard, that it makes sense to do so. Paranoia plays out in gentle and subtle ways in most cases: the person in every meeting, every week who says, "Yes, but...?" because of fear of the group landing itself in a situation unaware of all the possibilities of what can go wrong—keeping the group safe is territory the Six views as his responsibility.

Counterphobic Sixes go against their fear, in the most overt manifestations they can often look a lot like Point Eight. The intense discomfort of being trapped in fear is so disturbing, almost annihilating, that they go into whatever is frightening them, in order to alleviate the discomfort. If you're a counter phobic Six and scared of heights, you'll take up bungee jumping. When you are in the fear then you can overcome it. If you're scared of water, you go sailing across the Atlantic on your own. These are extreme, but real life examples. If there's been an argument in a meeting before the repercussions can even begin to settle, the counterphobic Six is challenging you for your response. They need to know what's certain and safe—they can't leave the argument unresolved.

Now most Questioners report that they have both elements, they are both phobic and counterphobic, although one style usually predominates. If the counterphobic Six can come across as a Point Eight in energy and style, *all* Sixes are look alikes of Eights when it comes to authority issues. The difference is subtle. Both Six and Eight can be rebellious students, or belligerent adults, the ones who always want to challenge you. Eights live life in terms of a power struggle and challenge in order to establish who has power, will they be fair, and how far can they push the authority. Sixes challenge in order to find certainty and safety, pushing others to find out if there is solid ground where they are standing.

The Questioner educator's authority issues play out in the classroom. Students come into class one day and something has happened to the teacher at home, he's off the wall on the fear scale so the whole class is taken off that way. The questioning gets sharp, there's a suspiciousness about everyone in the classroom, an edginess to all interactions. The next day, the domestic situation is resolved for the Questioner, he comes into the classroom as if everyone's a good buddy: so let's all sit back and have fun. As authority figures Sixes oscillate between being too lax and too authoritarian. Students often don't know where they stand, and this can be disconcerting.

The avoidance of the Six is being seen as different—deviant. This seems strange in terms of a counterphobic Six who goes against his fear, doing outrageous exploits, so that you can't help but notice him. But deviance is much more a sense of an internal misalignment around authority. The world is seen in terms of me and the *authority*. It is easy to see how this is part of a fear-based strategy, "Time is the authority, my schedule for school is the authority, my boss is the authority. Life is the authority." Sixes give away their power to the authority, far more power than the authority has over them. Then they get resentful and the oscillation picks ups, back and forth, back and forth. In one faculty meeting the Questioner will be on her feet the whole meeting questioning, arguing; the next meeting she won't say a word. It depends upon where she is in her internal debate, the eternal tennis match around authority issues.

If you are a Six student your inclination is to submit everything you are told to an argument, counterargument, debate-like scrutiny. Much like Point Four, many Sixes have a low self-esteem and sense of deficiency, they don't believe in themselves. Verification is important. On a math problem in an exam, unless the student has done it several times previously, she is not going to believe that she can do it. It's a chicken and egg dynamic.

In writing papers, Six students set up a proposition in the first paragraph or statement, then knock it all down in the second, only taking out of it what they still feel is valid, put that into the third, so a back-and-forth argument ensues with themselves. If as a teacher you don't make some allowance for this natural way of thinking in whatever assignment you're giving, whether it's history or math, the Questioner student is going to have difficulty in your class.

Sixes are among the great procrastinators of the Enneagram. Unlike Point Nines, the other great procrastinators, who are poor self-starters and only the consequences of not meeting that ultimate deadline gets them to hand in the assignment one minute before midnight, Sixes procrastinate because when something is completed, it's out of their head, it's in public, they become a target. Among the situations Questioners avoid is drawing the attention of others toward themselves, because of the fear of unforeseen repercussions. Anybody can take a potshot at you, so you keep your head down, keep holding back and holding back. When it's almost too late, when you absolutely must, you turn in the assignment.

Another characteristic of Six students and teachers is a tendency to self-sabotage: the student who takes twelve years to complete a doctoral thesis and then at the last minute doesn't hand it in. The teacher who applies for a top position in the administration, get's it, then decides to stay in the classroom. It is fear of putting oneself out there, of being noticed.

The attentional focus of the Questioner goes to scanning to seek certainty, as if there's an internal radar system always running. For Sixes this survival mechanism satisfies their sense of seeking safety. This type of scanning is quite different from, for instance, a Point Two whose scanning is relational. It's a ceaseless scanning for danger that obviously becomes a part of the Sixes' conditioning. However, a gift of the Six is present in the continual scanning; if others give the Questioner room to speak up. Particularly in organizations, in meetings, in class discussions, Sixes should be allowed to voice their doubts and to troubleshoot. They are the best troubleshooters on any team and will define the problem so everyone gets to clear and logical conclusions. Six students will push you too. If as a teacher you are not rigorous enough in your thinking it's almost an affront to them, they'll question you, pull you up. Teaching students to think and think through ideas, helping colleagues not to jump to conclusions, these skills are instinctive to the Six.

### Shift to Point Nine (Security)

In the shift to Point Nine Questioners are able to relax, to let down their defenses, open their hearts and access the universal, unconditional love and peace the Peacekeeper exemplifies. This is felt energetically throughout the body. There is an openness and trust present, almost a counterintuitive stance for the ever-vigilant Six.

When I feel safe, it's in my heart, my heart will gradually start to open, I feel that it's a movement energetically that happens once the heart starts to open, it filters up and filters down. Once that occurs, it's completely safe and it feels great. But just to get to that space there is a whole process of scanning and sensing to feel comfortable. Once I'm there it's fantastic.

Even though Point Sixes shift to Point Nine when they feel secure, they can access the defense mechanisms of Nines: obstinacy, losing their own agenda, and difficulty with prioritizing.

### Shift to Point Three (Stress)

With the shift to Point Three the Questioner steps out of her head and moves to action. She performs, gets the job done, often because of looming deadlines. Oftentimes Questioners can look like the Performer in action, but it's a dogged, determined one foot in front of the other way of achieving tasks, not the natural go-getting style of the Three.

What happens with procrastinating, I let it build, build, build, and then I go into a Three mode where I go like crazy, go for it, tackle it, and get it all out of the way. I think for me when the procrastination takes place or hold, there's an energizing moment when I say, "Okay, let's go." If it's set up and structured for me, it's a piece of cake, I can go right in. But if it comes to me to set it up, structure it, and do it, that's when I procrastinate.

Even though Point Sixes shift to Point Three when they feel stressed, they can access the gifts of Threes: leadership, energy, envisaging hope on behalf of others, and belief in themselves.

### Key Characteristics

*Fear*

The world is a frightening place, and most Sixes are amazed that other E-types don't know this, or heed the dangers if they're told about them. Fear plays out in all aspects of the Questioner's life; interestingly enough many Sixes don't know that they are afraid and assume the habitual practices of their E-type intelligence: scanning, doubting, worst-case scenario imagining, questioning are sensible tactics in a life-long battle against keeping disaster at bay. This Six educator was surprised by his counterphobic behavior in a teaching dynamic, he relies on going toward his fear to help him in front of a class.

My driver is fear, in retrospect fear is what drives me. When I began to examine my teaching style I was always comfortable in front of a room, but *how* I would attack authority, *how* I would go after dissenters, *how* I would deal with security issues, *how* I would go toward what I was afraid of made the counterphobic part obvious for me. It helped me focus to be more effective to accept my driver, how I can work with my fear. I like to entice people into a situation to get them to think creatively, how to engage, to push people to go beyond their usual means of thinking. I love being in front of a room full of people because I'm afraid of it, so I get pushed toward it. Mental or emotional fear I experience as challenges and go right toward them.

Like our first speaker, this Six also recognizes the counterphobic nature of her reaction to fear, and how blind she is to what frightens her.

When I get fearful, I reach out and attack. One day when I was attacking somebody verbally, totally in their face, it just clicked, "I'm a counterphobic Six." This is why I move out when I'm fearful, why I'll push out and attack to protect myself this way. It's been something that I constantly, constantly see in myself, how I push out the fear that I feel inside and don't recognize as fear.

Here is a description of how out of panicked moments great mental clarity can arise. Many Sixes describe how they need to be pushed into panic before the energy surge rises to lift them to action, or thinking with total clarity.

My stomach gets upset, but I don't feel like I'm going to throw up because I think I'm too afraid to. But my chest gets real tight, my voice gets shaky and my hands get sweaty, I have this heat rush through me and I talk to myself a lot. That self-talk is important, it's as if I have to tell my mind to quit this. At first it's this total rush, an energy I can turn into task, or into tuning in. For example, I remember once being panicked about everything, everything was racing through me. I sat on the front porch and had one of those moments where I said, "Oh...I see that life happens on all of these levels, I see the squirrel and think that's one level, then I see a car going by and wonder where the people are going, and a suddenly there is a wholeness that comes out of the panic."

This following clear description contains a vivid accounting of how fear is experienced physically, what it feels like in the body. The emotional line between fear and rage is almost nonexistent, they are so close. This Questioner, like many other Sixes, is frightened of other people's anger because he knows how powerful is his own. Finally he describes the acute nature of his E-type conditioning—scanning, his attunement to "uneasiness."

The unknown always creates fear in me, it doesn't matter what it is even if I've done it before. This happens quite often in the lecture room. Walking into the lecture hall, standing up in front, the class starts and finally I say the first word, and then it's gone. I know that will happen. But the stomach clutching, the dry mouth, if I'm frightened quickly, it feels like it's below the stomach and goes up to my throat and it will even explode, or come out, or it will just rip my throat, I'll have to swallow and stop. Occasionally I stand up and my knees will shake, my hands will shake. I started to work on some of this and the first thing I realized was that I didn't know when I was afraid. Fear wasn't a word in my vocabulary. It took me a while to learn that I was afraid. The other thing that's happened is I often can't tell the difference between fear and rage. I can recall many scenarios where I know that my internal reaction was rage, but I was conditioned as a child not to let it out. The fear about the rage is that it can be turned toward me, and that's only fair. Often times I would say I was afraid, but what I was afraid of was the rage. When I walk into a room if I start to feel uneasy, I have to look around and if there's no reason inside of me, intellectually or physically why I should feel uneasy, then I'll start to look around to find somebody else's anxiety.

### Authority

Many Sixes feel powerless in the face of Life's capriciousness. This feeling expands into a general sense of themselves as Life's underdogs. From this point of view Life becomes the authority, a rubric that can include many phenomena. From here you are always up against the wall, underprotected, watching your back, scanning for safety. Sixes give away their power to authority, view authority as more powerful than they are. It's most often a case of "me against them," except when Questioners align themselves with underdogs or underdog causes then it's "us against them." If the Questioner feels safe with an authority, he will abide by the rules, but if the authority shows any signs of disarray, the Six becomes uneasy and wants to leave. Some Sixes are deliberately rebellious to test the authority, not as in a power struggle, but for safety and security with the authority. These speakers describe how issues around authority can be intertwined with many other key characteristics of the Six—for instance, for this speaker with trust.

Everything is an authority. I'm in the car, I'm late, the clock is the authority: how am I going to explain this. The police officer who stops me: the fear rush comes up and by the time he gets to the window, I'm all warmth and affection. What brings the rage up for me with authority is anyone saying, "Do it this way." I didn't understand that until I went on a rafting trip. I was up in the front of the raft and there were six of us. Our direction was down the river, down the rapids. I found out that the man in the back, our leader, this was his first time he had his own raft. Suddenly I knew I wasn't going to trust him. He was a young man, and he's telling us to do either back paddle, or forward paddle. I knew no matter what he said to me, I was going to do what I felt was correct. So he'd keep saying, "Now paddle." All that meant was that we were going to spin around, so I would do the opposite. I got a lot of flak from everyone in the raft. We stayed dry but the issue is that he was probably going to be wrong, there was something I didn't trust about him.

Blindly obeying authority can inculcate feelings of inchoate anger.

I always obey authority. An interesting thing is that I thought I was the most trusting person in the whole world, I trusted everybody. I didn't realize that all the questions had to do with not trusting, I thought I was just becoming clearer. I know I get resentful when my time is taken up, or my energy, or someone has authority over me. I think that's when rage comes into me, when everybody is demanding something from me including the clock, or whatever. That's when I find myself angry.

For this speaker, like our first, authority issues are shot through with trust issues. She also describes another characteristic of the Questioner. In relationships with Sixes, it is difficult to build up a track record that will counter the inevitable bumps along the way. One small incident is enough to dislodge five years of trust, you have to start all over again.

Authority is my huge issue. I can trust authority until there's something that they do that doesn't feel right to me, or that I perceive that they're doing. It might be after years of feeling totally comfortable with that person: my principal didn't come to a weekend workshop I organized as he said he would. Now I doubt everything he does. He supported me on some other things, he's supported me for five years and he still supports me, but that incident made me feel a little betrayed. And I doubt him now. So I don't know what it would take to get my trust back except that he's going to have to continue to support me and it will take some time. My biggest fear is having the rug pulled out, that when I do trust, someone will pull the rug out on me. When that happens, it's just awful. No matter that 99 percent of things have been good, once that rug gets pulled out, it reconfirms that I shouldn't have trusted, that I knew that and I didn't think it through enough.

Here is helpful advice for teachers interacting with Six students: rules are anathema to the Six unless they are explained, and the underlying logic or reason for the rule, is clear. Very often, sharp questioning from the Six student has less to do with gaining information, and more to do with scanning for intention. As a teacher it is useful to be aware of this motivation of Questioner students, and to be precise and specific in your responses.

Authority to me is rules, following rules. What I think my issue with authority was when I was growing up and in school was that the rules they upheld there, they'd never explain what they are for. Since I require safety, I'm questioning why do we have to do this? What's it for? Why this? Why that? It was not having the whole picture explained that caused me trouble. If somebody steps in and explains something to me and goes step by step, presents a picture, then it's more comfortable for me. But what I found in my learning experiences in school was that it was rare to find teachers who would spend the time describing their intention in trying to get me to learn from them. If they do, I can step into that and say okay, let me sit here with you and I'll learn it. But when somebody comes with rules, it's almost like a barrier pushing out. I have trust issues, I don't want to go in some place where there are rules.

This educator see herself as nonauthoritarian. Unfortunately for her, by being the teacher she is perceived as an authority figure by her students. Sharp questioning is seen as aggression, she sets herself up for "them against me" situations. Sixes' oscillation with authority—now the one in charge, now one of the gang—is disconcerting for students.

I think I generate a pretty nonauthoritarian classroom. I'm comfortable with not being in charge of everything that's happening, and not having to decide for people if they need to go to the bathroom, or need to go over there and get a book. I try to develop a fairly level, nonauthoritarian type of relationship with the students. Every so often,

I do notice that people feel I'm quite aggressive, which always surprises me, because I don't think I'm aggressive. But when I question them, they start feeling insecure or defensive, as if I'm trying to expose that they're wrong, that they hear me imputing blame to them, or being critical of them in a way that I'm not quite sure why. I mean I don't think that I put that out there. In other words in my anxiety to get them thinking, they feel the questions are sometimes too sharp, they see them as if I'm questioning them personally.

### Scanning

The focus of attention of a Questioner goes to scanning the environment for hidden dangers, the unexpressed intentions of others toward you, the host of unexpected occurrences that can ambush and assault you. A previous Six speaker reported the concept of scanning accurately when he said, "When I walk into a room if I sort of feel uneasy, then I have to look around and if there's no reason inside of me, intellectually or physically, why I should feel uneasy, then I'll start to look around to find somebody else's anxiety." Many Sixes may project *their* fear onto someone else, finding evidence that the person is hostile to them when no such hostility is present. The sentry in the sentry box often raises the alarm, when it's only the wind moving shadows. This can also occur in relationships: the Six tells you what *you* are thinking, when you haven't been thinking that at all. An important antidote to scanning and projection for the Six is to seek reality checks from those she trusts. Of course this E-type intelligence strategy can be seen as intuitive, useful, for instance, in finding the soft edges where students need assistance before they themselves know to ask.

In the report below the Questioner educator is aware that he scans his classes to apprehend those who are not paying attention, not for vindictive reasons, but to help them to become more attentive. He is aware that his scanning can be viewed as overvigilance and suspicion. In effect, as he tells us, in sharing with students key aspects of his E-type he is asking for a reality check.

I'm alert to what everybody is doing, I think that's helpful in that I may pay attention enough to know where they're at and what they're doing, or what they're thinking, and when they're not with me. So that when I've done something and they haven't understood it, I'm quick to realize it, and do it some way differently so they get the idea. Sometimes this works against me in that I treat them oversuspiciously when it appears to me as if they're doing something totally different, doing A's homework in B's classroom and B's homework in A's classroom, they're not paying attention. When I start trying to pull the students in, sometimes they feel I'm treating them terribly suspiciously, and that's where it becomes a difficulty. How to pull them in, pull their attention in without kind of setting up a case of I'm accusing you of not paying attention. Some students take any comment or any interaction as an accusation, so it's particularly difficult with them. But oftentimes I've felt that too many students have felt suspected. One of the things that I've done in the past year or two a bit more is that I've actually talked to them about the Enneagram. I tell them about my own personality, "I have a tendency to be overly suspicious, so if you think that's what's happening, try pointing that out to me." Sometimes this helps to have reality come through, suspicion falls away.

### Procrastination

Questioners procrastinate for several reasons, all of them having to do with the Six being unable to let go of mental prohibitions to taking action. The fear is of becoming a target, of being public. When ideas are still in the Questioner's head they can be submitted again and again to a process of argument and counterargument, but once they've been made public they cannot be retracted, the Six is fearful she has not thought through all the scenarios, that her words will be misinterpreted, misrepresented.

With Six educators, procrastination can occur in areas such as grading papers. Assessment and grading put Sixes on the spot because of the doubting and questioning of the grade: this one, or that one? What's appropriate? If I decide on this grade, then I doubt it's the right grade. I question—why am I doing this at all—I retrace the whole argument trying to understand why I'm doing this. Grading those papers can build and build until it becomes a huge mountain. Educators may wonder why some of their colleagues take an hour to grade a set of papers and others three days, this is one of the reasons. It is extremely difficult for a Six educator to grade a set of papers.

As a teacher, grading papers, often they just sit. I use the excuse that if I write comments which will take me forever, I have to go through and think of each part of the comment. If I want to write a long comment and I do it for somebody, I need to do it for everybody, it's just overwhelming. I let the papers sit, then I pass them back with a star or something because I think: well it's just the process that important, it's not the results. I know the parents are going to see all of the comments I write; I don't want that out there.

Sixes employ numerous strategies to overcome procrastination. Questioners can easily manage to do tasks, reach short-term objectives if a structure is present. Setting clear objectives and goals for the Six is a way to help them overcome procrastination. The following speakers break the grip of prohibitions by creating short-term tasks.

If I keep tasks short and focused, the energy stays high. Longer term tasks are hard, I do the last-minute things first to create that energy, to push it forward. The task I'm supposed to complete is like a dead body in my car. I'll be driving along all happy until I start to sniff it, then I remember and get in a panic and I'm totally energized and I get it done.

Like the previous one, the following speaker also reports that she accepts the fact that she procrastinates, but notes how she relies on the pressure of deadlines to get her moving.

If I have company coming, I don't worry myself, I *know* I'll be ready, I'll slip into that frantic mode at the last moment, but it's probably not healthy when I go crazy. If I'm having company my house is a mess until the hour before people arrive, then I'm screaming at everybody to help me, I'm madly getting things done that I haven't done for ages. For three weeks before someone's coming, I used to carry this heavy responsibility. Instead of picking up a room at time (it's not like I'm a horrible housekeeper) but I just carry this. Or if I have a paper due, now I know I'll be up to 3 a.m. the night before it's due and I sort of let it go, that seems to work.

This Six has a contrary take on the process of overcoming procrastination, for him structure is a safety net, but he still skirts disaster by not taking action.

When I get the structure set up, I say the job's done, I put it aside until the last minute and that drives me crazy. I find myself consciously trying to make things work for me time-wise but I'm always late. Another thing about procrastination that strikes home is the aspect that when it's complete, it's out of my hands, I have no more control over it and I can become a target. I don't think about it, but that's exactly how it feels.

### Self-Sabotage

Self-sabotage is related to the aspect of the Six conditioning around procrastination. If you're too successful you'll become a target, so you don't let yourself win the race, you need someone else to push you over the finish line (the metaphoric races in life as well). This person can then also be responsible for whatever outcome your success brings.

I used to race barrels on my horse and I'd reach a point where I would right before the finish line and I'd pull up the reins, I was winning too much, feeling self-conscious of that, suddenly I was conscious of being out there. Later on I went to finish school and during the last month of my student teaching I'm wanted to quit, "I will not do this." My husband said, "I'm just not letting you quit." It took someone else to shove me to the finish line.

Six students need teachers to structure a sense of safety around them if they are to show their creativity.

I think from the teacher perspective if you have a Six student, probably the best thing to do is to watch what they put out originally because it's not their best. Once they feel safe their best will definitely come out. They have two levels of achieving. The first level is just what they want you to see, but the second level is for themselves, there's so much more there and it's a gift to have a teacher who can stick a hand out and say, "It's okay come on in." The blossoming that can occur then is just fantastic because you'll see the true potential.

## *Safety and Trust*

To this E-type intelligence it makes sense that *as* you are afraid of being victimized, and are therefore constantly vigilant, *if* in the environment in which you operate (as is to be expected) you are not given the opportunity to express your questions and doubts then you must keep up your guard and wait for your worst expectations to materialize. Your wariness is a self-fulfilling prophecy. The obverse is also true—if you can feel safe, which to a large degree means being able to express your opinion, doubts, fears, and questions, you can let down your guard, be spontaneous and creative.

It is interesting how Questioner Six educator after educator states this precept as a golden rule of their teaching.

Part of my teaching style is hearing everyone's opinions, creating an open format so that there's room for expression. Safety issues are important. I'm antiauthoritarian—this plays a big role—people must feel safe in my classroom, feel that they are learning. Expressing more is important, then they can achieve more because they are able to gain knowledge from other people's opinions, we all learn from one another. I feel that is the greatest strength I have, I value other people's opinions. If somebody is not open to listening, I have difficulty in knowing what it is to get them to motivate themselves.

Safety is achieved by simultaneously holding a different awareness for each student in the class.

One of the advantages of allowing everyone to speak is that you can actually teach a whole class because everybody is participating, so I can keep in my mind thirty lesson plans, thirty discipline plans all operating at different levels. My thinking is powerful enough to keep all that information in my head and to be able to take each student through a different process. Another great thing about having people reveal themselves by having the environment safe is that you can test woolly thinkers by asking questions that are on the mark, that give enormous information. So it's not only that I question, but I ask good questions. So if you're trying to present something to me and there's no structure or framework, no thinking, then that will get taken to pieces. So I teach people to think logically, research accurately, and be able to explain a framework consistently. This all comes naturally to me.

Humor is often a trait associated with Sixes. This Six educator makes use of humor as a safety valve in the classroom.

My classroom has been described as wacko, eccentric, on the fringes, but protective and supportive. I encourage people to say strange, outrageous, funny things. My classroom is a funny place, it's often off-beat humor, it's hilarious, there's an interconnecting humor all the time in the classroom.

While this educator is aware she is overly defensive in the classroom, that her classroom doesn't always feel safe.

What I have to work on in my teaching style is to say a few key things, to ask a few key questions which will help me to understand where their difficulties are. I get into difficulties in the classroom when I get into arguments, I haven't learned to back up, I attack all the time. My first challenge is to try to listen 25 percent of the time instead of talking so much, because I'm talking about things that may be complicated to them. A problem I have sitting in a conference, I'm concerned that they understand the details when they probably don't want to understand all the details. I can overkill the lesson by going overboard and not shutting up and letting them say what they want to say.

### Creating Safety

Six educators create safety in a number of ways, among them are several strategies that tie in with their E-type intelligence. Looking someone in the eye is one strategy.

I make sure that I make contact with the person eye to eye. I ask them questions so they can bring forward what their fears are. I'm aware of when people are not feeling comfortable, I draw them in and make them feel comfortable by asking them questions, or asking them to ask me questions. But I try to draw them out first. I use humor a lot, make fun of myself. I find when I do that, it breaks some barriers with people. I share my own experiences.

Note the countervailing rationalization in this Six educator's comment.

The only way to feel safe, is to run things. I just want to be safe: let's make it my football in my backyard so I won't get hurt. It's not because I want to run the thing, oftentimes I get into struggles with people who say I'm on a power trip, but that notion is far from the inner part of me. I don't want anything to do with the responsibility of being a leader. I know it's a safety thing.

### Loyalty

Tied up in the concept of loyalty are the concepts of faith and trust: if you are loyal you are faithful, you can be trusted. A characteristic of Sixes is loyalty, but especially loyalty to the underdog and underdog causes. Fundamentally to trust is counterintuitive to Sixes. The idea of trust is just *so* stupid, you don't trust yourself so how are you going to trust anyone else. You can take the word *trust* out of the dictionary, it doesn't exist. Many Sixes are bewildered by questions about trust; as they have never trusted, they are unaware that they don't have trust. Sixes are loyal, it goes with the territory of being responsible. Once you are committed then you are responsible to see a relationship, a job, through. There is certainly a sense of loyalty to the family, to intimates, to a close circle of friends, although trust issues play an important role, too.

I'm fiercely loyal and committed in relationships, and to causes. I show a protective, but I hope not overbearing concern for the welfare of the person or cause.

Loyalty can have a less personal, but still subjective twist.

I know I have tremendous loyalty, but this doesn't always play out in the good sense of being loyal to my family and friends. I can be loyal, loyal to myself, to my welfare, or to my ideas—I have waded through these ideas, I have refined these ideas. So as a teacher, this is what is important to me is that you will understand these ideas this way. My loyalty is to the material that I have refined.

Six educators also report loyalty to an ideal.

I know in my personal relationships loyalty is a key factor, so my rebellions have always been hidden rebellions. In the classroom I feel my principal loyalty is to try and get students to think for themselves, to evoke their independence, that's what I continue to do, no matter what happens. In a sense the loyalty I have is to a concept that they can think for themselves.

Disloyalty can be particularly irksome and disturbing. This is how this educator regards his students.

There's a feeling that despite my having built a relationship with them over a long period of time and having trusted them, they aren't taking an interest in trying to improve. I feel it's disloyal, and that particularly bothers me. I find myself struggling to get out of that frame of mind when I'm going to meet a group again, when we've had a negative interaction the last time. I have a tendency to go forward and attack, and that doesn't help. What does help is that I've discovered I can pull back and look again at the interaction and try to get a different perspective on it. To see that maybe they weren't attempting a personal attack. I might come in the next day and discover that they've forgotten all about it—that often throws me.

### Logical Thinking

The following categories are all reflective of the central preoccupation of the

Six, thinking and thinking clearly. Obviously for Questioner educators this is the area that carries the greatest charge for them in the classroom. Several educators explain how this preoccupation plays out for them.

*Clarity and Logic.* One of the things I keep looking for in my students is clarity in their thinking, "What is the main idea here?" "What do these equations translate as?" "What's the logic of the sequence for evidence, for constructing the evidence, or for the theory and then how do you use the theory?" It appears to me that's essentially what I'm trying to do, to give them a skill, or at least train the skill of observing situations and drawing conclusions from the information, making more exact information from less exact information, seeing how that leads to the conclusions one draws. Often students come in wanting to know what the conclusions are and ignore the connection between the evidence and the conclusion. Essentially I teach them how to deal with the evidence and organize the theory logically.

*Mentally based Classroom.* My classroom is quite mental in approach: I'm into their thinking, and thinking clearly. I give them the liberty to think, but some people need to be taken past the stage of an approach to life where they say, "Oh well, I can't think." Somehow that's a learned response that needs to be gotten past. I encourage them to see this, "Originally you may think you can't, but if you try, I think you can figure this out." I find that some students need presentation and performance, that's one of their big things, and I suppose I don't reward that whereas I reward people who volunteer answers that can be applied to the question that they are looking at. I would say that the people who have the most difficulty in my classroom are people who have learned this idea that they're someone who can't think. I have people who write on end-of-the-year evaluations, "Could say more"—people who want me to dictate the question and then dictate the answer and think it's unfair for me not to do so. I tell them it would be unfair of me if I did.

*Skepticism.* A lot of schooling, it seems to me, has prepared students to look simply for the answers without a connection between the evidence and the conclusion, so I'm skeptical that simply because I've given them the evidence that they've reached the appropriate conclusion. I want to make sure about that. I'm never sure that they've got the point until they show me that they've got the point. The fact that I've done it in front of them—I mean, over and over again I've realized that people don't learn what you thought they were going to learn from something you know obviously showed the point. I'm forever verifying what I was trying to show them: "This is how I thought this showed it. Is that how you saw it?" Or, "What happened when it got to you?" "Try to link the evidence with the conclusion, and don't jump the steps in-between."

*Building an Argument.* As a student, being in a creative learning environment was important for me, but I never took things at face value. I was a strong devil's advocate always challenging and questioning, not to bring authority or the facts down, but to make sure that what I was hearing was truthful and accurate. I find on the other side as an educator that the devil's advocate shines through strongly for me as a way to challenge the person or issue I'm supporting, not to bring it down, but to make sure it's refined so when it's out there it can withstand a battering.

### Worst-case Scenarios

The following story by a Six speaker illustrates clearly the Questioner mind at work spinning worst-case scenarios from innocuous situations.

We had gone to Mexico. It was the first time I'd left the country and I was excited to do this. I'd always wanted to go but was always a little afraid, so I had to learn the language a little better before we went. We got stopped at the border and I understood just enough Spanish to know they were debating upon whether to mess with us and take everything out of the car. They didn't and we drove on down. It was a Sunday, people were drinking, I watched every car, I noticed that there were five guys in a truck drinking beer, jumping out and peeing so I knew that they were drunk. I panicked, "Which are the cars with the drunk drivers?" The next morning a plane flew overhead, a camouflage plane. I thought, "Great, I've brought my family to a revolution." And then I see ships and planes landing. The fog lifts and it's only a man from Alaska who likes to fly his airplane around, and some rocks out in the ocean. It all worked out, but that's how my mind works.

### Questioning and Doubting— "Make a decision and you doubt yourself, make a decision and you doubt yourself. It is an unending and unsatisfying process."

This Six educator reports that she avoids working in groups because of the fear that she won't be allowed to voice her doubts.

Being part of organizational or administrative groups is difficult. I find it hard to express my opinion because I like to tell the truth, so it's hard to find a format where I can express the truth and have it not be pushed aside. It's hard for me to be in a structure and not be heard, so I tend to stay away from groups.

This Six educator tells us what it is like to live with a mind that is constantly questioning. She is aware that she plays the devil's advocate for others, and of the consequences of her actions.

I find myself at a department meeting scanning the others for what they are thinking, or what I think they're thinking and I'll ask questions for them. I can sense that they've got a question, that they can't ask the question, but I don't care if I look silly if I'm asking it for them. I have been accused that I'm shooting them down by asking questions, but the questions immediately come to mind, they just start rolling. This bothers a lot of people, people can't finish asking their questions, because I'll finish them. Part of it is impatience, irritation at their slowness. I'm in my head and I already know what their question is. This drives people crazy. The other part of the question for me is a procrastination device that I've seen myself use. The more I ask, the longer it will be before I have to take that step of implementing the answers.

### Dealing with a Rebellious Student

This educator has sound advice for colleagues who find a rebellious student in their midst. It is good to be aware of the cautionary note she sounds with regard to teacher sensitivity.

I was that rebellious student; in the last two years I've had somebody review for me the impact of what it feels like to be with me. If you do this with a student, do it sensitively, because if you don't the student will take it that you don't like her, that she's a troublemaker. If you can go to that student and somehow have a scenario where she can see herself, see her impact and how others are affected by it, it's a real lesson because she'll realize that by doing what she does how much she pushes people away. Again it's for safety. I'll keep filling the space in with questions because I don't feel safe, I neglect the people around me. I know for myself it was a sensitive and hard issue to address because I didn't realize that I was doing it for safety and trust reasons.

### Protecting the Underdog

Sixes often view themselves as Life's underdogs, after all they give away their power to authority and what is an underdog if not powerless. From this position it is easier to explain the fear, the doubts, the negativity, all the other mental constructs that arise with a constant necessity to question the world. This Six educator is acutely aware of his inner motivations and how they manifest themselves.

In a classroom it's interesting that my focus is on relationships, because relationships are where I can get security. A set of strategic relationships can establish my safety zones. I can remember walking out of school as a sixteen year old and saying I'm going back to teach because I'm never going to allow students to be bullied as I was bullied. I was determined that I was going to go back and run a school where every kid was heard and every kid was safe. I did, I went into a school where there were knives and guns and bullying. I stood in the middle of the playground and I set up the mental antennae and I could hear every conversation and see every kid and I was able to run an entire pastoral program that made the place safe. In my classroom I made sure every kid was allowed an opinion even if it was strange, then we got into whether it can be justified by the evidence, whether it's a good argument or a bad argument. My primary concern in teaching is not the material, but that they experience the material in a safe environment. My anger comes at those students who don't value the safety, who put another kid down, or are bullies.

This Six educator is aware of the danger of his becoming a bully in his zeal to protect the underdog.

My work is with training adults. I tend to be almost like a protector, I tend to lean toward protecting the underdog, let everyone have a chance to speak up, attack the ones who seem to be overbearing. Toward the hierarchical bully types, I become the bully. The upside is I've become a good mediator between the mousy ones and the overbearing ones. Perhaps the downside is I tend to pick sides and root for the underdog, which strips away my objectivity and makes me less effective.

### Growth Path: From Fear to Courage

Growth for Sixes occurs when they can act with courage. Questioners describe courage as the ability to move into action without thinking, because so often thinking replaces doing. The conditioned response to fear is cowardice, it is cowardice that keeps the phobic Six hanging back and what gets the counterphobic moving toward confrontation.

The administration was about to fire a colleague accused of sexual harassment without giving him a fair hearing. Before I knew what I was doing I organized a protest meeting, demanded an interview with the principal, helped this man get legal assistance. Afterward people remarked to me that I was brave, it seemed to them that I acted without any thought of my own position. Looking back I can see I did act with courage, it was a courageous course of action, but I acted out of loyalty, I felt responsible. Besides if he could be dismissed without a fair hearing, I could be next.

### Quality of Essence: Faith

The essential quality of faith for the Six is present when the uncertainty, doubting, and questioning die down in the Questioner's mind and is replaced by a sense of security and safety. Watchfulness falls away as a state of *knowing* replaces *thinking*. Acting in faith is to rely on that safety being present: to feel it in the whole body, not only in the mind.

Faith is trust, a belief in being able to get to that place where in a universal sense you're able to believe that something is safe, something is certain. That's faith.

## What Questioner Students Say

### Authority

In my experience as a student, I don't find the educator to be the authority, I dance with authority more than I battle it. Authority issues, I've always done a dance with authority. I'll align myself with the authority figure, but if I feel I've been damaged or hurt, I can turn right around and go after that person. I've been told that my behavior is unpredictable, but I know exactly why I'm doing some-thing.

and

In school the teachers who impact me the most are the ones who have the ability to listen and give freedom of expression and create a space for creativity, a space to create. Structure is important, but the space to be able to create is more important.

and

From the minute teachers walk into the room, I'm scanning them. If they present whatever the plan's going to be, and don't present it in a quick, sharp, right way, then I lose something with them—I feel as they are going to be a drag, or how can I trust them, or they're not as bright or sharp as I think I am.

### Verification

In track this season, I think the reason I didn't succeed was that there was a specific part of the race I needed to work on. In practice I never proved to myself that I could overcome this barrier which was making the third lap faster. I think that in order to overcome barriers in learning I have to know I can do it. If I want to overcome an obstacle of feeling nervous and knowing how to to do something: by doing it several times, I just have to show myself I can do it.

### Doubting

I don't conform, I don't think; I mean of course I do, because most teenagers do in some way or other, but compared to other people I don't like the feeling of conforming.

*Thinking*

The first fifteen pages I was fine, and then my mind started wandering, it's as if I'm on two completely different levels. My mind is way out there, I'm kind of reading it, but I'm not absorbing it. I think I have trouble getting down to the work and getting it finished. But once i'm absorbed in something, I'm committed to it, I feel a connection to the material, I can concentrate. Now I know it's part of my type to be a procrastinator, I worry about the procrastination; I think about it, I think I'm going to procrastinate.

and

In my head I feel there are several layers of what I'm thinking about. Then sometimes I'll think to myself is there any way I couldn't think about that, then I know it's going to come back again and again. I do things like that, little mind games with myself. I definitely think a lot and I don't understand what it would be like not to think as much.

### Brief Interview with a Questioner Educator

*Q. What is your teaching style?*
A: My teaching style is interactive, dialoguing, attempting to get people to think.

*Q. What do you look for in your students?*
A: What I look for in my students is a willingness to undertake some thinking, rather than try to mimic my thinking, to actually look up information and construct some new constructs, and so on.

*Q. What is important in the way you present material?*
A: What is important to me how I present material is that it catches their interest and that it be clear, that the central idea is clear to them, and that it pulls everybody into the material.

*Q. What will students say of you?*
A: Students will say of me that I try to get them to think, and not just parrot material or repeat back things that they learned.

*Q. Why do you teach?*
A: I teach because I enjoy dialog with students. I enjoy group thinking and individual thinking and how individuals look at thing differently.

*Q. How do you communicate?*
A: My communication style is questioning, you know? I'm forever trying to come up with better questions so as to get them thinking more, and then to get

them to come up with questions for more thinking, more good skepticism.

*Q. What is your attitude to preparing teaching plans?*
A: To prepare plans is total frustration, I don't enjoy it. I have this plan book to do, it contains a certain amount of information, but of course part of it is there for someone else to look at. But to make up plans for myself—what I'm looking for is to figure out what are key ideas or new strategies I can find that would get these ideas to work. My plans will never go from minute-to-minute. They'll forever be kind of open to whatever happens, the actual situation.

*Q. What do you like about the classroom?*
A: I've figured out a way to be reasonably relaxed in the classroom and interact comfortably with students, a feeling of not being attacked, of students feeling comfortable with me.

*Q. What don't you like about the classroom?*
A: What I don't like about the classroom is the tendency of students to treat me as in charge of them. In charge of them personally, or in charge of them in terms of controlling them, or in terms of giving them the thinking—all these different ways that the students want you to be in charge of them rather than being in charge of themselves. What I don't like is because I allow then freedom often students come up with a lot of complaints. They want to tell me how bad I am, or how bad everything else in the world is. You open yourself up to receiving a lot of whining. The students I find the hardest to be with are the ones who do that pathetic approach, the ones who say, "I can't do this," or "this is too hard." The message I receive from them is they're not willing to try something else simply because It's too difficult. I want them to try.

**Practical Tips**

*For the Questioner to Work with Themselves*

- Be aware of when thinking replaces doing.
- Be aware that you may be projecting your fears and emotions onto others; get reality checks.
- Be aware of asking questions too sharply, you may know that you're after logic, but others may feel personally attacked.
- Find a process to help you structure your way out of procrastination.
- If you are an educator you are seen as an authority figure, find a consistent way to model this role.
- If you are a student you may be seen as rebellious when you are voicing doubts; modify the way you challenge others.
- Try to get in touch with your body and emotions; an exercise program and interpersonal interests are important for balance.
- Try to be more spontaneous with your emotions and appreciation.

- Be aware that loyalty, trust, and faith are two-way streets.

*For Others who Work with the Questioner*

- Create an environment where Questioners can feel safe to express their doubts and questions.
- Create an environment where Questioners can feel free to be spontaneous and creative.
- Help structure short-term tasks and goals as a way to short-circuit procrastination.
- Give constant feedback and reality checks when projection comes your way.
- Give constant reassurances of the Questioner's standing in your mutual relationship.
- Help Questioners sort out real danger from imagined threats.
- Be consistent in what and how you delegate tasks to the Questioner; show you are aware of the pros and cons.
- Be aware that the Questioner has given you undue authority and feels weakened herself.
- Don't let the Questioner shoulder too much responsibility and overcommit.

## *ENNEATYPE SEVEN: THE OPTIMIST*

- TRIAD: *DETACHER*
- ATTENTIONAL FOCUS: Plans. Pleasant options
- GIFT: Optimism
- AVOIDANCE: Pain
- GROWTH PATH: From no limits to restraint
- ESSENCE: Commitment to work
- SHIFT TO SECURE POINT: *THE OBSERVER FIVE*  (Detacher —against arrow)
- SHIFT TO STRESS POINT: *THE PERFECTIONIST ONE* (Defender —with arrow)
- WINGS: *THE BOSS EIGHT* (Defender)
       *THE QUESTIONER SIX* (Defender)

## EXAMPLES OF OPTIMIST SEVEN EDUCATORS: EVERY CLOUD HAS A SILVER LINING

### Ebullient, Mercurial Me

Dick T. chose to be a teacher because he has four months off each year to pursue his many other interests. He likes young people and teaching pays his bills, but he learned from colleagues that aspects of teaching could often become a chore, so he makes sure teaching is enjoyable. Dick keeps creating challenges for himself. Each year he has new students, who bring fresh perspectives. He enjoys planning and evolving different ways to teach the same material; he never teaches a course the same way twice. He teaches freshman Spanish in the Modern Languages department of a large state university. Dick studied Spanish in Spain, and is also fluent in French and Chinese. On the side he maintains a small business as an illustrator and translator of children's books.

Dick's passion is travel, and both through his teaching and his work in the book world he manages to travel extensively. Dick views the world as his oyster to be crisscrossed on a whim. Shortly after he began a love affair with a young French lecturer, he surprised her with a three-day weekend in Vienna. They both loved to dance, enjoyed good food and wine, and seemed amazingly compatible. Dick broke off their relationship at the height of its promise; he felt too young, too carefree to settle down, to fetter himself with a serious relationship. Besides he would never know who else was coming down the pike if he commited himself to one person now.

Dick's charm, his easygoing way with people in general, but young people in particular,  his energy and enthusiasm are appreciated by his students, and not lost on his peers. He sees himself on a par with others and treats learned professors and graduate students alike with an irreverence that verges on rudeness. But Dick knows where to draw that fine line. He gets away with it, and most people seem more amused than miffed. Before he was thirty, Dick was headhunted by a college in Hawaii and offered a senior position in the Dean of Students office. Dick jumped at the opportunity to meet new challenges, to explore another physical environment, to be closer to Asia. Even as he was signing the contract he had planned and fantasized his life in Hawaii.

While his colleagues were bewildered by the rapid change in Dick's career path, and the alacrity with which he accepted the position, Dick was not at all surprised. It seems to him that his life moves on a gilded path, opportunities present themselves without his having to work for them. He has never shared his colleagues' concerns about job security, or building a career. He cannot see much point in setting limits for himself. Dick has great faith in his continued good fortune. "You create your own luck," he says, "you have to be fluid, unencumbered, not tied down with commitments and responsibilities to other people."

**The Helium Balloon**

Lucy W. is in her mid-thirties, she teaches now and has had an interesting career to arrive at this point. At college she was fascinated by the creative and performing arts and eventually majored in film and dance. She took time off during her undergraduate years and toured the country with a folk music revival troupe, where she danced, sang, played the guitar, and did stage management. The troupe went bankrupt in New Mexico, so Lucy worked her way back East in various jobs, from an office job in a silver mine, to a clown's assistant with a circus in the Midwest, to a fire-watcher in Idaho, and a waitress in Chicago. Lucy is fascinated by the pathways that interconnect to form her life's journey. "My curiosity about people, my sense of adventure, the life of freedom on the road, all these speak to the vagabond side of my nature," she says in a wistful way, allowing for the possibility of further travel to faraway places and new adventures that await her.

Lucy studied for a graduate degree combining a training in education with theater. She chose to work with preschoolers because, as she says, they are open and spontaneous, free as the wind, able to fly with her into a fantasy world that they can create together through dance and song. Her first job as a kindergarten teacher did not last long. Lucy felt angered to have the process of free-flowing growth she wanted to develop in the classroom curtailed in any way by the institutional regulations all teachers in schools are expected to uphold. Lucy simply did not see herself as an authority figure, "We are all children together in here, exploring the world through magic song and dance." She felt it corrupting and limiting to have her small pupils line up and walk in single file through the hallways.

The concept of a magic circle intrigued Lucy for many years. After she resigned from her school job, she went to Stonehenge in England to experience firsthand the power of the sacred circle of large stones. This journey started her on a path of travel and study that evolved into a small performing company. she called *The Magic Circle*. The magic circle begins with drums that children beat while sitting in a circle. They move on to explore reeds and other musical instruments that have some circular dimension. Lucy experiments with circles within circles. She has amazing rapport with small children, helps them to create a world of imagination where through storytelling, movement, and song they express freely their anxieties, their dreams, their exuberant life force. Lucy believes forming associative patterns, and seeing interconnections between ideas are as intrinsic to everyone's thinking as they are to her own.

Lucy is hired by many preschools and kindergartens in the school districts where she lives, but latterly her word-of-mouth reputation has grown so large she is feeling overwhelmed. She does not want to have to do the administrative work herself, or hire an administrative assistant. She views the almost-filled appointment book and accounting procedures that flow out of it, as the walls closing in on her, her instinct is to cut loose so she can keep her options open. She is beginning to talk of closing down *The Magic Circle* in its present form so she can explore the options of bringing this work to older children, young adults, even to adult education. One area she is certain about, "I don't want to work with sick children and the really elderly." She adds that their circumstances dampen her ability to be creative, she asks, "How can my mind soar with them?"

### THE OPTIMIST STRATEGY

| *Strengths* | *Weaknesses* |
|---|---|
| Optimism | Evasive |
| Plans, visions, dreams | Entitled |
| Conceptualizing processes | Feels superior |
| Upbeat energy | Charm to disarm |
| Entertaining storyteller | Trouble with commitment |
| Renaissance thinker | Tends to live in a fantasy |
| (interconnections) | world |
| Multioptional thinker | Lives in the future |
| Egalitarian | Avoids (emotional and |
|  | mental) pain |
| Creative imagination | Addicted to excitement and |
|  | change |

## THE E-TYPE SEVEN PROPOSITION

### General Description

### *Futures and Options; No Limits and Knuckling Down*

It is almost impossible when you first encounter Sevens to think (or for them to think) that they are a fear type. There are subtle mechanisms at work here. The blind spot, the projection or illusion for the Optimist, is the idea that if he makes his world upbeat, positive, and energetic, if he throws his ideas, fantasies, and plans at it, if he keep his options open, that becomes the way of the world. He doesn't have to be touched by fear, or fearful manifestations like pain—especially pain, he'll be able to avoid pain, mental pain, emotional pain.

Optimist Seven speakers model the paradox of this position that although Sevens can appear to the world as carefree and entitled—to the extent that people wonder if all Sevens have had an easy life to be this upbeat and positive—often the energy and outlook are a response to circumstances which in some way have given the Optimist the ability to use their E-type intelligence to see other possibilities. There is a preference to move toward powerful mental constructs. Although Sevens may appear to be loose cannons going solo without regard to the group, in fact in the Optimist's teaching, interactions, and relationships there is concern about how others are operating, about leveling and equalizing the group so everyone belongs. This produces a tension for Sevens, because often their future-looking energy doesn't allow them to stay with the agenda in a way they'd like, but the concern for others is definitely there.

The Seven E-type intelligence directs the Optimist to live in the head, to spend as much time as she can there, fantasizing, imagining, planning. While both Points Five and Seven are mental types, Observer Fives like to make connections in order to put a big picture together, while Optimist Sevens like to see the interconnections in associative patterns of ideas. Seven teachers love to plan lessons; they sit for hours planning all the possible ways to come at the material, or a particular course. This educational application of the Seven energy makes good sense. The passion for options, plans, and escape into the world of the imagination plays out as a desire to never teach a course the same way twice, the joy is in planning how to frame change and opportunities that change presents. Every year there is a new group of students, a new perspective, a new way to look at how the dynamic affects the material, how to change the material, to keep options open. Seven educators bring a gift of tremendous enthusiasm, firing of the imagination, opening of the mind, allowing for options—any idea that surfaces is looked at as an option.

Another gift of the Optimist is upbeat energy, bushy tail, and bright eyes from the moment they awake until they go to sleep, if ever they do go to sleep. The energy is palpable, it can drive other people crazy, but it's certainly present, and moves one along. The Seven energy is mental, the mind races on so many divergent tracks that it's often difficult for students to prioritize an understanding of what's important. The Optimist educator regards all ideas as simply ideas of equal standing out there. But most students, most people want to know what is important, "Should I study this, should I study that, where do I put the emphasis?" Seven teachers often leave the lesson open-ended.

The Optimist mind is working so fast that it can trip over itself. There are many circuits running at the same time. A Seven on a panel described how in a workshop she followed a guided visualization: every one had to close their eyes and imagine an empty house. They were to decorate and furnish, walk through the house and visualize each room, the color, the shape. The Optimist says that after she'd been sitting for thirty minutes she'd finished, fitted, furnished, lived in three houses in different parts of the country, while the group leader and everyone else were still working on that one house. This characteristic is often evident in the written work of Seven students. They fail to write down the associative leaps between ideas that their minds take. As readers and evaluators, educators are often at a loss to understand what looks like (oftentimes severe) elliptical thinking they see on the page. This racing mind can be a problem for Seven teachers too, who get so caught up in their own mental energy that they tend to leave their students and others behind.

They need to be reminded of this. The Optimist teacher outlines a plan that in the moment seems great for the lesson. Then a student will ask an interesting question and it can hijack the whole unit for three weeks in a totally different direction. Now that's fine for students who are Sevens, but for a Six, for example, if the teacher has just given an outline for a three-week unit that is thrown out the window seemingly on a whim, no Six is going to feel safe. There are many E-types in the Seven classroom who are not going to feel safe. On the other hand there can be no classroom as exciting as that of the Optimist's, because nothing will ever be done the same way twice.

Sevens can split attention instinctively. An Optimist student can seem to be concentrating and present in the classroom, and she is, but in fact her multitrack mind is split, and a whole other fantasy world is unfolding for her. In our hierarchical, bureaucratized classrooms often it's not acceptable behavior for students to have a multioptional take on the lesson, their minds in many different places, not wanting to sit in their seats, energy running that keeps the foot or pencil tapping. It's a relentless, off-the-wall energy, coupled with being oblivious to its affect on others, a diffuse way of paying attention which doesn't seem to focus on any one particular thing.

In their drive to keep their options open Optimists encounter another blind spot, which can be perceived by other E-types as the Sevens' lack of commitment. For instance, the Optimist's habitual pattern of lateness is rationalized away: I want to keep my options open until the last moment. I will say that I will be at the meeting at 11:00 a.m. and in that moment I mean that I will be there. But if at 10:15 a.m. someone calls and something else comes up, life becomes exciting. I have to be at a meeting at 11:00, but maybe if I get there at 11:15 it will be okay, then I can still fit in this option and do the meeting. Commitment can be a painful button pusher for Sevens.

When a commitment has not been met, the picture gets a bit broader, reframed by the Seven: 11:00 a.m. today? It was next Wednesday, right? The Optimist believes being a little slippery around the edges to avoid the consequences is a well-disguised ploy, but it can be noticeable to others. Sevens reframe the facts. Optimists think they're being creative and original, justified in reframing, because they're avoiding the consequences of causing pain to anyone. Reframing is a Seven blind spot.

The Seven gift is optimism and an ability to enliven the lives of others through storytelling, putting over a great story. Sevens attract people to them, they have many friends, even those people they've met recently are friends, but once out of sight, out of mind. Another notable trait of Sevens is they are egalitarian, they don't see the world in terms of a hierarchy, everyone is on the same level. This can cause problems when it comes to fulfilling authority roles, "No, I'm not an authority figure", says the Seven teacher. The Optimist's bias to equality can skew a classroom culture, an institutional culture. There's a lack of a sense of safety for many E-types in a school where everyone is regarded as equal. At the other end of the scale, Optimist students are often the cool customer in your class who has no respect for you as the authority figure. *You* earn *their* respect, not the other way around.

Sevens are rewarded in the culture and climate of many American schools, by being glib, superficial, able to do the instant presentation, to answer the question as soon as it is asked. Many Sevens, both educators and students, are the icon of the institutional culture: upbeat, mercurial, interactive, taking charge, always bouncy, willing to cooperate. Yet there is more to this Seven than meets the eye. In an interpersonal setting Sevens think themselves into other peoples' minds. This is different from the emotional triad who match others relationally. Sevens mentally model how other people think, how and why they're interacting, reacting. A Seven teacher tries to figure out what every student is thinking, how they make patterns of association, so she can mirror back their thinking, whether big picture, detail-oriented, conservative, or more liberal.

There are several look-alikes on the Enneagram model including the Seven and Three. Both E-types have high energy, a multitask ability, express and embody enthusiasm and positivism, and use rapid speech patterns. These are the obvious similarities; the key difference is that Sevens are all about process, Threes about goals. Sevens love planning the process, the task is done for many Sevens once the planning is over, they don't have to implement the plan to have a feeling of completion. Threes are not particularly interested in planning, they are far more interested in on-the-job decision-making. The planning stage hardly exists, the job's done when the task is completed.

### *Shift to Point Five (Security)*

When Sevens feel secure and they shift to Point Five they relish privacy. Once alone the Seven mind does not slow down, but speeds up, a monkey-mind ballet ensues with the Optimist leaping and cavorting among the tree canopy (free-form ideas) interconnected by vines on which the Optimist swings to and fro in a dizzying display of mental gymnastics.

In my middle and old age I'm allowing myself the time and space to do things which I always felt a little bit guilty about—to read and write. This may sound strange because I am after all an academic. It feels almost a self-indulgence or a luxury to say, "Yes, I can write a few days a week." This is a gift I give myself. I like to be alone, I like to process my thoughts when and how they lead me without the constraints of the form of a stylized academic article for instance.

Even though Point Sevens shift to Point Five when they feel secure, they can access the defense mechanisms of the Five: a disconnect from people and emotions, and relentless pursuit of knowledge.

### Shift to Point One (Stress)

When in situations of stress Sevens shift to Point One, the relentless self-criticism (so familiar to Perfectionists) comes into play. As with Ones, stressed out Sevens do not take kindly to the criticism of others, because nothing you can say is as damning as the internal criticism they've already leveled at themselves.

> Since I was a kid I felt horrible when I made a mistake that I didn't realize I was making. If I realized I was making it, if I could say, "You are absolutely right I did that," I can own up to that. If I do something that I am not aware I am doing, I feel awful about it. Since I was small I would go over it in my head. I replay it almost enough times that it comes out differently. I imagine myself doing the same thing differently, not having made the mistake I made. So I go over it again and again in my head. Or I explain it and explain it, I have conversations in my head with the person that I did this to, to help him better understand why I didn't intend the outcome. Those kinds of situations tend to get me stuck. I can't find another process for being wrong.

Even though Point Sevens shift to Point One when they feel stress, they can access the gifts of the One: ethical and moral correctness, and keen analytic ability.

### Key Characteristics

### Optimism

Sevens are almost unrelenting in their determination to see the bright side, to put a positive spin on events, particularly those events they deem to be painful or depressing. Their optimism is rooted often in the desire to escape from pain. While Sixes employ a strategy of worst-case scenario thinking to contain their fear, Sevens employ a strategy of best-case scenario thinking. They can't bear to be negative, not while the lifelong defense mechanism of escaping into a mental world filled with limitless options works so well for them. This speaker remarks on how she has a need to make the wake she is attending a less gloomy occasion.

> I can recall on many occasions going to wakes and funerals, and granted while people are there who are in a glum sort of way, I have a need to make it better, to talk about the accomplishments of the person, or what they contributed. It has to be positive, it can't be negative because in my mind I can't conceive of not ever seeing that person again,

it's painful. It's a whole lot easier for me to be able to have others see the better side of the worst side that they are looking at.

This speaker is aware that her optimism, her "up energy" is at odds with her husband's response. He needs time to stay in the moment, she needs to move on. It is painful to her to be around his state of mind.

My husband has a different personality to me, he does get depressed, and he kind of sinks into it. He needs the time to process, sometimes it can take days or weeks. I have learned to let him do that, but there's a point where I just say, "Okay enough. We've been doing this for three days, you've gone over those problems. I feel sorry for you, but can we move on? You need to do something about this." I think my husband would say there are times when I'm too up-energy. I just want to move him on.

### Commitment

It is not that Sevens are not commited, it's that they see potential in other options, but once they say they'll be there, they will, *because it is their choice*. This teacher is commited to her job because of the possibilities of change it offers her.

What keeps me in teaching is that things change all of the time. You have a new group of students with different ways of seeing things. There are new things that I have read that have changed my perspective. You can go deeper and deeper into it. There are so many levels to this job. I can spend a whole career and never feel as though I have exhausted this subject, I just think the variety and complexity are fascinating.

Commitment lasts for as long as the Optimist decides he should be there. In a powerful mental construct Sevens can feel they have fulfilled their commitment by completing *in their heads* what they have undertaken, they don't have to actualize it in the world.

I can be committed when I'm aware of the fact that I'm making a commitment. But I know for myself that I will make commitments, then when it's no longer a commitment, I'll just move on. One of the more interesting things about me is that I've always felt that if I can't do it, I don't need to do it, I don't need to prove things. Once I get it, understand it, and I can see myself doing it, that's it, I don't have to have the fact of doing it. I figure out a lot of things in my mind and never have to do them. It's about seeing it all and then not having to do it.

The following speaker describes his process of completing his Ph.D. dissertation. He was commited to getting it done, but on his terms of no limits and keeping his options open.

My dissertation was published before it was approved. It addressed probably twenty questions that had never been asked before and only one of my advisors was helpful to me. He said, "Each of these is actually a paper, write them up as papers, and get them published." I was having such a hard time with the rest of my committee who wanted me to make it smaller and I wanted to make it bigger. He was right. I published all of my papers. A study came out of who was publishing in my field. There were senior people, and me, and I still didn't have my Ph.D. But I had published all of my papers. In fact they finally let me graduate; they said, "Well, put all of your papers together."

### Reframing

For Sevens their worldview is not simply a question of saying this is true and that isn't, or, yes, the world is a terrible place, yes, the world is a wonderful place. Sevens pay attention to a certain aspect of that reality, but one where the possibility exists that at a future time a brilliant plan will come together to interconnect the whole. In the meantime it makes sense to reframe reality to reflect the possible perfect future. Reframing can be denial, rationalization, or thinking things out in a way that isn't true—not to see a different side, but to hold onto the glorious possibilities that are present. This Seven educator teaches us a fundamental truth about Seven students.

A Seven child won't say something is "painful," they'll say it's "interesting." They'll instinctively put on a positive spin, even if it was an awful experience, they'll reframe the negative to give it a more positive view. If you have a student who reframes a lot you may want to ask them if something painful is going on. It's their way of getting out of the pain.

This Seven knows she reframes reality, and she puts a positive spin on the benefits of doing so. But she helps us understand that what appears to others as denial, has a definite rationale for the Seven.

You can reframe things in a way which is simply denial: oh well that didn't happen., it was a learning experience, now I can move on. The fact is reframing can be positive. Maybe you couldn't have gotten to where you are now unless you passed through that pain. I tell students that the point about drafts for their papers is to get it down; and I believe that for myself, then you can look at it and it may not be the way you want to organize the book, or the course, or the article, but you have to have done that before you can move. So I think it is a technique and a positive one to incorporate past experience.

### No Limits

In many ways the Seven energy feeds on itself, so there is a constant need to replenish a high level of excitement—intellectual and emotional—interest, and options. This state of mind can be described as gluttony, a desire to sample the positive opportunities life offers without limits. Sevens are uncomfortable in situations where they feel limited.

If something doesn't work, I'll try something else, I don't linger too long on it. If I'm working with a student outside of class, and the suggestions that I give her don't work, I'll find some other approach. I think sometimes I can probably be overwhelming to kids in that way, because I'll abandon one plan, try another one before they have exhausted the possibilities, or understood what I was trying to get at with the first. That's such a natural place for me to be. If something doesn't work, then I try something else. I am never wedded to one thing so much that I can't abandon it and do something else if that doesn't happen to be working. Even if it's working well I might do something else that doesn't work quite as well because it seems more interesting to me.

Feeling free to taste from the smorgasbord of life is part of the Seven E-type intelligence.

From my own experience I would do anything that gave me a rush and took me out of the moment, including drugs, or driving motorcycles at a one hundred some odd miles an hour. Experimenting was no scary thing to me as a kid, I mean it certainly was part of the "smorgasbord" of life, I wanted all of my options. It got turned on me though; I realized how certain choices may limit my options in a drastic way, like getting killed, or becoming an addict, and I didn't want to do those things then.

This free-floating lifestyle, like a helium balloon without a string, can have negative consequences for the Seven. In a paradoxical sense, inherent in the experience of a life of no limits is in itself limiting. Milan Kundera well described this state of being in the title of his 1992 novel, *The Unbearable Lightness of Being*. As this Seven educator explains.

I feel as though I've spent a lot of my life planning, thinking of things: unfinished articles, unfinished books, unfinished drawings, unfinished ideas for conferences that will never happen. In fact I got rewarded because I received prizes, tenure, book contracts on the potential of my ideas. At a certain point you feel afraid because it's fine to be twenty-five and even thirty-five and be valued for your potential, but as you move into the forties you want to feel you have actually done something. I'd like to bring projects to a conclusion and feel that enormous satisfaction. I'd like to finish that article, have it published to see that I have turned my experience and thoughts and understanding of patterns into meaningful form which is visible for others. I want the public manifestation, visible, concrete, so it's not just airy and connections, and so on. Now if I say I'm going to do something, it saves me an enormous amount of energy if I actually do it.

### Limits

Limits are discomforting; the following speaker felt constrained by her inability to master Spanish.

I had an experience on my sabbatical of trying to study Spanish. but I wasn't any good at it. I was in Mexico, I had to speak it, and I got all bottled up. It was horrible. I got incredibly depressed. I was limited by my own expectations of myself and my inabilities in a new field. I didn't like it at all. I found a way out. I was there with a friend, so I decided to defer to her and let her speak for me. I couldn't dwell there without being enormously uncomfortable. That's the first time I recognized that in teaching I have a job that fits my personality well because teaching is a work situation that allows me the kind of flexibility to go into a different direction and try something new, it fits my strengths. I don't know what I would do if I was stuck in a job where I felt the way I did when I was trying to learn Spanish because it was awful.

### Entitlement— "It's not entitlement, it's making sure all of us are equal, that everybody has the same experience."

Optimists do not easily recognize that they carry a sense of entitlement. They find it difficult to put into words their sense of this characteristic. In many ways entitlement is tied into their desire to be egalitarian. Feeling entitled to assume an equal footing with anyone else is a way of lessening any authority's power over them, including those that set limits. Optimists feel entitled to ignore rules, disregard limitations, take risks. If others don't achieve certain results because they stick with the rules, Sevens can't see why they should be similarly constrained.

If something good happens to me I accept it with good cheer instead of rejecting it, or feeling I don't deserve it. Other people are envious, or angry at me, in a rage, because they didn't get it. I think, so what's the problem already, you could have gotten it. I don't think the rules apply to me, if somebody else is too fearful to try, then they think I've a sense of entitlement because I ought to feel as constrained by the situation as they do. But truthfully I don't.

### Egalitarianism—Equalizing Authority

Sevens are part of the fear triad, one of the ways their E-type intelligence directs them to lessen their fear is by equalizing authority. If everyone else is on the same level as the Seven, the Optimist can use a charm and disarm approach to move the authority to their side. Sevens can become markedly anti-authoritarian if the authority seems to want to limit or restrict their options in any way. Feeling entitled and superior are two strands of this overarching strategy that Optimists use to justify their own behavior. Sevens bring the authority inside, they claim it as their own. *They* choose to commit themselves, *they* decide on this option or that one, *they* keep the deadline—permission is internal.

For me I am my authority, it's never a question. If I'm in a situation where authority is an issue I equalize authority. I call myself a faculty member not an associate professor, I talk about colleagues, as opposed to people in different levels of the organization. I feel I do that with students, being equal on a path together with different gifts and strengths and weaknesses.

Varying explanations of why Sevens have these characteristics take interesting twists. This Optimist equalizes the social setting because she projects her own fear of being left out.

I realized one day when I was working in a self-esteem program and trying to make a child feel comfortable in the rest of the group, that I am that child I was trying to protect. I remember what it was like to be left out, I don't want others to suffer the same experience.

### *Planning and Options*

We have seen why the Seven E-type intelligence directs Optimists to having many options, but there is an equal drive toward planning. This is the focus of attention of the Optimist. Many Sevens use the words "fluid" or "fluidity" to describe the way their mind works. The planning patterns are like pieces of mercury rolling on a table, there is fluidity of movement, the mercury can take any shape, it picks up smaller pieces of itself, and like fluid lets the drops dissolve into the greater whole. Those smaller pieces may be fascinating daydreams, intricate thoughts, futuristic ideas, all parts of planning. What may look to others as evidence of scattered thinking, to the Seven are the pieces before the plan coheres.

My teaching is fluid, and big. When I sit down to plan a unit that I do, I'll take a two-three week period of time and construct it around an idea. There may be other things I want to do in that block of time, but there is always a central idea. We can drop other things into it. We can go into a place that the students want to go, some other direction. I'll bring it back at the end so that the idea has closure. It's a longer block of time, it's not a fifty-minute period. The other thing that I try to do is help them make connections and see patterns. I'll ask, "What connection does that have with anything else that you have learned before? Brainstorm: does it remind you of anything? Is there a similarity here to anything that you have learned before?" Quite often, they will bring things in from the beginning of the year when we discussed it for five minutes, but they will make a connection.

The next three characteristics are part of the way Sevens pay attention through planning.

*Fascination with Ideas.* My fascination with ideas plays out in my own work in that it frames the way I think. I've never taught a whole unit the same way twice. I may use particular articles, or selections from the text, or documents over again. I have a stack of twenty notebooks for each course I have taught. I always find something interesting that changes the way I construct the class. One year a boy I taught figured out an issue that changed the whole way I taught that unit the next time. I brought new readings into it because they were more helpful and understandable. Every time I come across a compelling idea it takes me in a different direction, it becomes the framework for how I teach the class the next time. There are a handful of interesting ideas that change the way I see my students, change the way I see the material I'm teaching, change the way I frame a problem.

*Flying Ideas.* The students that I have difficulty reaching are kids who are stuck in a concrete, detailed place— those kids who don't get to the ideas. They don't see the patterns easily. They are a challenge for me. I work hard with them, I meet with them after class. They are more challenging than the students who take some risks intellectually, see the patterns easily, or are willing to try. In terms of relationships with my colleagues, I think that I get impatient with people who are fearful of change, they want to do the same things over and over again because it is safer, at least that's my interpretation. I do get impatient with that, I want them to take a risk and to try something new and to let go. I want them to be responsive. I do get impatient with colleagues, but I don't get impatient with students because I have a different role in my relationship with kids.

*Interconnections (Patterns of Ideas).* I think that information doesn't have meaning except when you make a pattern of it. Each individual class finds a different pattern. I organize my courses around whatever pattern happens to strike me from one year to the next. I try to find a way to not make my pattern the rule, so that the students are able to see their own patterns in what they are learning. Ideas are the patterns that they make out of the information— when the students are focused, when they are working on an idea, when they are talking to each other about it, when they are getting deeper and deeper into it, and they can articulate it, and see it as their own articulation. I think that's a big plus.

### Modeling Students' Thinking

Seven educators know that their interactions with students are mainly on a mental level. Optimists read others mentally.

I try hard to get to know how each student thinks, how they see themselves, what are the components of their thinking, to understand why they frame a question differently from how someone else in the class does. What particular issues interest them is important. Whether they are detail people, or big-picture people, or like to take an alternative perspective and see themselves as a conservative and therefore frame everything that way. I try hard to figure out how each student approaches an issue, to help them understand, and the rest of the class understand, so they can either challenge the perspective or develop it. My best interactions with students are around my appreciation of their individual thinking.

### Racing Mind (Mental Energy)

This feature of racing mind is generally regarded by Sevens as a huge plus. They gain great pleasure from their ability to think fast along different tracks. The joy lies in making the interconnections between concepts— "knowledge is in the links." The following description is a clear articulation of this process.

My mind and how it works— the image of knowledge and the mind that I have is shaped like the Internet, a web, I'm constantly going out adding more links to Web pages. I find people who do their own Web pages and do their own research to make it interesting, I couldn't do that, I find it constraining, restrictive, but I can make a link to it. I find knowledge is in the links, not in the stopping places. My mind is like a net that covers a wide place, and then it's like a net that is weighted down in certain places. My talent is making links all over.

This Optimist, a senior administrator in a large school, has had to learn from others that her mental drive can be so strong it's sometimes discomforting.

My energy is absolutely intellectual. I have had to learn that through other people. I am comfortable with my own energy level, I operate there well. I do know that I am too fast for lots of people. When I find that happening in a classroom, the students will let me know that they don't understand, that I have to slow down, then I will slow down. Colleagues have an emotional response to this. I'm a senior administrator and they feel as though I am bulldozing something through, or I am taking control, or being too powerful. I have had to learn that through feedback from them. I have had to learn to slow down to give them time and space to respond not only to the idea that I am presenting, but also to the emotional energy that they are feeling. When that happens, the process is in my head. I say to myself, you know this person, to them you know it feels as though you are trying to railroad something through, I deal with it rationally. They respond to it emotionally. I have had to learn that through other people explaining it to me. It's not something that I understood myself.

A similar phenomenon is also true for another administrator, the head of a junior high. It is interesting to note the sense of entitlement evident in her final statement.

> The speed of my mind, I've had a certain amount of problems with that. Not with students so much, because one of the things that's interesting is trying to figure out all different kids; that's so intriguing that while your mind is doing that, you're doing a pretty good job of teaching. When I was in the classroom, before I became a school principal, I was good at reaching students, knowing where they're coming from and slowing down for them, also being open enough that if they said, you're going too fast, I'd slow down, I kept open communication. But with adults I don't cut that same slack, or I didn't in quite the same way. I assumed they could follow, or that it was as interesting to them as to me to go off on tangents. People would either think I wasn't listening, or they would tell me you're going way too fast. I'd have to teach people how to give me feedback. At first if people told me, "You don't listen, you just talk to yourself," it sounded harsh and painful to me, it was extremely hard to hear. But then in order to avoid future pain—which is a big important thing to me anyway—is to learn how people work with me. I always say to my faculty, "You've got to slow me down." I work closely with a school counselor in my role as head. She puts on brakes for me all of the time with all of her questions, especially when I want to change the whole grading system. She comes at it from a desperate point of view of getting the students into high school. But her questions are just what I need. I learned to help people see where their value is to me as a thinker, and line up the right people to put the brakes on me and slow me down.
>
> Because I can have at least three different tracks in my mind at once, literally have whole conversations with people and be thinking of something else, so I don't know what I'm saying, I've taught my husband and children to verify appointments and such—if it's something important. They must ask, "Mom are you there? Now repeat it back ... you're picking me up at 3:00 from soccer today." It's pathetic, but they've learned where they're going to get left high and dry, and not to assume I heard it. They write things down for me; you have to train people.

This Seven educator gives sound advice about allowing Seven students some latitude to play with the ideas racing in their minds.

> In terms of teachers with Seven students, it's important when their minds are racing in sixteen different directions to be given a chance to play with that because if they don't, there's no fun in learning. What happens sometimes in my job now is that as a teacher or as a student,

my mind races so fast and gets beyond people, and that drives them nuts. They say, "You're not listening to me," or the teacher might think you're off track, but you know you can write the paper the night before if you've known the topic long enough to allow for this play time in your mind. It's important to have that space to play between when you have to perform.

The following example serves as a sound illustration of the Seven's penchant for making concrete interconnections—in this instance, her Picasso-like attitude to reformatting her dolls!

I was a child of creativity, I grew up when we didn't have all of the extras that we have now, computers and the kinds of things that are wonderful for kids. There I was with my clothespins, making an airplane, or doing things with chalk on the driveways, seeing everything as pieces you put together and have fun. I can remember pulling doll heads off and putting one doll head on another's body to make it different. It wasn't made that way, but I liked the way it came out.

### Challenge—Being Motivated and Keeping Motivated

Optimists generally agree on two key facets of how they are motivated: one is that they have to be interested and find challenges to keep them curious, and the other is that *they* have decide to take on the project.

My motivation needs to come from within, it can't come from outside. Once I want to do something, I can be incredibly focused, but it's got to come from myself. I have a huge responsibility to meet all kinds of deadlines and run programs on time, I still think of a million different ways to do it. But in order to come through I have to narrow some of my options. I say, "Okay, I'm going to write this handbook for this program, I've got to get done, I'm going to give myself one week to revise it, I'm going to do it in this way." I discipline myself because otherwise I'll continue to play, play, play out ideas all by myself. In a classroom, if a teacher let me play around with ideas and let me keep coming back and doing it a lot of different ways, I could be brilliant.

This speaker sharply defines the connection for the Optimist between sparking interest and staying motivated.

When I was twelve years old I was supposed to go to the prom and my mother left me in my dress in the afternoon and I happened to be reading the Girl Scout magazine called *Polly Pigtails*. When she came back my entire closet was taken out, clothes strewn across the room at which point I lost interest. It was a tremendous effort to get things back into the closet. You see you get everything out ready to do and then you lose interest. It's hard to bring things to closure. That closet at age twelve has been a metaphor for how I operate in my life. It isn't to say that I don't get things done, the business of pressure is one thing, another is the difference between someone telling me to do it and me deciding myself. As long as it's interesting there isn't a problem. It's a completely internal permission, an internal deadline that is most effective. With external deadlines it's not my most productive work or free-flowing creativity.

Life should preferably be fun, Sevens tell us, fun is in new interests, new mental challenges, living in the future, not being dragged down in mundane matters of the present.

I've taught 1st, 2nd, 3rd, 4th, 5th grade, and more. My favorite time was teaching 1st grade and 8th grade algebra at the same time, sometimes with both groups in the same room. You move on to a new challenge. The fun is to move into an area of incompetence, for others it's frightening, and to me it's frightening when I start thinking, "Gee I like this job, what I'm earning now, but what if I run out of challenges, I know I won't want to do it anymore." I like the people, the place, but I know if I'm not challenged, I don't want to stay there. I look for new challenges. People are always relieved when I say at the end of the year, "Boy I can see that we have some new challenges." I literally ended the year-end faculty meeting telling my teachers, "You know that thing about closure, about coming to the end, for me closure is about thinking of all of the pieces that we're going to go on to next year." The teachers were reeling, "Lord, we haven't even put our grades in the grade book and you're planning how to start the first day of school."

### Avoiding Pain

At base many of the positive characteristics of the Seven mask a flight away from fear. Pain arouses the greatest fear, it is avoided at all costs. By being upbeat, talkative and bright, intellectual and rational, Optimists avoid what is painful. There is a fear that if they go too deeply into one area they will be found lacking, which is painful, so they become fascinated by many ideas and interests. The same dynamic is at work with commitment, they fear commitment and the pain it may bring so they seek options and no limits. Many Sevens do not know they are missing a fundamental element of life: open, emotional commitment to both what is joyful and what is painful.

We do a good tap dance, so that you don't know that we are afraid or that something is hurting. We are good at pushing pain down, but as we get older we know that growth doesn't happen until you start feeling the pain.

This Seven became aware of his disconnect with essential aspects of being alive. What was extremely bothersome to him was that he had no way into the world of emotional experience.

Well, until about four or five years ago, everything was great, life was great, life is still great, but there is a difference. About four years ago I realized that I couldn't identify my feelings, that I was so disconnected from people, from my family, from my children, from the losses in my life, from the longing in my life for the things I didn't have that I wanted to have, that it was too awful, too painful to even think about it. I couldn't get there, there was no way for me to get there, I had no pathway in. Anything about going to the feeling of loss, or what's lost, the longing in my life for the things that aren't there, for the bad things I've done in my life. That's the pain for me, that's the pain I avoid.

This next speaker cites a poignant circumstance where she knew she was keeping pain at bay through an intense effort to intellectualize her mother's death. She watched other people to see how "to do" emotions, or how to set up a framework for commiting her ideas to paper.

When my mother died, I was twenty-one and the priest came to our house. I had to talk to him about what was needed to be done. We spoke on an intellectual level, about funerals, rituals. I was not dealing with the whole idea that I was the oldest of three children and that I had a responsibility to them and that our mother was dead. To me the event was experienced on an intellectual plain as an interesting conversation about rites. The priest is telling me all of these things I have to do and think about. I want to alleviate the pain for everyone else instead of feeling it for myself. I didn't have the words to talk about my emotions that other people do. It's one of the reasons why I get into the interesting, intellectual aspects of whatever sad is happening. So something I've done is listen and watch other people who can be with their emotions. There are other painful parts of my life, writing is a painful experience for me, to put my ideas in writing. I watch other people who seem to do it better than me and I try it on, I use their words and watch what they do because it gives me a structure for what I wouldn't know how to do.

This Optimist school principal shares two painful situations, one public, one personal, and what she learned about her pattern of avoidance. It is interesting to note how often Sevens state that they watch others to learn—in this instance, how to show emotions.

This year we had a student die, a 6th grader, it was painful for everyone. But what's been hard for me and it bothers me, is talking to the child's parents now when they come to school, it's hard for me to be close to their pain. There are students at our school who are so much better at dealing with this than me. I'm learning by watching other adults and children who can get into the pain in a way that I can't and I noticed that the fear is that it will be too painful.

I have to experience the pain in private, I'll be the person who doesn't cry in the public moment, but it will get triggered at a different point and I will just cry and cry and cry. It happened on the same day that this boy died, my dog died. For about a week after the boy died I delayed mourning the dog. People thought I was so efficient, I could handle this so well, I was so steady. The second week I was dysfunctional. I cried constantly, I didn't stop crying about the dog. It was through the dog I allowed myself to feel the pain of the student who died.

The other way that I try to avoid pain is that I move on. When I was in college and high school, I always dropped my boyfriends, I moved on. Of course, there's always another option and falling in love is a new possibility and that's exciting. I know that I avoided the pain that maybe he'd get tired of me before I got tired of him. This does seem central. I'm always thinking of new ideas, if I imagine that my husband might die, I have a plan of what I'm going to do. Since we've been married I've told him, "If you die here's my plan. Maybe it sounds morbid to you, but that's how I make sure that I can cope." He doesn't think that way at all, he tells me how he'd shut down, his reaction is different. I'm always in a future place, I think that has something to do with what might happen if I stayed present long enough and it was painful.

### Growth Path: From No Limits to Restraint

An Optimist's growth path is to move from an expectation that the experiences life offers are a cornucopia of delights created expressly for the Seven's tasting, to a sense of finding some fulfillment in the routine, in knuckling down to doing committed work. Sevens need to let go of trying to stoke the inner excitement, of being entitled to the first bite and the first taste of everything, to the idea that the world is my oyster and I sail through the world. They need to develop a sense of restraint, a type of sobriety: I will say no to those options, I will commit myself, I will follow through on this.

It's almost as though there are so many options open to you, the world is a banquet and you want to taste everything, you're excited about everything, you want to do everything, you think you can do everything, it's very exciting. When I got married I was a painter, and my husband thought he married an artist because I did that for a while, I got good at it. Then I decided I liked cooking, so I became a cook, and I started catering the best parties. Then I wanted to do something else, work with children, that's where my love is, so I don't change as much now, I'm much more commited.

### Quality of Essence: Commitment to Work

The essence quality of the Seven is a commitment to work—to sobriety—to quieting down, to creating fulfillment of being by being present in the moment. This state is achieved by being emotionally and intellectually present, not fleeing into one's head, but constrained willingly by narrowed options, and not taking the mental escape route into planning.

Here it is summertime, the best time, I love summer, but my mind is racing already to fall's coming; and when fall comes, winter is around the corner, and I will talk to people about that. I'm three months ahead of time, I think it might be the same way with pain. Here's some pain but oh, there's another option, things are going to happen three months from now when my mind's not in the pain, my mind is three months ahead of time. I wish often I could stay in the moment, quieten my mind, appreciate what I am experiencing.

## What Optimist Students Say

### Multitask Mind

I draw pleasure from having a schedule which I have to adhere to. It's kind of weird, I think, but when I have things to do, places to go, people to see, I tend to get excited: "Wow, this is pretty cool. I've got things to do, I'm not sitting around doing nothing, I'm getting involved, doing stuff. And that's cool, I like that."

### Equalizing Authority

As a student in junior high school I decided that teachers had to prove themselves to me. I'd go into the classroom, I didn't care about the authority; they would start teaching and the ones who taught I would listen to, the ones who were dull teachers, it didn't matter. I thought of these people as people just like myself: they drive to school, they go home at night, this is the job they have taken. The ones that I respected were the ones who were teaching.

and

For me to regard someone else as an authority figure that person has to get my respect. When I first meet somebody, it's as if, "You're just another person and you're my equal." But if that person shows they're worthy of being an authority figure and worthy of respect I'll follow them and heed what they're saying.

### Commitment

Commitment is working hard on something, doing something. I'll do something: write a paper, read a book, write a speech, because I want to do that, not because someone tells me to do it. I don't commit myself if I don't want to do something. A lot of times if I find it's not interesting, I'm not going to do it. There's so much happening around in the world and life is kind of short.

### Split Attention

I don't usually tune out in class that quickly. I have a pretty good attention span. If I'm not interested, my conscious mind switches off and I withdraw a little bit. I go back into my head and start thinking about different things rather than what's going on in class.

### Mental Energy

When I have deadlines I think I'll do something by myself and do it in my head and work it out. I'm in my head a lot, I think in my head, I do a lot of analyzing of what's going on in other people's heads, or I try to. When I'm feeling I have more space I'm more apt to go out and talk to people and get their insight.

### Creativity

I think teachers should allow for my creativity. In my educational process, when I get a syllabus which is the regime—go from step one to step eight—I always put it in a different order because that's what makes sense to me. I do a lot of discussion in order to prove my point. I can't learn traditionally, I can learn quite a lot in depth but I have to do it juxtaposed, it has to be in my order to make sense. I realized from when I was a kid that I see things differently from other people. I spent quite a bit of time until I convinced the individual teacher that if you wanted to get the optimal out of me, I had to learn how to do it my way. For example, I can remember kindergarten and having a teacher say we're going to learn the alphabet. I learned it backwards, purposely, because it was different from everybody else. When the next day came I was the first, I was so excited, I put up my hand, I demanded to be first and I started off, *zyx*, it freaked out the rest of the kids who forget how to do it *abc*-wise and I got a kick out of that. But this is me—this is me starting out and my whole school life is like that.

### Interconnections

I see lots of connections, I want to ask what do artists think about this, what do anthropologists think about this. Most teachers know their subject well and don't link it to other disciplines, or other subject matters, or historically. So for me a lot of my teachers don't know enough, they haven't considered things. One teacher in high school told me, "You don't understand the impact you have on these other teachers, you make them feel ignorant because you're basically saying to them why haven't you thought about this, or that." The idea that as student I was making my teachers feel ignorant was unbelievable, because I have this sense that I'm never done, I've never finished finding out, making connections.

### Curiosity and Fun

I had a lot of curiosity and as a toddler, I was attached by a harness to an apple tree. I'd wrap the harness around a tree, run one way and then the other, break it and toddle off to my neighbors. I've always had that curiosity and interest.

and

I don't like memorization at all, it is not something I do well or easily. If I can ask questions, if I can explore ideas and find out answers from people, then I feel I'm learning and can move myself on. I'm at a large college, big classes, all multiple choices, so I couldn't ask questions. I changed my major from the sciences into the humanities where I could read on my own with less memorization.

### Brief Interview with an Optimist Educator

*Q. What is your teaching style?*
A: My teaching style is fluid. I'm not an authority in the classroom. I feel as though I'm an equal with my students to the extent that they each bring a perspective into the classroom. I certainly am an authority in terms of my knowledge of the material—it's greater. I understand it's my responsibility to frame the questions, to frame the discussion, to choose what goes into what they read, and the kinds of questions that start a discussion. I feel as though I am a learner along with them each year.

*Q. What do you look for in your students?*
A: What I look for in my students is investment in their work, energy, the desire to understand something, and a unique perspective.

*Q. What is important in the way you present material?*
A: What's important to me in the way I present material is coherence, I'm not comfortable with discrete bits of information that don't connect, there has to be a pattern to it. That changes all of the time, not from one day to the next, but certainly within a unit of time, within a semester, within a year. The pieces have to fit together.

*Q. What will students say of you?*

A: Students will say that I love what I do, that I have a passionate interest for history, that I care about them. I encourage them to think independently. Sometimes it feels risky, and it always feels challenging to them. I do ask them to think for themselves. I don't give them as much guidance sometimes as they might like.

*Q. Why do you teach?*
A: I teach because I love it, I love the kids, and every year is different.

*Q. How do you communicate?*
A: My communications style is verbal, articulate, pretty tightly reasoned, precise. My use of language is precise. I frame ideas carefully and articulate them carefully, but I feel as though I am always listening for the nuance, the greater complexity, the change of direction.

*Q. What is your attitude to preparing teaching plans?*
A: Preparing teaching plans is a joy. I read something, it takes me into a new direction, how to organize this is great fun. I love thinking about how I'm going to do something in class. How I will teach this differently, about what I would do with this document if I have used it before, taking it into a new direction, about how I am going to incorporate the perspective I put on something last year into something this year. I can spend hours sitting at my desk thinking about how I'm going to do this. I go through these intricate plans. I now type them out on a computer and paste them into my notebook, then I can cut and paste and change more easily. When you write things down, then you have to write in the margins, now that I can use a computer, I can just go back three steps and change something because I might have changed the way I thought about it by the time I got to step five or six. I love doing it.

*Q. What do you like about the classroom?*
A: What I like about the classroom is the students. I love talking with them about ideas, about the difficulty they might have figuring out why something is the way it is, or how to understand it, or hearing their ideas, seeing them in action.

*Q. What don't you like about the classroom?*
A: What I don't like about the classroom is that sometimes things don't end up coherently, the bell rings, or you can't finish something for another reason. I hate to leave good ideas hanging there and not resolve them.

## Practical Tips

*For Optimists to Work with Themselves*

- Be aware when planning and fantasizing replace doing.

- Find ways to make mundane tasks interesting, so you see them through.
- Be aware that you try to keep your options open.
- Once you have the plan, commit yourself to a course of action.
- When you know you are reframing facts, get a reality check.
- Make yourself accountable, don't try to slip through the cracks.
- Encourage others with your optimism and energy.
- Be aware your energy can be too high-octane for many others.
- Be respectful, even if you regard everyone as an equal.

*For Others who Work with Optimists*

- Help Sevens ground their energy through structuring tasks into interesting, disparate projects.
- Give Optimists a safe place to play with the many ideas racing in their minds.
- Let Sevens express their buoyancy and enthusiasm.
- Call Optimists on it when they reframe reality.
- Call Optimists on it when their sense of entitlement causes them to ignore or belittle others.
- Help train Sevens in the discipline of meeting deadlines and seeing through a process.
- Appreciate the Optimist's gift of spell-binding and entertaining storytelling.
- Help Sevens get in touch with their emotions; ask "What are you feeling?" not "What are you thinking?"
- Try to keep Optimists present in the proceedings of the moment; make them aware when you notice they've escaped into a fantasy world.

## *ENNEATYPE EIGHT: THE BOSS*

- TRIAD: *DEFENDER*
- ATTENTIONAL FOCUS: Power and control
- GIFT: Harnessing their force to empower others
- AVOIDANCE: Vulnerability
- GROWTH PATH: From excess to trusting sufficiency
- ESSENCE: Truth (Fairness and Justice)
- SHIFT TO SECURE POINT: *THE HELPER TWO* (Attacher —against arrow)
- SHIFT TO STRESS POINT: *THE OBSERVER FIVE* (Detacher —with arrow)
- WINGS: *THE OPTIMIST SEVEN* (Detacher)
  *THE PEACEKEEPER NINE* (Defender)

## EXAMPLES OF BOSS EIGHT EDUCATORS: WHO'S IN CONTROL HERE?

### The Justice Seeker

Molly M. found it intolerable. She wanted to find a place for herself as an educator, but she could not deal with the public school system. All those rules established God only knows how many years ago, to protect the so-called power of the authority, doing little to enhance the cause of learning. The whole bureaucratic system bent her out of shape—you met deadlines and wrote in preparation books, students ate the same cardboard lunch at the same time, everyday, because that's the way it was always done. Molly couldn't abide the small-mindedness of the system.

The students in her junior high classroom saw a different side of Molly. Despite her discontent, her passion was huge for helping them to learn. The classroom was her territory and she made the rules there. Molly believed education was about empowering students her way, largely this translated into allowing them to operate within a framework she controlled so everyone was treated fairly. Big words for Molly are *truth* and *fairness*. Every year the students had to stand and state their commitment to keeping the classroom environment safe, physically and emotionally, to do all their homework all the time, to support each other. If a commitment was not honored, Molly set up a procedure to process the broken agreement. There was no punishment, the student simply had to tell his fellows what it felt like to break a commitment. The other students shared with the "culprit" how it felt to be interacting with him/her. Molly believed in justice. Moral issues were black and white for her; putting people on the spot taught them to speak the truth for themselves. Truth was the great lesson, the way to empowerment. She particularly wanted the students to understand that they had a voice in the procedures of their classroom. The test scores of her students rose every year. Despite their perturbation about Molly's forceful challenges, and their bemusement about her unorthodox approach to teaching, Molly's principal and superintendent had to support her as a teacher.

Years went by, Molly continued to try to take on the school system in toe-to-toe combat. But in the end, the slow-moving inertia of the system wore her down. One year, over Christmas break, she resigned suddenly. Friends told her that the powers that be were pleased to see the end of her, long since she'd been labeled as a troublemaker. The thought of abandoning her current crop of commited junior high schoolers bothered her, but she rationalized that as they'd had a full term of commitment, many were empowered already.

For some time Molly had been interested in the new alternative high school that opened in her town. Around New Year she marched into the director's office and volunteered to start a special education unit. She loves alternative education. The students are underdogs in the system, in the same way she felt she had been. They are the ones with learning disabilities, gifted children who need a place where they can fit, where they can belong, where they can find their strength, find the part of them that is strong and empower it. This is a place for her too.

### I'm in Charge

Marty V. is a dapper man, lean, lithe, of medium height, yet his presence is large; you can feel his forceful, almost belligerent energy preceding him as he walks through the halls and across the school grounds. He's been teaching at the school for almost thirty-five years, with a couple of breaks of several years each, when he ventured into other fields. His most recent stint, with breaks for sabbaticals, is twenty years. When asked why he returned to the same school, he barks his answer with a self-deprecating laugh: "I love the place. I love the kids. I love teaching. It took me a while to find that out."

Marty always wears a jacket and tie, he seems put together from a handbook for Ivy League teachers. But generations of students will attest that this is no laid-back preppie. Marty is a passionate man, his passion is intellectual, he drives his students forward in a continual battle to lead them to victory over the body of knowledge they should conquer. Marty's own vocabulary is peppered with military terms—plan our campaign strategy, wage war on sloppy writing, I'll take no prisoners at exam time, conquer the GSAT or come back on your shield, we have to hold the line against the creeping soft-headedness of the television generations.

This latter admonishment has become Marty's signature tune in department meetings. His great battle is being waged against not allowing reading to become redundant in this age of visual learning, to keep to past standards of reading requirements, to closely guard the great canon of Western literature and thought. Marty is relentless in his pursuit. Provosts, deans, assistant deans, department chairs, departmental colleagues, colleagues in other departments—all are accorded the heat of Marty's passion for his cause.

This is the same intellectual energy and strength of will Marty brings to the classroom, which results in strong reactions—his students love him, hate him, admire him, are scared of him. He holds equally strong opinions about them. If Marty feels a student has more potential than she is putting out in the class-room, he will push and prod, challenge that student until he sees the results he wants, or the student quits. To those strong enough to stand up to Marty's with-ering intellectual fervor, he becomes a friend. Each semester Marty has his inner circle of trusted students who drop by weekly for coffee and casual conversation. Marty's end-of-the-semester parties are legendary, as much for the excesses of provisions, as for the wild fury of the word games, and the rollicking toasts which roast many an ego to ashes.

## THE BOSS STRATEGY

| *Strengths* | *Weaknesses* |
|---|---|
| Take-charge leadership | Excessive behavior |
| Forge a path for others to follow | Can be authoritarian |
| Ability to confront | Blaming others |
| Being direct | Denial of limitations |
| Protective of underdogs | Lag time in acknowledging feelings |
| Passionate about beliefs | Damaging, direct anger |
| Seek justice and uphold truth | Keep a lid on vulnerability |
| Loyal to those they trust | Extreme—no middle ground |
| Empowering others | Vengeful |

## THE E-TYPE EIGHT PROPOSITION

### General Description

*Take-Charge Energy, Power and Control; Hiding Behind Ex-cess and Trusting Sufficiency*

Point Eight, the Boss, the so-called confrontational E-type intelligence, ex-hibits out-there-in-your-face direct anger. Point Eight and Point Nine are next to one another, and in the same triad on the Enneagram model, yet the two styles are so different. Bosses use confrontation as a way of establishing zones of safe-ty and certainty, of where they stand in the world. Peacekeepers do everything possible to avoid conflict. The Eight E-type intelligence leads Bosses to believe the world is a threatening place. Therefore power and control are important to the Boss, in fact it is their focus of attention—who has power and will they be fair? This is where the Bosses attention always returns.

In the context of the classroom, Point Eight teachers can often come across as abusive, because as they report to us, confrontation is not frightening to them, they use it as a way of stirring up their students. Often they push too far and then realize that they have to engage in damage control. As confrontation isn't frightening to Eights, it's hard for them to understand how they can devastate a whole room with their anger. There's an excess of energy, all that belly energy is available to them in a split second. Eights don't count to ten before moving into action, they seldom count to one. The "react" response is combative and almost involuntary. This is an Eight blind spot, an illusion; of course, reaction can be delayed. It's important for Bosses to work at being able to contain themselves. Eights need to embody the idea of containment, not to allow their energy to spill over and destroy everyone and everything around them.

Bosses need a large theater of operation—part of their energy translates into a take charge leadership style and they are territorial—a classroom becomes *my* classroom, students become *my* people, "I can berate you and yell at you in my classroom, but I will go to bat for you against anyone else." If a student of an Eight is accused of any lesser, or more serious, misdemeanor, they'll hear from the Boss, but so will the dean or principal, on the student's behalf. We can extrapolate this behavioral trait to any situation where the Eight is in charge—department chair, dean, provost. Eights are gifted in their ability to be protective of those who form part of their territory, those who are part of their space.

The Eight E-type intelligence directs Bosses to establish rules, tangible evidence of their power and control, but the rules are there for other people to follow, not for the Boss. "You come to my class on time, or else you don't get into my classroom, I'll shut that door in your face and you can't come in. But if I run over time, it's okay if you're late for some other teacher's class. You can't use swear words in my classroom, but it's OK if I do." On the other side of the learning dynamic, Boss students are the ones who challenge authority in those first days and weeks of the semester. They are the student who sits in the last row, legs up on the rail in front of him, balancing on the chair, with a sullen look on his face, glowering. (He sits in the last row, so he can see the whole classroom and what's going on.) Eventually he will come up to you and say something like, "Okay, how are we going to deal this semester?" He's pushing you, he wants to provoke a confrontation. This is an important moment because if you don't stand firm and hold your ground, you've lost that student, you've undermined yourself. From the Eight perspective the question arises: if you can't or won't stand up for yourself, how can I trust you to stand up for me?

If somehow in the moment when they choose to mount the challenge, you can meet it, you will have earned their respect and have someone on your side in the classroom. Otherwise, you can expect belligerent behavior, as an Eight student describes himself, "Loud, obnoxious, noisy, boisterous." Once this jockeying for power is over and you've held firm, Eight students can be invaluable in helping you organize whatever needs to happen. Bosses have an innate ability to take charge and make sure everyone has what they need, that they are where they need to be.

Boss Eights are driven by a need for justice. Like Point One Perfectionists they have a moral sense of right and wrong, but it's based on what's fair, not on avoiding error. Situations, decisions, issues are either just or unjust, there is no middle ground. Fairness for what's right is a passion. For instance, in an administration meeting, while everyone's studying a balance sheet, a figure jumps out at the Eight dean. Without regard for where the discussion is, she'll slam her hand on the table (Eights are the great blurters of the Enneagram—the words are out of their mouths without a nanosecond for second thoughts) and ask emphatically, even angrily, "What the hell? Where did this figure come from?" The whole meeting gets swung around onto this one detail, this one figure on the balance sheet. Through the power of their presence Eights can hijack the meeting. Everyone who isn't an Eight in the room is shaken up by the overt nature of the charge. The business manager responds and the Eight dean sits back and says: "Okay, let's go on." She's not angry with anybody in the room, her passion was directed at the decision that led to that particular figure. Others find it harder to regroup. The charge of energy is still present, as well as ruffled feelings. Nobody wants to come forward to speak.

This is critically important to remember about Bosses: their passion is for the cause, or the idea, it's not directed personally. It's a defense of a belief system, of what's fair, or perceived as fair by the Eight. When someone is standing six inches from your face and bellowing at you, it's sometimes hard to remember this. But Eights tell us that energy engulfs them around a cause, or defending something that isn't right. Eights know the bull-in-the-china-shop effect is something they need to work on.

Bosses belong to the Defender triad, their energy is outer-directed, defending their space. We see a larger-than-life presence, a prickly, strong figure, a bull terrier, while inside the Eight knows she's a cute spaniel wanting her tummy rubbed. The avoidance of this E-type intelligence is being vulnerable; the Boss protects herself by trusting few people. If the world is threatening, you can't be vulnerable, you'll be jumped. This is another Eight blind spot, but it does explain why Eights avoid vulnerability. A small inner circle, a trusted few, see the vulnerable spaniel side. In a classroom where the Boss feels comfortable, those students have a different experience from other classes where the Boss is less defensive. Avoiding vulnerability can also play out as denial of reality. The Eight sees the world as she believes it should be—neither illness, weakness, disappointment, nor setbacks stop the juggernaut. Sheer excess of will can carry the day. Part of this denial is to shift blame away from oneself. Bosses can rationalize reality by casting blame. It is good for Eights to remember that when they are pointing a finger at others, three of their own fingers are pointing back at them.

Eights' gift is harnessing his/her force to empower others. There can be few more empowering personalities than someone who has control of their energetic strength. Another way to understand this is to liken an Eight to a crashing wave, always moving forward onto the beach. The forward power is positive, so different from the retracted power of the passive aggressive anger of the Nine, or the retracted power of the Five, which are equally strong, but drain energy negatively out of situations.

Eights' inner world is flat. The goalposts of life are clearly marked. The Bosses' energy moves forward like a bulldozer, unstoppable, surmounting whatever is in the path. There is never a question in the Bosses' mind that they will not arrive at where they want to go.

In organizations if Eights don't feel appreciated, if they sense they are not being heard, their energy can go underground in a way that's political, undermining, damaging. All of their energy goes into bringing down the authority. Backroom politics, rumormongering, priming the bombs, these are the discontented Eights at work earning their paychecks. Before the situation reaches a point where they have to leave, they will have tried to blow up the whole place. Political intrigue is juicy for Eights, as is plotting and executing revenge. Eights will never forget a slight, or a betrayal—again it goes back to the justice issue. Even if it takes two or three years, the Boss will get back at you.

### *Shift to Point Two (Security)*

When Point Eights shift to Point Two they allow themselves to be vulnerable, needy and open. They also take care of others in a loving way, different from their usual combative protection.

I find that I connect with classes much more on an interpersonal level now. I'm much more emotional, letting out tenderness. I enjoy it a lot more, but it's been a long process to be vulnerable, to be open. I trust a lot more openly than I used to.

Even though Point Eights shift to Point Two when they feel secure, they can access the defense mechanisms of Twos: not knowing their own needs, and manipulation and hypocrisy.

### *Shift to Point Five (Stress)*

When Point Eights move to Point Five under stress, it is usually after they have spoken their truth with more belligerence and aggression than they knew, metaphorically resulting in bodies lying all over the floor. Eights shift to the privacy of Five, like a bear with a sore head retiring into a den. They stay there until their excessive energy has dissipated, emerge smiling, and wonder why everyone else is walking so gingerly around them. Eights also go to Five when they feel stressed from the depletion of their energy. Note, however in the following example, the ten videos in two days. Even when recouping Eights live life on a larger scale than other E-types.

At times I move right down to Five where I have to cave in, go up to my room and put on ten videos in two days, until I recoup myself. My energy level is such that I have to force myself to stay in one place during a lesson; I spend an awful lot of energy to keep in one spot. I'm here, I'm there, but I can be ten thousand other places mentally.

Even though Point Eights shift to Point Five under stress, they can access the gifts of Fives: rational thinking and objectivity.

### Key Characteristics

*Empowering Others*

When Eights harness their energy, vision, and leadership on behalf of others, they are powerful educators indeed. Eights like to bend the structure of an institution to set up rules that suit their own style. This Boss educator sees her job as jump-starting students' visions. She feels empowered herself when others respond to her energy.

I think the most difficult situations for me in working with students have to do with the structure of what I'm working with being too rigid. What I mean by that is if there's a set curriculum that I know we have to use and I can't be flexible in how I teach. Or if students are so used to a curriculum that's rigid, and they can't be innovative, or excited about alternative ways of looking at things, that's difficult for me. I have a gut sense that allows me to shift my energy, to push at the edges, so learning can occur. What works for me is when I can work with students to find out where they want to journey to. What do they want to become, how do they see themselves doing that, and being able to support what I call the empowerment of that process of their journey, I get excited about their excitement. I start feeling successful. The whole thing starts to unfold.

Inherent to this Boss's definition of education, is that it is a process that opens people up to become who they are.

I've taught students from third grade on up through college, and adult education, too. Education is opening a person up to who they are and having them realize that who they are is fantastic. It's not about that they have to become something different, but that they can gain skills and bring who they are forward in a way that works for them. To me, that's what people want. That's what education is.

*Motivating Others*

This Eight educator takes it upon herself to find a vehicle to motivate students. Note how she will make available to students her not inconsiderable force and energy "to do whatever it takes to support someone if they want it." Misunderstandings can arise sometimes when the Eight educator wants the motivation more than the student! But most of the time students are content to be taken under the protection of the Eight.

I teach from the part of me that I feel has been empowered, that seems to know what kind of structure is necessary, and is able within that structure to move freely and have the students move freely with me. I'll do whatever it takes to support someone if they want it. What's difficult for me is when I get a student who doesn't feel they can learn, because either their desire has been discouraged, or they don't know what they want. I see their potential, and sometimes they don't. It's the same with adults for me. I see their potential, but it's hard for me to get them from point A to point B, if they're not motivated. I get upset with myself for not being able to figure out a way to make that happen. I take the responsibility to find a vehicle that motivates them. I take it on myself to motivate them, because I think everyone has to learn to motivate themselves. I do feel responsible as a teacher to find a vehicle that will get them motivated.

Here is an example of what I referred to above—if the student doesn't want to get motivated, or be empowered, the Boss teacher will become confrontational because (s)he is so convinced that everyone has to be motivated, to move to our full capacity.

If students don't get motivated on their own, I have been known to get pushy and aggressive, I will do some pushing in order to get their juices flowing. If a person is subdued and I know there is something there, and he or she is not willing to come out, I will push. I think that as I have grown older I don't push as hard as I used to, because I think it can be a little damaging. But a little pushing doesn't hurt. I don't think it hurts with the younger students either. I believe that most of us don't know where our capacity is. I don't think we ever move to our full capacity.

### Excessive Energy

In Enneagram literature, Eights are often described as "lust" types. In this instance, lust has little to do with excessive sexual appetite (although that can be a characteristic of some Eights), and more to do with a lustiness for life —more is never enough. Eights are aware of their energy as a high-voltage charge. They're constantly seeking ways of release—food, drugs, sex, sport, play, work, laughter, troublemaking, and so on. This Eight makes a poignant statement of how his energy drives him.

I have such energy it can drive everybody to drink. I notice at home, I'm moving all the time, my wife says, "Where are you, what are you doing?" There's just so much energy. I tell you I feel like I have to get right out of my skin, I just can't sit there any longer. It's a real problem at times.

This Boss educator describes in a general way how she's aware through feedback that her energy is large, excessive. She teaches us well about Eights who have some degree of self-awareness that if they consciously "go quiet inside," they allow space for others to come toward them. This Eight can then meet the energy of others, rather than have her energy overpower them.

As far as being with students or other teachers, I have to be aware of my energy, because my energy is big; people say they feel me coming before I enter a room—and I believe them. I feel energy in my body strongly, I can feel someone else's energy, especially when I'm teaching. One of the things I do is that I go quiet inside myself and give the other person a sense of being able to come toward me, so that I meet their energy rather than push at it. But it's only recently that I've felt safe enough within myself to do that.

This Eight educator recognizes that she is so intent on making every one of the fifty-five minutes of the lesson count that she never gives her students any downtime.

A month ago I attended a reunion of a class that I had taught as ninth graders in science and again as seniors in government. It's been twenty years since these kiddos were in my class and they were saying to me that the thing they remember the most is they never dropped their pencil, or else they'd be two weeks behind. It was so intense that I never gave them any downtime. My thinking was that I've got them for fifty-five minutes, it's my obligation to get as much done, give them as many experiences as I can. Twenty years later they can remember, "Yes, yes, you did, you did."

### Authority Issues

Many of the E-types have authority issues, but for Eights authority is representative of power and control in their lives. Eights do not want to be controlled. Therefore Bosses have a constant need to challenge authority mainly to test whether the authority is fair and just. The Boss's perceptual lens sees the world as threatening, so you don't let down your guard, you don't trust easily, you don't show any vulnerability—otherwise you're a deluded fool, and the threat will manifest itself like a self-fulfilling prophecy. You'll be controlled, you deserve getting whatever is coming to you.

The Eight E-type intelligence directs Bosses to chafe under the illusion that life itself is an authority. There is a constant testing of the limits, this is part of the root of the defense mechanism of excessive behavior. Eights lock horns with life, with authority (in its myriad forms) in order to establish who has control and if they'll be fair. The following speakers enlighten us on the inner workings of this dynamic for Eights. Our first speaker accurately states how authority is fine with her if she shares the belief system. Otherwise she assumes her confrontation mode.

For me, authority is fine if it's in alignment with me. If it's not in alignment with me—in other words if their values and their ideas are not in sync with me—I have a difficult time with that. I will keep confronting it and confronting it in hopes that it will change. It has been a downfall for me because I realize that some authority, no matter what it is, like the public school system, isn't going to change. It's going to stay the way it is. Rather than me asking it to change, what's important for me is to find a place where I fit, to try not keep hitting up against that.

*Authority Issues—Rules.* Eights have much to say about rules. This speaker gives sage advice to educators of Eights. He explains how Eights need to trust authority to uphold the rules fairly.

If you're going to have rules, make sure you keep them. Don't bend them; if it's a rule, it should be a rule, the moment you start wavering, that's it. Rules are important because if there are different rules for different people then I can't trust anything you say, and then that's it. I don't think the rules apply to me, and if you let me get away with it, then that's bad. If you set the rules and you allow some people to break them, then I've already lost your trust. If someone's done something bad, handle it in the moment, because I want to see that it's handled. If I don't see it, then I don't think that you've handled it. Being in control of the classroom, it doesn't have to be that everybody is sitting there rigid, but if someone goes for you, don't deal with it afterward, take control right there.

This Boss educator tells us bluntly that she makes up her own rules and that she's always believed that rules are made to be broken. The alternative structure for student disciplinary participation she envisioned worked well, because it was what she believed in. Like this Boss, many other Eights report that it's impossible for them to support anything they don't believe in.

I had a difficult time in conventional education, and I didn't last long actually, because I did like to make my own rules. I also felt that some of the rules set for the students were not productive. I feel that people learn in different ways, certainly I did. I always thought rules were made to be broken. It was difficult kind of holding the structure of that as a teacher, and believing that too, because certain rules have to be followed. I have to say that I wasn't as rigid on the rules as most people are. Alternative education allowed me the place to let students participate. They were part of hiring and firing teachers, part of setting up the discipline committee—which I felt worked much better than having a principal decide what the rules were going to be. The students decided on the rules, they'd helped us carry out the disciplinary actions around other students. It worked well. It worked for me because it was part of what I believed in. If I don't believe in something, it's hard for me to do it. In fact, I think it's probably impossible.

*Authority Issues—Trust.* Eights do not trust easily, and trust is tied up with ethical behavior in whatever is that Boss's paradigm.

I've worked for a lot of different superintendents. Some want notoriety, some want to publish, some want the test scores to come up. I don't care what they want. What I care about is creating a learning environment where every single child's ability is maximized. So once I find out what they want, then I present my vision in a way that supports whatever makes them feel good. In my part of the country most of the administrators are male; this is the first time I'm working for a woman, and it's been wonderful because we share the same vision. I don't even have to ask her, I know she trusts me and I trust her and I know I'm headed in the right direction.

In handling the power and authority issues there's always somebody on top of me and there are also many people who report to me. When I first started out in administration, or even in the classroom twenty-four years ago, it was my place. I was much more in control then than I feel I am now. I did leave the last place I worked, because I felt the person I worked for didn't have a real sense of ethics and would put people out on the limb and chop it off, if it was not politically convenient in the community. I couldn't work for that kind of person, there were other places and other things that I could do.

*Authority Issues—Fairness.* If an authority isn't perceived as fair by the Eight who is interacting with them, mayhem breaks lose. This minisaga describes an Eight dynamic—the supervisor is not deemed fair, but rather than walk away, the Eight stays put out of loyalty to others still involved in the situation. The discontented Boss resorts to plotting and intrigue to undermine the authority, bring it down. Anger is directed at gaining revenge.

If you're so good at what you do, you know that even if they have authority over you, they don't. I definitely do that; I pretend that they don't have authority over me, I pretend that I can do anything that I want to do. My primary concern is who do I report to, and is that person fair and can I work with him? I have this huge fear of getting into a situation where the authority isn't fair and it's just a disaster. I'll try and bring him down as quickly as possible, cut him into shape, and then we can either move on from there, or we don't. I usually struggle with that for a long time. I have a tendency not to leave, because there will be other things that will be keeping me there. I'll have friends there that I don't want to abandon, I'll say, "Well, they need my help against this jerk." But eventually if I can't find a way to bring this person into line, then I do have to leave. It's a difficult situation, I do try and sit there and say, "Okay, let me try to be objective about this. What's it like sitting in that person's position right now having to deal with me?" I try to put myself into her shoes. Sometimes I can do it, sometimes I can't, it depends on how angry I am at the person.

This Eight educator tells us she's concerned with fairness in what works in supporting her students. She'll do her utmost for them. The issue is everyone getting a fair deal, this is a central precept for Eights. But this raises the question of whether this is fair to other students who don't have an Eight advocate.

Fairness in what works with the growth of the individual is what's important to me. I will do what it takes to support that. If I feel a connection with a student, God knows what I will do. I'll bring parents in, I'll bring whoever it takes in, the authorities, and try to work with them around creating a place where that student can work to better themselves.

*Authority Issues—Control.* Ironically, Bosses can become dictatorial and authoritarian themselves when they are in control. They tend to paint the world black or white. Either you're doing your job, or you aren't, there's no middle ground, its *my way or the highway.*

There are some people in the field who will sell out a student to preserve a program. I won't, I'll close it, I won't use the program any more, I'll just tell them point blank, "You're not working honestly with the students." I had one supervisor, for example, she and I and a student met together for a midterm evaluation. She asked, "Can I see you for a few minutes after the student leaves?" She proceeded to tell me she was lying. She didn't want to hurt the student's feelings because he had all kinds of problems. I said, "I won't accept that, we need to talk to the student about it, we need to deal with it." She got defensive, I asked her to bring in her director, I told him I wouldn't work with her anymore. They ended up firing her. To me that was perfectly appropriate, she was not doing her job. With my own employees I'm honest and flexible, but we're not going to beat around the bush. You're either doing your job, or you're not, and it's not my fault, it's your problem, your choice. If you're not doing it, then we'll deal with it, and you'll leave. To me that's pretty simple.

On the other hand this Eight is an advocate for the student, against an authority she considers unfair in its use of control mechanisms that defeat their own purpose.

If control is just set there by conventional means because it's what's been there for one hundred years, or twenty years, and it doesn't make any sense, and it's not working for people, and it's not fair to a student, then I can't uphold it. For example, if I have a student with an emotional problem, and he loses control, and starts yelling at a teacher, or even swears at a teacher or whatever, and he's suspended in the public school for that, that rule defeats the purpose of why the student is in school. The student stays to learn what is appropriate. How can that student learn that if he is not in a situation where someone can sit down with him and explore other ways he could have expressed his anger? To me that's fair. But it's unfair to suspend him because he broke a rule made for whatever reason because a teacher is going to be insulted or hurt. If our mission here is to empower students and to teach them how to be in the world, you can't teach them if they are at home suspended.

*Authority Issues and Feedback.* The following Bosses report that they welcome feedback and can ameliorate their behavior when the result of their style is pointed out to them. This Eight sheds light on how to get him on board: don't tell him he's wrong, tell him of someone else's need.

> With me it is always to go to the vulnerability rather than trying to power back. If you say to me, "Someone else needed to express themselves and they didn't get the opportunity because of how forceful you were, and I'm wondering if there's any other way you can be?" I will hear that. If you try to make me wrong I'm going to come right back at you. But if you go to my vulnerability, I'll hear the need, and I'm interested in other people's needs and having them come forward too.

### Protecting Myself

This Eight poses a neat conundrum: he perceives himself as embracing his students in a great protective bear hug, yet the menace of the bear hug becoming a death squeeze is present if one reads between the lines of all he says. Eights often are unaware of the intimidating force they inadvertently show to others.

> When I'm working with students there's no sense of vulnerability, I don't need to protect myself. First of all I'm older, I'm bigger, I'm stronger, and I know I don't need to force the issue, so I don't feel vulnerable. I want to protect them all, like my family. I have a lust for life, I live my life for other people. In the classroom I reach out and grab all of those students and say, "You're mine, you're mine." I know they feel that encompassing energy. Everybody knows where I stand. If they don't, I'll tell them. They won't cross my path because they know where I stand. My students will tell you that if they ask me one thing today and ask it a month from now, my answer will be the same. When I go into the classroom, I react in a consistent manner. But once having said that, if I can bend the rules to help somebody, I'll go right around everyone.

### Confrontation

Simply put, an intrinsic part of the Eight E-type intelligence is to use confrontation as a strategy to root out threats, to enable the Boss to find safety zones. Confrontation is not scary to Eights, it's a way of life.

> I think when I go into any kind of teaching situation, I assume that, sooner or later, there's going to be a confrontation. It doesn't disturb me that it's going to happen. In fact, I kind of look forward to it because I feel that the people who will confront with me oftentimes are the ones who learn the most, and are usually the ones who open more

quickly. So for me, confrontation isn't a negative thing, it's a positive thing. I look for it in people. People who withdraw from me and don't come toward me, I find more difficult to work with. Sometimes I'll keep poking at them, poking at them, until they will come toward me, everyone does confrontation differently. I am comfortable with it, I don't get particularly upset with it, I find it exciting.

### Anger

For Eights, anger is tied into their passionate belief in truth-telling—speak directly, don't mince words, let others feel the full force of your anger. When Bosses see the effect of their anger, they are often remorseful. Eights learn to say they're sorry, but often it's too late to mend the fences. Not many people stick around for a second blast of anger. Bosses need to learn to count to ten before they lash out. In the classroom, dealing with the fragile egos of adolescents, the Eight's direct anger can be damaging.

I think my anger in the past, and still sometimes in the present, has been perceived by some people as being abusive. I think actually it was. I think that there was a time when there should have been an end to moving beyond to where I moved to. I have had to spend a lot of time saying I'm sorry in my life. Much of it has to do with the passion I feel about a certain situation, I'll get too carried away emotionally. Also, I don't realize that for most people, confrontation is a scary thing, because for me it's not. It's not meant to be. When I'm confronting, it's because I'm defending a belief system, not because I want to hurt any person. It comes across sometimes as hurting the other person. So I've had to say I'm sorry—a lot.

### Being Heard

Like the other members of the Defender triad—Nines (who need to be listened to) and Ones (who need to convey the specifics correctly)—Bosses have a need to be heard. This is the triad of self-forgetting, this is why it is so important to be able to track that they have others' attention.

When I am in front of a room, it's important to me that people are listening, that they are hearing what I am saying. Often, if people aren't paying attention, I will stop, and that's when confrontation can arise. I will ask them if they can please respect that I am speaking now, and I will give them a chance for their say. This is my turn, and what I have to say I feel is important.

### Passion Around a Belief System

In working with, or in relationship with, Eights, it's important to understand that their anger and passion are not directed personally, even if you are the one upholding the view that the Eight is shooting down, it is the belief they are attacking, not you. When Eights are in attack mode because of their belief system, they want you to defend your position with commensurate passion. Many other E-type intelligences simply do not express high-voltage passion. This is where the confrontation can escalate.

My passion is so great for what I believe in, I come across with such intensity; very, very, very seldom is that intensity geared or directed to you personally, it's directed to this passion. I want someone to come back and not just agree with me to agree with me, but to show me another side, another point of view. When I'm in one of these situations I see that people are so overwhelmed they shut down, and it's not a personal attack. I expect and want you to come back with the same passionate belief. In fact I'm concerned about people (I want to write them off) who never have any passion about topics. It is that respect for passion that drives what I do and I expect to get from you that same kind of energy.

### Passion Around Truth

Eights are equally passionate around issues of truth.

When people are lying to me, I know immediately, and I'll either choose to ignore it or confront them with it. I get a sense in my stomach, I know immediately. I do try and listen to my intuition. I don't always, but I try to and it's actually most often right.

Smoothing the waters, finding a subtle way to deliver the news, being diplomatic—all these forms of expression raise the Eight's level of suspicion. If possible be direct, and straightforward, ambiguity is taboo in the Bosses' vocabulary. They don't want anything to do with hidden agendas.

When people get married, they make all kinds of commitments to each other. I said to my wife, "I have only one commitment I want you to make to me. I don't care what else you do, but I never want you to be ambiguous with me. If you've got something on your mind, tell me. Don't allude to it, don't work around it, just tell me what's on your mind."

### Blame

Bosses blame others for personal setbacks. It is part of the Eight E-type intelligence that directs them to always appear powerful and forceful, to ignore limiting factors that will take away from that stance. Eights deny their own deficiencies, or their own role in an argument, in order to protect the space their self-defenses have created for them to appear strong in the world. The following speaker articulates this stance clearly.

Part of why I blame is out of protecting the space that I'm in.

When I'm pointing the finger at the other person, my space is protected and I don't have to take responsibility, or be accountable. Part of it comes from protection of this vulnerable, fragile place inside, which I think doesn't often come across. People who have known me over a long period of time, or take the time to be close to me, know that place inside of me. I think that over time I've created so many defenses to protect that place. It's almost like I break easily—I do—I'm like good china, I crack easily. Most people don't perceive me that way, so I create space to take care of myself, and what I've had to learn is to do that within myself, not to have to keep doing it out here.

The following speaker highlights an interesting Eight take on blaming others to get themselves off the hook. While it is essentially true that the recipients of the Eight anger and confrontation are allowing themselves to be intimidated, Eights are not blameless in their behavior of going after people. A cautionary note, if you are an educator you certainly don't want to be labeled a wimp by your Eight students.

People say to me, "Well, you intimidate me." I'm not doing anything to you, I can't intimidate you, you're letting yourself be intimidated. I've learned to get over that behavior a little because it might not win me friends. But that's how I feel: why are you being a wimp? I don't like wimps. Wimps are wishy-washy. It's one of the worst names I can call you. I would rather you came at me with your own energy, I'll respect you. If you wimp out, I won't even annihilate you, I'll dismiss you like a little fly: go away. You've got to meet the energy. There's the wimp and there's the underdog. They're two different things. An underdog is someone who needs my help and I'll do anything for them, I will. But the wimp is someone who has no backbone. There's a distinction there whereas the underdog needs help, a wimp is just a wimp.

### Bosses as Students (Advice for Educators Who Aren't Bosses)

*The Insurrectionist— "I got it finally that all you have to do is do what they ask you to do."* I was the student who was always in trouble. In addition I have to move around to learn, and we sat at desks, we never got to get on the floor. I tried to set the school on fire when I was in the fourth grade. My parents, the teacher, and the principal said, "You will not be able to go on to junior high with your class." Finally that was enough of a consequence that it grabbed hold of me and I asked, "There's no way?" They responded, "Yes, we'll let you have a tutor all summer and if you can pass the test at the end, we'll let you go. But it will be on probation." So I went to summer school, had the tutor, I passed the test, intelligence is not the issue, it's the will, a strong will. In elementary school I was a problem child and when I got it finally that all you have to do is do what they ask you to do, then basically I changed from being the rebel kid.

*The Rebel— "I rebelled against being told I was a failure, because I knew I wasn't a stupid person."* I was thrown out of kindergarten, unfortunately I wasn't quick to figure out that you did what the teacher wanted, so I got thrown out right through high school. It wasn't until college that I figured out a way for me to be able to be successful as a student. I am hyperactive, I rebelled against being told I was a failure, because I knew I wasn't a stupid person. As long as I didn't have any trust in them so as far as authority goes, I didn't listen to them. I always believed I had power. I may not have the power to get the teacher to like me, but I have the power to be the way I needed to be. In college I could create my own curriculum, I could do it my way. After the first six months of college I was on the dean's list and won a full scholarship and graduated from my master's program second in my program, primarily because I had the freedom to do it my way.

*The Troublemaker— "If they couldn't control the classroom then I would go for them, because I wanted to show everybody else in the classroom that I was the strongest."* When I was a student, if I was bored, I would provoke the teacher. I could read the room and see whether the teacher was a wimp or not. Once I found out they were a wimp I would lunge forward, provoke them like crazy. I was always going to the principal's office. On a couple of occasions a teacher beat me up; he got fired. If the teacher was powerful enough and strong enough to control the classroom, I was okay. But if they couldn't control the classroom then I would go for them, because I wanted to show everybody else in the classroom that I was the strongest. I would go for them and provoke them until they were absolutely crazy.

*Taking Control— "By the time I got to college that was a different story, because then I could take over the classroom."* The main reason I went to a parochial high school was otherwise I would have had to go to the public high school where my mother was teaching. There was no way that I wanted to be in the same school where she was, where people were going to know that. I did well in school, but I only worked for those teachers I respected. By the time I got to college that was a different story, because then I could take over the classroom. I remember when an instructor decided we were going to take an exam and he wanted us all to bring in questions. It was a small class, I got together with everybody afterward and we decided we weren't going to do it. So the next class we just told him that we weren't going to do it and there wasn't any problem. We just changed the format. It was a matter of if you didn't like it, you changed it.

## *Vengeance and Revenge*

Plotting and executing revenge ties in with the Eight defense mechanism of being strong and infallible in the eyes of the world. If someone has let you down, bettered you, caught you off-guard, taken advantage of you, if you plot revenge you can keep the dynamic going in your own mind, you *can* have the last word.

> I told my dean, "Never go behind my back. If you have an issue, come to me, and we'll settle it." She went behind my back, I didn't talk to her for three years—three years. All the time she's asking everyone else, "What's wrong with him?" I cut people off, or if you're not careful, I'll have a tendency to go after you. But I try not to do that.

## *Advocating for the Underdog*

Eights are territorial, they establish their space, if you fall within their ambit, they protect you. Bosses also exert themselves on behalf of others *they* perceive as being treated unfairly. This speaker was not asked by the new faculty member to intervene on her behalf, he did so of his own accord. He thought she was being treated unfairly so he went to bat for her. Notice how he turns this exchange into a power play with the department chairperson.

> I'm big on sticking up for the underdog. I will advocate for anyone that I feel is being unjustly treated. In the department I'm probably the biggest advocate for my students, I will lie for them, cheat, absolutely anything. I will do that for the children with special needs whom I teach. I will do it for other faculty members too. This year a brand-new faculty member came aboard. There's a real conflict between the faculty member and the chairperson. At some point after this was surging, I decided that I would intervene on behalf of the faculty member. I went to the chairperson and I said, "I think you're treating this person unfairly and I'm going to act on her behalf from now on. I want you to know that right up front. Anything I tell her, I'll tell you, but I want you to know that I'm now part of this. I will advocate for the underdog."

In the following instance the desire on the part of the Eight to keep the student in school has as much to do with the student's cause as with his own issues of power and control, of establishing who is the stronger authority in the school.

> This past semester there was an experience with one of our seniors who got in some trouble; he accepted the responsibility for the fight. The police were overreacting, he wasn't getting a fair shake. The administration, which should have been behind him in many ways, was questioning even letting him go from school, which would have been double jeopardy. I hired a private investigator and paid for the attorney. The point was I wasn't going to let anything happen to him and he

graduated—he'd been accepted at graduate school. There was no way that the school was going to screw him, it wasn't going to happen.

This Eight in a way becomes an advocate for his colleagues.

When other teachers can't deal with a student, they'll call me in to talk with that student. I will talk openly, frankly, I won't mince my words. But I notice that the others in my department, they want to talk all around the issue without every addressing what the real problems are. What I find in my department is that I'm the enforcer. Somebody's got to do it.

This Eight educator tackles head on the question of whether he advocates for students as part of his own agenda, or for other reasons. It is an interesting insight that he can advocate on behalf of others, but not for himself.

I don't believe that it's my ego when I'm advocating for students. I'm going to hold them accountable, I'm going to deal with them, but I am going to advocate for them and it's not my ego. It's much easier for me to advocate for them than it would be for myself. I wouldn't get into that kind of power struggle battle.

This Boss educator describes how open he is to help others, but how difficult it is for him to ask for assistance.

I probably write more recommendations a year than any other faculty member. I don't say that carelessly. But now I'm going up for a promotion and I find it the most difficult thing in the world to ask somebody else to write one for me.

### Learning Patience

As probably the most outer-directed of all the E-types, Eights find difficulty in cultivating the virtue of patience. When they can sit back and wait, they learn the passive stance has its own rewards.

One of the greatest lessons that I've had to learn is patience. As a teacher it would be push, push, push, push and with some students you can't do that. You have to give them the space to come toward you; that's been a lesson I've had to learn and put into action.

Like Point Threes, Boss Eights can drive themselves beyond the point of collapse. Both Threes and Eights can learn from Fives about energy management.

I'm now learning to see when I'm about to collapse, so that I can pull back before the collapse happens. But usually I'll have so many balls in the air, that finally I can't do it anymore and need to take a day off. After many years of hitting collapse, I've started to figure out: okay, I'm getting toward collapse. A lot of times I'll take little time outs almost to force myself to stop.

### Intuition

The energy of this triad is called instinctual, or gut, because of the intuitive ability of these E-types. A Nine Peacekeeper speaks of being able to "feel into" her students. A One Perfectionist says, "There's something I know that other people don't. I can't explain it, it's all sensing and feeling, it's reliable." This Eight Boss speaks of how she can, "sense into what the person needs." In this case she knows instinctively that striking a deal with her students will work.

As far as my teaching style is concerned, I think it is intuitive, sometimes I will take a risk and try something. I don't have always to be right in the way which I work. If I find that's not working I'll go to something else. But usually I sense into what the person needs, or where the person is, and will try again to meet them there and see what it is that excites them, what it is that they want to learn, and how they want to learn it, and I'll go there. An example, I taught a group of what we called emotionally disturbed adolescents. There were fifteen boys in the classroom, they aged anywhere from thirteen to sixteen years old. One of the things that I discovered was that to teach them reading, writing, and the basic skills, if I made a deal with them they would buckle down in the morning and we would learn that material; in the afternoon, they could choose what they wanted to do, whether it was to go out and shoot some basketball, or whether to go downtown and do comparison shopping. They got the best results in that school. It was neat to see that motivating factor that worked for them.

### Self-forgetting

Eights can be hard on themselves. In moments of truth they know what is the cost of excessive energy, direct forcefulness, putting out energy for others.

I hear a lot about abuse that I do to others, and I don't talk about the abuse I do to myself. I'm more critical of me than I could ever be of anybody else and it's difficult. Even with the energy, I will burn myself out, unless I actually block off times in my daytimer book that are quiet times for me, because otherwise I will keep going until I drop, and I wouldn't even know that I was in pain. Part of my training over the past couple of years has been to listen to my body and not abuse myself. The pattern for me is always to go to the abuse, always go to the excess, always go to the addiction, whether it be with others or with myself. I feel so sad, part of it is the sadness I feel is for myself.

The poignancy of this speaker's comment lies in the phrase "when things are the way I think they should be," in other words "when I'm in control everything's okay." She takes personal responsibility for anything that goes awry.

When everything is going well and I'm happy, when things are the way I think they should be, I'm right out there and loving. But when there is difficulty, if there's a problem with my children, my grandchildren, my significant other, I go to a place of such despair. It feels like going down into a dark cold well and not being able to get out. And that's such a painful place.

### Positive Gifts in Teaching

This Eight educator describes how her take-charge leadership style—with some adjustments—allows others' visions to become reality.

I think that what makes me effective is that I can describe and enroll people in a vision and not move in any other direction until the vision is accomplished. Regardless of what happens, I'm still moving toward the vision with energy and enthusiasm, hopefully bringing a team of people with me. I've had to learn to temper my energy so I don't chew people up along the way, or I couldn't be in a public school system. I don't think I'd be where I am if I didn't learn some adjustments to my leadership style.

This Boss educator knows herself well, she admits her energy may be hard to take, but you can count on her when *her* students, *her* program, *her* school needs support.

As a public school teacher, I think one of my strengths is that I'm willing to try anything that's new and large enough. For instance, we've just got in an interesting new reading program and we're working with the local university. The program was actually designed with a sense of largeness about it. I became an advocate and started to move the program through the system, certainly through the sixth grade, with unusual energy. So if a program is large enough I will support it in any which way.

I'm also willing to support the underdog; often children who don't have a chance someplace else, have a head start in my classroom. I'm willing to work and support in any way I can that person whom I feel has not been given an equal opportunity. My energy may be hard to take, but you can always count on me.

### Growth Path: From Excess to Trusting Sufficiency

The growth path for Bosses is from relying on excess—too much (energy, force, time, laughter, power, food, narcotics)—to taking risks, trusting there'll be sufficient to meet their needs. (For instance, many Eights hate running out of provisions, and buy in bulk to make sure they never do.) If they can stay with an innocence that trusts they're not going to get a knife in their back, this allows them to move forward in an open way. Learning not to indulge in excess to test whether you're alive means it's okay to be vulnerable, to be passive, to receive.

I think the issue around vulnerability in the past for me has been feeling exposed, fragile. I think most people perceive me as powerful and strong, if they ever knew that inside was this little mush ball, they would understand that when I am being vulnerable, it's a tender place for me. It used to be difficult for me to move there, in fact I would only go there with certain people. Now it's much easier because I have found the place inside myself, that no matter what happens it's okay. Because I'm perceived often as strong and unhurtable, people will come after me when I am in that space of vulnerability. For a long time, that's why I wouldn't do it. Now it's okay. If they come after me, they come after me, but I am not willing to give up that part of me. I think it's an important part. I cherish it.

### Quality of Essence: Truth (as in Fairness and Justice)

The essence word for Eights is truth, which ties in with issues of fairness and justice. Basically truth for Eights means that in the moment they are present to themselves, they can know who they are, abide with that knowledge, and not have to forge their way in the world through direct force and vigilance. This speaker states the essence quality succinctly.

To find that sacred space inside myself where I can create safety, so then I can be in the world as who I am and not as my defenses.

## What Boss Students Say

### Power Play

Life's a game in that there are pawns to be used and there are people who will use you, and you have to fight against that—it's a matter of being the one who moves the chess pieces, of being one of the movers and shakers, one of the people who gets things done. I want to be one of those people.

### Survival

If I learn, I become educated and then I can have intelligent conversations with intelligent people and survive in the world.

### Force

It's very hard for me to argue something I don't agree with. If I'm in line with that view, I'm right out there, I'm arguing, I'm letting the other side have it. For some reason I work much better that way.

### Forceful Presence

When I get behind something I'm a force—I do stuff—I'm strong, loud, boisterous, perhaps even pushy and obnoxious. But I'm there, I'm a presence.

### Combatitive

You give a person a chance to prove that they can do the job, and if they fail, if they show that they're not capable of it then you get rid of them. If people are going to be weak and not able to get things done then you can't deal with that. It takes too much out of you. You have to find capable people who won't always require you to be pampering them and be on their back.

### Being Heard

I hate to be belittled, especially when I know I'm right. I hate people who argue in a way that doesn't listen to my point of view, I hate to be not listened to. I'd rather have someone hear me and disagree than not hear me at all.

### Capable

I want to avoid that sense that I haven't done it to my utmost, that I haven't been able to do it right, to do it in such a way that he or she (the teacher) wants in order to get the job done, to be capable. Capable is a big word for me.

### Deep Emotions

Emotionally when I feel something I feel it strongly, just as when I'm behind something, I feel love, I feel hate, I feel sadness. When I get into moods, I may change quickly, but while I'm in them, they're deep. When I get into something my whole sense goes into that feeling.

### Brief Interview with a Boss Educator

*Q. What is your teaching style?*
A: My teaching style is innovative, intuitive, spontaneous, powerful. It tends to be toward aggressive and empowering.

*Q. What do you look for in your students?*
A: What I look for in my students is what touches their soul. What moves them toward their greatness, and what they want from me as far as supporting them.

*Q. What is important in the way you present material?*
A: What is important to me in the way I present my material is that it be exciting, powerful, that it meets the needs of the person that I am working with, and that it gets results.

*Q. What will students say of you?*
A: Students will say of me that they think in the beginning that I am tough, and that sometimes I want something more than they do. What they find is that I am vulnerable, and caring, and loving, and supportive.

*Q. Why do you teach?*
A: I teach because I love teaching. I love seeing people transformed, I love seeing people find out about themselves.

*Q. How do you communicate?*
A: My communication style is very direct, sensitive, and I guess one would say somewhat controlling.

*Q. What is your attitude to preparing teaching plans?*
A: Preparing teaching plans is a torture for me. In fact I never do them. So it is difficult.

*Q. What do you like about the classroom?*
A: What I like about the classroom is that it's a place where people can transform, become empowered. It's a place for me to express my views, my beliefs.

*Q. What don't you like about the classroom?*
A: What I don't like about the classroom is that I find it is too contained. I like to expand the walls of the classroom. I also don't like that there are certain rules which don't work for me.

**Practical Tips**

*For Bosses to Work with Themselves*

- Be aware that your energy is overwhelming to most other people.
- Be aware that your passion around your belief system blows away most other people.
- Be aware that your presence looms larger-than-life and that stance is intimidating.
- Learn to trust being open and vulnerable, people will find it easier to approach you.
- Be aware when you are blaming others, you are usually in denial.
- Try to inculcate patience and passivity, let others come to you, you receive more that way.

- Try to be a team player, support the ideas of other people, your leadership can be invaluable.
- Catch yourself when the instinct for revenge becomes powerful, cut the political intrigue, you can damage yourself and others.
- More is often too much—curtail your excesses in whatever form they take; don't you be at their mercy.

*For Others Who Work with the Boss*

- Give Eights feedback as to the impact of their anger.
- Ask the Boss to champion an underdog.
- Use the Eights' energy and take-charge leadership style to accomplish a vision.
- Go toe-to-toe with Eight colleagues and students, otherwise you'll be dismissed as a wimp.
- Be direct in your dealings with Eights; they intuit ambiguity and it makes them suspicious.
- If Eights think you have betrayed them, they will plot revenge. (They don't necessarily act on it.) Constantly reinforce your position with reality checks.
- Structure a process whereby Eights can be helped to see where they were wrong and to shoulder their part of the blame.
- Set a framework of rules to govern your interactions and do not deviate from them.
- Help Eights to see that when their excessive, all-or-nothing behavior becomes a compulsion, they are usually in denial.

## ENNEATYPE NINE: THE PEACEKEEPER

- TRIAD: *DEFENDER*
- ATTENTIONAL FOCUS: The agenda of others
- GIFT: Unconditional love
- AVOIDANCE: Conflict
- GROWTH PATH: From being asleep to oneself (acedie) to right action
- ESSENCE: Universal love
- SHIFT TO SECURE POINT: *THE PERFORMER THREE* (Attacher against arrow)
- SHIFT TO STRESS POINT: *THE QUESTIONER SIX* (Detacher with arrow)
- WINGS: *THE BOSS EIGHT* (Defender)
  *THE PERFECTIONIST ONE* (Defender)

## EXAMPLES OF PEACEKEEPER NINE EDUCATORS: DON'T ROCK THE BOAT

### Keeping the Peace

Brett S. is the associate director of the music department of a large public school. He's in charge of the voice program, and every year he puts on a full musical or operetta production, conducts the glee club, separate boys and girls à capella groups, and the chamber singers. Brett is in his early thirties, he has a strong tenor voice and often joins in ensemble singing with the students. He is a much-loved figure—colleagues and students alike value his warmth, his support, his enthusiasm, his giving of himself in the classroom and in performances.

Brett's music room is a mess: collected assortments of programs, musical sheets, posters, lie in dusty piles around the floor. Odd pieces of stage props are festooned with various period costumes. On a raised platform at the back of the room, tiers of varying heights stand ready for the students. A scuffed grand piano that has seen better days dominates the room. Music invariably booms from a large CD player. Brett's computer is surrounded by stacks of papers on his desk. A closer scrutiny of the desk reveals many photographs of singing groups and musical productions, but pride of place is given to photos of Brett's wife and their two small children.

Brett makes it clear that he is one of the gang with his students; more often than not it is he at the bottom of a scuffle of boys on the floor, or teasing the the girls while showing off costumes from their musicals. To an outsider Brett's classroom is a chaotic place with often off-the-wall energy and activity, but he says it's controlled chaos, that he can't teach without movement, and that he knows where to find everything on his desk. Deadlines for grading periods, attendance at faculty meetings, keeping school rules of discipline and decorum have a Teflon effect on Brett: they don't seem to stick. He handles pointed reminders and even reprimands from administrators with shrugged shoulders and a smile: let them get excited about such matters if they must, it's not important in the overall scheme of life.

Brett is aware of his organizational problems—try as he does, he can't seem to prioritize, or keep order and structure, because nothing appears more important than anything else, and it's certainly not worth the effort to beat yourself up over it. A year ago the school's chamber singers were invited to an international competition in Poland with a singing tour of the country to follow. Brett stumbled when it came to working with the travel agent and tour organizers in Poland. Put simply, he was unable to have all the documentation ready when they wanted it, he found making decisions onerous, he started blaming others for being unreasonable. He could feel himself zoning out as requests for this and that grew shriller and shriller. The trip almost unraveled, but at the last moment Brett rallied and everyone got safely onto the plane and off it again two weeks later.

Now Brett jokes that he has a buddy system in place, he has an assistant in the voice program because it has grown so large. "She's quite different from me," he grins, "she loves details and procedures and schedules and timetables. Actually it's a real relief to have her around. She helps me keep the peace."

### The Mediator

Mary R. is an assistant dean in the academic office of a large Midwestern, rural community college. Mary rose through the ranks from a secretarial position in the same office about twenty years previously. She finished her undergraduate studies and master's degree in education by taking courses at night. She is the single mother of four children, all but one in the workforce now, her youngest is away from home at a state college. Her husband left her years ago, complaining about her "passivity."

Mary's friends describe her as an earth mother—she is always a shoulder to cry on, she goes to great lengths for her friends, remembering birthdays and other important events with a well-chosen card or small gift. Mary is an excellent, instinctive cook, she rarely uses recipes, and loves to cater for informal parties as long as someone else organizes them. Mary thrives on other people's energy. And people like to come to her home, which is truly "homey"—what you see is what you get—you can take your shoes off and relax, you don't feel you're imposing on any order or image. There are always dogs and cats underfoot, the local branch of the ASPCA often calls Mary to take in a stray animal, and she seldom says no.

The academic dean, Mary's boss, values her support, she carries through his ideas and instructions with good grace. He has learned to give her long lead time on important projects and to check in periodically to see where she is in the process. As long as he helps her structure her progress he knows she'll do the job. Where Mary is invaluable to him is in her role as a mediator. As with any academic environment, at times the dynamic among administrators, or between administrators and faculty, can become political and conflict-ridden. The dean asks Mary to seek out the opinions of as many of the parties as she can. He has learned to trust absolutely her gut feel for their positions, as well as her ability to report accurately her understanding of their arguments. Latterly, the dean has included Mary more often in high-level meetings. Her warm, open disposition, the fact that she is trying to support everyone in the group to come to a resolution that is best for the whole community, rather than to beat a drum for any one agenda, make her an ideal mediator.

For the most part Mary finds her life satisfactory. She feels comfortable that as long as she keeps afloat in safe and predictable waters, she'll be okay. Life is pretty flat and ordinary, and to tell the truth, Mary likes it that way. As she's gotten older she is aware at times of stabs of discomforting energy coursing through her body. If she thinks about it, she can name resentment and sometimes even anger. Why is she always there for everyone else? Why do other people not seem available when she asks tentatively for help? Perhaps her ex-husband was right, she is a doormat. Mary is frightened of that energy, of what conflict it might engender. She escapes from it by tuning it out by listening to her favorite operas, reading another P.D. James mystery, taking a nap.

## THE PEACEKEEPER STRATEGY

| Strengths | Weaknesses |
|---|---|
| Unconditional love | Asleep to oneself |
| Accepting of others | Contain energy by inertia |
| Supportive | Lose own position |
| Predictable | Obstinacy |
| Good listeners | Passive aggressive behavior |
| Fair—see all points of view | Procrastination |
| Slow to express anger | Inability to prioritize |
| Energy on behalf of others | Difficulty coming to personal decisions |

## THE E-TYPE NINE PROPOSITION

### General Description

#### Mediation and Support; Asleep to Oneself and Right Action

Point Nine is another member of the Defender triad, the instinctual triad. The Peacekeeper Nine E-type intelligence is skilled at using the body's own knowing as an indicator of how to respond to situations. There is an instinctive connection with this energy. Unlike the Point Eight Boss who utilizes the energy fully, Point Nines are wary of the energy; they don't want to disturb the peace, they dislike being carried away, they tamp it down, so the energy has nowhere to go—this is the root of the passive-aggressive behavioral pattern of the Peacekeeper. The passive-aggressive mechanism demonstrates the power of retraction, of letting energy drain away, becoming flaccid, so other people have to come after you, then the Nine counters by accusing them of being aggressive. As we have noted, many Point Sixes say that fear is not necessarily paralyzing, but can often be a charge to help them find courage, so this instinctual energy for Nines can be a charge helping them to take right action on their own behalf, albeit passive-aggressive action.

Point Nine is called the Peacekeeper and there is a seeming paradox here. How can the E-type intelligence that promotes harmony, peace, avoiding conflict as a survival strategy also exert control through obstinacy and the retractive force of passive-aggressive behavior? Nines are the peacekeepers of the Enneagram, but on another level they are angry and resentful, their anger takes a diffuse form that can drain the energy out of many interactions. A major blind spot for Nines is that they deny they are angry. Many Nines, if you ask them, "Why are you angry at me," they are absolutely astonished. "I'm not angry at you," they reply, "I'M NOT ANGRY." If you ask, "But why are shouting?" the denial and shouting escalate.

When you speak in a flat even tone, meander as you make your point in a saga-like description, people tune out. Peacekeepers report that they can sense this happening. A cardinal sin against Nines is not to be listened to. They become angry and respond by digging in their heels and being passive aggressive. Peacekeeper speech patterns mirror their interior world. Nines live in a world which has the appearances of a level terrain. Time spreads out, there's no urgency—if it doesn't get done today, it will tomorrow, nothing is of more importance than anything else. Nines convince themselves that time is part of this terrain, events are that way, people are that way, the gestalt is flat and even, diffuse. There's always enough time, there's always another event, there are always other people. In the Nine E-type intelligence there's little of the Point Eight bulldoze movement forward. The worldview is uniform and even, no peaks and valleys. The idea of highs and lows, or periods of great or less intensity, these are not part of the inner framework of the Nine. Instead there's a sense of wanting to level out the world, smooth it out, keep it flat. Inherent to this tendency either in professional life, or as a student, is an inability to prioritize, or a reluctance to prioritize, to give more importance to one project over another. Nines are the primary procrastinators of the Enneagram. In our Western society with its emphasis on prioritization and deadlines, Nines run smack into institutional problems.

How do Nines meet deadlines? They operate in a world where there are institutional rules, societal rules, other rules, so there are consequences for procrastination. Nines complete the task in their heads in good time, the problem arises in actualizing it in the world. If Nines have a sense that there is a deadline, or a task has to be done in a specific order, it disturbs their inner sense of wanting to keep everything even and flat, of not giving more importance to any one thing over another. Nines write lists, adding to lists that grow ever longer. The longer they become, the harder it is to cross off the top item, so the lists collapse of their own inertia. Peacekeepers keep deadlines by becoming champions at the last-minute save. They kick in the Point Three energy and work for twenty-four hours straight to meet the ultimatum that's been given often after the deadline has passed.

The reason for maintaining an inner, level tenure is that it allows you to go to sleep to yourself. If you convince yourself you live in a comfortable world, you can avoid conflicts. Avoiding conflict is the key Nine defense mechanism and blind spot. The Peacekeeper E-type lens sees no conflict, so there is no conflict. This is an illusion, for we live in a conflictual society. Nines move to the beat of a different drummer. Nines perceive anything and everything as having potential for conflict—querying bills, wanting to change an appointment with the school principal, a student asking for a conference. Procrastination starts up, the conflict level builds, because the more they avoid it the more potential for conflict there is. By the time they actually grab the bull by the horns, in their own head the conflict has escalated. Nines are often surprised, "Oh, she was so nice about it."

If you sit on the fence, if you try to mediate, try to find the smooth spots in a dynamic situation, you are indeed a peacekeeper. In the dynamic of a classroom, Nines have the ability to sense intuitively where there is resistance, and they can get everybody working together to create harmony—so there is no conflict. Peacekeepers can easily take on the position and perspective of each student in the class, see a problem from many points of view. This helps in mediation, but it can be a handicap in decision-making.

Nines have a gift of universal love given unconditionally, of universal acceptance of others. They are the most supportive of the E-types, words like competition, me-first, or ego don't have the same charge they do for other E-types. They act on behalf of others without much concern for their own sense of achievement or success. Nine teachers can be dynamite because they take on the agenda of the class as a whole. While Point Twos potentiate certain students by meeting their needs, Point Nines buy the whole agenda. The class motivates the Nine teacher, it's the consequence of not being there in the morning that motivates the Peacekeeper to get up and go to school. To outsiders, Nine educators are the embodiment of a committed, dedicated teacher who will go the whole way for that class—that's the agenda they've taken on. Taking on the agenda of others is the Nine focus of attention.

The converse also applies. Other E-types who teach Nine students should be aware that they will often take on our whole agenda. Nines merge with the agendas they take on. It seems as if they have lost their boundaries, but the fact is that because their self is so laid back, or asleep, it's not themselves who have merged, *the inner self is not present*. Nines are on automatic pilot and the self is replaced by the agenda they've adopted. It's up to others to draw boundaries, to set the consequences of certain (in)actions. One suggestion to help Nines is to develop a powerful buddy system. If you're a Nine teacher, you should ask a colleague to work with you, to help you to set priorities, to keep you to your

218 The Enneagram Intelligences

commitments, to make sure that you're on time. Typically at the end of grading periods, Nines are among the people who never hand in their grades on time and this drives the whole studies office crazy. Here's an instance where a buddy system comes in handy. And an intervention that works with Nine students is to require a draft or even a predraft, as well as some guidance in how to select a topic. Or sit down with them and discuss their work, before the test, or the paper is due.

Peacekeepers like to do things for people, but they don't like to be told what to do, they like to be asked. This is key in interactions with Nine colleagues and students. The first approach is important. Otherwise the obstinacy dynamic kicks in, "I'll do this for you, but that doesn't mean I've agreed." A Peacekeeper starts to feel, "Why am I here and why am I doing this? I don't want to do this." The passive-aggressive pattern takes hold. By ostensibly buying your agenda, but then holding up everything because they don't want to be on board, Nines adopt an aggressive, controlling stance.

### Shift to Point Three (Security)

When Nines feel secure they shift to Point Three and access the Three energy, drive to achieve goals, ability to prioritize and perform. But they don't take on the Three competitiveness or success-failure syndrome. Usually Nines feel secure when they have bought someone else's agenda and use their energy to further that agenda. They report that they function in high gear in total immersion experiences.

Parent's Day was coming up, the class decided we should turn the classroom into an experience of Ancient Egypt. I thought that was a great idea. We had a week to pull it off. I worked for twenty out of twenty-four hours for five days, we built a small pyramid, made a papier-mâché sphinx, created the topography of the River Nile around a crack on the floor. The students made costumes from diagrams in the the pyramids, we performed Act One of *Antony and Cleopatra*, we taped Egyptian music. Work that week was a real high.

Even though Point Nines shift to Point Three when they feel secure, they can access the defense mechanisms of Threes: self-deceit and avoiding failure.

### Shift to Point Six (Stress)

When Nines shift to Point Six under stress, their natural inertia is exacerbated by worst-case scenario thinking, and the Questioner fear and paranoia can be paralyzing.

The atmosphere among the faculty was so conflict-ridden, most mornings I didn't want to go to school. I started coming later and later, missed giving my lectures, dragged my feet on grading papers. I got a call from the dean's office. It was probably a routine matter, but all my worst fears came up to haunt me. They are going to fire me. I agreed to see him next week, but I know I won't keep the appointment, and matters will just get worse and worse. I know, I've been here before, it's a vicious cycle.

Even though Point Nines shift to Point Six when they feel stressed, they can access the gifts of Sixes, courage, and logical thinking.

## Key Characteristics

### An Even Terrain—Seeing the World Globally

Among the major drivers of the Peacekeeper E-type intelligence is the avoidance of conflict. A sensible strategy to avoid conflict is to maintain an even tenor to all that is happening around you, to view the world through a diffuse lens. By not paying more attention to any one feature of the interior or exterior landscape, Nines keep their environment flat, even, and uncontentious. This Nine educator reports on how everything she does seems equally important to her.

I've always got about twelve different things going on at the same time. I'm in my classroom, the bell rings, it's my planning period, I'm surfing the Internet looking for material I can use next year. At the same time I've got a tape over here that I'm dubbing because I want to show it next period, I jump up and run out to the Xerox machine. I don't tend to do things in a methodical order. All of the steps seem equally important to me and I try to do them all at once. That's why my classroom is a mess because I always have nine or ten different activities going on in the room at the same time. If you start putting materials away you just have to take them back out again. I mean they're all happening, it's not like we're done with one. There's no sense putting things away and then taking them back out. We need it, so we just leave it there.

This Peacekeeper is aware that she is flouting the institutional norm by the seeming disorder of her teaching environment, but her energy and attention go to the activity of learning, rather than the outer appearance of an orderly classroom.

My desk is a mess. It's controlled chaos. The actual process of learning is more important than the way my desk, or my room, looks. The activity is the important thing. Often there's so much going on in the room, that's more important than that everything is in its place. It's something that I have made myself accept that material isn't always put back. That's not one of my strengths. I judge myself on it, I always have in the back of my mind what will other people think when they walk into the room. I've had to teach myself not to be worried about what other people might think, to teach the way my talents lead me.

### Others' Agenda

The Peacekeeper's focus of attention is to take on the agendas of others. Others' agendas replaces being awake to oneself. Nines can utilize enormous energy, be decisive and forceful, show passion—as long as it is for others. They use others' agendas as a screen, because they want to avoid conflict by not drawing attention to themselves. For this teacher her agenda is obviously her students' learning—she is passionate on their behalf.

> I think my talents are that I'm flexible in the classroom. I can create a space where everybody feels that their contribution has value. I don't get stuck with a rigid plan, "This is what we have to do today." If something comes up and it seems important, those are the teachable moments. I'm good at taking those on. I think that they need to learn to work in groups, to get along with each other, to be creative, to express themselves visually, through writing and speech. In the process of completing a project, seeing what they can accomplish from their idea—that's what I want them to learn.

The following speaker succinctly describes how it feels to take on another's agenda at the expense of looking out for oneself. She also describes how resentment of this position can kick in.

> I will not take lunch if my boss needs something done. I mean I will go from 7:00 a.m. till 8:00 p.m.—go, go, go—never aware of what I need. Besides I never know how I can present to her that I need something, knowing that she needs all of this from me. That's where my attention always goes. The one thing is when I focus on somebody else's agenda, my attention is totally there. It's almost to me as if it's a crime to say I need something. How can I dare? How I can find the balance and not care what that other person thinks? That's where my mind goes, what are they going to think?
>
> I get resentful and then I say to myself: she made me do this, she made me do that. She is constantly asking me to do things (which she probably is) but it's also my responsibility to say, "Hey, wait a second, you know this and this and this is what I have to do for myself, well, it's not getting done." It's hard not to get angry. It's hard to find out where the anger is directed and not always point it out, to stop and ask, "Wait a second—what part is mine and what part is the other person's?" Usually a lot of it is mine.

This Nine is beginning to claim "pieces of herself" which is scary to her because she doesn't know how to handle the conflict such claims might generate.

> I had no agenda of my own, it wasn't something that I knew how to do at all. Now I have found an agenda, not just what I'm researching, but personal pieces, but I don't know that I know how to fight for

them. I've not been in a position where I've had to do that. I can stand there quietly and claim them, but if somebody attacks them, looks at me as if I'm crazy, then my position no longer has any force. In terms of direct conflict, if I'm one of the people directly in line, I don't think I know how to do that.

### Unconditional Love— "I just love my students."

Among the gifts Peacekeepers bring to the table is an ability to give love and support unconditionally. This educator shares a poignant anecdote of how he tried to salvage the self-esteem of the person in his class with the lowest grade.

I can remember twenty-five to thirty years ago inventing a Myron C. Peterson with a Social Security number who always got the lowest score in my class. He was at the bottom of the list, so that poor devil who was next to last didn't feel as bad.

### Motivation

It is almost a truism in Enneagram literature that Nines are reluctant self-starters. The following speakers report on what motivates them. Particularly helpful to other educators are the responses and suggestions for the teaching-learning dynamic. For this speaker the students' expectations and her own desire to promote harmony in groups are what motivate her.

What motivates me into action when I'm in the classroom is the fact that I'm in the classroom. Often I will get up in the morning wondering "what am I going to do today?" But as soon as I'm in the room, the students and their expectation are there, I push a switch and I'm there, too. I think what motivates me as well is that I want them to see how much value each other has, I want them to get along with each other. These students are all coming from different kinds of environments. I want to see them working together in a positive, productive group.

Likewise, this Nine educator finds it's the students' expectations that get her going.

I actually ask people how do they get up in the morning. It's hard for me to get up. I don't like to, I would rather lie in bed and be comfortable. Once I drag myself up, once I get myself up and into the classroom, it's the expectation of the students that gets me moving. I mean if they were fine without me in the room, if they could all get along there, be happy in the room together without me doing anything, I'd probably not come. It's their expectation that gets me moving, gets me planning.

The following Peacekeeper shares ideas about how he teaches. The most important aspect is that he provides a safe place for students to fail—this is key in motivating Nines. He wishes he had had a teacher who knew this. The fact is that allowing someone to fail in a nonpunitive way is so contrary to our institutional and societal conditioning. But what a gift to give a student—a place to feel safe enough and not deficient when you are unable to fulfill the teacher's expectations, when you want so badly to get there for the teacher, but you know your mind doesn't work the way she expects—and that's OK for her.

One of the ways I learn is the way I teach, too. The idea of deadlines and consequences is linked to choice-making. Much of my schooling was me being told what to do and then me being told how I didn't do it as well as the teacher wanted it done. If I had felt that my opinion, choices, thoughts, failures, attempts had mattered, I would have invested more of myself into school. So that's what I end up trying to do in teaching, leaving a lot to my students. I pull them along gently, or they don't learn how to walk themselves. If in school I could have made my own choices and decisions and failed safely and learned from that failure, I could have learned that way. But school was being told what to do, doing it, aching for praise, sometimes getting it, and then wanting to do exactly what I did again not for myself but for that person's agenda.

This educator underlines the points made by the previous speaker. She articulates clearly the inner workings of the Nine process of learning.

Setting consequences is good for me, but if I either don't understand, or it doesn't fit with how my processing works, I'll deliver, but it won't be anything good. I will fulfill your expectation, I know how to do that, I'm quick enough to do it, but I'll do barely what's required if you put a deadline on me. My processing method is different, putting consequences on me forces me further into thinking that there's something wrong with me. I can pass your course, but I can't actually learn it in any way that's going to be useful to me. And I won't. I can absorb a tremendous amount of information quickly and almost not know that I'm doing it. I don't know how to synthesize it, because there's no structure for it to be processed. If you can give choices and make some space for my process, if you encourage me, allow it to be safe to fail, this is the way to reach me and teach me. My mind doesn't work in a goal-oriented way.

The way Nines learn mirrors their E-type perception of a diffuse, global view of life. Many other Nines, as well as this speaker, report on their inability to structure a framework made up of discrete steps. This is one area where educators can be directly helpful with Nine students and colleagues.

The way I learn is if there's a huge body of information, let's say it's history, I will take a little bit of information from many areas. In the beginning I can't make sense out of it, I don't know which piece of information is more important than another piece and I need to have that spelled out for me. Otherwise, it's overwhelming for me. The way I learn is by building up the foundation over and over again from this sea of information—that feels like something I have to do and it takes large amounts of time. If somehow a teacher could structure this (I can't set my own priorities) then there's a framework into which I can take all of these bits and pieces of details, and it will make sense to me. But I cannot build my own framework. If I'm sitting there in class and taking notes from a lecture, I'll take every single word if I possibly can because I can't get to what is the dominant topic, what is the subtopic, I can't do that. I need help with doing that, that's the way my mind runs throughout my whole life.

### Being Listened To

Peacekeepers want the reassurance that they are being listened to. If Nines sense there is conflict or potential conflict in any interaction, they will pursue the interaction with relentless obstinacy until they sense the potential for conflict is past, or a resolution has been found. Little else makes Nines as uncomfortable as having unresolved issues dangling in front of them. In order for teaching /learning to take place, Nines need to to be reassured that they are listened to.

Being listened to is important to me. I feel as if generally I'm not listened to very well, but I have the ability to listen pretty well to other people. I think that's key in any kind of teacher/student relationship. If the teacher listens to the student I think that's important, because a good teacher will get a sense of what that student wants to do and is capable of doing. They will have a good relationship. Are you interested that the student ends up on page 35 by Tuesday? Is that the number-one priority, rather than the fact that the student is doing some daily reading? I think if the teacher is clear with what she or he wants, and communicates that to the student and then listens to the student, learning will happen.

### Communicating

Nines have a communication style that can be characterized as meandering in saga-like anecdotes that threaten to lose contact with the main thread of what they are trying to say. It does not occur to Nines that they can get through to other E-types without all the diffuse detail. Many people tune out to this long-winded, indirect style. If Nines sense they are unheeded, conflict arises, and an unfortunate dynamic is set in motion.

My husband, my friends, my students have learned to ask me what's the point of what I'm saying. I've learned to welcome that moment with a lot of grace and to get to the point. I love the words meandering, wandering, wondering, embroidering, all of those, weaving, spinning, I think those words describe my speech. Those are metaphors that I use all of the time for conversation, for writing, and for speaking.

This Nine speaker describes his response to others' tuning out. Nine educators can be verbose in their presentations and lose their audiences.

If I could see a little green light coming on your forehead saying, "I'm listening to you, I understand," then my stories would be short and succinct. But there is no light, so I'll embroider the story, make it interesting because I don't want to lose your attention. If I make the story interesting, I'm going to hit some of the spots that you can relate to because that's happened in your life and you're going to continue to listen to me and this is going to be good. If you start to drift, I'm going to have to do something, like get in front of you or something, but I'm not confrontative, so I have to embellish my story to be more interesting. Your best bet is to say, "Hey, cut to the chase, what's the bottom line, where are we going with this?" I'll respond, "Oh, you're right," and I'll start another story.

### Conflict

Here are some direct reports on this key Nine defense mechanism, avoiding conflict. In the Peacekeeper's perceptual lens, conflict invariably brings up anger. If you become angry you wake up to yourself and other people take notice of you which can lead to more conflict. So part of the Nine intelligences is to contain the anger, and the energy, by avoiding conflict if at all possible. This educator sees instructing her students about getting along as an area of informal teaching.

I try to keep the conflict down, I tend to go after the conflict once it's happened. I begin to make a long speech about how important other peoples' feelings are, how important it is not to bring evil into the world. I can go on and on, the students interrupt, "Okay, alright, we've got it, we'll be nice." I tend to go after conflict from more of a mental place where I'm trying to convince them about how unreasonable it is for them to be creating this nastiness.

This Nine put herself directly into conflictual situations to experience how she handles conflict.

I was in a support group and there were many different personalities. I loved all of the women, but I would leave there feeling so stressed. I realized early on that the reason why was because there was so much conflict in the group. I didn't like it, we'd be in the middle of a meeting and I would want to run. I actually stayed with the group because I'd made a commitment for two years and I felt it was important for me to sit through the conflict, to sit in the middle of everybody going after each other. Around then I started taking tae kwon do and I loved it. I like to exercise. It helps me with getting the energy moving. Before

I lived in typical Nine style, I would go to work, go home, lie down, and stay in that position until it was time to go back to work. But the struggle with tae kwon do, as much as I loved it, was eventually I had to buy gear so that I could spar. This was horrifying to me, but there was a certain little tingle of excitement in it, it was scary. When I took my black belt test we had to write a paper and I wrote actually about wanting so badly to avoid conflict that I had to call on a warrior self, because I'd made a commitment to it. I run from conflict; even now that I feel I've done a lot of work on myself, it's still not something that I would choose to put myself in.

## Passive-Aggressive Response

Nines are often disconcerted by the energy that arises when they become angry. If they express the anger directly it is sure to lead to conflict, so the Peace-keeper E-type intelligence directs Nines to express their anger in passive-aggressive behavior that drains energy out of the situation. This way they won't have to do what they don't want to do, *and* they gain the moral upper hand by making the other party frustrated and angry. This Nine speaker articulates a remarkably clear understanding of this dynamic. We can extrapolate what she is saying into any Nine clash around authority issues.

Lately I have tried to put myself into situations where I can engage in conflict, because I have found in myself a strength that I'm willing to face the discomfort of coming up against someone else. The person who taught me how to do this was my mother, she was the flint that allowed me to find my flame. She was quite controlling, a beautiful, wonderful mother and she liked to have her way. In order for me to have any life at all I had to learn how to stand up to her. I wasn't able to do so until I was fifteen; until then I don't think I ever engaged in any conflict because I knew I would lose. I began to try to stand up for myself a little and after I got married I put my husband between me and my mother—a brilliant maneuver—I learned to find the courage to come up against her. It was in fighting with her and saying, "No, not that, it's not that" —that I learned to find my own position.

It was a desperation move because I felt pushed to the wall, it was not acceptable to be pushed that far and not have any say in my own life. I had to find a way to be myself and often it was in a passive-aggressive way. My mother loved to know everything, so I would hold out on her and not tell her the things I knew she wanted to know. I was slow, I think part of being slow is a passive-aggressive act. My mother would stand in the doorway with her arms crossed as I was getting dressed, waiting to go for an appointment or something and she'd say, "You're as slow as molasses in January." I was trying to move, at least I thought I was trying to move, but I was like a slow motion picture—I couldn't find anything, I was paralyzed. I think it was because I didn't like being pushed around. So I slowed down.

### Obstinacy

Likewise this speaker articulates clearly why and how Nines become obstinate. She has some sound advice for educators interacting with Nine students.
Simply because I've said I'm going to do it, or because I've agreed
with you that it's a good thing to do, doesn't necessarily mean that I've
bought into it. Many times I've told all these people that I would do
these things because they seem like such great things to do, but when it
comes time to do them, I'm not committed to them. It's so hard for me
to figure out when is this *my* commitment, when this is *my* passion,
and not something I think is a good idea of somebody else's. I struggle
with other people seeing me as being lazy, or not keeping the commitments I make. What they don't understand is that it looks to them like
I've made a commitment, but I haven't made a commitment. So what
I'm struggling with now is having integrity with the way I speak. For
instance, in saying, "I can't do that", if in fact I'm not willing to make
a commitment to do that right now. One of the interventions I would
encourage other teachers to do with students when they give you answers like, "I can't," is to ask them, "Are you willing to do this or not?
If you're not willing to do it, say: 'I'm not willing to do it.' If you are
willing to do it, and you're making a commitment to it, understand
what commitment means."

### Peacekeeper

This Nine relishes being able to use his natural gifts of a peacekeeper. Note
how easily he plays this role on behalf of others.
About twenty-five years ago, I was part of a new university that
opened up and there were a lot of problems, a lot of conflict. The dean
didn't like conflict so he did what deans normally do—passed the buck
to me. He put me in charge of a committee of *Common Concerns*
which is a nice way of saying of all of the bitching. The interesting
thing was that I loved it, I learned a valuable thing about myself: when I
had people coming in ranting and raving—I was the peacemaker. The
conflict didn't bother me at all as long as it wasn't directed at me.

### Harmony

Part and parcel of being a Peacekeeper is having an E-type intelligence that
directs you to promote harmony. This Peacekeeper describes how one measure
of success for her is when everyone is working together and she can sit back and
watch.
I feel like I've had a successful day when everybody works together.

There are certain days when everybody is just into it: nobody's distracted, nobody is more interested in writing a note to their girlfriend, everybody is excited about what they're learning. Those are the days when I feel I've been successful. It has more to do with them, their movement, their interaction than it has to do with me. Often when I've had the best days, I say "go" and I just sit there and watch, and they run around, go back and forth, and do what they have to do, and it works out great.

Harmony and peace—a prescription of sanity for Nine educators
I like peace. We're working together, we're not angry with each other, there's no conflict, sometimes it's chaotic and noisy, that's actually the way I like it. I don't like it to be too calm, then it feels like I'm not being productive. I like it to be peaceful, but not calm, we're all happy, we like each other.

## *Inertia and Energy— "Festina lente" (Make Haste Slowly)*

Peacekeepers sit on huge reserves of energy, akin to the pilot module of a spacecraft sitting on huge reserves of rocket fuel. If that energy is released it can explode like a firecracker, blowing others away in a firestorm. It can create conflict, involve Nines in all sorts of unpredictable, uncomfortable, and unwelcome consequences. Some Nines will admit that they suffer more from fear of success than fear of failure. Success tends to raise expectations, demand more energy, and set people up for disappointment. The world expects more from successful people. It is safer and more comfortable to coast. So the Peacekeeper E-type intelligence directs Nines to tamp down the energy on their own behalf, and only to use it on behalf of others. This is why many Nines appear highly energetic and enthusiastic. The form this tamping down takes when it comes to their own agenda is inertia, going asleep to oneself, not being present. The following speaker describes this process with clarity.

As a teacher I feel as if I'm sitting behind the wheel with one foot on the gas and one foot on the brake. Go, stop, go, stop, go—it takes a lot of energy to keep the car on the road. I know that I have energy, but if you look at me there doesn't always seem to be a lot there. Another image I have of myself is standing like Atlas, holding up the globe, making sure that the world stays where it's supposed to stay. That takes a lot of energy, in fact. I can pull energy from another person; I love to be around high-energy people because I feel juiced up and alive when I'm near them and it's a lovely feeling. But whether or not I could sustain it—I have a feeling that my lining would burn out. There's so much energy coming through the system, I'm so excited, then I go back and it's like someone let the air out of the tires. I pull energy from those around me.

This Nine educator shares his observations of the process of managing his own energy. Nines react with defensive anger to the label of laziness.

I feel as if sometimes I have so much energy I'm going to explode, so I need to do something with it to defuse it—I go to sleep. It's not a lack of energy, it's there, I can sense it, I resent being called lazy, because, well, yes, I am lazy, but I don't want somebody else to tell me that. I remember my mother calling me lazy quite a bit. I think one of the saviors is to be in a job where the structure is predictable and I have a lot to do. At all moments in the school year I am running, running, running, almost on overdrive, go, go, go, so you would never see a lazy moment. But the minute school is over, sloth comes into my life, to tie my shoe is a big deal. It's an amazing transformation. I certainly hardly recognize myself in June compared to April.

### Being Open

With Nines it's WYSIWYG—what you see is what you get. This Nine educator has learned to share the state of her mood with her students.

The way I come into the classroom depends a lot on what my mood is. I can come into the classroom excited and full of enthusiasm, but at other times I come in and I have no energy. I'm honest with the students, they know. I tend to make it clear, to be honest with them about how I'm feeling and try and help them understand where I'm coming from, so that we'll have a peaceful day anyway. If I'm stressed out because I was stuck in traffic, I try and let them know, so if they do something and I jump all over them, or bite their heads off, they don't take it personally. I want them to understand.

### Merging

Nines describe how they can merge with another person, literally lose their boundaries so that they feel as if they become that person—their moods, their energy, they can even anticipate thought and speech patterns, and know what the other person is going to say before they do. This is one area of behavior where Nines and Twos can be confused as look-alikes. But Nines take on the whole agenda of the person, situation, or group, whereas Twos home in on what other people need and alter themselves to fulfill those needs. This Nine educator reports on how she can viscerally "feel into" her students. She responds to the class as a whole even though approaching quieter students is difficult for her.

I develop a sense of my students as the year goes on. It's not as if I walk into the room and boom there it is. On the first day I'm usually motivated by my agenda. I have these things that I have to do, and I don't even know how much attention I pay to the students that first day. I can be task oriented at the beginning of the year. It's not until the next week when I start to feel into them individually. It's not until they start moving around the room that I begin to get a feeling for them. The sense I get from them is in their reaction, what's going on once we start moving around. Then I can figure out who's interested. The still ones are hard for me. I want there to be peace and love in the room, so once I can get the moving ones moving, I'll go over to the still ones and try to draw them out individually. The quieter ones I have to go after them. I don't tell students where to sit in the room. Some of them will be right up front, eager little beavers, and some of them will be in the back of the room, leaning back. I let them sit where they want to sit and then I go get them. It's hard to go after the quiet ones. I do it because I feel like I need to. I would much rather let them do what they're doing. They're quiet, they're minding their own business. I would much rather let them be. There's a big open space between us, and I find myself saying, "Okay, just walk over there they're not going to bite you." It's hard for me sometimes to realize that I'm the teacher, the grown-up, that they actually want me to go over there and talk to them. They're probably shy like I was. I have to psych myself up sometimes to go over, but I know that that's what they want, so I do it, but it's hard.

This Nine reports a similar phenomenon.

Among my greatest strengths is being able to walk into any situation or any group and know where everybody is before they do. I can't tell you intellectually how I do it or what I do, but I know what to do and it comes through to me. In that instance I think what happens is that I push whatever my brain is telling me my priorities are—usually details that are not important—out of the way to make enough space to take in all the energy of the situation. It's about me, about making space to be able to run that group and direct that play by moving things out of the way. If I'm forgetting myself in that, I'm willing to do so, because what I gain for myself is much greater than the piece I let go.

And another similar report.

Merging can be so intense for me that I know the words before they come out of the other person. It's not only being able to sense them, it's to get in there. It makes people nervous.

## Anger

Peacekeepers can express direct anger, but note how it is usually on behalf of others. This Nine educator also touches on how she can become angry on her own behalf around authority issues.

I get angry in the classroom when there's meanness. I try to be responsible with it, but I let them know it's there. Unfortunately they don't always take it seriously because it shows up so rarely. Outside of the classroom my anger shows up when people are treated unfairly. I get angry when people are not tolerant, even when there is just cause for impatience or anger. I'm such an exercise in contradiction here because I know that I can be judgmental too. I get angry when other people are judgmental. I get angry personally around authority issues, I have authority issues. I don't like to be told what to do. I love to do things for people, but I like to be asked in a certain way. I don't like for people to assume that they can dictate the way I do things.

This Nine educator shares a saga describing instances of his anger.

In a classroom environment with adults, for instance, I had one guy walk in, slam his computer down, forty-five minutes late and start saying, "Listen, I need this done and I'm not going be able to do it because it's not working properly." I said, "Look I've got this other system set up for you over here." I'm trying to be nice to this guy, but for the next maybe forty seconds to a minute and a half, he's loud, arrogant, pompous, and I know I don't deserve this. So I put my face right into his, I was seething, I said, "Listen, this is my classroom. If you want what I have you golly, gee, darn well, better sit down, NOW, here." This is about as angry as I can get, it's not loud, just intense. Afterward, when I reflect, I think, I could have handled that another way. I always thought there's something wrong with me. It wasn't anger: I don't ever remember being angry except once—at whomever you want to call God—because I was over in Vietnam and my friends were getting killed and I thought you son of a gun! And that was the one time in my life where I was angry because I felt if there is a God, this is not justifiable. There is no excuse for this kind of thing, and that anger is still there.

### Procrastination

In a society and institutions that place value and importance on being able to create priorities as a way of achieving goals, and keeping deadlines as a way of reaching those goals, most Peacekeepers are out of step. Procrastination is particularly sharply etched in the educational dynamic where meeting deadlines is an essential way business as usual is conducted. Nine educators are articulate and aware of their misalignment in this culture.

I think I do have quite a lot of organizational skill focused around my teaching and I do have very beautiful teaching notes. I keep my daybook quite religiously; I even write up classes after I've done them. If it's a new class I'm doing for the first time, I'll write it up afterward so I'll have the record the next year with key questions, activities, everything. But that daybook is the only area of my life that is beautifully organized and there are many other areas, vast areas, of neglect and that does include most of my home and garden. I rely on my husband to remind me of things. Choices are also a problem, priorities and choices are a major problem. I think he's learned to ask me what I do not want to do. "Which one of these do you not want?"—if there are three choices for dinner. If there are five things you could buy, he asks, "Well which of these colors do you not want?" "That one!" Eventually I can maybe get around to what's left, I'll take what's left because I can never sit down and say "I want that."

Peacekeepers take comfort in the conventional wisdom of keeping lists to help them plan and impose structure on their lives—but this methodology, too, can misfire. An interior world that is diffuse, not formed from peaks and valleys, is not easily able to impose a sequential pattern of importance on outside commitments and events.

I'm a real list maker. I make lists all the time, I have all these lists, and this is only the small pile. Every once in a while the piles get so big that I can't keep them all together and so I consolidate them into one list. I will actually go back and read the list and check something off that I've done on that list. There's a great sense of accomplishment when I've done that. I feel good that I can actually put that thing away and move on to some other things on the list. Even though I prioritize that list, the priorities aren't that important to me. The things on the list as a whole are important to me, but not necessarily in the order in which I put them down. Even though I know that some of them may be more pressing than others, I do try to focus on the ones that are a priority at the top of the list, but invariably reality strikes and those don't necessarily get done first. Bits and pieces of all the things on the list do get done all the time. Eventually by virtue of moving forward and moving the mounds of paperwork and the other things that are on that list, things do get done. But they don't get done in the order or in the stream of which I'd like them to get done.

This Nine describes what it's like to be on overload. It is not that Peacekeepers cannot come to decisions, for instance, on what to work on first, but it is helpful to them if someone can offer them a slate of choices. What they select to be first becomes the priority, and so on down the list by a process of elimination. Our speaker needs someone to check in with her, to help her prioritize and keep to her agenda.

Yesterday I had five different projects going on at the same time. My boss calls me and asks, "Are you busy?" What do I say: "Yes?" Now I've got five different things going on and I say, "No," because I know she wants what she is calling about, done. I'm looking at all these projects and I know I'm not going to get one of them done today. I got angry, I was upset. So finally I called her up and said, "Listen, I need your help, which one of these do you want done first?" I always need help with prioritizing. Getting a buddy is the best thing in the world that I've done so far. Otherwise it's a nightmare, I can start cleaning and pick up a photo book and start looking and the thought of cleaning is gone and that could be an hour. But if someone reminds me of what else I've got to do that day, the hour will not disappear on me.

### *Going on Automatic — Spacing Out*

Inertia, not being present to oneself, spacing out, how do Nines describe these inner states? Here are several examples. This speaker describes how taking on the agenda of directing a school play causes him to be asleep to most other parts of his life.

> I direct a play at school each year, last year there were 300 students in the cast and we have one month for rehearsal. I have the best time producing, it's fun, I focus totally on the students. I've done this for three years and every year I space out on everything else in my life. I had a flat tire that stayed flat for seven weeks, so I just didn't drive, I walked everywhere. I've had my phone cut off because I forgot to pay my bills during that time. It's hard to explain because it's not like I forget to pay, it's more unconscious, nothing is as important as doing this play with these 300 students.

This speaker describes what spacing out feels like in her body.

> It's a physical spacing out and it feels as though I've been drugged. It's difficult to recover from that and I'm not quite sure what prompts it. I mean I can guess. Sometimes it can happen for hours. Other times it's a milder form of spacing out. I have practiced listening to everybody to make sure that I stay present all of the time because my mind can go off. I only realize it when I realize that I've missed whole sentences.

This speaker describes how her energy can be siphoned off and absorbed in inessentials, at the cost of getting essential tasks done.

> Gone! My mind will be gone somewhere, but it's completely unfocused. I can have awareness of somebody wanting something from me, it could be an emergency. If I'm gone I'm not in control of clicking myself back in and moving forward. My husband used to joke about this. A number of years ago I bought him one of those little video handheld games. We determined that he had to take it away and hide it because it was life-threatening, I would get so absorbed. I think it's a reaction to stress and tension, that I can't take the intensity, so I do anything that I can do to shut it all down. My mind will wander a little bit, but there's no plan; if you asked me after it happens, what was going on in my brain? I have no idea at all, none.

### Acedie — Asleep to Oneself

This Nine educator shares a description of what it is like to sense that one is asleep to oneself. Note his terror that if he stops he won't be able to start again. Also note that because he's so out of touch with himself, he has little idea of how he's coming across to others. This is a major Nine blind spot, misjudging their impact on others.

There's tremendous motivation for me in the fear of stopping dead and not being able to move again. I don't know whether it's because of other people's expectations, or childhood experience, or what it is, but it's so painful for me when I stop that I've begun to learn to do almost anything to get out of it. Any kind of movement dissipates the feeling that I won't be able to move. But sometimes I'll overreact, I'll throw myself forward, do way too much, because I'm so terrified that if I stop, I won't be able to get it going again, I won't find my energy. It's less so now but for many, many years I had no clue how to find a way to force myself to do something. I don't know where the energy is, I know it's in there, I just don't know how to find it.

One of the issues that gets in the way of my relationship with students is that sometimes I don't know how I sound to them. I will find out later maybe that I spoke sharply to someone, hurt their feelings, which I had no intention of doing. That's happened to me in other times in my life, not just in the classroom. I see myself as this peaceful, loving person and it startles me when other people express that they are getting anger or a sharpness from me. I don't hear myself that way, I actually pride myself in not being that way, it always startles me when someone tells me that I've hurt their feelings or that one of the students says to me, "You didn't have to say it like that."

### Growth Path: From Being Asleep to Oneself to Right Action

The growth path is from being asleep to oneself to right action on one's own behalf which, of course, then translates to taking action on behalf of others. Nines need to be able to line up the facts with their intuition, to decide what is the right action in a particular set of circumstances. It's difficult work for Peacekeepers to find their own agenda, all too easy to find someone else's. This teacher's need for there to be harmony leads him to move to right action instinctively.

If students are fighting at my school, I don't know why but I always wind up being the one to step into the middle of a fight. I won't run from that because I hate for people to get hurt, I want them to be peaceful, to like each other. I always wind up stepping into the middle of a fight, jacking up some kid twice my size and saying: "If you hit me, I'm gong to kill you." It's empowering and scary and I usually do it before I have time to think about it.

### Quality of Essence: Universal Love

One of the great gifts of the Nine is universal love, universal acceptance, unconditional love, acting without competitiveness, accessing energy in an almost pure way to use it on behalf of others. Nines ride high on that energy and it can go on for weeks and months. This educator knows her love of her students is her great asset.

> I think one of my strengths is that I care about all of the students and I love them a lot and I think that they know that. I think that's probably my best strength.

## What Peacekeeper Students Say

### *Consequences*

> You go day-by-day and there's someone (a teacher) pushing you every day. Usually what that person pushing me does is to get me to a situation where I know if I don't work there'll be consequences, or that it's an obligation I have to do something, or I'll be in trouble.

### *Procrastination*

> I was grateful and I wanted to write a thank-you letter with no one telling me to. I was planning on doing it, I just never got round to it. Nothing was going to happen to me and I'll probably never see her again. So it was hard for me to ... and I would think about it once in a while ... I'd say, "I'll do it later, at the end of the day," but I'll never just get up and do it.

and

> Every once in a while I do get home and run through my assignments, while I'm fresh and energetic and then I have time for other things. But usually I won't start work until dinner's over. I'll start after 8.00 p.m. and I'll be fine. But if I watch TV for a while, or sit around and wait, then it gets hard.

### *Taking Action*

> Sometimes I can get directly to what I have to do, and do it. This can be one day a week, or two days a month, or a period before exams when I'm cramming, cramming everything. I can work seemingly endlessly. I get on a roll and stay there. It's a natural high, the energy feels potent. I surprise myself, because othertimes I look back at periods like that and I wonder how I was ever able to pull it off, taking action for a prolonged time like before exams. Most times there's a roadway jammed with many unimportant things infront of me. I get side-tracked into doing other things instead of what I need to do, like homework. I move between the unimportant things, trying to do a bit of each. To others it looks like I'm not doing anything, but I know I'm trying to get to my

homework which, believe it or not, is my priority.

### Obstinacy

I didn't see any point in doing the homework, because it wasn't going to give me any answers, it wasn't going to make me better, or happier in any way. But I do like learning and I do like school and the achievement that comes with it. I like improving myself. But it doesn't always have to be in the areas that other people feel are important for me.

### Global View

Success for me is personal satisfaction, knowing that I can be good, that I poured so much work into it and I got this direct tangible result. Overall I do want to learn everything there is in school—because obviously it's worthwhile or they wouldn't be teaching this. A lot of times I don't have enough interest in it so that it's the obligation of getting good grades, getting into a good college that's driving me to sit down and work. What is frustrating is that I can't learn everything in school, and making choices about what to study is hard for me.

### Structure

One of the things that strikes me as a student is my knowing when a teacher is completely, absolutely so frustrated with me because I can't do what she wants me to and I know it. I can remember one instance of feeling I'm never going to make this woman happy. I can't do it because I know that I haven't done this work and that and all of it is due. It's at the point where another teacher had to come in to understand where I am. He asked me, "What do you want to do? How is it that you want to put these projects together, because you have to get them all done?" It's tough because I said I'd do it and I'm not doing it. I think that a good teacher would say, "You're telling me that you're doing this, but I don't see where or how you are doing this. Can you tell me? What have you done so far?" Because I guess it's the structure and the understanding that I don't have internally. I don't have it. Then I feel I'm bad or I'm wrong and I'm never going to get it done because I don't have this structure.

### Passive-Aggressive Behavior

Usually I don't pay much attention to rules and regulations because they are meaningless, they don't bring happiness, or it's not going to give me anything to do certain things.

### Inertia

I do what it takes to keep up a good grade and to keep being a good student. I think I'm a good student in that sense because in a way I always end up performing well. On the other hand I think that I'm not a fully achieving student. Like the other kids spend hours and hours working and I can't even imagine it and I don't want to do it. So I don't know if I'm a great student in terms of my potential; I could spend hours and hours more working.

### Brief Interview with a Peacekeeper Educator

*Q. What is your teaching style?*
A. My teaching style is chaotic to someone looking in from the outside. Lots goes on at the same time, lots of little lessons happening at the same time in the room. I rotate around the room because I want to give them all what they need, what they want at the time. I want to please everybody.

*Q. What do you look for in your students?*
A: What I look for in my students is movement, energy, enthusiasm, and a willingness to get along.

*Q. What is important in the way you present material?*
A: What is important in the way I present material is that I put it across so they can understand it.

*Q. What will students say of you?*
A: Students will say of me that I care for them. I pride myself on getting along with my students. I know that I have students who are problems that other teachers don't even want to see them coming. But they'll see me in the hallway and say, "Hi ...," they're all sweet, I have a good rapport with them. I think that's because they know I love them.

*Q. Why do you teach?*
A: I teach because I want the world to be a better place.

*Q. How do you communicate?*
A: My communication style is meandering. I communicate well most of the time as it's important to be understood. I can rephrase other people's comments so they are better understood.

*Q. What is your attitude to preparing teaching plans?*
A: Preparing teaching plans is frustrating because what I plan is hardly ever what happens. Usually what happens is better than what I had planned, because planning on paper is not as exciting as when it happens. You can't write that

down ahead of time.

*Q. What do you like about the classroom?*
A: What I like about the classroom is that it is mine and I can pretty much do what I want to do. I can keep experimenting.

*Q. What don't you like about the classroom?*
A: What I don't like about the classroom is conflict. What distracts me most in the classroom is when the students start to go after each other. They start making those little snide remarks at each other, or one is picking on the other—that can get me totally distracted. So it's important to me that there not be conflict between them. It makes me sick. I can literally feel myself getting nauseous when it starts. Conflict exhausts me. By the end of the day sometimes I'm totally wiped out from the struggle with how important it is for there to be peace.

## Practical Tips

*For Peacekeepers to Work with Themselves*

- Be aware when inessential activities replace fulfilling your commitments.
- Do some form of body work to help uncork your energy.
- Practice speaking with intonation in your voice, be aware when you are talking in sagas and meandering.
- Try to structure manageable short-term goals for yourself, have a fallback plan if you don't keep to them.
- Learn to make decisions for yourself, voice your own opinion, notice when you defer to others.
- An urge to gather more and more information is a cover-up for procrastination around decisions.
- Try to finish projects, be aware when your energy and attention are siphoned off.
- Be aware when you dig your heels in and become stubborn.
- Learn to handle anger better, go off and punch a pillow, or dig in the garden to lessen the charge.

*For Others who Work with Peacekeepers*

- Give Nines unconditional support through providing a safe place to fail. They believe in themselves when others believe in them.
- It is essential to conduct regular feedback sessions.
- Remind Peacekeepers of their personal needs and rights, they lose sight of these easily.
- Nines absorb a lot of information and can see a "big picture" but need

help in structuring the pieces of how they got there.
- Together structure a framework of short-term objectives to help Nines achieve their goals.
- Point out how in unstructured time inertia comes on and energy drains away.
- Nines are excellent at conflict resolution, use them to help articulate many points of view.
- Help Nines to learn that saying "No" does not necessarily lead to conflict.
- Encourage Nines to find—or even pair them yourself with—a buddy in a buddy system. Reality checks and checking in are extremely beneficial to Nines.

## *ENNEATYPE ONE: THE PERFECTIONIST*

- TRIAD: *DEFENDER*
- ATTENTIONAL FOCUS: Correcting error, a right/wrong mind-set
- GIFT: Moral compass
- AVOIDANCE: Error
- GROWTH PATH: From criticality and judging to serenity
- ESSENCE: Perfection
- SHIFT TO SECURE POINT: *THE OPTIMIST SEVEN* (Detacher —against arrow)
- SHIFT TO STRESS POINT: *THE ROYAL FAMILY FOUR* (Attacher—with arrow)
- WINGS: *THE PEACEKEEPER NINE* (Defender)
  *THE HELPER TWO* (Attacher)

## EXAMPLES OF PERFECTIONIST ONE EDUCATORS: GETTING IT RIGHT

### The Moralist

David W. is the business manager of a large independent school, he oversees a budget of $75 million. David is known as a cautious man who pays meticulous attention to detail. He works best when surrounded by order and neatness, and it took him three years when he began this job to have the office space remodeled to suit his taste. He likes clean, white walls. He dislikes loud noise, so he moved his private office as far from the school corridors as he could. Telephones are muted, soft carpets drown the sound of heels clacking, soundproofing muffles conversations. David's assistant business managers and secretary are in close proximity, but have their own offices. David thinks the era of open office space is a bad idea.

In his own office neatness is a prerequisite. His desk top gleams; once a week he wipes the dust off the leaves of the office plants with meticulous care. Files are neatly labeled, and pages color-coded. Order can only come out of order, chaos out of chaos—this is one of his favorite maxims repeated endlessly to his staff.

David dislikes the role of salesman. He delegates to an assistant the task of presentation, whether to the executive committee, or the trustees, or even at the occasional faculty, or department meeting, but David is on hand to field questions, to make sure no one gets the wrong end of the stick, to spell out the facts, and accurately detail the figures. David relies on detailed memos—that way the facts speak for themselves, there can be no errors in miscommunication. He is intense in his desire to avoid error. Since he has been in his position, and especially in the latter years as his leadership has became more established, the school's financial procedures operate with hitherto unknown efficiency, and the financial records are models of clarity. Accountability and responsibility are the two bywords of his business style.

There are perhaps two other people in the world who know that once a week David plays the bagpipes at a local gathering of Celtic musicians on the other side of town. His fellow musicians are mostly artisans and artists, no one there knows anything about David's professional life. He arrives dressed in his kilt and other Scottish regalia, and plays the bagpipes as if he were entreating Heaven's gates to open. David finds enormous relief in being able to escape into the world of making music.

### How Perfect This Could Be

Susan McC. supervises a large, rural school district in one of the Western states. At the elementary school level, many students travel long distances from ranches and farms to community schools where teaching K-8 under one, or two, roofs is usually the norm. High schoolers are weekly boarders at their schools, or stay with families in the small towns. Susan herself is constantly on the road driving vast distances to visit the schools. She doesn't resent the time she spends in the car; she can be productive. She speaks rapidly into a tape recorder, dictating letters and notes to her secretary, and so catches up with her correspondence. She always travels with a large number of self-improvement cassette tapes that while she listens to them reassure her she is learning the lessons of motivating self and others, understanding and exercising the responsibilities of leadership correctly, communicating effectively, and so on. Occasionally she'll play a jazz tape, she loves music, but only after she feels she's earned the time to relax.

Susan has an internal sense of how to dress for each occasion. If asked she wouldn't be able to describe how she has arrived at this rubric, but she knows intuitively what is right and what is wrong. It is right to wear her most expensive suit and jewelry when she visits the departmental offices in the state capital, it is wrong to wear pants when school personnel are coming to meet with her in her office. It is all right to wear a pant suit if she is a houseguest while on business travel, but not all right to do so when she visits a school. Often Susan is unaware of the internal judgments she makes of others because of what they are wearing—to the manor born, she'll think approvingly of the principal of one school; a farmgirl who's never grown up, of another; a slut, she can't hide it and doesn't want to, of a third.

Usually Susan keeps her criticism and judgments to herself, but if she is angry she knows that she can become irritated and "shrill," as her most recent secretary accused her. The accusation of shrillness pierced Susan like a knife. She felt such mortification, as if the secretary had found out a most damaging truth about her. It is true that she has difficulty in retaining staff, their greatest complaint is she doesn't trust them. She does, but she has a compelling need to go over what everyone has done, to make sure it is right. "After all, if I'm responsible for this school district I have to exercise that responsibility." Aware of how devastating criticism is to her, Susan tries to be gentle when pointing out error to others: yes, it is true, she probably looks for error even in places where no one has looked before, but it's part of her nature to be obsessive.

In the state education department, Susan has a reputation as an outstanding district supervisor. She can be a tigress on behalf of the teachers and students she serves. If there is any question of inequity in allocating funds, she will go toe-to-toe with legislators at budget time, spend hours knocking on doors to make her argument, rally the troops in the local schools. "Every child in my district has a right to the same education as those in any other, and I will do everything I can to ensure the system is fair."

## THE PERFECTIONIST STRATEGY

| Strengths | Weaknesses |
|---|---|
| Moral compass | Right/wrong mind set |
| Analytic ability | One-track thinking |
| Detail-oriented | Criticality and moral superiority |
| Honorable | Inflexible and rigid |
| Continual self-improvement | Overprepare |
| Help others see error | Inner critic measures performance |
| Take on causes—uphold justice, ethics, and principles | Indirect anger |
| Strive for excellence | Burdened by self-criticism |
| Can envision perfection | Procrastination from fear of error |

## THE E-TYPE ONE PROPOSITION

### General Description

#### *Being Right and Being Moral; Criticality, Judgment, and Perfection*

The Perfectionist One is an internalized point, the E-type intelligence takes subtle forms in this strategy—anger is *indirect*, Ones contend with an *internal* critic, they judge themselves and others by an *internalized* yardstick. There is a central preoccupation with rightness. This is different from Eights who ask, "Is it just, is it fair?" Ones ask, "Is it right?" Everything is either right or wrong. This is, of course, the primary Point One blind spot, because the world simply is as it is, the right/wrong construct exists only in Ones' heads.

Perfectionists belong in the Defender triad. As with Points Eight and Nine, they interact in an interspace that exists between themselves and others. For Perfectionists, the interspace is problematic, for when they brush up against others; there is potential for error. There's a wariness, an edginess, a scratchiness when Ones begin to interact with others. Potentially others represent a flaw, or a mistake: whatever it is that I'm going to be doing with you is open to error.

Avoiding error is the primary defense mechanism of the Perfectionist. While

Sixes live with the illusion that outside influences, even life, are authorities, and Eights live with the illusion that life must be challenged in order to establish their own power and control, and Threes *do* life as a task instead of living it with Ones life *is* potential for error. Each E-type is conditioned into being able to cope with their compulsions and defenses, most Ones function fine in the world. But internally there are stark patterns, such as, I have to keep this distance, because if we're going to be wrong, and I'm going to have to retract something, I must have the space to do so.

A major gift of the One is to be a moral compass, Perfectionists intuitively know what's right, they feel it in their bodies. Ones do have a sense of the moral and ethical shape of a project, they can move quickly to what is right or wrong. But the focus on error can often be a drawback. For instance, a One can walk into a classroom and even if the room is perfectly neat and tidy, except for chalk dust under the blackboard, the One's attention will fixate on the chalk dust and immediately the room is imperfect. Additionally, the focus of attention doesn't only go to what is wrong, the next step kicks in, "How can I correct this?" Avoiding error is a two-step process, "What is wrong here and how can I correct it?" Ones take on the burden of responsibility for correcting error, because they believe (another blind spot) that they can see how to perfect error. This belief can annoy others, especially if they're always being told how things can be corrected. If doing it right is not a particular concern of yours, you begin to react negatively against the One.

Believing that they are the only people who carry around a sense of perfection, of correctness, is the source of the Ones' anger. This is where the edginess and resentment comes in. Because they are "good boys and girls" they tamp down their anger. Anger comes out indirectly as criticism and judgment. The Perfectionists' tense body language—clenched jaw, stiff neck, rigidity around the shoulders, and staccato walking—broadcasts their discontent, resentment, judging thoughts, and the comparing that occurs internally. There is a continuous process of comparing self with others in a judging way: I work twice as hard as she, but she gets better grades/more and more money, so on.

Perfectionists are moral standard-bearers and their motto is, "I see the world as perfect." Anger arises because Ones can never make the world into the perfection they see, and they take that on as their responsibility, "If I'm the only one who sees perfection, and I can never make it as perfect as I see it, I get angry." Judgment and criticality, indirect anger about this impotence, wears away, erodes whatever is the closest target.

Perfectionists don't often see themselves as being critical or preachy, they are simply trying to help to make life as perfect for others as it can be. Many Ones report the burden they feel of this sense of responsibility, this great feeling of keeping the world on the right track. For instance, in a team effort like putting out a school newspaper, the One editor will say to herself, "Okay, I'll go along with the team as long as ultimately I can have a chance to check it that one last time." This is a real-life situation, not once, but several times, I've known Perfectionist student editors who work with a team of talented and responsible colleagues, but once the newspaper is ready to go to the printer, they go over it yet again, the whole paper, another four hours, to make sure it's correct. This example pinpoints several traits of One behavior—they are righteous, independent, believe that life is unrelentingly hard, that fun and play have to be postponed (sometimes indefinitely) until everything else is done. Ones can exercise rigid self-control, there is always room for self-improvement.

Many Perfectionists are drawn to teaching—in fact, I name in tongue-in-cheek fashion Perfectionists as the teachers and preachers of the Enneagram. They do convey a moral tone of, "You will learn." Perfectionists *will* people to learn, to see the world their way, sometimes overzealously, because they see it right, it's for your own good that you see it that way too. Perfectionists tend to have a preachy style in conversation, but they're not aware of this and are mortified when it's pointed out to them. They hear criticism as error, "I've done something wrong." Ones can come across as moralistic, annoying those who are constantly being talked to in a way that conveys the message, "You don't get this. I get this, and I can show you the right way."

Perfectionists live with a critical inner voice that directs a constant commentary on the way they conduct their lives, peppering the commentary with "oughts," "shoulds", "musts." This critical voice (a mental construct of their own consciousness) is the inner standard, the inner measure by which Ones weigh the rightness of every facet of their lives. Rules are important, but most often the inner standards set higher expectations than the rules. If you're a Perfectionist working for someone else, what's upheld as standards in the organizational culture has little to do with the level to which you're going to perform. Performance has everything to do with your own internal sense of standards. Part of this inner voice conducts an ongoing comparison to others. It is important that you know this about your One students, or your One colleagues. The internal comparing is unlike Point Three who asks, "How much amperage do I have to put out there to do the job?" The internal conversation runs more on the lines of, "I'm putting out all of this effort, you're not putting out nearly as much, yet you get the rewards, nobody appreciates how much I'm doing." No one is asking the One to go the extra mile, they're doing it to satisfy their inner critic, nonetheless they feel unappreciated. The cycle of resentment and indirect anger can kick in if the feeling of lack of appreciation continues.

It is not surprising that an E-type intelligence based on precision and correctness also has a need for analytical accuracy which translates into thinking in terms of details. For instance, a body of knowledge, a project, a report is broken down into the details. This is a Perfectionist gift, superb critical analytical ability. Details allow all the pieces to be put in place, so the big picture forms slowly. Ones complete meticulously all the steps of a process. Attention is more on breaking down the task into manageable pieces than putting it together in a mental construct, as we saw with the Observer Fives (big picture thinkers) and Optimist Sevens (multioptional thinkers). This need for, and emphasis on, details (along with fear of error) is at the root of the One pattern of procrastination. Ones believe (another blind spot), "I can never have enough detail." Or, "If I've amassed all of the details that's even a worse dilemma, because which is the right order and selection into which to put them? If I make those decisions and complete a final draft, I'm going to have to hand in the paper. Then there's no chance of me being able to redo it again and I know some of it is bound to be wrong." Perfectionists wrestling with that final moment of decision, will often run over deadline while grappling with the question, "Is this error-free enough?"

There is a double jeopardy at work here, not only are Ones unsure about the details, but they know they are not going to get an "A" for every paper (or life effort). This is another cause of resentment and anger. With everything the Perfectionist undertakes in life, they think they can see the perfect way to achieve that "A." But they can't get there because they live with human imperfection, and are answerable to an inner critic, so they constantly berate themselves, because everything *should* be an "A," or even an "A+," it *should* be perfect.

Ones go through life with the mind-set of, I can see the "A+," I can see the "A," but I know I can't get there. I don't want to hand in any work, because once I've handed it in everyone will see the flaws. Yet, I can't be a bad boy or girl, so I'll wait until five minutes after the deadline, then I'll hand it in. Ones don't wait until the next day. They'll come at the end of the due period, and say, "I'm running down to the computer center to print out the paper." The unspoken message is that this is the last moment they have to hand in the assignment without the consequences of losing a grade. It's out of their hands now.

Every educator has seen Ones' disappointment with grades, their anger is self-immolating, they beat themselves up. A Perfectionist once provided a graphic description of this process, by describing himself in the shower where he recalls every word of a conversation he had the previous night and remembers that which he didn't say quite the way he wanted to. The shower water is stabbing through him, piercing him for everything he didn't say, that didn't come out right. He experiences the unstated and misinterpreted words as guilty unease stabbing at his body.

### Shift to Point Seven (Security)

When Perfectionists shift to Point Seven under situations of security, it is almost as if another person emerges—we see the playful side of the One. Often Ones need to be physically away from their normal daily round for this shift to kick in. Although they will still check their voicemail daily, in between phone calls they can have fun, be carefree, keep their options open, fantasize in a free-flowing way, generally let their hair down. Being anonymous in a strange place can give some Perfectionists enough of a safety zone to tell their inner critic to take a walk.

I have a pair of Mickey Mouse ears that I wear upon occasion. When I first got them I was with my husband walking through the Orlando airport, we were both well-dressed and I had on the Mickey Mouse ears. He was dying with embarrassment, and I was having the best time because I was on vacation. Being able to see the joy and the surprise of people walking towards us was terrific.

Even though Point Ones shift to Point Seven when they feel secure, they can access the defense mechanisms of the Sevens: avoiding pain, reframing, escaping into a fantasy world.

### Shift to Point Four (Stress)

When Perfectionists shift to Four energy in stressful situations, the longing for what's missing arises, as well as feeling like a victim, but the primary manifestation of this shift is that Ones feel adrift in a claustrophobic fog, unable to maintain a grip on their liferaft—the details. Previously repressed emotions kept under wraps by the rigid self-control of the inner critic are now exposed and threaten to sweep the One away. Ones report that this is a most discomforting place to find themselves.

Being treated unfairly produces such internal stress that I can become immobilized. Many years ago I received a poor—and wrong —annual performance review from my department head. Instead of immediately dealing with the situation, I went into a dark hole for several days. I felt totally out of control, couldn't concentrate on the simplest task. I felt abandoned by the department head with whom I'd had a good relationship, and I felt like a total victim. Finally I snapped out of the depression, gathered my thoughts, prepared my rebuttal, met with the department head, and had the review rewritten.

Even though Point Ones shift to Point Four when they feel stressed, they can access the gifts of the Fours: unique creativity and deep connections.

### Key Characteristics

### Inspirational Teacher

Of all the E-types, Perfectionist Ones are the natural teachers and preachers of the model. Their passion for excellence, sense of right and wrong, the enthusiasm and even zealousness with which they try to impart moral standards and life lessons, can make them inspirational teachers. This One educator pragmatically acknowledges these attributes and examines the role zealousness can play in her teaching. Note how convinced she is of the righteousness of her message. Many Ones share this belief.

I think students perceive me as energetic, real. Frequently, I get the term authentic applied to the way I teach. I've gotten "inspiring" for many, many years. When I ask students, for example, on a scale of 1-10, do you think I enjoy teaching, I get 15s and 20s. There has never been any doubt that I immerse myself genuinely into it. I treasure what I'm talking about, and they find themselves coming along. Some students, who aren't with me yet in appreciating the exquisite beauty in natural processes, sometimes feel that maybe there is a zealous nature to the way I go about what I am doing. Maybe I work too hard at convincing them; it's almost as if I were to take them by the shoulders and say, "You will see this won't you?" More often than not, it works. In my thirty years of teaching, I feel confident that tactic works more often than not. For those students for whom it doesn't work right away, or doesn't feel comfortable, I don't let them alone. I feel so confident that eventually even if they are determined not to see what I see, eventually they will see it. I don't let up on them. I don't give up. I can say it honestly, I want 100 percent of my students to treasure what I treasure for their own good, and for the good of life processes.

### *Responsibility To Be Prepared*

While Point Sixes take on the responsibility of keeping those around them safe by making them aware of hidden dangers, Point Ones take on the responsibility of making the world right, correct, and as perfect as possible. This educator describes her sense of responsibility around knowing accurately the details of her field, so she can handle any questions in the classroom.

When I prepare my classes, I do so for my own sake, for my own enjoyment of what I am teaching. I want to stay current in both of my subjects, because they change all of the time. So I do it for my own enjoyment, and also because I feel I owe it to the students to be up on what's happening now, and because I feel I need to be prepared for any eventuality that may come up in a particular class. If a student has a question about a certain aspect of how an enzyme functions, or why exactly chlorine atoms do damage ozone in the stratosphere, I feel that I owe it to them, I owe it to myself to be competent enough, to be able to handle that on the spur of the moment. Of course, I have grown comfortable with saying, "Well, I just don't know, but I will find out"—and I do. Promises that I make are important. If I say I'm going to do it, I will. My preparation seems almost unending. My husband would love to know why I spend so much time at my desk after all of these years. It's because I feel I owe it to myself and my students.

This educator gives a stark example of the Perfectionist's drive to be right, in order to validate to himself that he has the correct knowledge. He does not want to make any false claims to being an expert.

I have five master's degrees. I don't know anybody else who has that many. Five master's and there's another one that I could throw in that I didn't get the degree for, and now I'm getting my doctorate. Plus there are umpteen trainings that I've done on top of that. None of this has given me what I think is the basis of why I'm successful, or why I feel successful in what I do. That experience isn't learned in school. But it's been essential for me to get the credentials for two reasons. One is because I recognize that I need the information, that's certainly an important part, but there's also a piece here about needing to validate to myself most of all, and to others, that I do have this knowledge, that it's objective, that I'm not going to be caught off guard by not knowing as much as someone else, or claiming to be an expert if I don't in fact have that to back me up.

### Being Heard — "Some men see things as they could be and say why not?"

As with the two other E-types in the Defender triad, being heeded is important, underscored for the One by a responsibility of feeling they know what is correct.

I find that I want my students to hear what I have to say, I trust my own insights. I would like the world at large to hear what I say. I want people to hear what I have to say about what we need to do. I like the second part of the G.K. Chesterton thought, that some men see things as they could be and say why not. I'm saving the world.

### Postponing Fun

If you have an inner conviction that you have a moral responsibility to save the world from itself, it is hard to justify taking time off. Ones need permission to have fun.

I need to earn fun, to give myself permission to do something that isn't productive. Life goes by and I can think of so many instances of missed opportunities. It's a catch-22: if it comes into my view screen I own it, or I feel I own it, and then I'm sucked into feeling responsible for it, and worrying about it. For example, if somebody asked me to check into their classroom once a day while they were away, to see if anyone left papers or messages on their desk, if I agree, I own it, therefore I'm responsible for it. I check in much more often than once a day, and I worry at night: is the classroom unlocked so the students can leave message, and so on, all the details. I always feel much more calm in nature, because it's perfect without me being responsible. When I'm away in nature I give myself permission to have as much fun as I want.

Whereas this educator has another take on the matter. Postponing fun for her is an excuse to limit the influence of spontaneity from her life. Spontaneity is risky, it can lead you astray.

I think I've come to see this as having to do with an intense need to suppress instinct and suppress spontaneity and everything that's associated with what's not in control and in order. It's a defense against spontaneity. It's a defense mechanism: my god, going with the flow

248 The Enneagram Intelligences

feels risky. It can feel like that's the bad stuff right there and should be avoided.

### Fun or Spontaneity in the Classroom

This educator is good-humoredly aware of her own intensity, and how its effect on others needs to be ameliorated in the classroom.

I have the good fortune to team teach and the gentleman I team teach with teases me when I get too intense, too rigid, too structured; i can always rely on him to lighten up things. I notice that when he's absent, I try conscientiously to move myself to a place where I can win the students' approval, their admiration, and connect with them.

Here is a poignant statement on what an effort it takes for Ones to have fun.

About seven years ago my written objective was to make my classes more fun and I'm still working on that. I work on it every day and would say that about two days out the school year I succeed in that. I'm trying hard.

### "Trapdoor" Effect

Life for Ones can be unrelentingly grim and rigid. When the tensions become overwhelming, many Ones develop a "trapdoor" release mechanism, a way to release all that pent-up anger, self-criticism, and judging. They do find a way to have "fun," usually at a physical distance from the place where they conduct their daily lives, such as on a favorite Caribbean island where no one knows them, they can dress casually, and behave spontaneously, going with the flow of wherever that leads them. This One tells us fun is an escape, the opening of her "trapdoor."

I felt such a deep imperfection about myself for much of my life that I choose not to join in. It isn't around the fun, fun is an easy place for me to join in, it's escape. I think it is owning the inner part of myself that feels so imperfect, I don't fit. That's what I've struggled with for most of my life, I don't fit, I was dropped into the wrong world.

### Divided Self

The One shift to the fun-loving Seven energy in situations of security, finding that "trapdoor" to release tensions, and the sense of a divided self are all interrelated: a rebellion against the strictures of the inner critic. Essentially, Ones live with a divided consciousness. On the one side the punitive inner critic pushes down real emotions, stamps on anger, sexuality, permissiveness, which get translated as temptations to bad behavior. The other side is a private consciousness that evolves in which these forbidden emotions are acted out as fantasies. This educator describes a personal metaphorical construct to explain this concept of the divided self.

I always thought of myself as part German and part French. The German side of me drives me to do things right. Whereas the French side of me says, "No, come, let's have fun in our life." I am constantly at war with those two sides of me. They are pulling me in both directions. So that the standards that I go by are whether the Germanic, or the French, side of me is operating at any given moment.

### Inner Critic

When Ones find their place on the Enneagram model and learn of the concept of the inner critic, many are shocked that not everyone has this internal feature of consciousness. Then comes anger that they have to live with this phenomenon. We all talk to ourselves to some degree, but Perfectionists live with an inner critic constantly commenting on their lives. This educator eloquently specifies the details of what she calls her "demon."

When I'm teaching, when I'm preparing, actually when I'm doing anything in my life, there is some inner voice always directing me to do it as well as I possibly can. I sometimes feel burdened by that voice. I have on occasion called it my demon, and would not mind at all if someone could help me exorcise that demon. It is painful, and yet it drives me to do things well. I have gotten a lot of outside accolades for doing what I do well. That is valuable. But, I don't think in the balance it is worth all of the intense efforts that I undertake. I would like to do things with a lot more ease, and graciousness, and flair, and spontaneity, but there is always the voice, the inner critic, the demon telling me, "Do it right, do it now, do it thoroughly, or don't do it at all."

There was a dream I had that I think is the perfect metaphor for this demon that I speak of driving me to do things way beyond the realm that they have to be done. I was sitting at a desk with my head down, probably doing school work. As I turned my head to the side, I saw a parade passing by—I'm from New Orleans so it was kind of a second-line type of parade where people were twirling colorful parasols. They were gesturing to come join them. I said, "No I can't come, I have to do this." What the dream said to me was that I was so immersed intensely in the details of what I had chosen to do with my life, whether it's teach or anything, that my life represented by the parade was passing me by while I was focused on unnecessary details.

This teacher has learned how to accommodate to the inner voice by rationalizing its message.

When you're in your fixation you're absolutely sure that the inner voice is absolute truth. It helps to question it, to state simply when it gets going, "Okay, but that isn't God, it isn't absolute truth or absolute authority." Be skeptical of the voice, don't fight it that much, accept that it's there, but you can make a choice about heeding it.

### Bottling Up Anger—Self-Forgetting

As we have seen, the E-types in the Defender triad embody variants of the self-forgetting theme. Eights are not into vulnerability and openness, the self is kept under powerful lock and key; Nines lose their own agenda in the agendas of others, and Ones tamp down their emotional energy, mainly anger, lest it bursts forth and they be seen as bad. The denial and repression of anger take a huge toll on the One psyche. With an E-type intelligence that directs you to good behavior, you cannot risk the consequences of out-of-control anger. This Perfectionist makes a clear distinction between good and bad anger.

I've come to the conclusion that the problem I have with anger is that it always ends up hurting someone else, and for me the ultimate wrong is causing somebody else distress. I can immediately, instinctively see when I've hurt somebody, and I just die. It's so instinctual and boom, before you know it, somebody's bleeding there, and I had no idea that that was going to happen. It just did. Good anger is anger on behalf of someone being hurt by someone else, or who's being treated unjustly, that's righteous anger, oh, very cleansing. I can do that one, no problem.

This One teacher clearly expresses one of the Perfectionist blind spots around anger. Note how she believes that she is able to express anger openly, but the moralistic tone of her accusation of, "How do you think that makes me feel", is typical of the inherent criticality and blaming of this E-type intelligence.

Anger is one of the capital sins, and if you're a quintessential good little girl you don't get angry. I'm talking about tantrum anger building up, fatigue, stress, you lash out at your family, or whatever. You feel unbelievably bad because indeed you've hurt people you love and you've lost your control. What's behind the business about control is the overriding principle that you must be good. I've come to terms with the fact that anger is a feeling and feelings happen. As an adult I have learned to express anger for myself, calmly, rationally, whatever. I'm angry, but I don't act on it, I don't have a tantrum with it. I'm perfectly capable of saying, "You made me angry when you said you were coming for dinner, I cooked dinner and you didn't show up, how do you think that makes me feel?" I'm able to express legitimate anger, but in a way that doesn't assault others, there's a big difference. I don't deny it, and I'm not afraid of anger any more.

### Zealous Righteousness: Willing Students to Learn

If emotional energy cannot find natural release in the spontaneous expression of anger, then it must take less overt forms. Zealous righteousness, expending energy on behalf of a cause, or belief system, is one such form. This educator exercises her moral will in the classroom because of her inner conviction.

> One of my former principals, when asked to describe how I teach, said, "She wills her students to learn," and that is true. In willing my students to learn, I will them to learn this detail or that fact, only insofar as that detail or fact allows them to get to the bigger picture, I want them to appreciate the aesthetic of it all. When my willing them to learn doesn't seem to work, sometimes I will focus on that particular student, catch that student's eye, personalize the message, to get to that person to be part of the group. What makes me feel so strongly about willing students to learn anything that I'm teaching, but especially now that I'm in life science and environmental science as well, is some conviction that there is a bigger scheme here, that there is some important part that each of us has to play in treasuring life, and in keeping life processes going on earth, so that the degradation that I see as a possibility doesn't set in.

There is no doubt in this educator's mind that her students will work together harmoniously. This is different from the Nine wanting the same result but as a conflict avoidance strategy. Note the moral tone with which this teacher imbues her message.

> I have no tolerance for unkindness in my classroom. I put it in global terms to the students, "If we can't get along in this small community and be good to each other, what hope is there for the the Arabs and Israelis? *We will* get along in here."

### Righteous Indignation

The following two examples serve well to illustrate some alternate forms indirect anger can take. Both the examples pulsate with anger. The first speaker revealingly lets slip her aversion to direct anger—"I'd look imperfect, God knows." As you read you can hear the chill in her voice when she addresses her students.

> Teaching in a parochial school, all male, last semester some of the seniors began to vocalize that they did not see the need to take six years of theology. As I was listening to some of them vocalize this, my anger was like fire in my belly. My first response to myself was, "How dare they make such an insulting, rude judgment. Don't they understand that this school and its mission is wedded and espoused to the Gospel?" All of my indignation was bubbling up like a volcano. Of course, it didn't erupt, I wouldn't have shown that anger, because I'd look imperfect, God knows. But the anger was in my communication style: direct, clear, concise, succinct. "I will help you gentleman understand why

you're taking six years of theology" they could hear anger in my voice.

This teacher feels violated by her students' misbehavior. She is as angry about the breach of trust, as she is about the students squandering a chance to strive for excellence.

I'll share the example of musical theater, where I've put in some twenty hours a day that last week before the show goes on. I've had up to 98 people in a show, in *South Pacific*, for example. Then I find out opening night that some serious public acts of affection have been going on down in the dressing room. It's dishonoring to me because they can trust me not to police them, and they've taken that trust and thrown it on the floor. It's like taking a pearl I've given them and throwing it into the pigsty. It's horrifying to me and dishonoring to everyone else in the show. I don't understand why I have to supervise them, I don't think they should be watched, why can't everybody just do what's right—I don't understand that. They have taken the chance, the opportunity to be what they could be, and they've dishonored themselves. When you give trust, and they've dishonored themselves, they've become less than they can be.

### Passion for Excellence

This Perfectionist understands and clearly articulates the negative dynamic set in motion when he experiences resentment at not achieving what he knows is possible for himself and having that anger turn inward with no place to go.

The dark side of the intensity of the passion for excellence, for the ideal, is that when I'm zealous about something, convinced about the way things should be, and spend tremendous energy in a positive direction toward that end, and still can't accomplish the great things I set out to achieve, it's like coming up against a brick wall, and crashing and burning. I feel the anger inside. Then a phrase comes to my mind, which someone shared with me a long time ago, "Be careful of sacrificing the real for the ideal."

Living in a world of idealism can be wonderfully invigorating, but unless it's grounded for me, I find that it's easy to sacrifice a lot, and then lose the energy and sense of what *I have* accomplished. I know I need to be careful not to expend myself, or not come to a point where resentment takes over, because my effort hasn't been acknowledged, or achieved, to my best sense of what it can be.

### Instinctual Intelligence—I sense it in my gut

Many Perfectionists make a distinction between being disinclined to express their sensuality, while at the same time trusting an instinctual, or gut-level truth. The first speaker describes how distrust of sensuality is woven into her E-type intelligence that directs her to maintain self-control as a survival mechanism—a One blind spot.

In addition to self-control, I repress and suppress any kind of emotions that might seem to be a little bit not good. I think it's true for myself that there's a whole piece of sensuality that isn't available to me, because it's too scary, too out of control, it's no good for me. I disconnect from anything below my throat, because that's going to get me in trouble and I won't go there. The body isn't a safe place to be, because if you get on a roll, you may do something that's not good.

The following two speakers articulate their understanding of their intuitive knowing. The first can recognize a difference between the mental constructs of his "world of shoulds," and the place of knowing that he can tap into at will.

I have a gut intelligence that over time I've come to recognize as distinct from a mental intelligence. At times it's come across as a gut instinct—the visceral knowing of something—I know it's right for me, as opposed to the intellectualization that happens when I'm always trying to fit it into some sort of connect to understanding what the world should be. My world is constructed out of "shoulds"—I should be, I should do this, I should be that, they should be doing that—this is a different type of intelligence. The "shoulds" are obviously my own mental construct, a different physical sensation to the gut intelligence which is simply knowing. I haven't found that my tamping down of emotions has prevented me from tapping into that intuitive place. I've always had a connection to that, but I do know that there are times that I get so locked into my controlling state, or my way of looking at the world, that it's less likely that I'm going to be aware of and able to tap into that gut sense.

This next speaker echoes the first, he knows that following his "path of shoulds" is a mental process whereas "the something" that he trusts deep down is fundamental and life-sustaining, a source of good.

There is always something that I trust deep down and that seems to operate in spite of all of the other "shoulds" on top of that. That's one of the things that helped me to build a base of self-esteem, because in spite of having all of this self-imposed pressure to behave in a certain way, and the conviction that it is important to do so, nevertheless I do have that more basic sense that there is something right about me. There's a contradiction here, because to this day I operate still with a pretty strong sense of how things should be for myself. I couldn't tell you what the consequences might be if I didn't do that. I'm not going to Hell, life isn't going to turn awful, but there's a sense I have, that in order to be authentic and true I have to follow that path of shoulds. Yet there is something in that instinctual base that is life-sustaining and continues to give me a great deal of energy and enthusiasm for my life.

### *I Know I Am Right*

For many Perfectionists, their gut instinct translates into a conviction about being right. This is the root of the One characteristic of righteousness. This speaker describes the frustration of knowing she is right on a visceral level, but having to try to prove it to others through mental evidence.

I know instinctively what is right to do. Unfortunately in this society you can't take that gut feeling to the bank. In order to bring forth an idea, or solution, or a proposal, I need to go into my head, check details out in different ways, generate all the statistics, write down all the credentials, and more often than not, it comes out to the same conclusion as I knew from my gut. What I am learning about myself is to honor my gut feel more, and not go through this crazy looping process.

In sharing this anecdote, this speaker echoes the conviction of the former.

I trust my gut, my husband has learned to trust my gut. Twenty-five years ago he was in a position of having to hire a lot of people and he would ask me, "Please come out to dinner, meet these people, because I need your input." We'd come home and I'd say, "No way." He'd say, "How do you know, what to you mean, I don't see that in that person?" I'd say, "Trust me." Once he said, "No, I don't believe you, and I like this person." Six months later he came back, "You were right and I'm going to trust you now." I can't explain it, it's all sensing and feeling, it's reliable.

### *Details and Intuition*

This educator tries to provide us with an example of how she uses her intuition in the classroom, but cautions that trying to describe an intuitive process is by definition difficult, because the intuitive process itself is essentially beyond words.

It's hard to talk about intuitive levels of teaching because they are intuitive. I know Step 1, and I know Step 3, and I don't know what happened to Step 2, or how it came along. I suspect that the Step 2 going from the observation to the conclusion comes in, in two ways. One is that I myself convey a lot with my own body, I rely a lot on nonverbal communication, so I'm more sensitive to watching for that in students as well. Just the shift of the body can either say, "I've got it, or I'm uncomfortable, or I want out of here." Because I talk less and watch more, I think maybe I can discern that in them. I think everybody has intuitive skills, too.

### *Focus on Details*

A gift of Perfectionists is their ability to exercise accurately their critical abilities, to produce manageable details. Details build on details to form a satisfying whole that can be ever-expanding. This educator tell us categorically that the secret of her teaching is in the details.

The secret to my teaching is in the details. I find that in the functioning of a single cell, no piece of literature can be anywhere near as beautiful. If I were to describe my teaching style it would be on two levels. One level is the minutia, the detail level, the intricacies of the cell, the structures, the membrane, how the enzymes work, and so on. The other is the whole, sensing how nature works, how everything fits together and functions as a whole, or doesn't function at all. Then I have this tendency to extrapolate these examples to society. The social level of the wholeness of things is a metaphor for how the body politic should work. The pancreas doesn't say, "I'm better than everything else", nor does the brain. Because if they do, the body shuts down.

This educator is aware that as a student, and now as a teacher, he needs help sometimes to rise above the level of details. Note how in his description of a teacher he can trust, he aims for a role model of perfection.

I can get lost in the details. In the classroom if I'm in the presence of a competent teacher, and by that I mean someone who is able to present material and maintain a relational rapport, then I feel much freer, especially if that teacher can pay attention, give feedback, recognize positives, and also challenge me. Then if I make a mistake, or if I try something and it doesn't work, I have more freedom, because there is somebody else whom I trust holding the field, and keeping me from getting focused too narrowly.

### Perfection and Imperfection — A Perfectionist Wannabe

Much of the One E-type intelligence is interwoven with ideas, concepts, and mental constructs around perfection. This speaker describes what many Perfectionists report: their own sense that they cannot achieve the perfection they strive toward. The state is truly that of a perfectionist wannabe. (Note her awareness around issues of judging others, in this case, her husband.)

There's no judgment of myself. I think I become judgmental if I'm yoked with someone, or teamed with someone. If I'm performing alone and carrying the whole thing, I can do it the way I want to do it, or the way someone has asked me to do it, or what's required. But the team product is a problem. Even with my husband, raising our children together, I'll say, "Okay, we're going to see it two different ways." But then I think these are our precious children, and I start in on my husband, "You're going to have to shape up and get neater, because they're picking up from you osmotically." Then he says of me that I see only one right way. I never agree with that. I mean, you don't ask a kid what he wants to eat. You feed them nutritiously what they need. But I can hear certain things where I come across as dogmatic. Throughout my life people have called me a perfectionist, but they're always saying it to me when I'm aiming for something, not when I've succeeded. I don't seem to succeed, I don't get to that state of perfection I'm aiming toward it. I'm a perfectionist wannabe.

This One associates perfection with struggle, 100 percent is still not enough.

The first word that pops into my head around perfection is struggle. The standards are internal and have nothing to do with what anybody has told me to do. For me it's a struggle against a perfect standard, the ceiling is always going up, up, and up. As a teenager I got involved in sewing, it was creative and good. I was making a product, and it was in a way in which I could get something almost perfect. A workshop leader once looked at me after an exercise and said, "100 percent is enough." I now have that on my desk and I look at it many times a day. But for me, I never get there, I always go beyond the 100 percent; 100 percent doesn't mean anything, there's always more to give.

This One worries about the imperfections that others will see, if he goes away too often.

I was away for a two-and-half-week vacation, came back, and had about a week where I could catch up on my clinical work, before going away for two weeks again. I was feeling terrible guilt about saying to clients, "Well, I'm going to be away for another two weeks. I was careful to point out that I was going away to teach and attend conferences. If they'd respond with, "Have a nice vacation," I'd say, "No, no, no, I'll be teaching and going to conferences." Finally my colleague in the clinical practice said to me (this was just before July 4th), "Have a nice holiday," and I practically jumped down his throat, I told him emphatically, "I'M NOT GOING ON VACATION!" He said, "I'm only talking about Independence Day." It was a real moment of humility. It is so easy to get trapped into that fear that if people think I'm just going off having a good time, what will that say about me.

### Standards of Right Behavior

Previously, in discussing the inner critic of the One, a speaker alluded to the fact that working to internal standards has brought her outside accolades. This speaker shares the same view that on a positive level the inner critic in fact mirrors some of the societal expectations we all fall in step with.

My parents are immigrants, I'm the first born American in our family. My mother had a fourth grade, and my father an eighth grade, education. I was a girl, and their highest expectation for me was that I work for the telephone company, because then I'll get a discount. I was the perfect, good, compliant little girl. I don't think my parents ever went to a school conference, there was never any reinforcement by teachers saying to them, your daughter is a good girl. There was a voice inside that said, "The teacher said to do this, this is the right thing to do, do it." I felt good in that space, and apparently I had the ability to please the teachers, so I kept reinforcing how good it felt to do the right thing. I was respecting the voice inside me, it was born in there with me.

The moral of this tale is self-evident, but the speaker asks a poignant rhetorical question at the end of her account, for Ones criticism takes hold at a deep level.

When I was in third grade I absolutely idolized and loved the nun who taught me. In fact I was going to grow up to be like her, until one day I raised my hand and asked if I could be excused to go to the lavatory. As I walked in front of the classroom my foot hit the wooden phonics chart that was used to display all of the letters. I remember Sister saying loudly, "Clumsy."

I walked out of the room, closed the door, and all the way down the steps to the girls' lavatory, I cried and cried and cried. It seemed like three years that I stayed there. Sister sent my sister to find me (we were only eleven months apart and in the same class). My sister saw me crying and thought maybe I'd hurt myself or was ill. "And what is the matter with you?" she asked. "Sister called me clumsy," I said. She responded, "Will you snap out of it, will you get up and into the classroom!"

Sister is now eighty, or older, and we still write letters. Inadvertently, every time I write to her at Christmas, or Easter, or whatever, I'll always bring up that little incident. Do you think perhaps she still thinks I'm clumsy? She needs to tell me I'm not. She absolutely destroyed me.

### Processing Criticism

When Ones are criticized a painful process occurs to try to rationalize the criticism, to remove its powerful charge. But the pain remains around having caused the error in the first place that brought on the criticism. Ones assume they are responsible, if only indirectly, for the criticism they receive. The following speaker sheds light on an important facet of this E-type intelligence: criticism is internalized as a feature of the Perfectionist's psyche.

When criticism comes my way, I want to respond rationally —either change myself, because I want to be good, or perfect, or please in some way, but the shame is so huge that I absolutely go into a black hole and disappear, completely withdraw, and that pain follows me for years. I've only gotten to the place lately where I can let the criticism sit on my shoulder and see it as something external.

This Perfectionist teacher asks other educators to exercise restraint in criticizing their students, especially perfectionists.

My "As" in school surprised me, I never sought them, they were
lovely. But the one thing that devastated me was criticism. If a teacher
wrote something critical on a paper, if it was harsh, or if it was interpreted as harsh by me, it was devastating. As a classroom teacher I remember that. If you ever have to criticize a student who you think is a
Perfectionist, do it ever so gently, because you have to remember that
there isn't any voice that's more harsh than their own inner voice.

Here is a catch-22 for educators: One students don't ask questions because
they think they should know the answers already.

As a child I had no appreciation that there were other ways to be. I
don't ask a lot of questions, because I think I should know the answer.
Somehow if I had had some teachers or adults in my life who could
have taught me that it was okay to make a mistake, or shown me that I
wasn't going to die from making an error, it would have been okay. As
an adult, I still struggle with mistakes when it's not important and I
should forget about them. But it's the hardest thing to do.

*Judgment*

One of the functions of the inner critic is to offer a constant commentary
comparing the One to others around him. As a consequence Ones carry internal
judgments of others. Most often the judgment stays in the Perfectionist's mind.
Judgment helps to fuel the incendiary anger that has no place to go. This One
gives us a clear articulation of this process, his judging with regard to some of
his fellow teachers.

I don't remember a lot of difficulties in school in terms of teachers. But I've noticed as I've gotten older, and as I've been going on in
graduate school, I'm often in this position of being torn between wanting to be the good student, wanting to be the one who's there in a supportive way, who's identifying with the goals of the class, and knowing
how I should behave, while at the same time needing to deal with anger
that comes up especially in situations were I feel that the teacher is not
doing it right. If I have a sense that someone is well-intentioned I can
stand behind that person. But if that isn't there, and there's a problem in
method, or style, that's where I find criticism in me which stays inside
in the form of anger. Whenever the criticism comes up I immediately
question myself, "Well, that's true, this person doesn't know what he's
talking about, nevertheless what is it about me that makes it hard for
me to hear and accept this?" The part that I've had to learn is first of all
to be aware of that judgment, but also to be able to express the anger

rather than simply sitting on it.

### Focus on Error

The Perfectionist's focus of attention is on error, and then on fixing what's wrong. The primary defense mechanism, and avoidance of this E-type intelligence, is error. This speaker suggests that Perfectionist students can be eased advantageously into an acceptance of error as a normal occurrence of daily life.

I am so risk aversive, it's because I don't want the shame, the criticism, of doing something wrong. I would never try something new. I think if a child can be encouraged by teachers to take risks and there are no consequences, that is enormously helpful. Perhaps have a private contract with the student that she gets to make a mistake every day, an intentional mistake, and let her experience what it's like to make mistakes.

### Perfecting the World

Many Ones can be found in the ranks of those who work on behalf of social and political causes, from the local, grassroot level, to national office. Teaching others about issues, communicating the rights and wrongs of political decisions, taking action on behalf of victims of wars and natural disasters, fighting cruelty to animals, Perfectionists find legitimate outlets for their rage, anger, and sense of morals and ethics.

I have to make the world better. I put my energy into educating the community on every issue that comes up—writing to Congress, I know the representatives' phone numbers by heart. Marching in Washington, participating in the flotilla that reminds people of Hiroshima and Nagasaki, I wouldn't miss it for anything, because I must always do these things. I mean I won't buy a bottle of French wine, because France was exploding bombs in the New Zealand area, and blowing out Greenpeace, how many people know that? I could ask, "How could you NOT know it? That's my mantra. "You *need* to know that." We are the world, and we have a responsibility to do things better.

I remember waking up in the middle of the night and thinking: Oh, my God, the washing machine. My husband asked, "What's the matter?" I ran down three flights, he thought it was flooding. I came back and said, "It is a GE!" He said, "What's the matter with GE?" I said, "Don't you know that they make a profit from the sale of nuclear weapons? We've been washing our childrens' clothing, our precious angels' clothes in a GE!"

That machine went, and as every appliance broke down, a Whirlpool was put in its place, because their record for a social consciousness is terrific. I learned that I'd better avoid General Mills cereal, but my growth has been such that now I can go back to my Cheerios.

### Growth Path: From Correcting Error to Serenity

The growth path is from an indirect anger that takes the form of criticality and judging to a type of serenity. This indirect anger which focuses on error and is driven by the "shoulds" and "oughts" of the inner critic, and the sense of responsibility that comes with being the exemplar of perfection, carries commensurate resentment. Serenity encompasses a sense of letting go, of letting the world take responsibility for itself. As this speaker explains her growth, she has learned to let go of her anger; it is now in constant, if understated, release mode. She has let go.

I experience my anger as fire in the belly. Because of my strong belief in spirituality, because of my own personal prayer life, that fire probably now has become a steady, small pilot light. So even though I know I'm going to have to live with that for the rest of my life, I contain that. Rather than let that pilot light be destructive for me, I can rely on the source of that fire to be warm and glowing and that's what moves me to my serenity. The constancy is important. That doesn't mean that I don't get fired up, but that volcano doesn't bubble under the surface anymore.

### Quality of Essence: Perfection

The essence word for Ones is Perfection, not a striving for perfection, but Perfection in and of itself. Perfection is being present in the moment where everything comes together, a perfect balance of opposites, complete unto itself. A mirror of this essence quality is the Perfection of nature: flora and fauna, osmosis and evaporation, the food chain, the ecosystem. no one is responsible for the trees and the flowers and osmosis and evaporation. It all works on its own. It is Perfect.

To me perfection is an ever-expanding concept. Over time I've found that my vision of perfection is a rigid one. I've tried to manipulate my life, my choices, into some sort of conformity which is not perfection at all, but some expectation of the ways things should be. Now I define perfection as an ever-expanding awareness of the way things are. There is an inherent perfection in that, but it's not about fixing something the perfect way, or accomplishing the perfect thing, or creating the perfect life. It's about accepting the perfection of all of the chaos, the mess, and the emotion, and the connection. It's perfect in that it just is.

## What Perfectionist Students Say

### Inner Critic

I have an internal judge of what is right and what is the best thing

I can possibly do and I'm always trying to measure up to that. I always have high standards of my own. It's not other people's standards that make me work hard.

### Details

I tend to work longer on things than other people and pay a lot of attention to little tiny details that aren't noticeable, but are to me.

and

I put a lot of energy into small things that the normal person would never notice that I've done.

### Independence

I'm not a collaborative worker. It doesn't matter much to me what other people do, as long as I'm doing the best I can—the internal judge is more for myself than anybody else. It would only be in the case if I was working on a project with somebody and they were not putting energy into the project to my standards, then that would be a case where I would judge others, but mostly I judge myself much more than other people.

### Right/Wrong Mind Set

There is one way of doing things right for me. And that comes out in class too, because when it comes to participating in class I don't consider any opinion right. I know this sounds bad. When I speak myself I only want to say things that I think are right and that's probably why I don't talk that much. Everything's measured before I do it.

### Inner Standards

I have trouble producing massive amounts of work, because every little thing I do, every sentence I write, I delete off the computer, because I'm constantly measuring how good things are and that gets in the way of progress.

### Postponing Play and Fun

I'd say people are of secondary importance to getting the job done right. It's the "right" that is important, my work is not done until I've taken care of all the little details that I notice and drive me crazy. Even friends come after getting the job done. I have to get my work done first and then I can relax and be with my friends.

262 The Enneagram Intelligences

### Good Enough

I used to think that I couldn't play until my work was done. Well, it's never done. The school librarian said to me, "You know there's an endless supply of things to take care of, it will all be there tomorrow. You can't finish it today, you can't finish it tomorrow, you can never finish it." That sounds wise, but it's hard to put into practice.

### Compulsive Behavior

I think it's necessary for people to give us perfectionists a certain amount of room, acknowledging the fact that we're going to be a little compulsive. It's something I do, and it's not something I can change easily, I'm going to grate sometimes on people's nerves, in that I have to get things done a certain way. But it's only a characteristic, it's not anything I can do something about.

### Practicality

I never daydream, I'm always right on the material, underlining things, analyzing things, writing notes—I never let my emotions take me away, that's why I don't think I'm touched by a lot of work, because usually I'm thinking more about it and analyzing it than going inside it.

### Brief Interview with a Perfectionist Educator

*Q. Your teaching style is?*
A: My teaching style is person-centered. I have a certain content that I want to convey, but if I convey it or not almost doesn't matter. But whether the people in front of me catch the beauty and some of the exquisite details of what I am offering them, that matters.

*Q. What do you look for in your students?*
A: What I look for in my students is evidence that they see what I see, that they have taken this walk with me through the garden, that they have seen the exquisite beauty of natural processes.

*Q. What is important in the way you present material?*
A: To me what's important in the way I present my material is clarity, conviction, authenticity, and some grasp of the whole—how everything in itself fits together in the whole picture.

*Q. What will students say of you?*
A: Students will sometimes say of me that I am an inspiring teacher.

Sometimes they will say that I go over the top in expecting that they will be able to see what I see and put it all together, to make this gestalt, to see how everything fits together with everything else.

*Q. Why do you teach?*
A: I teach because to me it is pure pleasure to convey to other people what I see. I have the deep conviction that when they see what I see, then they too will treasure it as I do.

*Q. How do you communicate?*
A: My communications style is sometimes zealous, sometimes subtle and understated. My communications style is whatever it takes in a given moment to convey a particular concept. If it's an enzyme that I'm talking about, it has to be very detailed, it has to be technical and analytical. If I'm conveying something about the processes of a beating heart or the cerebral cortex of the brain, then it might just be interspersed with metaphors and poetic expressions.

*Q. What is your attitude to preparing teaching plans?*
A: Preparing teaching plans is something I can do without. At this point in my career, my lesson plans might fit on a postage stamp. In my head, it's very, very detailed. I know at any given moment exactly what I'm going to do, what eventuality might occur, and how I'll deal with it. Plan A, Plan B, Plan C, and Plan D are all ready, even if not written.

*Q. What do you like about the classroom?*
A: What I like about the classroom is that I can close my door and have a little world in which we can take a trip together the way I would like the trip to be taken.

*Q. What don't you like about the classroom?*
A: What I don't like about the classroom is that it is confining, that the real world is not necessarily in that classroom. We can talk about it, we can use diagrams, and pictures, and models, and so on. The real world to me would be better conveyed sitting under a tree.

## Practical Tips

*For Perfectionists to Work with Themselves*

- Find a way to release your anger when it first starts to build.
- Internal judging and comparing are signs that you are angry.
- Be aware that you can come across as being morally superior; curb criticism of yourself and others.
- Find ways to lessen the grip of the internal critic on how you conduct your life.

- Try to find a balance between outer expectations and your own internal standards.
- Build in body work or exercise to release the tension that builds, especially in your neck and shoulders.
- Sometimes your attention to details is overkill, remember 100 percent is enough.
- Practice letting go—a mistake is simply what it is, a mistake.
- Practice being imperfect, deliberately make mistakes in front of others.

*For Others who Work with Perfectionists*

- State your criticism gently, repeating that it is constructive feedback.
- Try to get Perfectionists to share their thoughts about your feedback. Short-circuit the berating inner critic.
- Give genuine praise for their striving for or achieving excellence.
- Show appreciation for their powers of critical, analytic thinking.
- Ask Perfectionists their input in decision-making, trust their intuitive response. Ones can be a moral compass.
- When you give them responsibilities make sure they understand the limits, otherwise they feel personally responsible (and burdened) for the whole project.
- Ones can get stuck in the details, help to raise their gaze to the big picture.
- Help Perfectionists to see the gray areas, the right/wrong mind-set can be limiting.
- Give them permission to have fun.

# 4

# ATTENTION PRACTICES

What do I do now, what's the next step? This is the question most people ask me when they finish a workshop and conclude they know their E-type. The first step is to try on your E-type identity, to see how it fits you. Let the knowledge sink in, practice becoming aware of your focus of attention, of where your energy goes, of how your defense mechanisms, your avoidances, and gifts operate in the world. Watch yourself interacting with others. Learn to be self-aware.

The inner discipline of awareness, of understanding the emotional and mental habits of your E-type, helps you to know yourself. Self-awareness is your guide to knowing your type, how to work with your fixation, how to come back to yourself, how to develop that neutral place, that safety zone from which you can operate proactively (and not reactively) in those charged situations you deal with every day. In coming to understand the concept of an inner-safety zone, knowing the etymological roots of the words *education* and *discipline* is helpful to people.

*Education* means to *lead out*. In this sense all educators, parents, caregivers are leaders. We lead out from within ourselves, as well as call forth the essence/being of others with whom we are interacting, in whatever our teaching dynamic. The etymological root of the word *discipline* shares the same root as the word *disciple*. In this sense, through self-awareness, through the cultivation of inner discipline, a discipleship forms around whatever it is we know about ourselves. And the Enneagram provides us with precise knowledge.

When I conduct workshops it is touching and gratifying to see the way in which people wrestle with the responsibility of this powerful tool, the Enneagram system. They recognize the extraordinary potency of the model, both for themselves and for others. Every day we interact with the generation currently being educated, and it is hoped that many of us will be around to educate the next generation, too. We do have a huge responsibility. I believe Enneagram knowledge begins with ourselves. I want to emphasize this—*know thyself.*

Knowing the Enneagram opens wide the shutter of the perceptual lens, allowing us to see the 360 degrees of human possibility, but that knowledge also gives us added responsibility; we know our own E-type intimately, but also the eight other E-types with whom we share the classroom and our lives.

I am convinced of the efficacy of people identifying an E-type for themselves. It's your personal journey. You have to own your E-type. None of us should type others. It's almost impossible once you know the system not to try to type the people closest to you, but don't tell them of your discovery—that first moment of recognition belongs to them. We all know our curiosity at being with a class of students for a semester, or a year. *How are they as individuals? How are they going to learn? How are they going to behave?* Now we have a model that gives us that information empirically. I ask you to use the knowledge judiciously. The more important work is to get to know yourself —absolutely, deeply. Know yourself, feel comfortable with who you are, even if Enneagram knowledge has brought you some initial discomfort. For the rest, it's simply enough to know that there are eight other E-types in the world, and your responsibility is to figure out how *you* interact with them.

## INNER PRESENCE/SELF-AWARENESS

How do you come to know yourself? One aspect of the Enneagram system that separates it from any other model of personality is that it indicates a growth path for each of the E-type strategies. Chapter 3 of this book contains a description of these nine growth paths. The path is there for us to walk along. In order to be able to access the path, we need to be able to come into a quiet place inside ourselves, and to do this, we need to cultivate the idea of self-awareness. Attention practices lead to self-awareness, and will help us acquire objectivity so that when our fixations come on us the strongest, we can step back, and have a choice as how to respond. We can step onto the growth path. In many cases we can become self-aware enough to allow proactivity to be the new order of our lives.

Working with the defense mechanisms is like building a muscle. If you want to build a muscle, you go to the gym. If you want to stay on the growth path, you practice self-awareness. For instance, Twos are under the illusion that they need to have their selves validated by others. In order to do so, they have to win approval, and will create needs for another person that they can fulfill, so as to receive back approval. When the fixation becomes strong, Twos can become manipulative. Other people see the manipulative ploys, but Twos are operating within a blind spot and feel secret pride in how well they are meeting the other's needs. Twos feel naked when someone mentions how proud they must feel about meeting Xs' needs. When Twos are in their fixation they can't step back and see how the old pattern is repeating itself. But if they have some self-awareness they can stop, and step back, and say to themselves, No, I won't do that for X. I have boundaries. I have freedom, and the will to exercise that freedom.

This is their growth path—to move away from compulsively meeting the needs of others, and toward exercising will and freedom on their own behalf. Self-awareness allows Twos the freedom to separate from others, to let others make do for themselves (which they probably prefer), and for Twos to feel validated from within. There are eight other growth paths, one for each of us to follow in our individual circumstances.

Finding the safety zone is as simple as breathing—literally. Breath is life, if we don't breathe, we die. The breath is our neutral reference point, it is always present. We can come back to it. It is our safety zone.

How do we cultivate a sense of space in our bodies that's tied to our breath? Try this short exercise. Sit comfortably with your feet on the floor, your hands on your lap, close your eyes and find the breath. Breathe in, breathe out. I want you to concentrate on your breathing, I want you to become so quiet you can hear your heartbeat. When the thoughts come, let them go without judgment and return to the breath. Breathe in and breathe out. Remember to become conscious of the breath. If you can remember to breathe, you can stop the fixation, short-circuit the cycle you're caught in. It's that simple.

Find the breath: perhaps it's useful to think of it coming through your nostrils as a silver or jeweled cloud moving down metaphorically through the belly, then turning around, and exiting through the mouth. Breathe in, breathe out, find your own rhythm. Now try to breathe into the belly, breathe deeply, breathe in, breathe out. If you like, place your hand on your belly. Forget about trying to hold your stomach in, breathing practice is not about maintaining a flat stomach. Concentrate on the breath. When thoughts or emotions arise, or concentration wavers, consciously return to the breath.

Try this breathing exercise for two minutes the first time, build it slowly over time, to ten, fifteen, twenty minutes. Return to the breath, the neutrality of breathing. Gradually, over weeks and months, you will find a spaciousness growing inside you, a safety zone, a place you can return to simply by finding the breath. This is also called centering practice. Let's do this again.

Close your eyes, come home to the breath, and get down, get centered by breathing through the turn of the breath in the belly. Try to practice this, any time during the day, if you have five minutes between a class, several minutes before you're going into a meeting. You don't have to close your eyes and become self-conscious, sit quietly at the conference table, find your breath, try to get so still inside that you can hear your heartbeat. Good, now you're centered.

Soon you'll be able to drop to the belly instantaneously, you'll be able to access that neutral place, your safety zone. It's the same practice for all the E-types. Come back to the breath, come down to the belly, drop your attention, find your center. The more you practice, the easier it becomes, until it's almost automatic. The next time a student comes to you and argues about a grade, you don't have to be at the mercy of reactivity, of triggering one of the nine patterns of defense mechanisms. You can drop your attention, find your center, respond proactively: Here I am, there you are. "Okay, now lets deal with what this is all about." It's not about me, it's obviously something about you. "Let's get to the bottom of this."

## ATTENTION PRACTICES IN THE SAFETY ZONE

Once you have the breathing practice under control, and some spaciousness forms in your mind when you practice, I want you to become aware of how many mental attentional states you already practice daily, albeit unconsciously. The purpose of this exercise is to help us name these states, even to call them forth at will, while we are attending to our breathing practice.

We are all advanced practioners of mental states development. Sit comfortably, find the breath, find your center, stay quiet for several minutes simply following the breath. We are going to begin with a mental state called *memorization*. Into the inner space of your mind, I want you to consciously remember, to visualize the face of someone you love and who you haven't seen for a long time. Remember their face. What do they look like How does the hair fall around their face? What is the shape of the planes of their cheeks, the color of their eyes? Are they smiling, or angry, or looking back at you with love?

Try to get as clear a picture in your mind of this person as you can. Stay with this, play with this for as long as you like. Keep that picture there, fill in the details. Keep following the breath. Now one final time come back to the breath, and slowly let the picture of the friend or beloved dissolve. We are all adept at the mental state of memorization.

The next mental state we are going to practice is called *imagination*. Close your eyes, I want you to come with me to a game park, an animal game park, in South Africa where I was born. Who are you with? What time of day is it—dawn, dusk? What can you imagine through the five senses—what are you smelling? What are you feeling—a nervous tug of excitement, awe at the primeval beauty of an African plain? What are you seeing—the morning dew drops glistening in pink colors on the tall grass as the sun rises? What are you tasting—the dust in the air from the movement of the motor vehicles? What are you hearing—bird calls, and the far-off roar of lions still hunting in the dawn? Why are you in South Africa at a game park? Can you see the grass, the lions, elephants, giraffes, zebras? Aside from what you've seen on the *Adventure Channel*, or *Animal Planet*, what can your own imagination fill in the picture for you?

Now keep the breath conscious and every time a thought comes, don't judge it, just let it go, and come back to the breath. The game park is gone, South Africa is gone, imagination is gone. My mind is clear. This is called *empty mind*. It's one of the most difficult mental states to attain, being present to oneself: awareness of much less of me, my personality, and much more of what's inside of me.

Through the imagination and through the breath, you can get yourself out of your own way. See how far you are already along the road of attention practices. You can distinguish between memory, imagination, empty mind, a neutral place, and all of the other deductive mental activities, reasoning and thinking, and planning and fantasizing, that you practice. All you need to do is ask the question: where am I? To find yourself, all you need to do is to get back to the breath, and drop to the belly.

## TRIADS ATTENTION PRACTICES

During workshops when I put educators together in discussion groups, among many of the topics I ask participants to discuss is how they can use their new knowledge of the Enneagram in the classroom, or other places of work. The most obvious response is the one we've already explored: to know yourself well, to try to ameliorate the impact of your personality on the other E-types in your classroom and your life.

Another response is that it is impossible in a fifty-five minute lesson or lecture to allow for, and cater to, the nine learning styles. Many groups follow up that caveat with a response that allows for exercises and activities that will tap into the energy of the Enneagram triads, and hence involve all nine E-types. The three triads—the body (gut) triad, E-types Eight, Nine, One (Defenders) align with the great energy of groundedness (the belly center); the emotional (heart) triad E-types Two, Three, Four (Attachers) align with the great energy of universal love (the heart center); the mental (fear) triad E-types Five, Six, Seven (Detachers) align with the great energy of visualization (the head center.)

We can engage the three centers in every lesson we teach at whatever level, with a small or large group, and in every discipline. Each one of us is capable of creating variants to suit our purposes with three basic exercises that follow. They don't all have to appear at the beginning or end, but can be peppered through the lesson. They don't have to follow this order either. Maybe one day you want to spend more time on one center, and not do the others, and so on.

The ideal is to do these short exercises in every lesson, every day, but even if you can manage only two or three times a week, over the period of an academic semester, or a year, you'll make a difference. I've seen this work in my own teaching, this access to and shift of energy.

### Engaging the Belly Center

During each lesson/lecture, for two minutes everybody in the class should stand up, raise your arms, stretch, move your shoulders, shake out your legs, do some conscious breathing to get into your bodies. This exercise is good for the Eights, Nines, and Ones; for the other E-types initially it's counterintuitive, or a bore, but they become accustomed to it.

### Engaging the Heart Center

During each lesson/lecture for two minutes everybody in the class should turn to the person next to them and interact, connect, share a thought about the work you are exploring, or about the teacher, the weather. Only connect. The Twos, Threes, and Fours enter into this exercise with enthusiasm; for the other E-types it can be a little disconcerting at first.

### Engaging the Head Center

During each lesson/lecture for two minutes everybody in the class should work privately with themselves, a one-to-one encounter with their own minds. Write down your thoughts for two minutes without lifting your pen, engage your mind. Have some conversation in your own head with yourself. For the Fives, Sixes, and Sevens this is home territory; but for the other E-types it can feel alienating at first.

## FURTHER EXERCISES

This set of exercises is more elaborate and designed for people who want to engage all three centers as an adjunct to their attention practices. It is a way to become acquainted with all three of the great energies of the Enneagram on a visceral level, a way to experience experientially the wholeness of the system. To practice effectively you'll need a small group.

### Body Center Exercises

This is the realm of the instinctual E-types. They need their space and have a sense of being Defenders of that space. Issues here have to do with anger. Anger is an energizing emotional mechanism for this group at the top of the Enneagram. They need to find a way of accessing that emotional energy at will, not only when the anger defense mechanism kicks in. The other E-types can also access the belly energy advantageously.

It is through breathing exercises that we access the energy in the belly. This is about grounded attention. Please stand. You want to place your feet firmly on the floor, sense your feet, visualize energy coming out of the ground, up through your feet, your legs, through the torso. Bend your torso forward, hands falling toward the floor. Draw a deep breath in through the nostrils so as to draw the energy in. Slowly raise your torso, and straighten up. Pull your hands up sideways to a V above your head, reach for the sky. Pull up the energy, sense where it goes. On the exhale, let it out gently, while you lower your arms to your sides with your hands facing palm down. You can make a sound on the exhale if you want. Feel all the tension flow out, breathe out through your mouth.

Put one hand on the small of your back and with the other hand rub your tummy area. This is the *kath*, the seat of energy, keep rubbing, you should begin to feel some heat under your hand. Take your hand away, and move it about an inch from your tummy. It should tingle, you should feel energy. You can put your hand here whenever you wish as a reminder of the grounded energy available to you.

### Heart Center Exercises

This is the realm of the image/emotional E-types. They are outer-directed,

Attachers, conscious of their image, and need approval. Issues here have to do with emotions. None handle their emotional life with ease, in fact they get mired in a morass of emotions. Chapter 3 describes the ways in which Two, Threes, and Fours play out the emotional theme. They need to find ways to connect that don't violate boundaries—their own or others. They need to access emotional energy at will, open their hearts, learn to be passive, receptive, to leave room for others to come toward them. The other E-types can also access advantageously their heart energy.

Find a partner. Look at his or her face, but you don't need to lock your gaze. After a minute close your eyes. What do you feel for this person? Can you feel that emotion in your body? What would you call that emotion? Is it hard for you to do this? Does it make you happy, or sad, or neither? Open your eyes again, look at your partner, repeat the exercise a couple of times. The objective is to be able to know and name different emotions. The connection, having to face someone else, is most important.

Find another partner, someone to talk to. Talk for one-and-a-half minutes each, three minutes total, stop. Where's your attention Is it on the other person? Is it on what you're saying? On what they're saying? Where's your attention while you're talking? This is what we want to establish here. Repeat the exercise, but this time while you're talking, open yourself to the other person. Now freeze frame the moment and connect to the other person without saying anything. Open your heart. Feel the connection through something other than mind, thoughts, words. Widen your boundaries to include the other person. Do you see how we rely on words to open up feeling? Open your heart.

**Head Center Exercises**

This is the realm of the mentally based/fear E-types. They are inner-directed, Detachers, who rely on the workings of the mind in order to feel safe. Issues here have to do with fear. For these E-types, it is both a blessing and a curse to be able to be in their heads. They can escape from their fears through living in their heads, but they experience a disconnection from the world. Chapter 3 describes the ways in which Fives, Sixes, and Sevens play out the fear theme. They need to access mental energy at will, still their minds, find that sense of inner spaciousness that has nothing to do with intellectual ability. The other E-types can also access advantageously the mental energy.

Outlined earlier in this chapter is the way to achieve the spaciousness of the inner safety zone through breathing practice, so I won't repeat it here. Rather we are going to practice what it feels like to detach, to live in the head.

Find a place against the wall, face the wall with your eyes closed, so that you can't see any-one. Imagine as best you can that you are the only person in the world. Detach. Get right up there into your heads. Don't think about how funny you look from the back. As soon as a feeling comes, let it go. *I am the only person in the world, and that's okay because I have my head.*

Open your eyes. Lower your gaze. Don't meet anyone else's eyes. Start walking around the room. Keep the sense of being in your head, and being the only person in the world. Note how difficult this is if you don't belong in the mental triad. And even if you do, because you've been conditioned to be interactive, it is difficult. Can you stay in your head?

Find a seat and share the experience with the person sitting next to you. These are typical of the comments that are heard: *It's hard, I never got there. It's easy, I'm always in my head. It feels cold and alienating. The world is out there, I cannot not focus on it.*

## Concluding Exercise to Align the Centers

Get on your feet once again. Stand still and imagine that you have a line running through you, from your feet to your head and connected to the ceiling—a length of string to line up the head, heart, and belly. Visualize this any way you want. In our society we all have an overdeveloped head center. Most of us stand with our heads a little forward. So try to move your head back more than you're used to, two inches further back than feels comfortable, and imagine a line going through the middle of your head, down your throat, through the center of your body into the ground, lining up the three centers. This will actually put you in balance.

For ourselves and for our students, we can access so easily these three great energy centers.

# 5

# THE ENNEAGRAM AND THE MBTI

The Myers-Briggs Type Indicator (MBTI) is the most popular and widely used instrument in the world for measuring individual personality preferences. The MBTI is based on the idea that one's psychological type determines and drives one's judgments and relationships in the world of cognition. My interest in the MBTI from the Enneagram perspective is not to try to forge a correlation between the two systems, but to try to understand how it has been introduced so successfully into mainstream business and education, both here in the United States and internationally.

The MBTI has a fifty-year lead on the Enneagram. I believe the Enneagram community has many lessons to learn from the MBTI community, and that it is unnecessary to reinvent the wheel, or repeat the mistakes of MBTI pioneers. Because so many educators know the MBTI, and other (less well-known) learning style instruments, the following overview serves as a framework to place the Enneagram system in the rubric of learning style models.

The MBTI and other typologies focus on learning styles. They seek to measure what learners need in order to learn, and how those learning needs can be met. Education, and educational psychology literature, is rich with books and articles on cognitive skills improvement, such as problem solving, critical thinking, and so on. Much of the research is excellent in identifying these learning style needs. Many educators and educational researchers have devised self-report personality tests to *get at* learning style characteristics. Here the MBTI is a leading instrument. Among others that are held in high regard are Kolb's Learning Style Inventory, the Learning Orientated-Grade Orientated (LOGO) Survey, Friedman & Stritter's Instructional Preference Questionnaire, and the Grasha-Riechmann Student Learning Style Scales. There are many others.

One typology that caught my interest attempts to categorize types of people by behavior, rather than by the way they function cognitively. This is the work of Mann and his colleagues (1970). Their type descriptions are based on student behaviors in the classroom observed through audio- and/or video-taping. The data were analyzed to find evidence of consistent themes in the way students interact with teachers. Mann et al. isolate three learning needs that underlie their typology. One is the need for structure and secure relationship with authority; another is to work independently and not be involved with peers; the third is a need for attention and approval, and to work cooperatively.

Like pioneering psychologist Karen Horney (1945) some twenty-five years earlier, it seems that Mann et al. through empirical observation found evidence that supports the theory of the Enneagram triads. In the work of Mann et al. (see Figure 5.1), the first cluster of learning needs fits the Detacher energy, see Compliant and Anxious Dependent (or Horney's "moving away from"); the second cluster fits the Defender energy, see Independent and Hero (or Horney's "moving against"); and the third cluster the Attacher energy, see Attention Seeker and Silent Student (or Horney's "moving toward"). I am not suggesting that the Mann et al. learning style descriptions approximate the E-types, although there are provocative similarities in the characteristics of a few of the categories. In Enneagram terms the Mann et al. descriptions are all over the map. The "fit" is most obvious in the latter grouping, but a case can be made for the other two. It is interesting to speculate on what Mann and his colleagues would have concluded from their observations if they had known the Enneagram model. But here, as is common in the research on learning styles, it is a case of the tail (learning needs) wagging the dog (personality behavior). Although some of the research does get at what some students need in order to learn, none suggest *why* students behave the way they do. The Enneagram system is the only personality model to do so.

The Enneagram model's typology descriptions differ from all the above learning style inventories, because the primary rationale is different. The Enneagram system posits that *who you are* is how you will learn, and teach, and behave in all areas of your life. This is a fundamental difference and a fundamental breakthrough. In order to understand how you learn, and how you teach, you need to know yourself. *Cognition is not E-type related.* Starkly different E-types can share, for instance, similar MBTI characteristics. There is no Rosetta Stone to match these two models (or any other). The following anecdote supports this conclusion.

In March 1997 I led a workshop for educators in the Midwest. One of the participants is a national figure in the MBTI world, and this was her first Enneagram workshop. She admitted that she was present because she was curious, and she wanted to see how the Enneagram and the MBTI lined up with one another. I had done some thinking on that score, but I kept my conclusions to myself.

She maintained silence and a look of polite skepticism until the final day when I was facilitating a panel of Ones. Someone on the panel was talking about a childhood incident around anger. The MBTI practitioner could not help herself. Her arm shot into the air. She seemed to almost jump out of her seat. I sensed that the question would not hold till the end of the panel, so I let her put it to the panelists. She inquired if any of them could remember taking certain actions to express their anger when they were children. Several panelists answered her positively. She sat back in her seat nodding, and shared with us that her granddaughter was a One, and that the panel had illuminated certain aspects

## Figure 5.1.

## Brief Descriptions of Mann et al. Learning Styles

**Compliant** — Typical student of the traditional classroom. Conventional, trusting of authorities, willing to go along with what the teacher wants. Focuses on understanding material rather than criticizing it, or formulating own ideas. Self-image is not well defined.

**Anxious Dependent** — Concerned about what authorities think of him or her. Low self-esteem and doubtful of own intellectual abilities and competence. Anxious about exams and grades. Class comments hesitant and tentative.

**Discouraged Worker** — Intellectually involved but chronically depressed and personally distant. Afraid destructive impulses will lead him, or her, to hurt others.

**Independent** — Self-confident, interested, involved, tends to identify with teacher and to see teacher as a colleague. Has firmer self-image than students in above three clusters.

**Hero** — Intelligent, creative, involved, introspective, struggling to establish identity, rebellious. Ambivalent toward teacher, erratic in performance.

**Attention Seeker** — Possesses a more social than intellectual orientation. Wants to be liked, to please others, to get good grades. Both self esteem and control depend upon periodic reinforcements from others.

**Silent Student** — Speaks in class only when sure teacher will approve. Feels helpless, vulnerable, threatened in relation to teacher; fears engulfment by instructor, but longs hopelessly for teacher's attention.

**Sniper** — Rebellious, but more defensive and less creative than the Hero. Low self esteem, afraid of introspection, attracted to authoritarian class structure. Uninvolved and indifferent towards class; stresses fact that course was required. In class, tends to lash out and then withdraw quickly.

of her granddaughter's behavior that she'd always found troubling and puzzling. The Enneagram model had became real for her.

At the conclusion of the workshop she stood and pronounced (these are her thoughts in my words) that the Enneagram and the MBTI are neither mutually exclusive, nor do they correlate with one another, in fact they are complementary, *because each seeks to describe something different about personality.* The Enneagram describes the gestalt of human possibility, the whole human personality including the motivations behind behavior. The MBTI measures the cognitive process—how information is acquired, processed, and disseminated. Her conclusions were congruent with my own. In fact there have been studies attempting to find correlations between the two systems, and none thus far are successful.

## MBTI—A BRIEF OVERVIEW

The MBTI was developed by Katherine Briggs and her daughter, Isabel Briggs-Myers before World War II. (The so-called Form A was published in 1941.) These two women, both Swarthmore College graduates, were heavily influenced by psychologist/philosopher Carl Jung's work on personality. A biographical history of the story of the development of the MBTI has been written by Frances Wright Saunders (1991) *"Katherine and Isabel: Mother's Light, Daughter's Journey."* Neither Briggs nor Myers were trained psychologists.

The current, popular version is Form G. The Forms start at A and go through to K now. Form K has some 20-27 subscales. There is also a children's version, called the Murphy Meisgeier Type Indicator for use with children ages six-twelve and is widely used in public school systems. Having undergone decades of testing and psychometric analysis, the MBTI is a mature typology. It is available commercially in ten languages, and in research form in eighteen others. The MBTI is administered to an estimated 3 million people per year. The primary intent is for it to be a "good news" instrument, to help people find out the work they are suited to, and to identify their on-the-job strengths. The MBTI is scored and inventory takers are told where they fit. With the Enneagram model people are encouraged to find which of the E-type strategies describes them.

## MBTI ORGANIZATIONS

There are three major, independent, international MBTI organizations: Consulting Psychologists Press (CPP), the Association for Psychological Type (APT), and The Center for the Application of Psychological Type (CAPT). CPP publishes the instrument, conducts research on new instruments, provides scoring services, and certifies training programs. APT is a professional organization which publishes a newsletter and a journal, has an annual convention, sponsors regional and local chapters, and offers training sessions. CAPT maintains research materials, offers scoring services, and training materials. CAPT has a research library that has over 5,000 research sites in which the MBTI is used for a variety of purposes, in a variety of settings.

Currently, there is one fledgling international Enneagram organization, the International Enneagram Association (IEA), which publishes a newsletter, holds annual conferences, and is beginning to sponsor regional chapters. There are other (large and small) Enneagram organizations directing outreach to the mainstream. These include Learning & The Enneagram Workshops (education), the Enneagram Professional Training Program, and the Enneagram Institute (both personal growth.)

## OTHER MBTI (DERIVED) INSTRUMENTS

The Singer Loomis Inventory has twelve types instead of the MBTI's sixteen. The Gray Wheelwright Test is a similar instrument to the Singer Loomis. Temperament Theory, devised by David Kiersey, is a condensed version of the Myers-Briggs and it proposes there are four types and sixteen subtypes, instead of the MBTI sixteen types. Since the early 1950s leading MBTI researchers such Isabel Myers herself, Gordon Lawrence, David Kiersey, M. Bates, and Mary McCaulley have pioneered applications of MBTI theory to educational settings.

Type theory and learning styles are predicated on the idea that seemingly arbitrary variations in approaches to learning are not chance occurrences at all, but can be observable components of mental activity. The differences arise from how different learners prefer to use their minds. MBTI adherents see patterns in how information is received, processed, and disseminated.

Currently, there are about twelve Enneagram testing inventories available, ranging from multiple-answer questionnaires to paragraph inventories.

## A DESCRIPTION OF THE MBTI

The MBTI model is built on four precise dimensions, each containing two pairs of opposites with contrasting preferences (See Figure 5.2). The first dimension is directed at our orientation toward information and ideas. The opposites are (E) Extroversion (which means we take our energy from the outer world of activity and action) and (I) Introversion (which means we take our energy from an inner world of reflection and contemplation). The second dimension is directed at our perception of ideas. The opposites are (S) Sensing (which means we perceive ideas through observable facts and details) and (N) Intuition (which means we perceive ideas through insight of meanings and relationships). The third dimension is how we process ideas. The opposites are (T) Thinking (which means we process ideas though conclusions based on logic and objective reasoning) and (F) Feeling (which means we process ideas through decisions based on subjectivity, human values, what is personally important). The fourth dimension is how the processed information and ideas are disseminated. The opposites are (J) Judgment (which means we send out information in an organized way that can involve plans, and closure) and (P) Perceptions (which means we send out information in an open, curious way, and are receptive, flexible, and adaptive). Everyone possesses all the qualities inherent in each dimension, but one set or combination is *preferred*. Thus the possible combinations of the sixteen MBTI types.

The MBTI is a highly structured, intricate, and evolved model. The four mental functions are exclusive. One function cannot be reduced to any other. They are also exhaustive, there is no fifth mental function. Thinking and feeling are polar opposites, so that if one is the dominant, the other will be the inferior, and the same holds true for sensing and intuition.

## Figure 5.2.

### The Sixteen MBTI Types

| | | | |
|---|---|---|---|
| ISTJ | ISFJ | INFJ | INTJ |
| ISTP | ISFP | INFP | INTP |
| ESTP | ESFP | ENFP | ENTP |
| ESTJ | ESFJ | ENFJ | ENTJ |

## THE ENNEAGRAM AND THE MBTI: POSSIBLE ALIGNMENT?

1. There are sixteen MBTI types and nine Enneagram types, they do not fold easily into one another.
2. The MBTI is well-defined, and the structure holds true across the work of a number of innovators, researchers, and practitioners. The basic Enneagram model is the starting point for a number of interpretations and "schools." What does hold true is the empirical evidence for the E-types. That aside, there are, for example, a lack of standard type definitions, a lack of agreement about how type is generated in the Enneagram model, and many arcane and esoteric theories that have little to do with the empiricism of the model. There is a lack of applied research, due mainly to the field being so young. This book is the first applied research of the system to education. There is no peer review journal.
3. The MBTI was first published in 1941. The first Enneagram books appeared in 1984.
4. When trying to put together a theory that integrates these two models, there is the problem of measurement. Each tries to measure something different.

## ENNEAGRAM LESSONS FROM SUCCESSFUL MBTI APPLICATIONS IN EDUCATION

The MBTI is a mature technology in education. It is used in professional development of faculty and administrators, with an emphasis on self-development, awareness, and teamwork. It is used in instructional design and assessment. There are precise tests used for student coaching and counseling. It is used to understand learning styles. Above all, the MBTI is used mainly for career counseling, and there is a large body of literature in this area.

The Enneagram model offers the same applications to education. The following brief guidelines are for those who may be interested in trying to introduce the Enneagram successfully into your institution. These steps follow the conventional wisdom as practiced in introducing the MBTI into a school, college or university, or school system (educational institution.)

1.  Start with a champion, one person in authority in the institution who is committed and wants to bring this information to his or her colleagues. Pick an area of the institution where you are likely to succeed, where it's likely to take hold, then build on successes.

2.  Train and enlighten the champion. Have the champion enlighten others, and when you've established a beachhead and are having some successes, bring in a credible outside authority.

3.  Spread this "soft" technology one department at a time. Customize your approach. Be aware that you need to "sell" the Enneagram differently to, for instance, the math or English departments, the academic or business offices. Know the flavor of the institution.

4.  Maintain support from the champion. Try to get top management to see the value of the system in terms of their personal lives.

5.  Don't rely on  support being there forever. Be sensitive to issues in the local institutional climate. Continually shore up the successes you've achieved.

# 6

# THE ENNEAGRAM SYSTEM—A LENS FOR THE 21ST CENTURY

As we enter the 21st century, we are on the cusp of a revolution in education. Think of the explosion in research and innovation to improve our schools, not only in terms of motivation and better student performances, but in understanding learning styles. The revolution is perhaps most noticeable on college and university campuses across the country. In the last decade almost 800 campuses have established centers to encourage excellence in college and university teaching. There are many rewarding and interesting initiatives in college-school collaboratives. Funding is available from many large and small foundations to support educational enterprise and innovation. Peer review journals proliferate and books on innovation in education represent a large segment of educational publishing. The list of sessions and workshops at the many educational conferences each year attests to this revolution. There is enormous interest, for instance, in the impact of computer technology and the Internet, in learning collaboratives, in distance learning, in any new technology that is seen as resilient enough to meet the challenges of the new era. From the reception accorded our work, working with personality styles using the Enneagram model is one such technology.

The emphasis of much of the activity outlined above rests squarely on students and learning styles. I believe we should be placing as great an emphasis on educators and teaching styles, because teaching and learning are two halves of the same equation. For instance, few, if any, graduate schools of education or teaching excellence centers concentrate on *how* teachers teach; their emphasis is on teachers interfacing with how students learn. It is as if all teachers emerge from the same cookie cutter and pick up the tricks of their trade on-the-job. In most cases this is exactly what happens. Again and again, as I go around the country conducting workshops, I hear from teachers at all levels that understanding their own teaching style is a vital, important missing piece of the equation.

There is receptivity among educators to find out how they teach. Largely this is due to the valuable, ground-breaking work that has been done on learning styles and identifying student needs. The technology around teaching styles flows naturally from the work on learning styles, and both teaching and learning styles are linked intrinsically to personality behaviors. But few teaching programs, or faculty roles and rewards programs and policies, are designed to take into account the diverse personality styles of faculty and administration. Yet, with this knowledge we can pinpoint with great accuracy *why* and *how* people behave the way they do. The Enneagram system describes varying personality strategies that have unique application to traditional teaching and, for instance, to name one of several other areas, traditional roles and rewards policies. The Enneagram offers a different perspective on the teaching/learning continuum—a new perceptual lens for understanding diversity and difference. The Enneagram model is playing a part in the revolution in education.

For hundreds of years educators have been, metaphorically speaking, teaching in the dark. Given the constraints and the context of how we teach, the majority of us do an adequate job. But, until now, we have not had the technology and the tools to be precise in understanding ourselves, and those whom we are entrusted to educate. There is another way to educate, a more enlightened way, a more humane way, both for ourselves as teachers and for all of our students. After having learned of the Enneagram, I cannot believe that you can go back into the classroom and teach students as if they were receptacles receiving the information you are required to put out to them, as if one size fits all.

What of the poignant appeal of Point Four Royal Family students who beg you to acknowledge that they're special in some way. Who can forget the Point Six Questioner teacher who said that all her years as a student she longed for a teacher to welcome her into a safe place? The Point Nine Peacekeeper's plea for a place where he can fail safely surely resonates with every educator. How do such requests sit with you? What is your reactive response? You cannot make adjustments to your teaching style to accommodate these needs if you do not have an understanding of how your personality works.

In the Introduction to this book, I named a list of educational pioneers of the 20th century. Each one stands on the shoulders of those who have gone before, those who took a bold step in innovative thinking to try to break the rigid, didactic, educational practices that have held sway for hundreds of years. A.S. Neill, in the early years of the century, built a school, Summerhill, in Britain, where all children learned only what was of interest to themselves, and at their own pace. Perhaps even more importantly he questioned deeply long-held beliefs on the meaning of discipline, responsibility, and morality in education.

In the 1950s, Swiss psychologist Jean Piaget in Switzerland investigated the stages of cognitive development in children and adolescents and created a model that has been of inestimable value to educational psychologists for the past forty years. One of his students, South African-born Seymour Papert, in the 1970s used Piaget's theories on early cognitive development to create the computer language LOGO. LOGO programs with their famous turtle changed the map of early math and spatially related teaching and learning.

Maria Montessori in Italy, a later contemporary of A.S. Neill, developed a child-centered school program for younger students. Her interest was also in the interdisciplinary nature of acquiring knowledge. Montessori students work experientially to explore the world and draw conclusions from their empirical evidence. Montessori schools are labor-intensive, but they continue to thrive around the world, usually as an alternative to mainstream education.

Rudolf Steiner and the Waldorf schools are perhaps even more well-known than the Montessori schools. Steiner, a philosopher as well as an educator, based his work on the three great energy centers. He called them the thinking center (head), the feeling center (heart), the being center (belly or will.) Steiner believed that all three centers need to be utilized and aligned in the education of every child. He developed a detailed curriculum that modeled the cognitive stages of child development to incorporate the development of these centers. He believed that we need to develop a spiritual component too if we are to be complete human beings. The Waldorf movement is a worldwide phenomenon. Steiner wrote many books and helped to found the Anthroposophic Society, which continues to publish books and actively promote Steiner's philosophy.

John Dewey, an American educator, spent a lifetime, through books and lectures, seeking to improve the profession of teaching. In many ways he broke the ground for the current work on students' needs and learning styles. In this area, Howard Gardner has made a large impact on mainstream education, inviting educators to consider the multiple intelligences evident in students' learning styles. He asks teachers to expand the classroom, so as not only to reward the traditional intelligences of linguistic ability and numeracy, but also to accommodate musical intelligence, athletic intelligence, and so on. Many educators ask me if there is a correlation between Gardner's multiple intelligences and the Enneagram intelligences. As far as I can see there is correlation in that you can have a panel of seven Point One Perfectionists, or any other E-type, and each may display a different (Gardner) intelligence. In other words, each of Gardner's multiple intelligences can play out in the nine E-type strategies. Therefore, linguistic intelligence, or any other, is not intrinsic only to, for instance, Point Six. Any of the E-types can show remarkable linguistic intelligence.

The enormous impact of the work of Isabel Myers and Katherine Briggs in refining the MBTI instrument is discussed in Chapter 5. The work of Myers-Briggs and Gardner has established firmly in mainstream education the notions of personality preferences based on cognition and multiple intelligences. They have paved the way for models like the Enneagram system, and for the idea of personality styles and behavior, and how they impact education.

In 1988 Ernest Boyer, a researcher at the Carnegie Institute, wrote a book *Scholarship Reconsidered*, which calls into question the basis of teaching in higher education. Historically, institutions of higher education reward those members who follow the research/publish/tenure track. Little or no attention is devoted to the professionalism of teaching. Increasingly, with the change in demographics of higher education students, teaching has assumed larger and larger importance on higher education campuses. There are many outstanding teachers who struggle with the research/publish/tenure requirement and do not receive tenure. Programs and policies continue to support the research/publish/tenure track, and the debate is ongoing to find a way to reward teaching proficiency. Direct results of the impact of Boyer's work are the establishment of teaching excellence centers on campuses, of organizations such as the Lilly Conferences for Teaching Excellence in Colleges and Universities, and an off-shoot of the American Association of Higher Education (AAHE) that concentrates solely on issues of faculty roles and rewards.

In many ways the Enneagram is one of the logical next steps in educational innovation. Below I cite several situations where the Enneagram is being used as a new perceptual lens.

### Faculty Roles and Rewards

In February 1998, I copresented with Dr. Joan McMahon (director of the Center for Instructional Advancement of Technology at Towson University in Baltimore) a session on Enneagram Analysis and Faculty Roles and Rewards at the AAHE Faculty Roles & Rewards Conference in Orlando, Florida. I had met Joan at a conference at Columbus State University in Georgia the previous year when she attended my session on the Enneagram and teaching and learning styles. She filled out the Enneagram Triads Personality Inventory (ETPI), found her E-type strategy, and as she began to listen to my description of the Enneagram model, I could see the lightbulbs going off in her head. Joan is involved deeply in the national debate on faculty roles and rewards, and speaks passionately on the issues. She made an immediate connection to the fact that current programs and policies are designed by Detachers (Fives, Sixes, Sevens) and do not cater to the personality needs of Attachers (Twos, Threes, Fours) and Defenders (Eights, Nines, Ones.)

At the AAHE conference the session objectives were for participants to find their E-type using the TPI, to understand their personality shifts when relaxed or under stress, to understand the avoidance areas of faculty work, and to determine ways to reward faculty for each E-type.

I explained the Enneagram background and context, and Joan laid out the parameters of the status quo with regard to Promotion and Tenure (P and T) Rewards (See Figure 6.1).

We categorize the prevailing Detacher culture thus:

| *Positive Traits* | *Under P and T Stress* |
|---|---|
| Personal privacy is important | Preoccupied with what can go wrong |
| Process oriented | Overly rational |
| Logical thinker | Inflexible |
| Excellent troubleshooter | Insistent on big-picture thinking |
| Focus on options | Scanning for hidden dangers |
| Loyalty to the group | Worst-case scenario thinking |

| Focus on keeping many balls in the air | Thinking replaces doing<br>Can be evasive if they drop the ball |

**Figure 6.1.**

**Traditional P and T Rewards According to Detacher Culture**

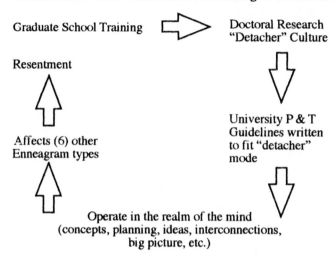

© McMahon, Levine, 1998

We then broke the session participants into groups according to their triads. About two-thirds of the group were Attachers, so we split them into two groups. Of the other third, 90 percent were Defenders, and 10 percent Detachers. I have found in general that with large groups of educators about 55 percent are Attachers, about 30 percent are Defenders, and 15 percent Detachers. We gave them all flip chart pages to stick on the walls, and asked them to discuss honestly and then to write up what rewards they would like to have for themselves. They were not made aware of the presenters' suggested rewards (detailed below) until after they had completed the exercise.

## What Rewards Would You Have for Defenders (8, 9, 1)?

### *Traits*

- They like to be heard.
- They have sound instincts.
- They are trustworthy.
- Some are take-charge leaders.
- They are steadfast—"WYSIWYG."

*Rewards You Recommend* (This is in-session data collated by AAHE participants.)

- See ideas implemented (as a measure of validation).
- Be rewarded for our contribution.
- Self-satisfaction is often its own reward.
- We are often tenured but not promoted. Why?

### Presenters' Suggested Rewards for Defenders

- Be invited to be members in Leadership Institutes.
- Provide Teaching Assistants (TAs) as a means to move forward.
- Be invited to a provost or presidential luncheon where their voices can be heard.
- Let them be part of team that implements their ideas.

## What Rewards Would You Have for Attachers (2, 3, 4)?

### Traits

- They are emotionally charged, many are creative.
- They are "people" people.
- They care about how they are coming across to others.
- They focus more on product than process.
- They are competitive.

### Rewards You Recommend

- Be given personal recognition; name recognition; invited to chair committees; publication acknowledgment.
- Be recognized for collaboratively designed products.
- Receive Teaching Awards.
- Student feedback.
- Receive thank you notes.
- Be rewarded for mentoring.
- Receive interpersonal public approval.

### Presenters' Suggested Rewards for Attachers

- Teacher of the Year at homecoming, have the Man and Woman of the Year present their "best" teacher.
- Dean's list reception—Dean's list students get to invite their "best" teachers(s) and have them acknowledged.
- Create technology fellows awards.
- Create (for example) technology center consultant awards.

- Have students' letters read at faculty meetings or other public gatherings.

## What Rewards Would You Have for Detachers (5, 6, 7)?

### Traits

- They are the culture.
- They are rational thinkers.
- They are logical thinkers.
- Some are ebullient, with childlike charm.
- They can be private and detached.
- They like concepts, imagination, and planning.

### Rewards you recommend

- We like it the way it is.

### Presenters' Suggested Rewards for Detachers

- Create faculty-in-residence programs.
- Provide technology tools.
- Provide certificates of proficiency.
- Publicize internally their journal citations/conferences, etc.
- Cite their student evaluation statistics.

It was gratifying to see how the spontaneous suggestions of participants verified those suggested by the presenters. The response of the Detachers is particularly interesting—they "like it the way it is." Of course they do, they fit right into the culture. During Q & A one participant, an Attacher, asked if so many faculty and administrators are Attachers, why hasn't the culture changed? The answer is that it has begun to change, albeit slowly. The answer was graphically illustrated by the composition of the groups in the room. The Enneagram model is a new perceptual lens for understanding diversity and differences. The faculty roles and rewards debate takes on a leading edge when personality differences and preferences can be empirically verified, and specific needs accommodated.

## ADMISSIONS

Admissions departments at the college and the K-12 level grapple daily with issues where personality plays a major role in interactions and decisions. Interoffice teamwork and the student interviewing process are enhanced greatly by using the model. Many admissions personnel have attended my Enneagram workshops. Below are comments that underscore the usefulness of the Enneagram model as a perceptual lens in this area of educational life. It is well to remember that most of the students you interview may be in their stress point when they visit with you. You can extrapolate these remarks to most areas of administrative school life where working as a team is important.

## Office Interactions

Having studied the Enneagram as a group, we now have a deeper appreciation for one another, can understand each other's behavior, and feel safe using humor to diffuse tension. Basically, the Enneagram has given us a *common language* which does not feel threatening and enables us to focus on the job at hand rather than on each others' personal style.

We gained an ability to recognize our own patterns of behavior and be less reactive to each other, particularly when the stress level is high.

We have a greater appreciation for the strengths that each of us brings to the office.

We have a better understanding of how we are received and perceived by others, and learned ways to improve communications.

I'm a Nine, many of my colleagues are Sevens, my boss is a Seven, we're so different in our reactions. He's always reacting in his head, to the figures, to the numbers, to long-range plans. This means little to me. I want to know what we are dealing with at this moment. I thought he was from another planet. Now I understand where he is coming from, and I've learned not to be so reactive.

As a Seven, I am now working on my issues around staying with a project once the initial excitement has worn off. Also I have a better idea of how I'm perceived by others. Before I thought what I had to say was endlessly fascinating to everyone and I wouldn't let them finish what they had to say.

As a counterphobic Six I recognize my patterns of behavior when I'm under stress and afraid of not coping. In order not to have to deal with the fear, I get angry at everyone around me. I've verified for myself now that instead of flying off the handle, I can look at what's happening and process my fear in an appropriate manner.

Having studied the Enneagram as a group, we act differently now toward one another. Before there were lots of closed doors and a feeling of secrecy. There's a deeper appreciation of one another. We understand each other's behavior.

## Applicant Selection

We read each others' write-ups with more understanding, and have a greater appreciation for how may different facets there are to each applicant.

We are more aware of the biases that each of us holds and how these affect our reactions to applicants.

## Student Interviews

I have a greater awareness that we may be jeopardizing whole categories of students from the selection process. In the interview process some brilliant kids will not come across as superstars and may never make it into the applicant pool because of their personality style.

I recognize that I brought too much enthusiasm to the interview process. Over the years my colleagues have asked, "Is there any candidate you don't love?" I'm an optimist, and I may have given false hope to some students about being accepted. Now I know to stand back, and everybody gains in the process. My evaluations have renewed credibility among my colleagues.

## MODEL AS A PROBLEM-SOLVING TOOL

Before we leave the arena of teamwork, I want to demonstrate how the Enneagram model may be used as a tool in decision making. This process was first suggested to me by two Enneagram colleagues (Louise Cochran and Ilona O'Connor, partners in the Ennead Group) and I have built on their suggestions. Any composition of your team in terms of E-types can make full use of this process. Ideally each of the E-types should be present, but that is almost never the case. If at all possible a representative of each of the triads should be on the team. For instance, a team may have no Twos, two Threes, a Four, no Fives, a Six, two Sevens, three Eights, a Nine and a One (three Attachers, three Detachers, five Defenders).

The whole group together undertakes this process. Think of the diagram of the model and start at Point One. Everyone on the team has to answer the question, what is wrong here? Let's define the problem. The next step is at Point Two—what do each of us need to solve the problem? Point Three—what do we have to do, what actions do we take? Then we start to refine the process. Point Four—we ask, what is missing from our previous analysis? Point Five—what facts and details do we need to undertake these actions? Point Six—what can go wrong? Let's use logic to troubleshoot the proposed solution. Then another round of refinement. Point Seven—what options do we have? Point Eight —what energy and power do we bring to get this rolling? Point Nine—let's sum up our plan, and make sure everyone's input has been considered.

This process works well with teams and is also useful when trying to arrive at personal or family decisions.

## PRESENTATION

How can the Enneagram help you in the classroom? As I said in the Introduction I am a Point Three and my Point Three high school English classroom was definitely oriented around tasks and achieving goals. But my personality bias was also present in the way I taught writing and presentation skills. I taught writing on the assumption that everyone wanted to be a published author (as I was). With every high intention, I reasoned that I was a role model. I had succeeded as a writer. My way was the way to go. I tried to teach the students that whatever the form of the exercise, they should present their best ideas in the most effective language up front, highlight those ideas with telling support, details, and examples in follow-up paragraphs; and tie it all together neatly in the conclusion. Tie it up with a bow, and hand it in smiling.

My Performer Three students scored high grades because they followed my instructions and did what came naturally to them. But what about the others? My expectations did not allow for them to mirror the way their minds work. Perfectionist One students work naturally in a form of presentation that focuses on analysis and details. Helper Twos try to meet the teacher's need and present what the teacher wants. They have to be encouraged to take risks, and present their own ideas. Royal Family Fours do have a distinctive creative ability and should be allowed to present their papers with an individual twist. Observer Five minds work in quite the opposite way to Threes. Their natural inclination is to produce a body, a corpus of work, where each idea stands on its own, and none assumes priority. Their opening statements are usually clear and broad enough to encompass the scope and intent of the body of work. Questioner Six students like to present papers in debate form. The first paragraph sets up a thesis, the second knocks it down, but saves a few sound ideas for the third paragraph. So the process goes, until a logical, well-argued presentation is concluded. Optimist Sevens prefer to present in anecdotal form, leaving conclusions open-ended and multioptional: the reader can make a choice as to the conclusion he prefers. Boss Eights won't want to do the paper the way you suggest, no way. They want to do it their way. You should let them take control of their presentation, but hold the line on the content and insist they fulfill the requirements of interpretation. Peacekeeper Nines will need help with predraft and draft deadlines, simply to complete the assignment. Let them fly (even wild) ideas during conferences without censure and help them prioritize and structure their presentation. Given enough structure, many Nines will produce original and interesting work.

For several years now, I have changed my expectation around writing assignments and presentations. At the beginning of the year I outline for my students (without mentioning the Enneagram) that there are many different ways of writing that naturally mirror the way they think—and that they should use their voice naturally in their writing. The results have been eye-opening.

## Grading Papers

There can be few such vexed areas in faculty workloads as grading. You may wonder why you and your colleagues have such different approaches to this task. Point Ones spend long hours grading, analyzing the work carefully before deciding what is right or wrong. Point Twos want to help the students, and gloss over glaring errors, concentrating rather on what is acceptable. Twos' grades generally tend to be higher than those of their colleagues. Point Threes whisk through a set of papers, trying each time to refine a more effective process to complete the task. There is often an element of self-competition: last week it took me an hour and half, let's see what I can do in an hour and a quarter this time. Point Fours don't like to give grades anyway, they do not see students as grades. Fours spend time writing elaborate comments to forge connections with their students. Point Fives like to applaud evidence of creative and lateral thinking. Their primary communication with students is long notes on papers. Grades are a necessary part of the ritual of the job. Point Sixes can get caught up in fear of worst case scenarios around grades. They are often late in returning papers. They dislike the thought of making themselves into targets once the grades and comments are public. Point Sevens would rather shoot the breeze with students. When they do grade, they look for connections between ideas. Grades do not figure high on a Seven's horizon. Point Eights use grades as part of a power structure. They will confront students over their work, or be protective of weaker students who try hard. Grades can sometimes be viewed as a measure of how they judge the student as a person. Point Nines find it hard to use a grading scale, each piece of work is seen in its entirety. It is difficult for Nines to prioritize among different papers.

## OTHER AREAS OF SCHOOL LIFE

### Dorm Life (comments from a dorm head)

One of the students was pushing the rules and testing the limits of the envelope constantly. Prior to knowing the Enneagram I would have had her in for a friendly chat. I regained control by standing in front of her squarely and confronting her on every broken rule. We have a much better relationship. She enjoys the confrontations. At first I hated being so aggressive, but now I'm more able to stand in that space.

In dealing with the House staff, I knew my hesitancy around making decisions drove many of them crazy. I would listen to the students and understand their points of view. Then I would hear the staff and side with them. How could I agree with two opposing points of view? Now I know not to act as a mediator but to find the middle way for myself.

### Dealing with Parents

One father was difficult for me; he behaved outrageously. I passed him on to the principal. I've now gained an appreciation for the situations I can't handle.

I've never been able to connect with the parents of one of my advisees. Now when I meet with them I don't try so hard. I have an appreciation that they need space to come toward me. So I take a deep breath, and let that happen in its own time.

There are many other dynamics in which self-knowledge of your E-type and the eight others smoothes the way for improved communication and interactions.

### The Enneagramatic *Hamlet*

The vast majority of world doesn't learn by sitting in a lecture, and yet by and large that is how we teach. We've all been students, spending our entire academic careers adapting to the personalities of our teachers. Now we have the technology as teachers to ameliorate the impact of our personalities in order to allow people to develop their own personalities while we teach them. Students can develop different senses of self-esteem, in which their personalities are allowed to work in their own way for each individual.

I know a Nine student (he identified himself on the model). He was sixteen years old at the time. He was struck forcibly by the idea that it was likely he was never going to fulfill his potential. He was a brilliant student, but did not perceive himself as such. He was the best writer in an exceptional class. His SAT scores were off the chart. Of all of the students to whom I've introduced the Enneagram, he was the one most negatively affected by it at first, because he was already aware of the pattern of procrastination and inertia in his life. His reaction was, "It's difficult to face the rest of my life knowing that I'm going to be like this." I encouraged him, "There is a way that you can help yourself, you have to structure short-term deadlines, work with a buddy system, and so on."

The following year he went to another teacher to do a course on *Hamlet*. At the end of the course he wrote a paper called *The Enneagramatic Hamlet as a Point Six*. I have not read a more brilliant, psychological analysis of Hamlet. He pulled together Enneagram theory and quotes from *Hamlet* to build a profile of Hamlet as a Six. Now he's through an Ivy League college, and we are still in contact. He's having a fine life, but on his own terms. He uses the Enneagram every day. He says it gives him a useful way to look at himself, to be with himself, to know how to help himself.

# REFERENCES

Addison, H. (1997). *The Enneagram and Kabbalah: Reading Your Soul.* Woodstock, VT: Jewish Lights Publishing.

American Psychiatric Association (1952). *Diagnostic and Statistical Manual of Mental Disorders* (DSM-1). Washington, DC: Mental Hospitals Service.

American Psychiatric Association (1996). *Diagnostic and Statistical Manual of Mental Disorders* (DSM-1V). Washington, DC: Mental Hospitals Service.

Bakhtiar, L. (1993). *Traditional Psychoethics and Personality Paradigm.* Chicago: The Institute of Traditional Psychoethics and Guidance.

Beesing, M., Nogosek, R., & O'Leary, P. (1984). *The Enneagram: A Journey of Self Discovery.* Denville, NJ: Dimension Books, Inc.

Boyer, E. (1988). *Scholarship Reconsidered.* Princeton, NJ: Carnegie Fund for the Advancement of Teaching.

Epstein, M. (1995). *Thoughts Without a Thinker.* New York: Basic Books.

Horney, K. (1945). *Our Inner Conflicts.* New York: W.W. Norton & Co, Inc.

Levine, J. (1997). *Learning & The Enneagram Workshops* Milton, MA: workshop materials.

Mann, R.D., Ringwald, B. E., Arnold, S., Binder, J., Cytrynbaum, S., & Rosenwein, J. W. (1970). *Conflict and Style in the College Classroom.* New York: Wiley.

Naranjo, C. (1990). *Ennea-type Structures.* Nevada City, CA: Gateways/ IDHHB, Inc.

Naranjo, C. (1994). Video-tape interview presented at the First International Enneagram Conference at Stanford University, August.

Oldham, J. & Morris, L. B. (1995). *The New Personality Self-portrait: Why You Think, Work, Love, and Act the Way You Do.* New York: Bantam Books.

Palmer, H. (1988). *The Enneagram: Understanding Yourself and the Others in Your Life.* New York: HarperCollins.

Saunders, F. W. (1991). *Katherine and Isabel: Mother's Light, Daughter's Journey*. Palo Alto, CA: Consulting Psychologists Press, Inc.

# INDEX

Compartmentalization, 130. *See also* Five Observer

Competition, 102-3. *See also* Four Royal Family

Conflict, 224-25. *See also* Nine Peacekeeper

Confrontation, 200-1. *See also* Eight Boss

Connection, 95-98; connecting to Five Observers, 133-34

Conserving energy and time, 131. *See also* Five Observer

Creating safety, 154. *See also* Six Questioner

Criticism, 257-58. *See also* One Perfectionist

Defender triad, 19, 38-41

Detacher triad, 18-19, 35-38

Detachment, 126-27. *See also* Five Observer

Details, 254-55. *See also* One Perfectionist

Dewey, John, 2, 283

Diagnostic Survey Manual (DSM), DSM-1, 12; DSM-IV, 9; DSM, correlation with Enneagram features, 13

Educational ideas, 2, 281; paradigm, new, 2; psychology, 2; reform, 2

Eight Boss, advocating for the underdog, 205-6; anger, 201; authority issues, 196-200; being heard, 201; blame, 202-3; Bosses as students, 203-4; confrontation, 200-1; empowering others, 194; excessive energy, 195-96; general description, 190-93; growth path, 208-9; in triad, 39; interview with Boss educator, 210-11; intuition, 207; key characteristics, 194-209; learning patience, 206; motivating others, 194-95; passion, 201-2; positive gifts in teaching, 208; practical tips, 211-12;

security, 193; self-forgetting, 207-8; self-protection, 200; stress, 193; truth, 209; vengeance and revenge, 205; way of being in the world, 10; what Boss students say, 209-10

Emotions, 127-28; emotional reactivity, 100-1

Empowering others, 194. *See also* Eight Boss

Energy, centers, 6; excessive, 195-96

Enneagram model, arrows, 25; attentional foci, 20-21; avoidances, 22-23; basic, 11; essence, 24; gifts, 21-22; growth paths, 23-24; inner workings,17-26; problem solving tool, 28; wings, 25-26

Enneagram psychology, 16-17

Enneagram Studies, 4

Enneagram Triads Personality Indicator, 27-31

Enneagramatic *Hamlet* as a Point Six, 292

Enneatypes (E-types in action), One 239-41; Two, 44-45; Three, 69-71; Four, 90-92; Five, 115-17; Six, 140-42; Seven, 164-66; Eight, 188-90; Nine, 213-15

Entitlement, 174. *See also* Seven Optimist

Envy, 101-2. *See also* Four Royal Family

Epstein, Mark, 14, 17

Error, 259. *See also* One Perfectionist

Essence quality, 24, One, 260; Two, 63; Three, 84-85; Four, 111; Five, 135-36; Six, 159-60; Seven, 182-83; Eight, 209; Nine, 233-34

Faculty roles and rewards, 284-87

Failure, 80-81. *See also* Three Performer

Faith, 159-60. *See also* Six Questioner

Fear, 146-47. *See also* Six Questioner

Feelings, 83-84, 100. *See also* Three

259; fun, 247-48; general description, 241-44; growth path, 260; in triad, 40-41; inner critic, 249; inspirational teacher, 245-46; instinctual intelligence, 252-53; interview with Perfectionist educator, 262-63; intuition, 245; judgment, 258; key characteristics, 245-60; over preparation, 246-47; passion for excellence, 252; perfection and imperfection, 255-56, 259-60; practical tips, 263-64; processing criticism, 257-58; right behavior, 256-57; righteousness, 250-51; secure, 244-45; stress, 245; trapdoor, 248-49; way of being in the world, 10; what Peacekeeper students say, 260-61

Optimism, 170-71. *See also* Seven Optimist

Others' agenda, 220-21. *See also* Nine Peacekeeper

Own journey, 26

Own needs, 53-54. *See also* Helper Two

Palmer, Helen, 9, 20

Panels of self-observers, 16, 43

Papert, Seymour, 2, 282

Passion, 201-2; passion for excellence, 252

Passive aggressive response, 225-26. *See also* Nine Peacekeeper

Patience, learning 206. *See also* Eight Boss

Peacekeeper, role of, 226

Perfection and imperfection, 255-56, 259. *See also* One Perfectionist

Performer Three, 2-3, classroom, 3-4

Personality intelligences, 6

Piaget, Jean, 2, 282

Planning and options, 175-77. *See also* Seven Optimist

Platonic tradition, 14,

Polyphasic ability, 77-78. *See also* Three Performer

Potentiating others, 55-56. *See also* Two Helper

Practical tips, One, 263-64; Two, 67-68; Three, 88-89; Four, 113-14; Five, 138-39; Six, 163-64; Seven, 186-87; Eight, 211-12; Nine, 237-38

Presentations and papers, Enneagram application to, 290

Pride, 57-58. *See also* Two Helper

Privacy, 130-31. *See also* Five Observer

Procrastination, 151-52, 230-32

Questioning and doubting, 157-58. *See also* Six Questioner

Racing mind, mental energy, 177-79. *See also* Seven Optimist

Rational assessment, 124-25. *See also* Five Observer

Reframing, 172. *See also* Seven Optimist

Right behavior, 256-57; righteousness, 250-52. *See also* One Perfectionist

Safety and trust, 153-54. *See also* Six Questioner

Selectivity, 56-57. *See also* Two Helper

Self-, forgetting, 207-8; protection, 200; sabotage, 152-53

Sequential order, 110. *See also* Four Royal family

Setting limits, 62. *See also* Two Helper

Seven Optimist, avoiding pain, 180-82; being motivated, 179-80; commitment, 171-72; commitment to work, 183-84; entitlement, 174; equalizing authority, 174-75; general description, 166-69; growth path, 182-83; in triad, 37-38; interview with Optimist educator, 185-87;

**About the Author**

JANET LEVINE teaches English at Milton Academy in Massachusetts. She is founder of Learning & The Enneagram, and the Director of the National Educators Institute for Enneagram Studies at Milton Academy.